Neal Bedford
& Janine Eberle

Vienna

The Top Five

1 Naschmarkt
Overload your senses at the city's premier street market (p185)

2 Hofburg
Explore the imperial palace, once heart of the Habsburg empire (p60)

3 Stephansdom
Visit Vienna's iconic cathedral, a masterwork of Gothic ingenuity (p53)

4 MuseumsQuartier
Experience everything a modern cultural complex can be (p75)

5 Schönbrunn
Discover the grandeur of the baroque palace and gardens (p99)

Published by Lonely Planet Publications Pty Ltd
ABN 36 005 607 983

Australia Head Office, Locked Bag 1, Footscray,
Victoria 3011, ☎ 03 8379 8000, fax 03 8379 8111,
talk2us@lonelyplanet.com.au

USA 150 Linden St, Oakland, CA 94607,
☎ 510 893 8555, toll free 800 275 8555,
fax 510 893 8572, info@lonelyplanet.com

UK 72–82 Rosebery Ave, Clerkenwell, London,
EC1R 4RW, ☎ 020 7841 9000, fax 020 7841 9001,
go@lonelyplanet.co.uk

© Lonely Planet Publications Pty Ltd 2007
Photographs © Richard Nebesky and as listed (p238)
2007

Printed by SNP Security Printing Pte Ltd, Singapore

Contents

The Authors

Neal Bedford

Landing in Vienna shortly after leaving New Zealand on his big OE, Neal spent his first year as an au pair learning the most important aspects of Austrian culture: *Wurscht* and *Schaas* are the two most important words in the German language; copious amounts of *Sturm* must be drunk at least once in your life; Austrian cuisine helps put on weight; and no place in the world invokes Christmas cheer like Vienna.

Like any relationship, his love affair with the city has had its ups and downs – he's left three times for what he thought were greener pastures, only to return to enjoy all that Vienna can offer. The magic of the city still manages to catch him unawares, particularly at night when cycling home through the quiet districts to his flat in Ottakring, and he has come to realise no matter how much he learns about Vienna, there is always an undiscovered pocket close at hand.

CONTRIBUTING AUTHOR
JANINE EBERLE
When Janine stepped in as Commissioning Editor for the Central Europe region in LP's London office, one of her first 'chores' was to spend a week documenting Vienna's shopping scene. Her credentials? A taste for glamour, an eye for a bargain, and a long-suffering credit card. The combination of cool trams, great wine, and shops filled with unbelievable amounts of old tat makes Vienna one of her very favourite places to plunge herself into debt.

PHOTOGRAPHER
Greg Elms
A contributor to Lonely Planet for more than 15 years, Greg finds shooting for city guides is like travelling with the fast-forward button pressed down. Armed with a Bachelor of Arts in Photography, Greg was a photographer's assistant for two years before embarking on a travel odyssey. He eventually settled down to a freelance career in Melbourne, and now works regularly for magazines, graphic designers, advertising agencies and, of course, book publishers such as Lonely Planet.

NEAL'S TOP VIENNA DAY
It all depends on the weather, but since it's my 'top' day, it would be a warm September Saturday.

A late breakfast of tomato- and paprika-omelette and Turkish tea at Kent with friends from the 'hood' starts the day off nice and gently, followed by a little shopping at the Bauernmarkt on Brunnenmarkt for seasonal fruits and vegetables. Cycling out of the city, I'd spend a few hours in the Wienerwald (Vienna Woods) working an appetite before stopping at a *Heuriger* (wine tavern) or *Gasthaus* (inn) to recharge the batteries. A quick break at my flat to refresh, then it's down to the Museums-Quartier to chat with friends, people-watch, and catch the last of the days' rays.

Some food at Saigon or one of the Asian diners on the Naschmarkt is the perfect appetiser for an evening out; I'd then choose a bar on Schleifmühlgasse before heading across the Danube Canal to one of Leopoldstadt's laidback *Lokale* (bars). If things are a little quiet there, I'd move on to the bar Flex before taking a long bike ride through the Innere Stadt – empty of people, I can enjoy its glorious architecture at my leisure. A final stop at rhiz to see if anyone's around for a late nightcap, and then it's off home.

Introducing Vienna

Northern province of the Romans; crown of the Habsburg empire; bastion of baroque and birthplace of *Jugendstil* and the Secession; to classical music what Nashville is to country and London to punk; queen of the Christmas cities; home to the most successful socialist system Europe has ever seen, and sight of some of the worst atrocities against the Jewish people. Vienna, a city of unquestionable historical significance and extraordinary beauty, is a mix rarely seen today.

Classical Vienna provokes a gamut of images in most people's minds. Angelic choirboys singing in perfect harmony while proud white stallions strut in measured sequence. The grandeur of the Habsburg imperial palaces, Hofburg and Schönbrunn, sitting comfortably beside breathtaking baroque architecture of the Schloss Belvedere and Karlskirche. Sublime *Jugendstil* (Art Nouveau) masterpieces executed by Otto Wagner and Gustav Klimt complement the sublime art collections of the Kunsthistorisches and Liechtenstein museums.

And of course strong coffee, delicate pastries and divine cakes are served in traditional *Kaffeehäuser* (coffee houses). Then there's the music. Just let it roll off your tongue: Mozart, Beethoven, Haydn, Schubert, Strauss, Brahms, Mahler, Schönberg. For lovers of classical music, it doesn't get *any* better than this.

But Vienna is so much more than its past. It certainly revels in its impressive history, but it's not about to spend all its time living on bygone eras. Like the rest of the Western world, the Viennese have acquired a taste for the exotic and want it on their own turf. Asian diners, kebab houses and conveyor-belt sushi restaurants compete with, but don't overpower, the traditional *Beisl* (beer house) and *Heuriger*

(wine tavern). The upwardly mobile while away the wee small hours in unpretentious bars alongside black-clad night-owls, before moving on to clubs where DJs spin the latest electronica. Modern art venues, like the MuseumsQuartier, constantly host thought-provoking contemporary artists who aren't afraid to push boundaries.

With almost half the city given over to green spaces (more than any other European capital), the not-so-blue Danube (Donau) slicing the city in two and Beethoven's inspiration, the Wienerwald (Vienna Woods), on its western fringes, this is also a city for the pursuit of the great outdoors. And then there's the vast expanse of vineyards, which makes Vienna the largest wine-growing city in the world.

It doesn't matter when you arrive, the city looks just as glorious – some would say even more so – under a layer of snow as it does under the gaze of a midsummer sun. And the constant turnstile of festivals and events rivals anything most other European cities can muster. Come Christmas the good burghers of Vienna roll out the welcoming mat to *Christkindlmärkte*, Christmas markets full of charm and grace, and the all-important *Glühwein* (mulled wine); when summer shines through so does a plethora of musical events. The granddaddy of them all is the Donauinselfest, a free – yes, free – concert attracting over three million screaming revellers. In between, cultural and musical festivities line up beside each other, all vying for attention. The only drawback to the summer is the holiday season: many of the city's world-famous institutions, such as the Vienna Boys' Choir, the Lippanzer Stallions and the Staatsoper, all take breaks, so a little planning can prove very advantageous.

Vienna is a place where culture, history, art and nightlife all mix together seamlessly. With only a few days on your hands, there is a lot to experience, but any time spent in this magical city will bring rich rewards.

MY ESSENTIAL VIENNA

- Heeresgeschichtliches Museum (p84)
- Zentralfriedhof (p97)
- Brunnenmarkt (p185)
- Cycling through the city (p113)
- MuseumsQuartier (p75)

LOWDOWN

Population 1.64 million

Time zone Central European Time (GMT + 1 hour)

3-star double room Around €100-120

Melange coffee Around €3

KäseKrainer €3.20

Opera ticket €2-254

U-Bahn ticket €1.50

Common sight Dogs, dogs, and more dogs

Don't Walk on the cycle paths – cyclists at full speed hurt

City Life

City Life

VIENNA TODAY

The brightest diamond in Europe's cultural crown for centuries, Vienna fell on hard times at the end of WWI with the decline of its keepers, the Habsburgs. With the exception of Red Vienna in the 1920s, when the city prospered under the most successful socialist government Europe has ever seen, the city wallowed in the cultural backwaters for much of the 20th century.

The previous 10 years has seen the city turn itself around, and in the 21st century, Vienna is once again looking peachy. Quality of life is high: Mercer Consulting, in its worldwide quality of living survey, ranked Vienna fourth behind Zurich, Geneva and Vancouver. Some Viennese would beg to differ. Nevertheless, the facts speak for themselves – the city's public transport system is one the best in the world, green spaces abound, the circus of public festivals and events grows larger year by year, rent and living costs continue to stay low and the socialist welfare system is strong.

The city's bar and club scene has never been healthier. Traditional pockets such as the Bermuda Dreieck have floundered in the wake of new locations opening up across the city, and now locals are spoilt for choice. The districts inside the Gürtel, in particular Wieden, Mariahilf, Neubau, and Josefstadt, have built up a strong concentration of progressive bars and live-music venues, while districts traditionally bereft of night spots, like Leopoldstadt, are currently experiencing a surge in nightlife. Electronic music, once the darling of Vienna's contemporary music scene, is, like the city, on the comeback. Clubs such as Flex and Künstlerhauspassage not only attract big names in the local scene, such as Kruder & Dorfmeister and the stars of Cheap Records, but also a regular troupe of international DJs and bands. Many of the smaller bars, rhiz, Fluc, and Cabaret Renz included, feature DJs habitually.

The Viennese, back from world trips, tired of schnitzel and began exploring the few Chinese restaurants and Turkish kebab houses in town. Before long, new flavours and spices were popping up all over the city (and continue to do so), whetting the Viennese appetite. In recent years the trend has reversed somewhat, with local cuisine making a comeback: today, modern takes on traditional dishes are in.

Art, a major link in Vienna's cultural armour, continues to go from strength to strength, and fortunately the councillors of Vienna have never been shy about forking out for art and public space. Their greatest achievements in the 21st century – the reopening of the Albertina, home to the world's greatest graphic art collection, and the completion of the Museums-Quartier, the eighth largest cultural complex in the world – have not only complemented the city's incredible art treasure chest, but helped to create an art scene of epic proportions.

Through all the improvements and new-found openness, Vienna has remained an incredibly safe city. Crime has risen ever so slightly in the past few years, but the majority of convictions involve theft and burglary, something that has had little impact on the freedom and safety of the Viennese. People can go almost anywhere night or day and feel unthreatened; women still walk home alone at night without fear of harassment, and the elderly ride the trams and buses well into the night.

Xenophobia, Vienna's Achilles heel, still lurks in the background. In recent years the Freedom Party (FPÖ), formerly headed by Jörg Haider, has played on this fear, targeting foreigners and asylum-seekers during

TOP QUIRKY EVENTS

- Fasching – a time to dress up as a tree, oil slick or your favourite comic character and bar hop across the city.
- Lange Nacht der Museen – one night in the year when museums across the country throw open their doors to all and sundry.
- Life Ball – outrageous outfits, celebrities galore, and all in the noble cause of raising funds for AIDS.
- Soho in Ottakring – a multicultural residential neighbourhood transforms itself into a centre for contemporary art and nightlife.
- Volkstimmefest – a surreal hippy/communist festival with a very laid-back feel and plenty of live acts.

election time. In 2000 it rode the tide of intolerance right to the doorsteps of parliament, forming a coalition government with the Austrian People's Party (ÖVP). This, however, seemed a catalyst for Vienna's sleeping liberals, who demonstrated en masse at Heldenplatz (some 200,000 turned up) against the FPÖ's racist platform. In the 2001 council and 2002 national elections, FPÖ lost major ground in the popularity stakes and Haider left the party due to internal fighting. In stepped HC Strache to fill the void. A young, charismatic politician with perfect teeth, Strache began his career as FPÖ leader with strong xenophobic rhetoric accompanied by weepy eyes and overwrought nationalism. His racially motivated campaign against Turkey's inclusion in the EU in both the 2005 council and 2006 national elections struck a chord with a surprisingly large community in Vienna. His party secured 14.4% of the Vienna vote in 2006, up an incredible 6.4%. Juxtaposing the city's small racist streak is its concern for the environment; the Greens still head off the FPÖ in the popularity stakes, receiving 17.1% of Vienna's votes in the 2006 national elections, and won the districts of Mariahilf, Neubau, and Josefstadt outright. However, it might be time, as Dirk Stermann (of the humorist duo Stermann & Grissemann) proposed after the 2006 elections, for a 'foreigners' party that hates Austrian nationals'.

Through it all, the Viennese saying *Wien ist ein Dorf* (Vienna is a village) rings true; traditional values are still highly regarded and at times it seems as though everyone knows everyone's business. It may be old fashioned, but its kinda comforting.

CITY CALENDAR

Vienna's calendar of events is a ceaseless cascade of classical concerts, jazz and rock festivals, balls, gay parades, communist gatherings and art happenings. The following is by no means a complete listing of annual events; check the Tourist Info Wien website, www.wien.info, for a more comprehensive list, or read the weekly *Falter* paper. For a full list of public holidays, see the Directory (p226).

JANUARY & FEBRUARY

FASCHING
The Fasching season, a carnival time of costumes and parties, actually runs from November to Ash Wednesday, but February is traditionally the time when most of the action takes place. Look for street parties and drunken Viennese in silly get-ups.

OPERNBALL
☎ 514 44 7880; 01, Staatsoper
Of the 300 or so balls held in January and February, the Opernball (Opera Ball) is number one. Held in the Staatsoper, it's a supremely lavish affair, with the men in tails and women in shining white gowns.

MARCH & APRIL

FRÜHLINGSFESTIVAL
Alternating each year between the Musikverein and the Konzerthaus, this Spring Festival of classical concerts generally runs from the end of March to the beginning of April.

INTERNATIONAL AKKORDEON FESTIVAL
☎ 0676-512 91 04; www.akkordeonfestival.at in German
Running from the end of February through to the end of March, the International Accordion Festival features exceptional players from as close as the Balkans and as far away as New Zealand.

An outdoor cinema in front of the Rathaus screens films for free during the Musikfilm Festival (opposite page)

OSTERKLANG FESTIVAL

☎ 427 17; www.osterklang.at in German
Orchestral and chamber music recitals fill some of Vienna's best music halls during this 'Sound of Easter' festival. The highlight is the opening concert, which features the Vienna Philharmonic.

MAY & JUNE
DONAUINSELFEST

www.donauinselfest.at in German
For the younger generation, the Donauinselfest on the Donauinsel (Danube Island) occupies the top spot on the year's events' calendar. Held over three days on a weekend in late June, it features a feast of rock, pop, folk and country performers, which attracts almost three million onlookers. Best of all, it's free!

LANGE NACHT DER MUSIK

http://langenacht.orf.at
For one night, usually in early June, bars and concert venues host a heap of bands playing every kind of music genre conceivable. Tickets (adult/child €14/12; available at venues) grant entry into all performances. An information booth is set up on Heldenplatz two days before the event. The 2006 event was held in September; at the time of writing the schedule for future events was not yet determined.

LIFE BALL

☎ 595 56 00; www.lifeball.org
This AIDS-charity event is one of the highlights of the ball season calendar and is often graced by international celebrities. It's normally held in the Rathaus around the middle of May and attracts some colourful and flamboyant outfits.

QUEER IDENTITIES

☎ 524 62 74; www.identities.at
Identities is easily Vienna's second largest film festival, showcasing queer movies from around the world. It normally takes place at the beginning of June.

REGENBOGEN PARADE

www.hosiwien.at in German
Late June Vienna is taken over by the Regenbogen Parade (Rainbow Parade), a predominantly gay and lesbian festival attracting some 150,000 people. Expect loads of fun, frolicking and bare skin.

SOHO IN OTTAKRING

www.sohoinottakring.at in German
The multicultural streets bordering the Gürtel in Ottakring come to life in May and June with Soho in Ottakring. Hairdressing salons, disused offices and fishmongers are transformed into art galleries, bars, band venues and art shops, all of which attracts an arty crowd.

VIENNA MARATHON

☎ 606 95 10; www.vienna-marathon.com
The city's top road race is held in May.

WIEN IST ANDERSRUM

☎ 0664-941 14 74; www.geheimsache.at
Wien ist Andersrum is a month-long extravaganza of gay and lesbian art, which takes up all of June every second year (the next is in 2008). Most performances stick to the genre of stage and song.

WIENER FESTWOCHEN

☎ 589 22-0; www.festwochen.or.at
Considered to be one of the highlights of the year, the Vienna Festival hosts a wide-ranging program of the arts, based in various venues around town, from May to mid-June. Expect to see quality performance groups from around the world.

JULY & AUGUST

IMPULSTANZ
☎ 523 55 58; www.impulstanz.com
Vienna's premiere avant-garde dance festival attracts an array of internationally renowned troupes and newcomers between mid-July and mid-August. Performances are held in the MuseumsQuartier, Volkstheater and a number of small venues.

JAZZ FEST WIEN
☎ 712 42 24; www.viennajazz.org
From the end of June to mid-July, Vienna relaxes to the smooth sound of jazz, blues and soul flowing from the Staatsoper and a number of clubs across town.

KLANGBOGEN FESTIVAL
☎ 427 17; www.klangbogen.at
The KlangBogen Festival ensures things don't flag during the summer holidays. Running from July to August, it features operas, operettas and orchestral music in the Theater an der Wien and Musikverein, plus a few other locations around town.

MUSIKFILM FESTIVAL
01, Rathausplatz
Once the sun sets in July and August, the Rathausplatz is home to screenings of operas, operettas and concerts. They're all free, so turn up early for a good seat. Food stands and bars are close at hand, which are swamped by hordes of people creating a carnival-like atmosphere.

VOLKSSTIMMEFEST
www.volksstimmefest.at in German
For a weekend in late August or early September, the Communist Party fills the Prater with music and art. The festival, which has been running since 1945, features some 30 live acts and attracts a bizarre mix of hippies and staunch party supporters.

SEPTEMBER & OCTOBER

LANGE NACHT DER MUSEEN
http://langenacht.orf.at
On the first Saturday of October, around 500 museums nationwide open their doors to visitors between 6pm and 1am. One ticket (adult/child €12/10; available at museums) allows entry to all of them, and includes public transport around town. You'll be hard pushed to visit all 83 museums in Vienna though.

VIENNALE FILM FESTIVAL
☎ 526 59 47; www.viennale.at
The country's best film festival, Viennale features fringe and independent films from around the world It is held every year in October, with screenings at numerous locations around the city. See p171 for more details.

NOVEMBER & DECEMBER

CHRISTKINDLMÄRKTE
Vienna's much-loved Christmas market season runs from mid-November to Christmas Day. See p188 for more details.

SILVESTER
The city council transforms the Innere Stadt into one huge party venue for Silvester (New Year's Eve). It's an uproarious affair, with more than enough alcohol consumed and far too many fireworks let off in crowded streets.

WIEN MODERN FESTIVAL
☎ 242 00; www.wienmodern.at
The Wien Modern Festival takes an opposing view to many of the city's music festivals by featuring modern classical and avant-garde music. The festival is held throughout November, with many performances in the Konzerthaus.

CULTURE

VIENNESE LIFE
Not only are the Viennese are a hard bunch to pin down (possibly a reason why Freud had so much material to work with), but on the surface, lifestyles in Vienna vary greatly. To take the pulse of the city, we posed a few questions on Vienna and the Viennese to some long-time residents.

Marion, a Viennese-born fulltime mother, lives in Penzing; Peter Berger has spent his 35 years living in Landstrasse and works as a bartender; Tom, a professor of analytical chemistry, moved here from Lower Austria 20 years ago; and Lisa, who works in the arts, was born and bred in Leopoldstadt.

Lonely Planet: What do you like about Vienna?
Marion: It's small enough to get everywhere within a reasonable time and it's big enough to give you anonymity. There are lots of things to do with the kids, and you have the benefits of countryside and city.
Peter: I like the public transport system – it works, it's good, and it's cheap. And the size of the city – not too big, not too small, Vienna is still a city you can walk. Half the week I like the cuisine, and the other half not.
Lisa: There are lots of things to do in the city, whether it be cultural, sporting, or simply relaxing.

Lonely Planet: What annoys you about Vienna?
Marion: The Viennese shop assistants, dog turds, not enough of a view from my flat, not enough playgrounds, a growing number of homeless, and too little integration of the poorer immigrants.
Peter: People try to interfere where it's not needed, and don't interfere when help is needed.
Tom: The grumpiness of the people is sometimes hard to take, and their unfriendliness.

Lonely Planet: How have you seen the city change over the last decade or so?
Marion: There are more homeless on the streets, and a lot of houses renovated. Shopping has changed; a lot of the little shops in the outer lying shopping streets, like Thaliastrasse, are dying out and being replaced by bigger shops or shopping centres in the centre. People dress better, there are more restaurants, bars and cultural happenings.
Peter: The city has grown bigger, which has brought both benefits and losses. There are now more possibilities, but also more poor, homeless and drug-addicted.
Tom: It has lost a bit of the open-air museum feel. It's grown younger in a way, there are new places to hang out now, which counterbalance the old coffee houses. It's also got a little bit more international.
Lisa: It has grown bigger as people have moved away from the centre looking for a 'house & garden' lifestyle and there are more nationalities in the city.

Lonely Planet: If you had to describe the Viennese people in one sentence, what would it be?
Marion: Grumpy but helpful and mostly courageous.
Peter: Sweet and sour, sometimes a little too hard.
Tom: They have a golden heart, but gold is very heavy.
Lisa: It's hard to say. The Viennese are multicultural and hard to pin down, a walk through Naschmarkt is proof of this.

Lonely Planet: Are the Viennese grumpy or full of *Wiener Schmäh* (Viennese humour)?
Marion: The better off they are the grumpier - the worse the situation, the more *Schmäh*.
Tom: Grumpy. They don't take the time to evolve the *Schmäh*, most seem stressed and don't take the time to relax.
Peter: Full of grumpy *Schmäh*.

THE LOCALS' BEST VIENNA DAY

We also asked our Viennese friends what they'd do with a cheeky day off in the city; here are their favourite ways of enjoying Vienna.
Marion: I'd go to a museum and the Naschmarkt (p185), rent a boat and picnic on the Alte Donau (Old Danube; p78), or go to Erholungsgebiet Steinhof (p112) to fly a kite, then to a *Heurigen* (wine tavern).
Peter: If the weather was bad, I'd seek out a good exhibition. If the weather was good, I'd head for the Lainzer Tiergarten (p99).
Tom: I'd have a very late breakfast at the MuseumsQuartier (p75), sit out the afternoon in a coffee house, and in the evening catch a film at the Votivkino (p172). If it was wet and rainy, I'd head to the Bücherei Wien (p91) and scroll through the newspapers and music.
Lisa: It depends on the weather. I'd head to the Alte Donau for inline skating (p174) or sailing (p173) if its fine; a museum if not.

A POLITE SOCIETY

For all their grumpiness, the Viennese love *Höflichkeit* (politeness). Shop assistants, waiters and the like greet people with *Grüss Gott* or *Guten Tag* (good day) and expect the same in return. Occasionally you'll hear *Servus*, but it's normally reserved for greetings between friends. *Auf Wiedersehen* (goodbye) will follow you out the door. People either shake hands on greeting or exchange pecks on the cheeks (even between men); *Prost* is the common toast, and eye contact is important when clinking glasses.

How sincere this all is is another matter. Brigitte Schreger, a Viennese from birth and teacher since 1976, is well placed to comment on the city's *Höflichkeit*.

'Most Viennese aren't actually that polite. Ride the U-Bahn and you'll notice how unfriendly they are. Twenty or 30 years ago it was quite different, with sayings like *Küss die Hand* ('kiss the hand', a very polite greeting from a man to a woman), *Habe die Ehre* (honoured to meet you), and very, very occasionally *Gschamsta Diener* (I am your humble servant), still heard on the streets. The latter dates from the Habsburg days. In some shops you have the feeling it's a privilege for you to enter and pay them money.'

'Of course, this isn't representative of the whole society. Many German-based firms and specialist stores still maintain a high level of politeness, and often supermarket assistants are quite friendly if you regularly frequent their store. With regards to the younger generation, I think it depends on the upbringing – it seems the more money the family has, the more outwardly polite they are. Culture also plays a big part; Turkish people have another way of politeness which some Viennese find hard to comprehend. We try to teach politeness in school and hope the kids take it with them.'

And the notoriously rude waiters? 'I have no problem, but then again, I'm a *Stammgast* (regular) at my local coffee house. It seems waiters like things just so, and perhaps foreigners upset the balance. If you're looking for a taste of traditional *Höflichkeit,* take coffee and cake at Demel (p140).'

FOOD

Vienna's cuisine is a conglomeration of the best of the old empire. At its base is the substantial food of southern Germany, but it features a plethora of dishes from throughout Central and Eastern Europe: the world famous *Wiener Schnitzel* arrived from Milan; *Knödel* (dumplings) originated in Bohemia; *Gulasch* (goulash) and *Paprika Huhn* (paprika chicken) crossed the border from Hungary; the delightful *Palatschinken* (pancakes) travelled all the way from Romania and the *Apfelstrudel* (apple strudel) from Turkey.

On the whole, traditional Viennese cuisine is heavy, hearty and strongly meat-based. A must for any visitor – vegetarians and vegans aside – is the Wiener schnitzel, the ubiquitous Viennese dish traditionally made with *Kalb* (veal) escalope, but often nowadays with *Schwein* (pork) or *Puten* (turkey). *Gulasch*, a beef stew with a spicy sauce flavoured with paprika, is also on most Viennese menus; *Knödel* seem to appear in every second dish, can be either sweet or sour, and are normally made with potatoes or bread. *Apfelstrudel* is a ubiquitous dessert that is hard to avoid (and quite frankly, who would want to) while *Palatschinken*, a thinner version of the common pancake, is another favourite; like *Knödel*, they are served sweet with jams or savoury with meat.

Aside from standard dishes, Viennese cuisine runs with the seasons. Spring is a time to enjoy crunchy asparagus from the Weinviertel's Marchfeld (see p210) and dishes seasoned with *Bärlauch,* wild garlic found throughout the Wienerwald (p210). Summer brings with it a grand array of fruits, in particular *Erdbeeren* (strawberries) from Burgenland (see p211) and *Marillen* (apricots) from the Danube Valley (see p205). At this time, divine *Marillenknödel* top dessert lists throughout the city. Autumn is blessed with the arrival of *Piltze* (mushrooms – picking them in the Vienna Woods is a favourite pastime of many Viennese), *Kürbis* (pumpkin), wild meats and sweet *Sturm* (cloudy fermenting grape juice; see p142). *Eierschwammerl* (chanterelle mushrooms) and *Kürbiscremesuppe* (cream of pumpkin soup) are dishes to look out for. *Martinigansl* (tender roast goose) is prevalent around St Martin's Day in early November and fish is normally served at Christmas.

Although the menus of traditional *Beisln* (beer houses), *Gasthäuser* (inns) and *Heurigen* (wine taverns) loyally follow the established culinary standards, Vienna's overall gastronomic scene is in flux. The last few years have seen an explosion of restaurants offering cuisine from around the world: Asian diners, Turkish kebab houses, Italian trattoria and Indian curry houses sprang up like mushrooms after a heavy rain. Yet the city's current

SAUSAGES TO GO

The *Würstelstand* (sausage stand), Vienna's equivalent of a fast-food joint, is a familiar sight throughout the city. They're the perfect place for a quick bite to eat on the run; a pastime imbedded in the Viennese way of life.

These shrines to fatty bangers may sell up to a dozen types of sausage. Each comes with a chunk of bread and a big dollop of mustard *(Senf)* – which can be sweet *(süss* or *Kremser Senf)* or hot *(scharf)* – and are washed down with a beer. Tomato ketchup and mayonnaise can be requested. The thinner sausages are served two at a time, except in the less expensive 'hot dog' version, when the sausage is placed in a bread stick.

Take your pick from the *Frankfurter,* a standard thin, boiled sausage; the *Bratwurst,* a fat, fried sausage; and *Burenwurst,* the boiled equivalent of *Bratwurst. De-breziner* is a thin, mildly smoked spicy sausage from Hungary. *Currywurst* is *Burenwurst* with a curry flavour, and *Käsekrainer,* a favourite of 3am snackers, is a sau-

Wurstelstand in the Innere Stadt

sage infused with cheese. *Tiroler Wurst* is a smoked sausage. Not a sausage, but sold at *Würstelstände* is *Leberkäs* (literally 'liver cheese'), a kind of meatloaf often made from horse meat.

If you want to surprise and perhaps impress the server, use the following Viennese slang to ask for a *Burenwurst* with sweet mustard and a crust of bread: *'A Hasse mit an Söassn und an Scherzl, bitte'.* But you probably won't get it – crusts are generally reserved for regular customers.

culinary climate is experiencing a 'back to the roots' phase and an upsurge in restaurants offering modern takes on traditional dishes. Leading the way in this new love affair with Viennese cuisine is Österreicher im MAK (see p127), Steirereck im Stadtpark (p129), and *neo-Beisln* like Gasthaus Wild (p128) and Goldmund (p133).

Traditionally the main meal of the day is lunch (heralded by *Mahlzeit,* literally 'meal time' – a greeting heard throughout restaurants at midday) and restaurants are well attuned to their customers' needs; a large percentage offer set menus *(Mittagsmenü),* consisting of a salad or soup and a main dish, at a good price. However, like any busy city, lunch can be a rushed affair – dinner, on the other hand, is an event where the food, wine and company are to be savoured. Most Viennese breakfast at home. Week-ends are the exception to the rule: many restaurants cater to a flood of people meeting over continental breakfasts or full fry-ups (p125). The Naschmarkt is a prime spot on Saturday mornings.

SPORT

The Viennese aren't what you'd call sports-mad, but the city does have its fair share of fanatical supporters, particularly when it comes to football and skiing, and plenty of locals enjoy walking, swimming, cycling, inline skating and racket sports.

Summer is pretty much a dead time for spectator sports. However, with the arrival of autumn and winter, things heat up, so to speak. The national football league, the Austrian *Bundesliga,* kicks off at the end of autumn and runs until the beginning of spring, with a break during the severe winter months; two of the country's better teams, Austria Memphis and Rapid, are based in Vienna. A local derby is quite an affair, and while the actual football isn't the most scintillating, the match certainly brings out the best and worst in fans.

With much of the country given over to mountainous splendour, snow sports are hugely popular in Austria. Almost every Austrian has skied since they could be pushed down beginner slopes, and the average child will literally ski circles around most tour-ists. The best skiing is in the western reaches of the country, where most competitions are held. Vienna has a couple of tiny slopes and a handful of mountains within a couple of hours' drive.

See Outdoor Activities (p173) and Health & Fitness (p175) in the Entertainment chapter for information on sporting venues and various outdoor activities.

MEDIA

The *Wiener Zeitung* (www.wienerzeitung.at), first published in 1703, is the longest running newspaper in the world. With such a long and solid journalistic background, it's no surprise that Vienna receives a wide and varied view on political and social matters from its media.

Founded in 1957, Österreichischer Rundfunk (ÖRF; Austrian Broadcasting Corporation; www.orf.at, in German), the country's independent public broadcaster and the dominant force in Austrian media for decades, has faced stiff competition since the privatisation of airwaves in 2002. It owns 13 radio stations (Österreich1, Ö3, FM4, RÖI and nine regional radio stations) and the county's only two non-cable and satellite TV channels, ÖRF1 and ÖRF2.

Austria produces 16 national and regional daily papers, many of which are Vienna-based. Most are owned by their publishing houses and stick to quality over quantity, which results in fierce competition and generally good investigative journalism. Unusually, papers receive state grants, but this is under review.

Neue Kronen Zeitung (see below), a thoroughly tabloid spread, is easily Austria's most-read newspaper. Together with the *Kurier,* its more bourgeois brother, the two papers reach around half the paper-reading population of Austria daily. *News,* owned by Germany's Gruner und Jahr publishers, has the highest per-household readership in Europe for a weekly news magazine. The Newspapers & Magazines section in the Directory chapter (p228) provides a short but succinct list of papers available in Vienna.

LANGUAGE

German is the official language of Austria, but each region has a distinct dialect. The Viennese dialect has many similarities to High German, but also many differences. It is slower and more relaxed than its High German counterpart (it has all the qualities of a lazy drawl), but it is also more charming. The Viennese love to sprinkle their dialect with lively, evocative words and expressions that are often gobbledegook to other native German speakers. It's also peppered with French words, such as *Melange* and *Tottoir;* a hangover from the days when Maria Theresia encouraged her court to throw a bit of French into the conversation.

Within Vienna itself there exists a further dialect, Tiefwienerisch: a thick, sometimes unintelligible dialect that slowly oozes out between the lips, weighed down with expressive sayings that would make your mother blush. This is the language of the working class, but the non-working-class folk of the city just love it and use it at every opportunity.

THE NEUE KRONEN ZEITUNG

The *Neue Kronen Zeitung* (*Krone;* www.krone.at in German), a celebrated daily tabloid, is a power unto itself. Its influence on the nation is said to be so great that no national decision or project can go ahead without its consent, which is ultimately that of its founder and owner, Hans Dichand.

The figures speak for themselves: of a nation of around eight million, three million buy newspapers daily and of that three million, one million purchase a copy of the *Krone*. In percentage terms, that makes the *Krone* the most widely read newspaper per capita in the world. The paper's owners, Hans Dichand and Westdeutsche Allgemeine Zeitung (WAZ) media group (each own 50%), also publish the *Kurier,* the country's second-largest paper.

So what's all the fuss about? It seems the Viennese, like the rest of the world, love scandal and gossip. It could be said that the *Krone* is a less-aggressive (but just as powerful) version of the UK's *Sun:* light on solid newsworthy items, heavy on attention-grabbing headlines, celebrity gossip, cars and sports. There's even a section devoted to dogs.

The real fuss, however, is the paper's power to influence. Some sectors of society have voiced concern that too much influence lies in the hands of Dichand, and his views are at times far too nationalistic. Dichand recently retired and left the reins to his son Michael, but the paper's substantial influence over the populace remains as strong as ever.

Vienna has been at the crossroads of Europe for millennia and all these comings and goings have helped to create a population comfortable in two, three and sometimes four languages. For around 22% of the population German is not their native tongue. This level of proficiency extends through much of society – you may find yourself being accosted by a beggar asking for money, who, upon your ignorance to his requests in German, will switch to English or French.

If you don't speak much German, or none at all, don't worry. Nowadays English is taught from kindergarten level and a high percentage of the younger population speaks English quite well. The older generation unfortunately did not have the same advantages, but they'll probably be able to understand your requests if you keep them simple. See the Language chapter (p233) for vocabulary and pronunciation tips.

ECONOMY & COSTS

Austria has one of the strongest economies in the EU and Vienna is Austria's financial centre. Citizens enjoy good welfare services and health care, and a benign pensions and housing policy.

Vienna earns its cash through precision engineering, metal products and the manufacture of electrical and electronic goods. Banking and insurance also chip in their fair share, as does the service industry. The port of Vienna is the largest facility for container translocating in inland Europe, and has increased in importance with the opening of the Main canal connecting the Rhine and the Danube (Donau). Tourism isn't high on the list of money earners, although, like the arts industry, it's on the increase.

By European standards, Vienna isn't a particularly expensive city. It's cheaper than Paris, London or Rome, and more expensive than Prague or Budapest. Shopping aside, accommodation will be the most expensive item on your budget. Food isn't

HOW MUCH?

Box of Mozart Kügeln (marzipan chocolates) – €7.30

One litre of unleaded petrol – hovering over €1

A *Frankfurter* at a *Würstelstand* – €3

A *Krügerl* (half-litre of beer) at a *Beisl* – Just over €3

An *Achterl* (small glass of wine) at a *Heuriger* – €1 to €1.50

Copy of Vienna's city newspaper *Falter* – €2.40

Ticket to the Opernball – €215

20-minute *Fiaker* (horse and carriage) ride – €40

72-hour transport ticket – €12

that pricey, and if you take advantage of *Mittagsmenü* (set-menu lunch) you'll save and still eat exceptionally well. Museum entry fees range from €1 to €10. Many theatres and classical music halls sell tickets at discounted prices a few hours before performances, and have a standing-room-only section where tickets go for a song. These options help to stretch your euro that little bit further; see also the boxed text It's Free (p54) for ideas. Note that children pay lower prices and students and senior citizens often receive discounts. Public transport is an absolute bargain in Vienna.

On average, staying at a 2- to 4-star hotel (double room), eating out twice a day, taking in a show and a couple of museums and downing a few cups of coffee will set you back around €170 to €250 per day.

GOVERNMENT & POLITICS

As well as being the capital city of Austria, Vienna is (and has been since 1922) one of nine federal provinces *(Bundesländer)*. Every Austrian federal province has its own head of government *(Landeshauptmann)* and provincial assembly *(Landtag)*, therefore the mayor of the city is also the governor of a federal province and Vienna's City Council is a provincial assembly.

The Viennese are the country's staunchest supporters of socialism and are generally a rather cynical, expressive and questioning bunch when it comes to politics. It's not uncommon to hear a heated conversation over the affairs of the state or city at restaurants and

WIEN IST EIN HUNDEKLO

John Sparrow could easily have had Vienna in mind when he penned 'that indefatigable and unsavoury engine of pollution, the dog' in a letter to the *Times*. For some, the streets of the capital are strewn with dog poo; approximately 8.3% of households own a dog, which, at a conservative calculation, equates to 65,000 dogs, and while the Viennese love their dogs, the majority are loath to clean up their mess.

The city caters well to dog owners – 870,000 sq metres of parkland in Vienna is designated dog-only zone. Yet poo is everywhere: on footpaths, between parked cars, on grass verges, in parks and even in doorways. Recently, a campaign under the slogan *Wien ist ein Hundeklo* (Vienna is a dog's toilet) collected 157,000 votes in a matter of months in support of its demands for a council cleanup program and penalties for owners who neglect to clean up after their pets. Unfortunately it has had little effect to date, but the groundswell of support may soon change the councillors' minds. In the meantime, a cautionary glance groundwards before stepping out is advisable.

bars. People are rarely shocked, or even bothered, with the private lives of their politicians and couldn't care less who is having an affair with whom – their concern is how policy-making will affect their day-to-day lives and the future of their city.

Vienna's current mayor is Michael Häupl of the Social Democratic Party (SPÖ). Elections take place every five years; the last, in 2005, resulted in the SPÖ increasing its number of seats to 55, the ÖVP coming in second with 18 seats, the Greens moving up to third with 14 seats, and the FPÖ dropping to last with 13 seats.

On a national level, the SPÖ have historically held power, but the parliamentary race has often been a closely fought battle. The 1996 election ushered in the first post-war coalition between SPÖ and ÖVP, the country's conservative political machine, and in 2000 SPÖ lost its hold on parliament completely when the ÖVP, in collaboration with the FPÖ, had enough votes to form a government. FPÖ has gained international notoriety under its former leader Jörg Haider, who has expressed admiration for Adolf Hitler's labour policies and made several trips to see Iraq's former dictator Saddam Hussein while he was still in power. Haider, the governor of Carinthia province, resigned as head of the FPÖ in early 2000, following the international outcry generated by the FPÖ's inclusion in the federal coalition government.

The 2006 elections turned up more than one surprise. To all and sundry, it looked like a shoe-in for the ÖVP; Alfred Gusenbauer's SPÖ trailed the conservatives in opinion polls right up to voting day, and the increasing popularity of the Greens looked set to steal support from the socialists. The SPÖ went on to win the election with 35.34% of the national vote, 1% more than their biggest rival. Haider had split with the FPÖ in 2002 to form another right-wing party, the Alliance for the Future of Austria (BZÖ), which looked out of the running next to his old party and its buoyant new leader, HC Strache. However, he and his party won 4.11% of the national vote and a place in parliament (the threshold for parliamentary representation is 4%).

ENVIRONMENT

THE LAND

Vienna (elevation 156m) occupies an area of 415 sq km in the Danube Valley, the most fertile land in Austria. More than 700 hectares are under vineyard cultivation in the Vienna region, and nearly 90% of the wine produced is white. The largest wine-growing area is Stammersdorf in the northeast of the city.

To the west and north of the city are the rolling hills of the Wienerwald (p210), the much-loved Vienna Woods. These are the only hill ranges to speak of and the rest of the city is relatively flat. The Danube divides the city into two unequal parts, with the old city and nearly all the tourist sights to the west of the river. The Danube Canal (p78) branches off from the main river and winds a sinewy course south, forming one of the borders of the historic centre, the 1st district (Innere Stadt; p52). The long, thin Donauinsel (Danube Island p82), which splits the Danube in two as it courses through Vienna, is a recreation

area populated with beaches, playgrounds and pathways. Just to the east of the island is a loop of water called the Alte Donau (Old Danube), known for its beaches and water sports in summer and its ice skating in winter.

Almost half the city is given over to green spaces, more than any other European capital. Major parks include the Prater (p79), a massive belt of green just to the southeast of the Innere Stadt, and Lainzer Tiergarten (p99), a forested area home to wild animals and enthusiastic walkers in the far western reaches of the city.

GREEN VIENNA

Recycling is well established in Vienna – 295,000 tonnes of waste are recycled annually. This isn't only dictated by conscience – Viennese are compelled to do so by law. Vienna's widespread use of environmentally friendly trams and buses powered by gas has helped keep the city's air reasonably clean, and the Wienerwald does its part as an efficient 'air filter'. The city's water supply, which flows directly from the Alps, is one of the cleanest in the world, although many of the older houses still have lead pipes. This has resulted in one in every 10 houses recording lead in the water supply, but levels are generally too low to cause harm.

The Fernwärme incinerator (p92), has one of the lowest emission levels of any incinerator in the world. This plant processes waste matter, burning 260,000 tonnes of it annually to supply heating for more than 40,000 homes in Vienna.

Arts & Architecture ■

Art & Architecture

The architectural history of Vienna is long and grand. From its early Roman beginnings to its 21st-century contemporary constructions, the city's good burghers have played with brick and mortar, often mastering, sometimes excelling, in their attempts. Aside from the Renaissance era, the city is embellished with a healthy array of architectural styles, many of which are within easy reach of the Innere Stadt. Highlights abound, but the peak periods of baroque and *Jugendstil* (Art Nouveau) that emblazoned the city with a plethora of masterpieces, are in a class of their own; for some, their collective brilliance outshines all other attractions in Vienna.

In many ways, Vienna's art has waltzed arm in arm with its architecture through the ballrooms of history. And, like its architecture, the city's art peaked in its *fin-de-siècle* years, spawning *Jugendstil*, the Secession (Sezession), the Wiener Werkstätte (WW; Vienna Workshop), and greats like Gustav Klimt, Otto Wagner, and Egon Schiele. WWII and Austria's voluntary embrace of Nazism have created another artistic generation altogether, one attempting to come to grips with its at times unsettling heritage. Perhaps the most vivid expressionists to rise from the group are the Actionism art movement, whose work revolves around violent self-hatred.

> ## TOP MUSEUMS & GALLERIES
> - Albertina (p63)
> - Österreichische Galerie (p86) at Schloss Belvedere
> - Kunsthistorisches Museum (p73)
> - Leopold Museum (p76)
> - Secession (p72)

MEDIEVAL & BEFORE

Vienna's architectural heritage begins with the Romans; in the 1st century, the powerful empire built Vindobona, a small military camp, on the site of the Innere Stadt. Romanesque, a style noted for its thick walls, semicircular arches and simple geometry, was predominant in Europe from the 7th to 12th centuries. Only a handful of buildings in the city retain hints of Romanesque – most were replaced with the medieval Gothic style upon the accession of the Habsburgs in the 13th century. Gothic features pointed arches, heavy stonework, lacelike patterns and a dynamic structure.

Vienna's meagre medieval art collection is typified by two-dimensional religious pieces and is bolstered by Europe's earliest portrait, a 14th-century depiction of Duke Rudolph IV. In the Renaissance period, the Viennese shifted their focus from biblical to natural; the Danube school, an active group of painters in Bavaria and Austria from 1500 to 1530, combined landscapes and religious motifs.

WHAT TO SEE

Due to the Habsburg's unquestioned desire to clad everything in baroque, little remains of Vienna's art and architectural legacy before the 17th century. Roman ruins are visible at Michaelerplatz (p58), Feuerwehr Centrale at Am Hof (p64) and Hoher Markt (p66). The 12th-century Romanesque Ruprechtskirche (p66), the city's oldest church, graces the Innere Stadt's old Jewish quarter. The crowning glory of the Gothic era is Stephansdom (p53), but further examples exist; Maria am Gestade (p66) still retains an elegant Gothic tower, and traces of medieval architecture can be seen in Michaelerkirche (p59) and the Minoritenkirche (p65). A rarity for Vienna, the remains of a medieval synagogue are the focus of Museum Judenplatz (p66).

The Orangery at the Unteres Belvedere (p87) contains a collection of Gothic religious art, and the Dom- & Diözesanmuseum (p55) is blessed with the earliest European portrait, dating from 1360. The back of the Verdun Altar in Stift Klosterneuburg (p103) features one of the earliest examples of medieval panel painting in the country, and the oldest secular murals in the capital, from 1398, are the Neidhart-Fresken (p67).

BAROQUE & ROCOCO

Unwittingly, the Ottomans helped form much of Vienna's architectural make-up seen today. After the first Turkish siege in 1529, the Habsburgs moved their seat of power to the city and set about defending it; strong city walls were built, which stood until 1857 before making way for the Ringstrasse (see p68). However the second Turkish siege was the major catalyst for architectural change; with the defeat of the old enemy (achieved with extensive help from German and Polish armies), the Habsburgs were freed from the constant threat of war from the east. Money and energy previously spent on defence was poured into urban redevelopment, resulting in a building frenzy. Learning from the Italian model, Johann Bernhard Fischer von Erlach (1656-1723) developed a national style called Austrian baroque. This mirrored the exuberant ornamentation of Italian baroque with a few local quirks, such as coupling dynamic combinations of colour with groovy undulating silhouettes. Johann Lukas von Hildebrandt (1668-1745), another prominent baroque architect, was responsible for a number of buildings in the city centre.

Rococo, an elegant style incorporating pale colours and an exuberance of gold and silver, was all the rage in the 18th century. It was a great favourite with Maria Theresia, and Austrian rococo is sometimes referred to as late-baroque Theresien style.

While Austria didn't produce the same calibre of baroque artists as other central European countries, some striking church frescoes were painted by Johann Michael Rottmayr and Daniel Gran. Franz Anton Maulbertsch, working on canvas, was well known for his mastery of colour and light and his intensity of expression.

WHAT TO SEE

It's hard to turn a corner in the Innere Stadt without running into a baroque wall. Much of the Hofburg (p60) is a baroque showpiece; In der Burg square is surrounded on all sides by baroque wings, but its triumph is Nationalbibliothek (p63) by Fischer von Erlach, whose *Prunksaal* (grand hall) is arguably one of the finest baroque interiors in Austria. Herrengasse (p64), running north from the Hofburg's Michaelertor, is lined with baroque splendour, including Palais Kinsky at No 4 and Palais Mollard at No 9. Peterskirche (p59), off the Graben, is the handiwork of Hildebrandt, but its dark interior and oval nave is topped by Karlskirche (p89), another of Erlach's designs, this time with Byzantine touches. Schloss Belvedere (p86) and Palais Schwarzenberg (p77) – two highly esteemed Viennese addresses – are also Hildebrandt creations.

Nicolas Pacassi is responsible for the masterful rococo styling at Schloss Schönbrunn (p99), but the former royal residence is upstaged by its graceful baroque gardens.

The Habsburgs were generous patrons of the arts, and their unrivalled collection of baroque paintings from across Europe is displayed at the Kunsthistorisches Museum (p73). Palais Liechtenstein, the former residence of the Liechtenstein family, now houses the Liechtenstein Museum (p92), which contains one of the largest private collection of baroque paintings and sculptures in the world, and is in itself a gorgeous example of baroque architecture. Not to be outdone, the Albertina (p63) houses a vast number of paintings byAlbrecht Dürer, Raphael and Rembrandt.

Sculpture's greatest period in Vienna was during the baroque years – the Providentia Fountain (p57) by George Raphael Donner and Balthasar Permoser's statue *Apotheosis of Prince Eugene* (p87) in the Unteres Belvedere are striking examples.

TOP NOTABLE BUILDINGS

- Schloss Belvedere (p86)
- Fernwärme incinerator (p92)
- Hofburg (p60)
- Karl-Marx-Hof (p103)
- Rathaus (p70)
- Schloss Schönbrunn (p99)
- Stephansdom (p53)

NEOCLASSICAL, BIEDERMEIER & THE RINGSTRASSE

From the 18th century (but culminating in the 19th), Viennese architects – like those all over Europe – turned to a host of neoclassical architectural styles. In the mid-18th century, archaeological finds – such as the city of Troy in Turkey – inspired a revival of classical (Greek and Roman) aesthetics in many forms of art. In architecture, this meant cleaner lines, squarer, bulkier buildings and a preponderance of columns (particularly popular in the late 18th century, when romantic classicism relied heavily on Doric and Ionic Greek-style columns).

Meanwhile, the Industrial Revolution was marshalling the forces of technological development across Europe to house its factories and workers. As mechanisation upped the pace of production in the manufacturing industry, the new capitalists demanded more and more factories to produce their goods. In Austria, people flooded into Vienna from the countryside, drawn by the promise of jobs. Demand for housing skyrocketed, and cheap, mass-produced homes swelled the city's newly formed suburbs. Innovations in the manufacture of iron and glass allowed for taller, stronger buildings, and architects took full advantage.

The end of the Napoleonic wars and the ensuing celebration at the Congress of Vienna in 1815 ushered in the Biedermeier period (named after a satirical middle-class figure in a Munich paper). Growing industrialisation and urbanisation had created a cash-rich middle-class eager to show their wealth, and coupled with severe political oppression (a backlash from the revolutionary wars), their expression turned inwards to the domestic arena. Viennese artists produced some extraordinary furniture during this period; deep, well-padded armchairs were particularly popular, but the governing doctrines were clean lines and minimal fuss. Ferdinand Georg Waldmüller (1793-1865), whose evocative, idealised peasant scenes are captivating, is the period's best known artist.

Revolution in 1848 rocked the empire and set in motion a building boom. Franz Josef I, the newly crowned emperor, was at the peak of his power: when he took it into his head to overhaul the city, the city was overhauled. His ambition to one-up Napoleon's makeover of Paris led to him planning what would become one of Europe's most homogeneous inner-city designs. In the mid-19th century, Vienna was still essentially a medieval city in layout, with an inner area surrounded by fortifications. Franz Josef's plan called for the fortifications to be demolished and replaced with a ring road lined with magnificent imperial buildings. A competition was held to design the new Ringstrasse (p68); once the winner, Ludwig Förster, was chosen, demolition of the old city walls began in 1857.

Although Förster was the overall designer, the buildings were created by a company of successful architects; Heinrich von Ferstel, Theophil von Hansen, Gottfried Semper, Karl von Hasenauer, Friedrich von Schmidt and Eduard van der Nüll all had a hand in the creation of Vienna's architectural wonder. Some of the earlier buildings are *Rundbogenstil* (round-arched

Twin spires of Votivkirche (p69)

style, similar to neo-Roman) in style, but the typical design for the Ringstrasse is High Renaissance. This features rusticated lower stories and columns and pilasters on the upper floors. Some of the more interesting buildings on the Ring stray from this standard however; Greek Revival, neogothic, neobaroque and neorococo all play a part in the boulevard's architectural make-up.

Work on the Ringstrasse and associated buildings comprised one of the biggest building booms in the history of Europe. Thanks to the sheer volume of architecture created during this period, Vienna – despite massive destruction wrought in two world wars, including heavy bombing raids by the Allies towards the end of WWII which damaged almost every public building in the city and destroyed 86,000 houses – is still a showcase of European neoclassicism.

WHAT TO SEE

The Hofmobiliendepot (p91) has an extensive collection of Biedermeier furniture, some you can actually try, and more examples can be seen in the Museum für angewandte Kunst (MAK; p78). Ferdinand Georg Waldmüller's Biedermeier paintings hang in the Wien Museum (p88) and Oberes Belvedere (see p86) and one of the few uniformly Biedermeier houses is the Geymüllerschlössel (p103).

Taking a tram ride around the Ringstrasse provides a quick lesson in neoclassicism. Neo-Renaissance can be seen in Heinrich von Ferstel's Herrengasse Bank, and High Renaissance in Theophil von Hansen's Palais Epstein (p71), Gottfried Semper's Naturhistorisches Museum (p71) and Karl von Hasenauer's Kunsthistorisches Museum (p73).

Von Hansen also designed the Ring's Parlament (p70), one of the last major Greek Revival works built in Europe (take a close look at the statuary out front – perhaps horse-punching was part of the traditional Greek Olympiad). Von Ferstel's Votivkirche (p69) is a classic example of neogothic, but the showiest building on the Ring, with its dripping spires and spun-sugar façades, is Friedrich von Schmidt's unmissable Rathaus (p70) in Flemish-Gothic. The most notable neobaroque example is Eduard van der Nüll's Staatsoper (p169), though it's also worth having a look at Gottfried Semper's Burgtheater (p170).

While Franz Josef was Emperor he had a new wing added to the Hofburg (p60). The architect, Karl von Hasenauer, stuck very closely to a traditional baroque look, though there are some 19th-century touches – a certain heavy bulkiness to the wing – that reveal it is actually neobaroque. Neorococo runs riot in the Hotel Imperial (p197), built in 1863 as a princely palace and these days one of the city's most luxurious hotels. The Technical University and Luigi Pichl's Diet of Lower Austria at 13 Herrengasse are also examples of the neoclassical style. Paul Sprenger's Landeshauptmannshaft next door at 11 Herrengasse is neo-Renaissance.

JUGENDSTIL & THE SECESSION

While the neoclassical style continued into the late 19th century, by the 1880s Art Nouveau was beginning to bubble up. The clean lines and elegant sturdiness of neoclassicism still held appeal for architects who appreciated history and tradition, but some designers were tired of the style's restrictions. At the same time, the Industrial Revolution had spawned a trend towards cheaply made, mass-produced architecture and design, and towards a philosophy of utilitarianism above aestheticism. While it rejected the tradition of neoclassicism, Art Nouveau was in some ways a very nostalgic, elitist movement, longing for the old days of individual craftsmanship and for style above utility.

Vienna's branch of the Europe-wide Art Nouveau movement, known as *Jugendstil* ('Young Style'), had its genesis from within the Akademie der bildenden Künste (Academy of Fine Arts). The academy was a strong supporter of neoclassicism and wasn't interested in supporting any artists who wanted to branch out, so in 1897 a group of rebels, including Klimt (1862–1918), seceded. Architects, such as Wagner, Joseph Maria Olbrich and Josef Hoffman, followed. At first, *Jugendstil* focused more on interior and exterior ornamentation than on the actual structure of buildings. Its motifs were organic – flowing hair, tendrils of plants, flames, waves – and signature materials included iron, stucco and plain and stained glass.

OTTO WAGNER

Otto Wagner (1841–1918) was one of the most influential Viennese architects at the end of the 19th century (also known as the *fin de siècle*). He was trained in the classical tradition, and became a professor at the Akademie der bildenden Künste. His early work was in keeping with his education, and he was responsible for some neo-Renaissance buildings along the Ringstrasse. But as the 20th century dawned he developed an Art Nouveau style, with flowing lines and decorative motifs. Wagner left the Academy to join the looser, more creative Secession movement in 1899 and attracted public criticism in the process – one of the reasons why his creative designs for Vienna's Historical Museum were never adopted. In the 20th century, Wagner began to strip away the more decorative aspects of his designs, concentrating instead on presenting the functional features of buildings in a creative way.

The most accessible of Wagner's works are his metro stations, scattered along the network. The metro project, which lasted from 1894 to 1901, included 35 stations as well as bridges and viaducts. Wagner's stations were to blend in with the surrounding architecture, wherever they were built. All of them, however, feature green-painted iron, some neoclassical touches (such as columns), and curvy, all-capitals *fin-de-siècle* fonts. The earlier stations, such as Hüttldorf-Hacking, show the cleaner lines of neoclassicism, while Karlsplatz, built in 1898, is a curvy, exuberant work of Secessionist gilding and luminous glass.

Wagner's Majolikahaus (1898–99) was one of his first Secessionist works. The façade of this apartment block, at Linke Wienzeile 40, is covered in a pink floral motif painted on majolica tiles. Inside, stair railings and elevator grilles are extraordinarily decorative, flowing like vines. Next door, the Linke Wienzeile Building at 38 was created by Wagner and Kolo Moser and is covered in gilded leaves and flowers – inside and out. Ten years later, Wagner designed another residence, this time at Neustiftgasse 40 – while the Linke Wienzeile blocks were designed for the elite, Neustiftgasse was built for workers. The contrast between the two – due both to the clientele and Wagner's shift in architectural focus – is striking. By 1910 Wagner was committed to a futuristic style, and Neustiftgasse is all flat planes and straight lines, with very little ornamentation. The well-lit interior is decorated with marble and metal in greys, blues and white, studded with metal rivets and floored with parquetry.

Perhaps Wagner's most impressive work is the Postsparkasse (p78) at Georg-Coch-Platz 2. Built between 1903 and 1912, this bank looms over the plaza, its exterior of thin panels of marble studded with aluminium rivets topped by statues of protective goddesses. Inside, a reinforced concrete and aluminium courtyard is roofed in glass; all the building's doors, balustrades and radiators are also aluminium.

By the second decade of the 20th century, Wagner and others were moving towards a uniquely Viennese style, called Secession. Many artists felt *Jugendstil* had become too elitist; others thought it had been debased by commercialism, as more and more '*Jugendstil*-look' artefacts were produced. Secessionism stripped away some of the more decorative aspects of *Jugendstil* and concentrated more on functionalism, clarity and geometry.

Olbrich (1867–1908) and Hoffman (1870–1956) had both been pupils of Wagner, but as the 20th century developed so did their confidence and initiative, and they eventually ended up educating Wagner in the Secession style. Olbrich designed the showpiece of the Secession, the Secession Hall (p72), which was used to display other graphic and design works produced by the movement. The building is a physical representation of the movement's ideals, functionality and modernism, though it retains some striking decorative touches, such as the giant 'golden cabbage' on the roof. Interestingly, many scholars believe that Klimt drew the conceptual sketches for the building, and that Olbrich took Klimt's ideas and turned them into architectural reality.

Hoffman was inspired by the British Arts and Crafts movement, led by William Morris, and also by the stunning Art Nouveau work of Glaswegian designer Charles Rennie Mackintosh. But by 1901 Hoffman had abandoned the flowing forms and bright colours of *Jugendstil* to concentrate on black and white and the square, becoming one of the earliest exponents of the Secession style. He is best known for setting up the Wiener Werkstätte design studio, but he was also an architect of note. His major work is in Brussels, but some of his lesser structures can be seen on the outskirts of Vienna. Hoffman's folkloric, anti-urban-sophisticate outlook on design later led to the founding of the *Hohe Warte* periodical and was picked up by the Austrian National Socialist Party – apparently Hoffman had no objection to his work being used to endorse Nazi principles.

The Wiener Werkstätte claimed a core membership of greats, including Klimt and Kolo Moser (1868–1918), who set out to change the face of domestic design. They wanted

Jugendstil to appear not only in galleries and public buildings but in homes (albeit only well-off homes) all over the city. Determined that art wasn't just for walls, they made curtains, furniture, wallpaper, tiles, vases, trays, cutlery and bowls into objects of beauty, declaring, 'We recognise no difference between high art and low art. All art is good.'

Highly ideological, the WW (as they came to be known) joined a Europe-wide anti-capitalist, anti-industrial movement espoused by designers such as English Arts and Crafts guru Morris. They promised equality of designers and craftsmen and paid their workers reasonably for their output. The WW thought they could improve the taste of the middle and lower classes – rapidly becoming accustomed to mass-produced, slightly shoddy home-wares – by promoting individual design and quality craftsmanship for everyday objects. Hang the cost, they held that style was paramount.

The result was works of sublimely simple beauty – pure, abstract, geometric pieces. At the same time, artists such as Oskar Kokoschka were working for the WW, producing postcards and graphic books influenced by Japanese woodcuts and Austrian folk art. Bickering over how to price these gorgeous items (the WW was constantly running at a loss) tore the workshop apart, and in 1907 Moser left. After 1915 the workshop popularised and became, in essence, simply an interior-design company. In 1932 the WW closed, unable to compete with the cheap, mass-produced items being churned out by other companies.

No-one embraced the sensualism of *Jugendstil* and Secessionism more than Klimt. Perhaps Vienna's most famous artist, Klimt was traditionally trained at the Akademie der bildenden Künste but soon left to pursue his own colourful and distinctive style. His works, which are a rejection of earlier naturalistic styles, are full of naked female figures, flowing patterns and symbolism and are decorated with gold finishing and strong colours. Even today, sales of his paintings cause a sizable stir in both art and media circles (p87).

A contemporary of Klimt's, Schiele (1890–1918) is classed as one of the most notable early existentialists and expressionists. His gritty, confrontational paintings and works on paper created a huge stir in the early 20th century. Schiele worked largely with the human figure, and many of his works are brilliantly executed minimalist line drawings splashed with patches of bright colour and usually featuring women in pornographic poses. Along-side his sketches, he also produced many self-portraits and a few large, breathtaking painted canvases. The other major exponent of Viennese expressionism was playwright, poet and painter Kokoschka (1886–1980), whose sometimes turbulent works show his interest in psychoanalytic imagery and baroque-era religious symbolism.

The last notable Secessionist – and the one most violently opposed to ornamentation – was Czech-born, Vienna-based designer Adolf Loos. In 1908 Loos wrote a polemic against the rest of the Secessionists, *Ornament and Crime,* slamming the movement's dedication to decorative detail. He was of the opinion that ornament was a waste of labour and material, and that high-quality materials were far more beautiful than any kind of decoration. Loos' work features minimal, linear decoration and geometric shapes. He preferred to work in high-quality materials including marble, glass, metal and wood. Up until 1909, Loos mainly designed interiors, but in the ensuing years he developed a passion for reinforced concrete and began designing houses with no external ornamentation. The result was a collection of incredibly flat, planar buildings with square windows that offended the royal elite no end. They are, however, key works in the history of modern architecture.

WHAT TO SEE

Aside from the designs mentioned in the Otto Wagner boxed text, his beautiful flourishes can be seen in the Kirche am Steinhof (p98) and the Stadtbahn Pavillons (p89). Vienna's public transport system is partly the handiwork of Olbrich, who also designed the West-bahnhof. Hoffman spent many years on the Hohe Warte urban planning project, and in 1903 he designed the Purkersdorf Sanatorium (now restored), a health spa built from largely undecorated reinforced concrete, with an emphasis on planes and lines and using only sparse ornamentation of black-and-white tile and delicate geometric fenestration.

A prolific painter, Klimt's works hang in many galleries around Vienna. His earlier, classical mural work can be viewed in the Kunsthistorisches Museum (p73) and at the Universität Wien (p69), while his later murals, in his own distinctive style, grace the walls of Secession (p72) and MAK (p78). An impressive number of his earlier sketches are housed in the Albertina (p63) and Leopold Museum (p76), and his fully-fledged paintings are in the Leopold Museum, Wien Museum (p88), and Oberes Belvedere (p86).

The largest collection of Schiele works in the world belongs to the Leopold Museum. More of his exceptional talent is on display at the Wien Museum, Albertina, and Oberes Belvedere; Kokoschka can also be seen at the Oberes Belvedere and Leopold.

One of the most accessible designs of Loos is the dim but glowing American Bar (p155), a place of heavy ceilings and boxy booths just off Kärntner Strasse. Also worth a look are his public toilets (p58) on the Graben near the Pestsäule. The Loos Haus (p59), built between 1909 and 1911, is his most celebrated example, and a stark contrast to the spectacle of the Hofburg opposite. Loos's *Raumplan*, or 'plan of volumes', was a system he developed for internally organising houses; using this plan he later built the split-level Rufer and Moller houses. The Wien Museum (p88) provides a look into the personal world of Loos, with a reconstruction of a room from the architect's own house.

Pieces by the Wiener Werkstätte are on display at the MAK and can be bought from Woka (p180) and Altmann & Kühne (p180).

> **BEST OF THE FIN-DE-SIÈCLE YEARS**
>
> - **Klimt** – *Beethoven Frieze* (p72); *The Kiss* (p86)
> - **Loos** – Loos Haus (p59)
> - **Schiele** – Anything in the Leopold Museum (p76)
> - **Wagner** – Majolikahaus (p90); Kirche am Steinhof (p98); Postsparkasse (p78)

MODERN ARCHITECTURE

World War II not only brought an end to the Habsburg empire, but also the heady *fin-de-siècle* years. Vienna was struck by great poverty and serious social problems, and the Social Democrats stepped in to right the situation. The new leaders set about a program of radical social reforms, earning the city the moniker 'Red Vienna'; one of their central themes was housing for the working class.

Between 50,000 and 60,000 apartments were built during the 1920s and early 1930s, many in gigantic apartment blocks. Designed as a city within a city, these superblocks featured central courtyards and community areas, and successfully solved the city's housing problem. Not everyone was pleased with the results; the right wing saw these mammoth structures as 'voter blocks' and potential socialist barracks, and some of Vienna's leading architects, Loos included, criticised the regime for failing to produce a unified aesthetic vision.

Fernwärme façade by Friedensreich Hundertwasser (p92)

Nevertheless, they are a lasting testament to the most successful socialist government Europe has yet seen.

Although Vienna experienced a mass of construction between WWII and the early 1970s (to replace war-torn damage), creatively they were lean years; most buildings were cheaply built and lacked any style to speak of. A rare few, however, sport colourful tiled motifs; the working-class district of Meidling is particularly rich in these socially accepted graffiti pieces.

In the early 1970s Viennese architecture felt a new burst of life, as architects took on the challenge of building mass housing that was both functional and beautiful, and creating shops and bars with individual flair. The likes of Hans Hollein, Robert Krier and Hermann Czech all expended their considerable energy and talent on such projects.

Since the late 1980s a handful of multicoloured, haphazard-looking structures have appeared in Vienna; these buildings have been given a unique design treatment by maverick artist Friedensreich Hundertwasser. Hundertwasser felt that 'the straight line is Godless' and faithfully adhered to this principle in all his building projects, proclaiming that his uneven floors 'become a symphony, a melody for the feet, and bring back natural vibrations to man'. Although he complained that his more radical building projects were quashed by the authorities, he still transformed a number of council buildings with his unique style.

With the arrival of the 21st century, Vienna is once again enjoying a building boom. While the Innere Stadt remains largely untouched by the brush of modernism (as a Unesco World Heritage site, it is obligated to retain its architectural uniformity), the outlying districts are experiencing an upsurge in contemporary architecture – some as entirely new edifices, others incorporating existing historical buildings. This new wave of clean, glass-and-steel creations juxtaposes the city's historical core, and to date is successfully dragging Vienna into a new architectural millennium.

WHAT TO SEE

The municipality buildings of Red Vienna are scattered throughout the city. The most famous is Karl-Marx-Hof (p103) by Wagner's pupil Karl Ehn, but the largest is Sandleiten Hof at Matteottiplatz in Ottakring; it contains a staggering 1587 apartments.

Among the earliest works of Hollein is the Retti Candleshop at 01, Kohlmarkt 8; its façade features sheet aluminium and a doorway of two R's back-to-back. The two jewellery stores Hollein designed for Schullin on the corner of Graben and Kohlmarkt have been described as 'architectural Fabergés': their smooth, granite façades appear riven and melting. The architect's best-known work is the Haas Haus (p53), whose façade seems to be peeling back to reveal the curtain wall of glass below. Hollein's message here is powerful and correct – modern architecture has a rightful place in the Innere Stadt – but its delivery is suspect.

Krier's low-line housing estates at Hirschstettnerstrasse in Donaustadt, built in 1982 and featuring inward-looking courtyards, are a striking example of Vienna's more recent housing projects. Czech's most celebrated work is the tiny yet immensely popular Kleines Café (p141).

Hundertwasser Haus (p85) attracts tourists by the busload, as does the nearby Kunst-HausWien (p85), but Hundertwasser's coup d'état is the Fernwärme incinerator (p92); opened in 1992, it's the most nonindustrial-looking heating plant you'll ever see.

Of the 21st-century architectural pieces, the MuseumsQuartier (p75) impresses the most. The Gasometer (p97) complex is another modern construction to adapt and incorporate historical buildings, while nearby at 03, Rennweg 97, Günter Domenig's T-Center, a long, slither of glass and steel lacking any soft edges, is classed as one of the city's top modern conceptions. Vienna International Airport is currently enjoying an overhaul, due to be finished in 2008, and is expected to be a welcome addition to the city's ever-increasing armoury of contemporary design.

CONTEMPORARY ARTS

Vienna has a thriving contemporary arts scene with a strong emphasis on confrontation, pushing boundaries and exploring new media – incorporating the artist into the art has a rich history in this city. Standing in stark contrast to the more self-consciously daring movements such as Actionism, Vienna's extensive Neue Wilde group emphasises traditional techniques and media.

Up-and-coming artist Eva Schlegel is a real name to watch. She is working in a number of media, exploring how associations are triggered by images. Some of her most powerful work has been photos of natural phenomena or candid street shots printed onto a chalky canvas then overlaid with layers and layers of oil paint and lacquer; they manage to be enjoyable on both a sensual and intellectual level.

One of Vienna's best-known contemporary artists, Arnulf Rainer, worked during the 1950s with automatic painting (letting his hand draw without trying to control it). Later

VIENNESE ACTIONISM

Viennese Actionism spanned the period from 1957 to 1968 and was one of the most extreme of all modern art movements. It was linked to the Vienna Group, formed in the 1950s by HC Artmann, whose members experimented with surrealism and Dadaism in their sound compositions and textual montages. Actionism sought access to the unconscious through the frenzy of an extreme and very direct art; the actionists quickly moved from pouring paint over the canvas and slashing it with knives, to using bodies (live people, dead animals) as 'brushes', and using blood, excrement, eggs, mud and whatever came to hand as 'paint'. The traditional canvas was soon dispensed with altogether and the artist's body instead became the canvas. This turned the site of art into a deliberate event (a scripted 'action', staged both privately and publicly) and even merged art with reality.

It was a short step from self-painting to inflicting wounds upon the body, and engaging in physical and psychological endurance tests. For 10 years the actionists scandalised the press and public, inciting violence and panic – but they got plenty of publicity. Often poetic, humorous and aggressive, the actions became increasingly politicised, addressing the sexual and social repression that pervaded the Austrian state. The press release for *Art in Revolution* (1968) gives the lowdown on what could be expected at a typical action: '[Günter] Brus undressed, cut himself with a razor, urinated in a glass and drank his urine, smeared his body with faeces and sang the Austrian national anthem while masturbating (for which he was arrested for degrading state symbols and sentenced to six months detention)'. This was, not entirely surprisingly, the last action staged in Vienna.

delving into Actionism, foot-painting, painting with chimpanzees and the creation of death masks, Rainer has more recently been photographing and reworking classic pieces by Schiele, van Gogh and Rembrandt. Rainer's work expands on the important Viennese existentialist tradition, started by the likes of Schiele.

Actionism has been an important movement in Viennese art since the late 1950s (see above). Once an important member of the group, Gunter Brus now uses the more traditional media of painting and drawing for his still abrasive, shocking message. Much of Brus's work these days is *Bilddichtungen* (image poems), combining lurid images with strong, graphic text that is an integral part of the picture. Some viewers may see Brus's work as violent, self-hating pornography; others comment on the brilliant tension he creates between desire and repulsion. Hermann Nitsch, another founder of Actionism, conceived the Orgien Mysterien Theater (Orgies and Mysteries Theatre), a pseudo-pagan performance involving crucifixions, animal slaughter, buckets of blood and guts, and music and dance. Like Brus's work, many find Nitsch's art incomprehensible, but since 1962 he has held around 100 such events.

While the Viennese have an unmistakable penchant for the avant-garde, there is still space in the city's contemporary art world for more-traditional works. In the 1980s, when painting was supposedly dead as an art form (replaced, apparently, by conceptual art, multimedia and installation art), the Neue Wilde group performed CPR on its still-warm corpse, creating a style of painting which was more about the paint on the canvas than the concept behind it. The Neue Wilde – which includes painters such as Siegfried Anzinger, Herbert Brandl, Maria Lassnig and Otto Zitko – is committed to maintaining the Austrian painting tradition, whether figurative or abstract, and their work crosses a variety of subject matter and styles. Brandl, for example, paints large-scale landscapes where literal representations of mountains and forests dissolve into abstract metaphors and symbols.

WHAT TO SEE

To get a great overview of what's happening now in Viennese art, visit the Sammlung Essl (p104) and the Museum moderner Kunst (MUMOK; Museum of Modern Art; p77).

Music,
Literature
& Cinema ▪

Music, Literature & Cinema

While the Viennese love their contemporary visual arts and cinema – regularly taking a look at both – visitors are more likely to encounter Viennese music. Contemporary pickings are slim (legendary DJ-duo Kruder & Dorfmeister are definitely the cream of the crop, while nobody can forget Falco's 'Rock Me, Amadeus'), but Vienna's musical history is rich, glorious and immensely accessible. Beethoven, Mozart, Haydn and the Strauss family all did their stints in this city, and Vienna isn't about to let you forget it. Visit the Vienna Philharmonic and you certainly won't want to.

Guilt, self-loathing, a pathological distaste for being Austrian and a fondness for dogs: these are the themes you'll see again and again in Viennese cinema, literature or painting. The legacy of WWII has left an indelible mark on Vienna's modern artists, and is particularly prevalent in the sadomasochistic obsessions of film director Michael Haneke and the general hatred of humanity in author Elfriede Jelinek's novels.

MUSIC

Above all else, Vienna is known for music. It is a sign of the perhaps disproportionate importance of music to this city that after both world wars, when resources were so low that people were starving, money was still put aside to keep up performances at the Staatsoper. Today, it's impossible to avoid music in Vienna; buskers fill the Innere Stadt's main thoroughfares and Mozart look-alikes peddle tickets to concerts at busy tourist spots.

> **TOP DOWNLOADS**
>
> - *'Choral'* – Finale, Symphony No 9 in D Minor; Beethoven
> - *Cradle Song, Op 49, No 4*; Brahms
> - 'Rock me, Amadeus' (on *Falco 3)*; Falco
> - *Die Vorstellung des Chaos'* (The Representation of Chaos), Part 1, The Creation; Haydn
> - 'Bug Powder Dust Remix' (on *The K&D Sessions*); Kruder & Dorfmeister
> - *Die Zauberflöte* (The Magic Flute; EMI Classics version conducted by Otto Klemperer); Mozart
> - *'The Trout' Piano Quintet In A Major*; Schubert
> - 'The Blue Danube Waltz'; Strauss the Younger

An unmissable Viennese musical experience is a visit to the Vienna Philharmonic. Rated as one of the best orchestras in the world, it plays to packed houses wherever it tours. Started as an experiment in 1842, it grew in popularity in Vienna but did not venture on its first foreign tour until 1898, under the baton of Gustav Mahler. The Philharmonic has the privilege of choosing its conductors, whose ranks have included the likes of Mahler, Richard Strauss and Felix Weingartner. The instruments used by the Philharmonic generally follow pre-19th-century design and more accurately reflect the music Mozart and Beethoven wrote. Most of its members have been born and bred in Vienna, making it a truly Viennese affair.

The Habsburgs began patronising court musicians as far back as the 13th century, and by the 18th and 19th centuries the investment was paying off. Composers were drawn to Vienna from all over Europe and music had become a very fashionable hobby. Mozart, Haydn, Schubert and Beethoven all came in search of the Habsburg's ready money; between 1781 and 1828 they produced some of the world's greatest classical music. The Johann Strausses, father and son, kept the ball rolling when they introduced the waltz to Vienna.

Vienna's *Heurigen* (wine taverns; see p142) have a musical tradition all their own – *Schrammelmusik*. Musicians wielding a combination of violin, accordion, guitar and clarinet produce maudlin tunes which form a perfect accompaniment to drunkenness.

Vienna's impact on international jazz, rock or pop music is minimal. Falco (1957–1998), a household name for 1980s teenagers, reached the world stage with his hit 'Rock Me Amadeus', inspired by the film Amadeus. A popular name in Vienna's rock circles is Ostbahn Kurti (or Kurt Ostbahn, depending on how he feels at the time), who sings in

VIENNESE COMPOSERS AT A GLANCE

If you want to strike up a conversation with a local while waiting in line at the *Bankomat* (ATM) or pausing over a *Melange* (the Viennese take on cappuccino) in a coffee house, memorise some of these facts and you'll be good to go.

Christoph Willibald Gluck Knowing about Gluck will really get you in good with the intelligentsia, because although next to no-one has heard of him, this composer paved the way for all the big names by reconstructing opera: he replaced recitatives (which broke up the story and placed the emphasis on the singer) with orchestral accompaniments that kept the story moving along. His major works include *Orfeo* (1762) and *Alceste* (1767).

Wolfgang Amadeus Mozart Not just the star of a blockbuster movie, Mozart (1756–91) wrote some 626 pieces; among the greatest are *The Marriage of Figaro* (1786), *Don Giovanni* (1787), *Così fan Tutte* (1790) and *The Magic Flute* (1791). The *Requiem Mass,* apocryphally written for his own death, remains one of the most powerful works of classical music. Have a listen to Piano Concerto Nos 20 and 21, which comprise some of the best elements of Mozart: drama, comedy, intimacy and a whole heap of ingenuity in one easy-to-appreciate package.

Josef Haydn People in the know think Haydn (1732–1809) is one of the three greatest classical composers; he wrote 108 symphonies, 68 string quartets, 47 piano sonatas and about 20 operas. His greatest works include *Symphony No 102 in B-flat Major*, the oratorios *The Creation* (1798) and *The Seasons* (1801), and six Masses written for Miklós II.

Ludwig van Beethoven Beethoven (1770–1827) studied briefly with Mozart in Vienna in 1787; he returned in late 1792. Beethoven produced a lot of chamber music up to the age of 32, when he became almost totally deaf and – ironically – began writing some of his best works, including the *Symphony No 9 in D Minor*, *Symphony No 5* and his late string quartets.

Franz Schubert Born and bred in the city, Schubert (1797–1828) really knew how to churn out a tune: he composed nine symphonies, 11 overtures, seven Masses, over 80 smaller choral works, over 30 chamber music works, 450 piano works and over 600 songs – that's over 960 works in total – before dying of exhaustion at 31. His best-known works are his last symphony (the *Great C Major Symphony*), his Mass in E-flat and the *Unfinished Symphony*.

The Strausses and the waltz The waltz first went down a storm at the Congress of Vienna (1814–15). The early masters of the genre were Johann Strauss the Elder (1804–49) and Josef Lanner (1801–43). Johann Strauss the Younger (1825–99) composed over 400 waltzes, including Vienna's unofficial anthem, 'The Blue Danube' (1867) and 'Tales from the Vienna Woods' (1868). Strauss also excelled at operettas, especially the eternally popular *Die Fledermaus* (The Bat; 1874) and *The Gypsy Baron* (1885).

Anton Bruckner A very religious man, Bruckner (1824–96) was known for lengthy, dramatically intense symphonies (nine in all) and church music. Works include *Symphony No 9*, *Symphony No 8 in C Minor* and *Mass in D Minor*.

Johannes Brahms At the age of 29, Brahms (1833–97) moved to Vienna, where many of his works were performed by the Vienna Philharmonic. Best works include *Ein Deutsches Requiem*, his *Violin Concerto* and *Symphony Nos 1 to 4*.

Gustav Mahler Known mainly for his nine symphonies, Mahler (1860–1911) – though German-born – was director of the Vienna State Opera from 1897 to 1907. His best works include *Das Lied von der Erde* (The Song of the Earth) and *Symphony Nos 1, 5 and 9*.

Second Vienna School Arnold Schönberg (1874–1951) founded the Second Vienna School of Music and developed theories on the 12-tone technique. His *Pieces for the Piano Op 11* (1909) goes completely beyond the bounds of tonality. Viennese-born Alban Berg (1885–1935) and Anton Webern (1883–1945) also explored the 12-tone technique. At the first public performance of Berg's composition *Altenberg-Lieder,* the concert had to be cut short due to the audience's outraged reaction.

Zentralfriedhof (p97) is the burial site of some of the most prolific and famous composers of our times

a thick Viennese dialect. The mainstream Austrian pop of Wolfgang Ambros, Georg Danzer and Reinhard Fendrich also draws large crowds.

From the late 1980s to the mid 1990s, Vienna played an important role in techno and the electronic scene. The city's connection to Detroit and New York led to the development of downtempo and avant-garde techno, and the resulting tunes played in clubs around the world. Artists on G-Stone Records and Cheap Records (Kruder & Dorfmeister, Patrick Pulsinger, Erdem Tunakan) proved a powerful source for new electronic music, but by the end of the 1990s Vienna's electronic heart had suffered a minor stroke due to over-commercialisation. In the last few years the city's scene has experienced a revival, with old and new artists once again creating waves in the electronic genre. Tosca, a side project of Richard Dorfmeister, is well regarded; DJ Glow is known for his electro beats; the Vienna Scientists produce tidy house compilations; the Sofa Surfers dub-hop tracks are often dark but well received; and the likes of Megablast, Makossa and Stereotype are going from strength to strength.

Evening view of the famous Johann Strauss Denkmal (p78)

LITERATURE

Lacking the variety of German literature or the vein of 'isn't tragedy hysterical?' running through Czech literature, Viennese writing seems to be bowed down by the weight of its authors' history. Living under an autocratic empire, dealing with the end of an autocratic empire, the guilt of Anschluss, the horror of Nazism, the emotional damage (and its legacy) dealt by WWII, neo-Nazism and the general nastiness of human beings and bleakness of life are all very, very popular themes in Viennese literature. Not content to deal with difficult subject matter, Viennese authors have regularly embraced obscure and experimental styles of writing. Overall, the Viennese oeuvre is earnest, difficult and disturbing, but quite frequently it is intensely rewarding.

The *Nibelungenlied* (The Song of the Nibelungs) was one of Vienna's earliest works, written around 1200 by an unknown hand and telling a tale of passion, faithfulness and revenge in the Burgundian court at Worms. But Austria's literary tradition really took off around the end of the 19th century, the same time as the Secessionists (p23) and Sigmund Freud were creating their own waves. Karl Kraus (1874–1936) was one of the period's major figures; his apocalyptic drama *Die letzten Tage der Menschheit* (The Last Days of Mankind) employed a combination of reports, interviews and press extracts to tell its tale – a very innovative style for its time. Peter Altenberg (1859–1919) was a drug addict, an alcoholic, a fan of young girls and a poet who depicted the bohemian lifestyle of Vienna. Hermann Broch (1886–1951) was very much a part of Viennese café society. A scientist at heart, Broch believed literature had the metaphysical answers to complement new scientific discoveries. His masterwork was *Der Tod des Virgil* (The Death of Virgil), begun in a Nazi concentration camp in 1938 and finished in 1945, after his emigration to the USA.

Robert Musil (1880–1942) was one of the most important 20th-century writers, but he only achieved international recognition after his death, when his major literary achieve-

TOP BOOKS

- *Dicta and Contradicta,* Karl Kraus (1909) – fans of Dorothy Parker and Oscar Wilde will want to get their hands on this book of aphorisms by the 1920s satirist and social critic. Selections suitable for toilet-wall scribbling include 'Art serves to rinse out our eyes'.

- *The Play of the Eyes,* Elias Canetti (1985) – the third in this Nobel-Prize winner's autobiographical trilogy, 'Eyes' is set in Vienna just before the Anschluss. Covering the span of human experience, many believe it is a work of genius.

- *The Death of Virgil,* Hermann Broch (1945) – not just a novel, but a complete overhaul of what a novel can be, *The Death of Virgil* is one of German-language literature's stylistic ground-breakers (though it has some similarities to James Joyce's English-language *Ulysses*). Covering the last day of the poet's life, this book is hard, hard work.

- *Bambi,* Felix Salten (1923) – banned by the Nazis but beloved by alleged Nazi-sympathiser Walt Disney, this is the book that launched the movie that launched a million crying sprees. Nonpurists should look out for the scratch-and-sniff version, *Bambi's Fragrant Forest*.

- *The Radetzky March,* Joseph Roth (1932) – a study of one family affected by the end of an empire, the themes of *The Radetzky March* are applicable to any society emerging from a long-hated, but at least understood, regime. In some ways, it is about life after God.

- *The Third Man,* Graham Greene (1950) – put some time aside to read the book Greene designed as a screenplay: there is a lot of intriguing and easily missed detail in this complex story of death, morality and the black market in the rubble of post-war Vienna.

- *Beware of Pity,* Stefan Zweig (1938) – almost Russian in its melancholic psychological complication, *Beware of Pity* weighs logic against emotion in this tale of a hedonistic soldier who lacks direction until he becomes accidentally entangled with a lame girl.

- *Across,* Peter Handke (1986) – another cheery Viennese novel, *Across* follows an observer of life drawn into 'real being' after he whimsically murders someone. Pretty darn postmodern.

- *The Devil in Vienna,* Doris Orgel (1978) – a book for older kids, *The Devil in Vienna* is the story of two blood-sisters in 1938 Vienna, one Jewish, the other from a Nazi family, and their attempts to maintain their friendship. May get kids all riled up, in a 'why is the world so unjust?' way.

- *Lust,* Elfriede Jelinek (1993) – she's a witty and clever writer, but Jelinek hates all her characters. *Lust* is the story of a rural woman preyed on by her husband and lover, told without a gram of sympathy for the filthy habits of humans. Jelinek also wrote the book upon which Cannes-awarded film *The Piano Teacher* was based.

ment, *Der Mann ohne Eigenschaften* (The Man without Qualities), was – at seven volumes – still unfinished. Heimito von Doderer (1896–1966) grew up in Vienna; his magnum opus was *Die Dämonen* (The Demons), an epic fictional depiction of the end of the monarchy and the first years of the Austrian Republic. A friend of Freud, a librettist for Strauss and a victim of Nazi book burnings, Stefan Zweig (1881–1942) had a rich pedigree. A poet, playwright, translator, paranoiac and pacifist, Zweig believed Nazism had been conceived specifically with him in mind and when he became convinced in 1942 that Hitler would take over the world, he killed himself in exile in Brazil. Arthur Schnitzler (1862–1931), another friend of Freud, was a prominent Jewish writer in Vienna's *fin-de-siècle* years. His play *Reigen* (Hands Around), set in 1900, was described by Hitler as 'Jewish filth'; it gained considerable fame in the English-speaking world as Max Ophul's film *La Ronde*. Joseph Roth (1894–1939), primarily a journalist, wrote about the concerns of Jews in exile and of Austrians uncertain of their identity at the end of the empire. His recently re-released *What I Saw: Reports from Berlin* is part of an upsurge of interest in this fascinating writer; his most famous works, *Radetzky March* and *The Emperor's Tomb*, are both gripping tales set in the declining Austro-Hungarian empire.

Perhaps it's something in the water, but the majority of contemporary Viennese authors (at least, those translated into English) are grim, guilt-ridden, angry and sometimes incomprehensibly avant-garde. Thomas Bernhard (1931-89) was born in Holland but grew up and lived in Austria. He was obsessed with disintegration and death, and in later works like *Holzfällen: Eine Erregung* (Cutting Timber: An Irritation) turned to controversial attacks against social conventions and institutions. His novels are seamless (no chapters or paragraphs, few full stops) and seemingly repetitive, but surprisingly readable once you get into them.

The best-known contemporary writer is Peter Handke (born 1942). His postmodern, abstract output encompasses innovative and introspective prose works and stylistic plays. The provocative novelist Elfriede Jelinek (born 1946), winner of the Nobel Prize for Literature in 2004, dispenses with direct speech, indulges in strange flights of fancy and takes a very dim view of humanity. Her works are highly controversial, often disturbingly pornographic, and either loved or hated by critics. Elisabeth Reichart (born 1953) is considered an important – if obscure and ferocious – new writer, producing novels and essays concerned with criticism of the patriarchy and investigations of Nazi-related Austrian guilt, both during WWII and more recently.

Many Viennese authors are also playwrights – perhaps the Viennese fondness for the avant-garde encourages the crossing of artistic boundaries. Schnitzler, Bernhard, Jelinek and Handke have all had their plays performed at the premier playhouse in Austria, Vienna's own Burgtheater.

The first great figure in the modern era of theatre was the playwright Franz Grillparzer (1791–1872), who anticipated Freudian themes in his plays, which are still performed. Other influential playwrights who still regularly get an airing are Johann Nestroy, known for his satirical farces, and Ferdinand Raimund, whose works include *Der Alpenkönig* (King of the Alps) and *Der Menchenfiend* (The Misanthrope).

Vienna has a huge range of federal, municipal and private theatres supporting the work of playwrights and librettists; in fact, the Burgtheater (p170) is the premier performance venue in the German-speaking world. The Akademietheater, under the same management, is a more intimate venue that generally stages contemporary plays. The Theater in der Josefstadt (p171) is known for the modern style of acting evolved by Max Reinhardt. Theater an der Wien (p169) favours musicals.

CINEMA

Modern Viennese cinema is a bleak landscape of corrupt and venal characters beating their children and dogs while struggling with a legacy of hatred and guilt. That's a slight exaggeration, but contemporary film does seem to favour naturalism over escapism, violent sex over flowery romance, ambivalence and dislocation over happy endings where all the ends are tied.

The film industry is lively and productive, turning out Cannes-sweepers like Michael Haneke, of *The Piano Teacher* fame, and festival darlings like Jessica Hausner, director of the confronting *Lovely Rita*. A healthy serving of government arts funding certainly helps, as does the Viennese passion for a trip to the *Kino* (cinema), where local, independent films are as well attended as blockbusters by Graz-boy-made-good, Arnie Schwarzenegger. A yearly festival, Viennale (p171), draws experimental and fringe films from all over Europe, keeping the creative juices flowing, while art-house cinemas like the gorgeous *Jugendstil* Breitenseer Lichtspiele (p171) keep the Viennese proud of their rich cinematic history.

That history has turned out several big names ('big' in that they've moved to America and been accepted by Hollywood). Director Fritz Lang made the legendary *Metropolis* (1926), the story of a society enslaved by technology, and *The Last Will of Dr Mabuse* (1932), during which an incarcerated madman spouts Nazi doctrine. Billy Wilder, writer and director of massive hits like *Some Like it Hot*, *The Apartment* and *Sunset Boulevard*, was Viennese, though he moved to the States early in his career. Hedy Lamarr (not to be confused with Hedley Lamarr of *Blazing Saddles* fame) – Hollywood glamour girl and inventor of submarine guidance systems – was also born in Vienna. Klaus Maria Brandauer, star of *Out of Africa* and *Mephisto*, is another native. And Vienna itself has been the star of movies such as *The Third Man*, *The Night Porter* and *Before Sunrise*.

These days, the big name is Haneke, whose films tend to feature large doses of sadism and masochism. His film *The Piano Teacher*, based on the novel by Viennese writer Jelinek won three awards at Cannes. Documentary-maker Ulrich Seidl has made *Jesus, You Know*, following six Viennese Catholics as they visit their church for prayer, and *Animal Love*, an investigation of Viennese suburbanites who have abandoned human

THE THIRD MAN

'I had paid my last farewell to Harry a week ago, when his coffin was lowered into the frozen February ground, so that it was with incredulity that I saw him pass by, without a sign of recognition, among the host of strangers in the Strand.' Thus wrote Graham Greene on the back of an envelope. There it stayed, for many years, an idea without a context. Then Sir Alexander Korda asked him to write a film about the four-power occupation of post-war Vienna.

Greene had an opening scene and a framework, but no plot. He flew to Vienna in 1948 and searched with increasing desperation for inspiration. Nothing came to mind until, with his departure imminent, Greene had lunch with a British intelligence officer who told him about the underground police who patrolled the huge network of sewers beneath the city and the black-market trade in penicillin. Greene put the two ideas together and created his story.

Shot in Vienna in the same year, the film perfectly captures the atmosphere of post-war Vienna using an excellent play of shadow and light. The plot is simple but gripping; Holly Martin, an out-of-work writer played by Joseph Cotton, travels to Vienna at the request of his old school mate, Harry Lime (played superbly by Orson Welles), only to find him dead under mysterious circumstances. Doubts over the death drag Martin into the black-market penicillin racket and the path of the multinational force controlling Vienna. Accompanying the first-rate script, camera work and acting is a mesmerising soundtrack. After filming one night, director Carol Reed was dining at a *Heuriger* and fell under the spell of Anton Karas' zither playing. Although Karas could neither read nor write music, Reed flew him to London to record the soundtrack. The bouncing, staggering refrain that became 'The Harry Lime Theme' dominated the film, became a chart hit and earned Karas a fortune.

The Third Man was an instant success, and has aged with grace and style. It won first prize at Cannes in 1949, the Oscar for Best Camera for a Black and White Movie in 1950, and was selected by the British Film Institute as 'favourite British film of the 20th century' in 1999. For years, the Burg Kino (p171) has screened the film on a weekly basis.

The film's popularity has spawned the **Third Man Private Collection** (Map pp260–1; ☎ 586 48 72; www.3mpc .net; 04, Pressgasse 25; adult/child €6/4; ☎ 2-6pm Sat; bus 59A), a small museum featuring props from the film, signed photographs from the stars, press releases, posters and cinema programs. A shrine to Anton Karas fills one room (his albums are everywhere), but the museum's prized possession is one of the original zithers Karas used for the soundtrack, recovered from a house where the musician once lived. Visitors can also watch an excerpt from the film on an enormous 1936 German Ernemann 7b projector.

Fans of the film can create a self-guided tour of the city, stopping at the **Riesenrad** (p80), the location of the classic confrontation between Lime and Martins, **Palais Palffy** (Map p169), where Lime fakes his death, and the doorway at Schreyvogelgasse 8 (near Rathauspark), Lime's first appearance in the film. A far more thorough tour, the **Third Man Tour** (☎ 774 89 01; brigitte@viennawalks.tix.at; €16), is conducted in English by Dr Brigitte Timmermann. It departs at 4pm Monday and Friday from the Stadtpark U-Bahn station (Johannesgasse exit). It covers all the main location spots used in the film, including a glimpse of the underground sewers, home to 2½ million rats. You'll discover that the sewers are not linked together, so unfortunately it's impossible to cross the city underground as Harry Lime did in the film.

TOP FILMS

- *Indien* (1993) – two of Vienna's greatest comedy artists, Hader and Dorfer, are government workers on the road around Vienna and the surrounding countryside checking kitchen hygiene standards. Very funny but quietly tragic. Directed by Paul Harather.
- *Lovely Rita* (2001) – director Jessica Hausner shot her first feature film on digital with a cast of non-actor novices and an improvised script. *Lovely Rita* tells the story of a young Viennese woman struggling to escape her bourgeois life through love, but who ends up murdering her parents.
- *Foreigners out!* (2002) – documentary about a protest event staged in Vienna in 2000 on the election of Jorg Haider. A concentration camp for asylum seekers was installed near the Opera; immigrants – in a parody of *Big Brother* – could be voted out of the country. Worth seeking out. Directed by Paul Poet.
- *Twinni* (2003) – a period piece set in 1980, *Twinni* is the story of a Viennese teenager who moves to the country in the midst of her parents' divorce. Achingly awkward Jana suffers the attentions of a boy and the scorn of the Catholic church in this sweet film. Directed by Ulrike Schweiger.
- *The Piano Teacher* (2001) – winning scads of awards at Cannes, director Michael Haneke's most recent film continues his preference for groundbreaking, eye-opening, discomfiting projects. From the novel by Elfriede Jelinek, this is the story of a masochistic young woman who suppresses, warps and destroys all her feelings in the search for artistic perfection.
- *Dog Days* (2001) – on Vienna's hottest day in years, the suburbs combust. Six intertwined stories of bondage, sexual abuse, private investigators, car theft and marital breakdown make up a surprisingly humorous film. Directed by Ulrich Seidl.
- *Siegfried* (1924) – Austrian director Fritz Lang turns his hand to the legendary *Nibelungenlied*. It may be silent, black-and-white and not have any special effects, but this remains one of the best action films ever made.
- *Funny Games* (1997) – another gritty Haneke film; a sadistic duo move from house to house in Salzburg's lake district, kidnapping, torturing and then murdering the families. Certainly no funny game.

company for that of pets. Lately he has branched into features with *Dog Days*. Hausner has made several short films and recently released her first feature, *Lovely Rita*, the story of a suburban girl who kills her parents in cold blood. Her films critique Vienna: she says the city lacks imagination and courage.

History

History

THE RECENT PAST

With its entry into the EU in 1995, Austria entered a new age of politics. This move was endorsed by the populace, who voted a resounding 66.4% in favour of EU membership in the June 1994 referendum. Support soon waned however as prices increased with the introduction of the euro, but most Austrians have resigned themselves to the fact that the EU is here to stay.

After the 1999 national elections, Austria suffered strong international criticism when the far-right Freedom Party (FPÖ) formed a new federal coalition government with the Austrian People's Party (ÖVP) under the leadership of Chancellor Schlüssel. The new administration, despite having been democratically elected, was condemned before it even had the opportunity to put a foot wrong. The EU acted immediately and imposed sanctions against Austria by freezing all high-level diplomatic contacts, while Israel withdrew its ambassador.

The problem arose from the then leader of the FPÖ, Jörg Haider, and his flippant and insensitive remarks towards foreign members of state and his xenophobic rabble-rousing. Many Austrians, irrespective of their views towards the FPÖ, were upset at the EU's preemptive move, believing that Austria would not have been targeted had it been a more important player in European affairs. In any event, sanctions proved not only futile but counterproductive, and they were withdrawn by the EU in September 2000.

In the 2002 elections the FPÖ's popularity took a nose dive, dropping to a mere 10.1% (from 26.9% in 1999). The ÖVP, with 42% of the vote, secured another term in government; Haider instantly offered his resignation, and soon after a second term of the ÖVP–FPÖ coalition began in earnest.

TOP BOOKS ON VIENNA'S HISTORY

- *A Nervous Splendour: Vienna 1888-1889* (1979), *Thunder at Twilight: Vienna 1913–14*, Frederic Morton (1989) – highly enthralling accounts of seminal dates at the end of the Habsburg rule. The first deals with the Mayerling affair, and the second with the assassination of Franz Ferdinand in Sarajevo.
- *Fin-de-Siècle Vienna: Politics and Culture*, Carl E Schorske (1980) – a seminal work on the intellectual history of Vienna in seven interlinking essays
- *Guilty Victim: Austria from the Holocaust to Haider*, Hella Pick (2000) – an excellent analysis of Austria during this period
- *Last Waltz in Vienna*, George Clare (1981) – a moving account of a Jewish upbringing in the interwar years leading up to the Anschluss
- *The Austrians: A Thousand Year Odyssey*, Gordon Brook-Shepherd (1997) – one of the few books to tackle the history of Austria from the Babenbergs through to the country's entry into the EU. Great for a general overview
- *Vienna and the Jews, 1867–1938: A Cultural History*, Steven Beller (1989) – an insightful look into the cultural contributions Vienna's Jewish community made to the city

The October 2006 national elections proved quite a shock. Most believed that, despite a close race, the ÖVP would once again lead the country. They were however pipped at the post by Alfred Gusenbauer's Social Democratic Party (SPÖ) who received 35.34% of the national vote (ÖVP gained 34.33%, the Greens 11.05% and the FPÖ, under new leader HC Strache, won 11.04%).

AD 8	1137
Vindobona, the forerunner of Vienna's Innere Stadt, becomes part of the Roman province of Pannonia	Vienna is first documented as a city in the Treaty of Mautern between the Babenburgs and the Bishops of Passau

FROM THE BEGINNING

THE EARLY YEARS

The 25,000-year-old statuette, the *Venus of Willendorf,* is evidence of inhabitation of the Danube Valley since the Palaeolithic age. Vienna, situated at a natural crossing of the Danube (Donau), was probably an important trading post for the Celts when the Romans arrived around 15 BC. The Romans established Carnuntum as a provincial capital of Pannonia in AD 8, and around the same time created a second military camp some 40km to the west. Vindobona, derived from the Vinid tribe of Celts, was situated in what today is Vienna's Innere Stadt, with the Hoher Markt at its centre and borders at Tiefer Graben to the northwest, Salzgries to the northeast, Rotenturmstrasse to the southeast, and Naglergasse to the southwest. A section of the southwestern border had no natural defence, so a long ditch, the Graben, was dug. A civil town sprang up outside the camp that flourished in the 3rd and 4th centuries; around this time a visiting Roman Emperor, Probus, introduced vineyards to the hills of the Wienerwald (Vienna Woods).

In the 5th century the Roman Empire collapsed and the Romans were beaten back by invading Goth and Vandal tribes. During the Dark Ages, the importance of the Danube Valley as an east–west crossing meant that successive waves of tribes and armies attempted to wrest control of the region, and as a result Vindobona foundered.

The rise of Charlemagne, the king of the Franks, marked the end of the Dark Ages. In 803 he established a territory in the Danube Valley west of Vienna, known as the Ostmark (Eastern March). The Ostmark was constantly overrun by Magyars, a nomadic band of peoples from the Far East who had settled the Hungarian plain, until King Otto the Great crushed the Magyar army in a decisive battle in 955. However, the region received no mention in imperial documents until 996, when it was first referred to as 'Ostarrichi'. The forerunner of the city's modern name – 'Wenia' – first appeared in the annals of the archbishopric of Salzburg in 881.

THE BABENBERGS

Some 21 years after Otto's victory, the Ostmark was handed over to Leopold von Babenberg, a descendant of a noble Bavarian family. The Babenberg dynasty was to rule for the next 270 years.

The Babenbergs were a skilful bunch, and it wasn't long before their sphere of influence expanded: in the 11th century most of modern-day Lower Austria (including Vienna) was in their hands; a century later (1192) Styria and much of Upper Austria were safely garnered. Heinrich II 'Jasomirgott' (so called because of his favourite exclamation, 'Yes, so help me God') was the most successful Babenberg of them all, convincing the Holy Roman Emperor to elevate the territory to a dukedom; Heinrich II moved his court to Vienna in 1156.

Vienna was already an important and prosperous city by this stage, welcoming clerics, artisans, merchants and minstrels to its population. Its citizens enjoyed peace and economic success; the Viennese were awarded staple rights in 1221, which forced foreign tradesmen on the Danube to sell their goods within two months of landing, allowing locals to act as middlemen for commerce downstream. In 1147 Stephansdom (St Stephen's Cathedral; p53), then a Romanesque church, was consecrated and a city wall was built. A king's ransom flowed into the city in 1192: Richard the Lionheart, on his return home from the Crusades, was captured by the then ruler, Leopold V. Richard had purportedly insulted the Babenberg ruler at the Siege of Arce, and an astronomical figure was demanded in exchange for his release. Leopold used the money paid to found Wiener Neustadt. Under Leopold VI, Vienna was granted a city charter in 1221, ensuring further prosperity.

1155–56	1276
Vienna becomes a residence of the Babenbergs; a new fortress is built on Am Hof	Rudolf I of Habsburg occupies Vienna; the Habsburgs reign until 1919

In 1246 Duke Friedrich II died in battle, leaving no heirs. This allowed the ambitious Bohemian king, Ottokar II, to move in and take control. He bolstered his claim to Austria by marrying Friedrich II's widow. Ottokar gained support from Vienna's burghers by founding a hospital for the poor and rebuilding Stephansdom after a destructive fire in 1258. However, he refused to swear allegiance to the new Holy Roman Emperor, Rudolf von Habsburg, and his pride proved costly – Ottokar died in a battle against his powerful adversary at Marchfeld in 1278. Rudolf's success on the battlefield began the rule of one of the most powerful dynasties in history, a dynasty that would retain power right up to the 20th century.

THE EARLY HABSBURGS

Rudolf left the government of Vienna to his son Albrecht, who proved an unpopular ruler – he removed the staple right and began taxing the clergy. His successor, Albrecht II, was far more competent, and while he gained the nickname 'the Lame' due to his polyarthritis, he was also known as 'the Wise'. The city, however, struggled under a string of natural disasters; first a plague of locusts in 1338, then the Black Death in 1349, followed by a devastating fire.

In his short 26 years, Rudolf IV, Albrecht's successor, founded the University of Vienna in 1365, built a new Gothic Stephansdom in 1359 and set about reforming the city's social and monetary environment. He is better known for his famous forgery of the *Privilegium maius*, a document supposedly tracing the Habsburg lineage back to early Roman Emperors. Albrecht V, the next in line, ruled in a time of upheaval when Hussites ravaged parts of Lower Austria and bad harvests befell farmers. The foul air may have led to Vienna's first pogrom (see The Jews of Vienna, p45).

In 1453 Friedrich III was elected Holy Roman Emperor, the status Rudolf IV had attempted to fake. Furthermore, he persuaded the pope to raise Vienna to a bishopric in 1469. Friedrich's ambition knew few bounds – his motto, *Austria est imperator orbi universo* (AEIOU), expressed the view that the whole world was Austria's empire. To prove this he waged war against King Matthias Corvinus of Hungary and initially lost; Corvinus occupied Vienna from 1485 to 1490.

What Friedrich could not achieve through endeavours on the battlefield, his son, Maximilian I, was able to acquire through marriage. Maximilian's own marriage gained him Burgundy, while his son Philip's gained Spain (and its overseas territories). The marriages of Maximilian's grandchildren attained the crowns of Bohemia and Hungary. This prompted the proverb, adapted from the *Ovid*: 'Let others make war; you, fortunate Austria, marry!' Maximilian, a ruler on the cusp of the Middle Ages and the Renaissance, encouraged the teaching of humanism in Vienna's university and also founded the Vienna Boys' Choir (p168).

With the acquisition of so much land in such a short time, control of the Habsburg empire soon became too unwieldy for one ruler. In 1521 the Austrian territories were passed from Karl V to his younger brother, Ferdinand, who soon faced problems of insurrection and religious diversity in Vienna. He promptly lopped off the head of the mayor and his councillors and placed the city under direct sovereign rule.

TURKS, COUNTER-REFORMATION & BAROQUE

Rebellion and religion were not the only problems facing Ferdinand. The Turks, having overrun the Balkans and Hungary, were on the doorstep of Vienna by 1529. The city managed to defend itself under the leadership of Count Salm, but the 18-day siege highlighted glaring holes in Vienna's defences. With the Turks remaining a powerful force, Ferdinand moved his court to Vienna in 1533 and beefed up the city's walls with star-shaped bastions.

Soon after the siege, Ferdinand went about purging Vienna of Protestantism, a hard task considering four out of every five burghers were practising Protestants. He invited the

1365	1420–21
Foundation of University of Vienna by Habsburg Rudolf IV	The first large-scale persecution of Jews in Vienna (Wiener Geserah)

THE TURKS & VIENNA

The Ottoman empire viewed Vienna as 'the city of the golden apple', though it wasn't the *Apfelstrudel* they were after in their two great sieges. The first, in 1529, was undertaken by Suleiman the Magnificent, but the 18-day endeavour was not sufficient to break the resolve of the city. The Turkish sultan subsequently died at the siege of Szigetvár, but his death was kept secret for several days in an attempt to preserve the morale of the army. This subterfuge worked – for a while. Messengers were led into the presence of the embalmed body, which was placed in a seated position on the throne, and unknowingly relayed their news to the corpse. The lack of the slightest acknowledgment of the sultan towards his minions was interpreted as regal impassiveness.

At the head of the Turkish siege of 1683 was the general Kara Mustapha. Amid the 25,000 tents of the Ottoman army that surrounded Vienna he installed his 1500 concubines. These were guarded by 700 black eunuchs. Their luxurious quarters may have been set up in haste, but were still overtly opulent, with gushing fountains and regal baths.

Again, it was all to no avail – perhaps the concubines proved too much of a distraction. Whatever the reason, Mustapha failed to put garrisons on the Kahlenberg and was surprised by a quick attack from a German/Polish army rounded up by Leopold I who had fled the city on news of the approaching Ottomans. Mustapha was pursued from the battlefield and defeated once again, at Gran. At Belgrade he was met by the emissary of the sultan. The price of failure was death, and Mustapha meekly accepted his fate. When the Austrian imperial army conquered Belgrade in 1718 the grand vizier's head was dug up and brought back to Vienna in triumph, where it gathers dust in the vaults of the Wien Museum (p88).

Jesuits to the city, one step in the Europe-wide Counter-Reformation that ultimately led to the Thirty Years' War (1618–48). Maximilian II eased the imperial stranglehold on religious practice, but this was reversed in 1576 by the new emperor, Rudolf II, who embraced the Counter-Reformation. Rudolf ruled from Prague and left the dirty work in Vienna to Archduke Ernst, who was highly successful at cracking down on anti-Catholic activity.

In 1645 a Protestant Swedish army marched within sight of Vienna, but did not attack – by this time Vienna was once more in the hands of the Catholics. Leopold I, whose reign began in 1657, emptied much of the royal coffers on buildings and histrionic operas, prompting the baroque era through the construction of the Leopold wing of the Hofburg (p60). Encouraged by his wife and Viennese Christians, he instigated the city's second pogrom (see The Jews of Vienna, p45).

Vienna suffered terribly towards the end of the 17th century. The expulsion of the Jews left the imperial and city finances in a sorry state and a severe epidemic of bubonic plague killed between 75,000 and 150,000 in 1679. Four years later, the city was once again under siege from the Turks. However, Vienna rebuffed the attack, and the removal of the Turkish threat helped bring the city to the edge of a new golden age.

THE YEARS OF REFORM

The beginning of the 18th century heralded further baroque projects, including Schloss Belvedere (p86), Karlskirche (p89) and Peterskirche (p59). At the helm of the empire was Karl VI, a ruler more concerned with hunting than the plight of Vienna's citizens who enjoyed few social

Dome of Karlskirche (p89)

1529	1670
First Turkish siege of Vienna; the city survives and construction of the city walls begins	Second expulsion of Jews ordered by Leopold I; the financial strength of Vienna is severely weakened and Jews are soon invited back

and economic privileges (the staple right had long been abolished). Close to 25% of the population were either employed by the court or closely linked to it, and the court payed poorly. Coupled with a severe housing shortage, a lack of shops (most were used for accommodation), and pedlars crowding the city streets, the average citizen struggled. Having produced no male heirs, his biggest headache was ensuring his daughter, Maria Theresia, would succeed him. To this end he drew up the *Pragmatic Sanction,* cosigned by the main European powers – most of whom had no intention of honouring such an agreement. After ascending the Habsburg throne in 1740, Maria Theresia had to fight off would-be rulers in the War of the Austrian Succession (1740–48). She had hardly caught her breath before the onset of the Seven Years' War (1756–63). The Habsburgs retained most of their lands, but Silesia was lost to Prussia.

Maria Theresia is widely regarded as the greatest of the Habsburg rulers, ushering in a golden era in which Austria developed as a modern state. In her 40 years as empress, she (and her wise advisers) centralised control, reformed the army and the economy, introduced public schools, improved civil rights and numbered houses (initially for conscription purposes). Her son, Joseph II, who ruled from 1780 until 1790 (he was jointly in charge from 1765), was even more of a zealous reformer. He issued the Edict of Tolerance (1781) for all faiths, secularised religious properties and abolished serfdom. Yet Joseph moved too fast for the staid Viennese and was ultimately forced to rescind some of his measures.

The latter half of the 18th century (and beginning of the 19th) witnessed a blossoming musical scene never before, and never again, seen in Vienna or Europe. During this time, Christoph Willibald Gluck, Josef Haydn, Wolfgang Amadeus Mozart, Ludwig van Beethoven and Franz Schubert all lived and worked in Vienna, producing some of the most memorable music ever composed.

THE CRUMBLING EMPIRE

Napoleon's rise in the early 19th century spelled hard times for Vienna. He inflicted embarrassing defeats on the Austrians and occupied Vienna twice, in 1805 and 1809. Due to the Frenchman's success, Franz II, the Habsburg ruler of the time, was forced into a bit of crown swapping; he took the title of Franz I of Austria in 1804 but had to relinquish the Holy Roman Emperor badge in 1806. The cost of the war caused the economy to spiral into bankruptcy, from which Vienna took years to recover.

The European powers celebrated Napoleon's defeat in 1814 with the Congress of Vienna, and the capital regained some measure of pride. The proceedings were dominated by the skilful Austrian foreign minister, Klemens von Metternich.

The Congress heralded the beginning of the Biedermeier period (see p22 for a rundown of the arts during this time), named after a satirised figure in a Munich magazine. It was lauded as a prelapsarian period, with the middle class enjoying a lifestyle of domestic bliss and pursuing culture, the arts, and comfort 'in a quiet corner'. In reality, censorship and a lack of political voice were taking their toll, pushing Vienna's bourgeois population to the brink. The lower classes suffered immensely: a population explosion (40% increase between 1800 and 1835) caused massive overcrowding; unemployment and prices were high while wages were poor; the Industrial Revolution created substandard working conditions; disease sometimes reached epidemic levels; and the water supply was highly inadequate. On top of all this, while the ideals of the French revolution were taking hold throughout Europe, Metternich established a police state and removed civil rights: the empire was ready for revolution.

In March 1848 it broke out: the war minister was hanged from a lamppost, Metternich fled to Britain and Emperor Ferdinand I abdicated. The subsequent liberal interlude was brief, until the army reimposed an absolute monarchy. The new emperor, Franz Josef I, was just 18 years old.

1683	1740–90
Turks repulsed at the gates of Vienna for the second time; Europe is finally free of the Ottoman threat	Age of reform under the guidance of Empress Maria Theresia and her son Joseph II

Franz Josef promptly quashed the last specks of opposition, executing many former revolutionaries. He soon abated his harsh reproaches and in 1857 ordered the commencement of the massive Ringstrasse developments around the Innere Stadt. His popularity only began to improve upon his marriage in 1854 to Elisabeth of Bavaria; nicknamed Sisi by her subjects, she became the 'It Girl' of the 19th century.

The years 1866–67 were telling on the empire's powers: not only did it suffer defeat at the hands of Prussia, but it was forced to create the dual Austro-Hungarian monarchy, known as the Ausgleich (compromise). Vienna, however, flourished through the later half of the 19th century and into the 20th. Massive improvements were made to infrastructure – trams were electrified, gasworks built and fledgling health and social policies instigated. Universal male suffrage was introduced in Austro-Hungarian lands in 1906. The city hosted the World Fair in 1873, which coincided with the major glitch of the era – a huge stock-market crash. Culture boomed; the *fin-de-siècle* years produced Sigmund Freud, Gustav Klimt, Gustav Mahler, Johannes Brahms, Egon Schiele, Johann Strauss and Otto Wagner.

The assassination of Franz Ferdinand, nephew of Franz Josef, in Sarajevo on 28 June 1914, put an end to the city's progress. A month later Austria-Hungary declared war on Serbia and WWI began.

THE REPUBLIC

Halfway through WWI Franz Josef died, and his successor, Karl I, abdicated at the conclusion of the war in 1918. The Republic of Austria was created on 12 November 1918, and although the majority of citizens pushed for union with Germany, the victorious allies prohibited such an act. The loss of vast swathes of land caused severe economic difficulties – the new states declined to supply vital raw materials to their old ruler and whole industries collapsed. Unemployment soared, not only due to the influx of refugees and ex-soldiers, but also because a huge number of bureaucrats, once employed by the monarchy, simply had no job to go back to. Vienna's population of around one million was soon on the verge of famine.

By 1919 the franchise was extended to women; now all Viennese adults could vote for the city government by secret ballot. The socialists (Social Democrats) gained an absolute majority and retained it in all free elections up until 1996. Their reign from 1919 to 1933, known as Red Vienna (see below), was by far the most industrious and turned the fortunes of many working class citizens around.

The rest of the country was firmly under the sway of the conservatives (Christian Socialists), causing great tensions between city and state. On 15 July 1927, in a very dubious judgment, right-wing extremists were acquitted of an assassination charge. Demonstrators gathered outside the Palace of Justice in Vienna (the seat of the Supreme Court) and set fire to the building. The police responded by opening fire on the crowd, killing 86 people (including five of their own number). The rift between Vienna's Social Democrats and the federal Christian Socialists grew.

THE RISE OF FASCISM

Political and social tensions, coupled with a worldwide economic crisis, weakened the Social Democrats, giving federal chancellor Engelbert Dollfuss the opportunity he was looking for, and in 1933 he dissolved parliament on a technicality. In February 1934 civil war erupted, with the Schutzbund, the Social Democrat's militias, up against the conservatives' Heimwehr. The Schutzbund were soundly beaten, and the Social Democratic party outlawed. However, Dollfuss' reign was short-lived – in July of the same year he was assassinated in an attempted Nazi coup. His successor, Schuschnigg, buckled under

1805 & 1809	1857
Napoleon occupies Vienna and removes the Holy Roman Emperor crown from the head of Franz I	City walls are demolished to make way for the creation of the monumental architecture of the Ringstrasse

increasing threats from Germany and included National Socialists in his government in 1938.

On 12 March 1938 German troops marched across the border into Austria, just one day before a Austrian referendum on integration with Germany was to be held. Hitler, who had departed Vienna many years before as a failed and disgruntled artist, returned to the city in triumph, and held a huge rally at Heldenplatz on 15 March in front of 200,000 ecstatic Viennese. Austria was soon incorporated into the German Reich under the Anschluss.

The arrival of the Nazis was to have a devastating affect on Vienna's Jews in particular, though many non-Jewish liberals and intellectuals were also targeted. After May 1938, Germany's Nuremberg racial laws were also applicable in Austria, and thousands of Jews and their property fell prey to the Nazis. Austria joined Germany's WWII machine from 1939 to 1945. In WWI Vienna felt little direct effect from the war; this time the city suffered a heavy toll from Allied bombing towards the end of the conflict. Most major public build-

RED VIENNA

With Austria's Fascist, Nazi and, more recently, far-right political history, it's surprising to learn that Vienna was a model of social democratic municipal government in the 1920s, the most successful Europe has ever witnessed. The period is known as Rotes Wien, or Red Vienna.

The fall of the Habsburg empire left a huge gap in the governing of Vienna. By popular demand the Social Democratic Workers' Party (SDAP) soon filled it, winning a resounding victory in the municipal elections in 1919. Over the next 14 years they embarked on an impressive series of social policies and municipal programs, particularly covering communal housing and health, aimed at improving the plight of the working class. Their greatest achievement was to tackle the severe housing problem Vienna faced after the war by creating massive housing complexes across the city. The plan was simple: provide apartments with running water, toilets and natural daylight, and housing estates with parkland and recreational areas. This policy not only gained admiration from within Austria, but also won praise throughout Europe. Many of these colossal estates can still be seen in the city; the most celebrated, the Karl-Marx-Hof (p103), was designed by Karl Ehn and originally contained an astounding 1600 apartments. Even so, Karl-Marx-Hof is by no means the biggest – Sandleitenhof in Ottakring and Friedrich-Engels-Hof in Brigittenau are both larger.

For the interested, the Architekturzentrum Wien (p76) organises guided tours of the main Red Vienna housing complexes.

1910–14	1919
Vienna's population breaks the two million barrier, the greatest it has ever been	Treaty of St Germain signed; the Social Democrats take control of the Vienna City Council

THE JEWS OF VIENNA

Vienna's love-hate relationship with its Jewish population is a tale of extreme measures and one which began almost 1000 years ago.

Shlom, a mint master appointed by Duke Leopold V in 1194, is the first documented Jew to have lived in Vienna. For the next few hundred years the Jewish community lived in relative peace inside the city, even building a synagogue on what is now Judenplatz. In 1420 the Habsburg ruler Albrecht V issued a pogrom against the Jews for reasons unclear in historical annals, although it is speculated that the motive amounted to acquiring Jewish money and property to finance the fight against the Hussites. Poor Jews were expelled while the richer class were tortured until they revealed their hidden wealth, and then burned to death. Over the ensuing centuries Jews slowly drifted back to the city and prospered under Habsburg rule. Both parties were happy with the arrangement – the Jews had a safe haven, and the Habsburgs could rely on Jewish financial backing. However, it all turned sour with the arrival of bigoted Leopold I and his even more bigoted wife, Margarita Teresa, who blamed her miscarriages on Jews. In 1670 Jews were once again expelled from the city and their synagogue destroyed, but the act weakened the financial strength of Vienna, and the Jewish community had to be invited back.

The following centuries saw Jews thrive under quite benign conditions (compared to those of other Jewish communities in Europe at the time); in the 19th century Jews were given equal civil rights and prospered in the fields of art and music. It was in Vienna that Theodor Herzl published his seminal *Der Judenstaat* (The Jewish State) in 1896, which laid the political foundations for Zionism and ultimately the creation of Israel. But the darkest chapter in Vienna's Jewish history was still to come. On 12 March 1938 the Nazis occupied Austria, and with them came persecution and curtailment of Jewish civil rights. Businesses were confiscated (including some of Vienna's better-known coffee houses) and Jews were banned from public places, obliged to sport a Star of David and go by the names of 'Sara' and 'Israel'. Violence exploded on the night of 9 November 1938 with the November Pogrom, known as the Reichskristallnacht. Synagogues and prayer houses were burned and 6500 Jews were arrested. Of the 180,000 Jews living in Vienna before the Anschluss, more than 100,000 managed to emigrate before the borders were closed in May 1939. Another 65,000 died in ghettos or concentration camps and only 6000 survived to see liberation by Allied troops.

For a brief rundown on the current Jewish community, see the boxed text Jewish Vienna (p80).

ings, including the Staatsoper and Stephansdom, received damage, around 86,000 homes were rendered unusable or ruined and around 3000 bomb craters dotted the cityscape. Almost 9000 Viennese died in air raids (many buried in cellars under collapsed apartment blocks) and over 2000 lost their lives in the defence of the city. On 11 April 1945 advancing Russian troops 'liberated' Vienna; raping and pillaging by the Red Army further scarred an already shattered populace.

POST-WWII

Soon after liberation Austria declared its independence from Germany. A provisional federal government was established under Socialist Karl Renner, and the country was occupied by the victorious Allies – the Americans, Russians, British and French. Vienna was itself divided into four zones; this was a time of 'four men in a jeep', so aptly depicted in Graham Greene's *The Third Man*.

Delays caused by frosting relations between the superpowers ensured that the Allied occupation dragged on for 10 years. It was a tough time for the Viennese – the rebuilding of national monuments was slow and expensive and the black market dominated the flow of goods. On 15 May 1955 the Austrian State Treaty was ratified, with Austria proclaiming its permanent neutrality. The Allied forces withdrew, and in December 1955 Austria joined the UN. The economy took a turn for the better through the assistance granted under the Marshall Plan, and the cessation of the removal of industrial property by the Soviets. As the capital of a neutral country on the edge of the Cold War front line, Vienna attracted

1938	1945
Hitler invades Austria and is greeted by 200,000 Viennese at Heldenplatz; Anschluss with Germany	End of WWII; Austria is re-established and Vienna is divided into quarters

spies and diplomats: Kennedy and Khrushchev met here in 1961, Carter and Brezhnev in 1979; the UN set up shop in 1983.

Austria's international image suffered following the election in 1986 of President Kurt Waldheim who, it was revealed, had served in a German *Wehrmacht* (armed forces) unit implicated in WWII war crimes. But a belated recognition of Austria's less-than-spotless WWII record was a long time in coming. In 1993 Chancellor Franz Vranitzky finally admitted that Austrians were 'willing servants of Nazism'. Since then, however, Austria has attempted to make amends for its part in atrocities against the Jews. In 1998 the Austrian Historical Commission, set up to investigate and report on expropriations during the Nazi era, came into being, and in 2001, Vienna's Mayor Dr Michael Häupl had this to say: 'Having portrayed itself as the first victim of National Socialism for many years, Austria now has to admit to its own, active participation in the regime's crimes and recognize its responsibility to act instantly and quickly.'

1995	2000
After resounding support from its populace, Austria enters the EU	ÖVP-FPÖ coalition leads to EU sanctions against Vienna

Sights

Sights

Vienna is awash with sights. From the Innere Stadt to its outer lying districts, the city offers a gamut of splendid palaces, churches, baroque and *Jugendstil* (Art Nouveau) architecture, museums, and parks, all easily enjoyed using the city's fast and efficient public transport system.

Imperial history abounds, from the proud Hofburg and magnificent Schloss Schönbrunn to the grand array of Ringstrasse architecture. Baroque design, the mainstay of Habsburg taste, not only shines in the likes of Schloss Belvedere and Karlskirche, but also on the streets of Josefstadt and in small pockets throughout the city. *Jugendstil*, the backlash against the pomp of baroque and neoclassical, also features heavily; Kirche am Steinhof and the Majolika House are classic examples.

It would take a month of Sundays to see all the museums in Vienna. The MuseumsQuartier, the darling of modern Vienna, houses the city's finest contemporary art spaces, while nearby the Kunsthistorisches Museum houses some of the finest paintings on the planet. But its also the little things that make exploring Vienna a pleasure; walking through a medieval quarter in the Innere Stadt, pausing in a city park, enjoying coffee and cake in an old coffee house, taking a tram to an unknown destination, stopping at a farmers' market.

Vienna has 23 *Bezirke* (districts), but to make things easier for ourselves and for the traveller, we've grouped them under geographical headings. First comes the Innere Stadt, the compact central district, followed by the Ringstrasse, a wide boulevard lined with grandiose architecture surrounding the Innere Stadt. We then move on to East of the Danube Canal, an area encompassing a residential district rich in Jewish history, fabulous public parks and the city's modern expanse to the east of the central city. Next

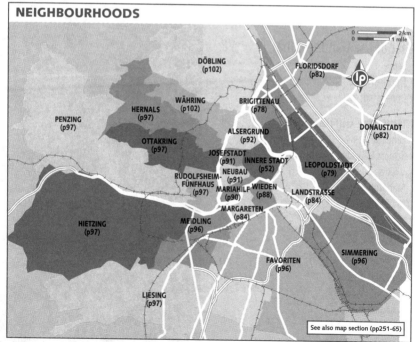

NEIGHBOURHOODS

See also map section (pp251-65)

A DIVIDED CITY

Vienna is comprised of 23 districts (Bezirke). Number one is the Innere Stadt, or 1st district as it's more commonly known, and the rest basically fan out from there in an almost spiral shape. Generally speaking, the higher the district number the further it is from the centre.

Districts not only divide the city geographically, but also socially. They often, but not always, signify social and financial status, and the numbers are no indication of any order. The 13th (Hietzing) and 19th (Döbling) districts are generally regarded as the crème de la crème, with the 18th (Währing) and 3rd (Landstrasse) coming a close second. Also-rans include the 8th (Josefstadt) and 9th (Alsergrund). The 15th (Rudolfsheim-Fünfhaus) and 16th (Ottakring) districts attract not only immigrants but also young Viennese looking for some ethnic diversity, while the 10th (Favoriten), 11th (Simmering) and 12th (Meidling) are regarded as the underbelly of the city and home to Prolos (a not particularly complimentary Viennese word for the working class). A resident of Hietzing would hardly ever venture into Simmering, and vice versa. The rest of the districts fall somewhere in between, except the Innere Stadt, which is a law unto itself. Viennese tend to associate it with tourists, shopping and an evening out rather than day-to-day living – except for the ones living there, of course.

Addresses come in three parts: district, street name and street number/apartment number in that order – eg 01, Kärntner Strasse 43/12 means flat 12, number 43 on Kärntner Strasse in the 1st district. We have stuck to this arrangement throughout the book. If you only have the postcode of an address it's possible to work out the district. Postcodes consist of four digits, with the middle two indicating the district; eg a postcode of 1010 means the place is in district one, and 1230 refers to district 23. Also note that the same street number may cover several adjoining premises, so don't give up if you come across an apartment block if you're looking for a restaurant as it may just be next door.

comes Inside the Gürtel, covering districts three to nine, which ring the Innere Stadt in a horseshoe shape to the west and south inside the city's multilaned road known as the Gürtel (literally meaning 'belt'). We finish with the districts beyond the Gürtel, cleverly titled Outside the Gürtel.

ITINERARIES
One Day
It's hard to know in which direction to head with only one day in your pocket, but it's best to start early at Vienna's heart, **Stephansdom** (p53). Wander its sublime nave and climb its steeple for views across the rooftops, before exploring the atmospheric back alleys directly behind the cathedral which date from medieval times. Meander your way along **Graben** (p58) and **Kohlmarkt** (p58) to the **Hofburg** (p60). Lunch at nearby **Café Central** (p139), one of the city's more esteemed coffee houses, then jump on tram 1 or 2 and circle the **Ringstrasse** (p68) for a brief but rewarding informal tour of the boulevard's buildings. Jump off the tram at Maria-Theresien-Platz, enter the **Kunsthistorisches Museum** (p73) and sample as much fine art as your system can possibly take. Before an evening performance at the **Staatsoper** (p169) enjoy a schnitzel at **Figlmüller** (p119), or a meal at one of the Innere Stadt's fine restaurants.

Three Days
After filling your first day with the must-sees of the One Day itinerary, start your second day with the **MuseumsQuartier** (p75) and a visit to the **Leopold Museum** (p76). Return to the Hofburg and discover the Nationalbibliothek's **Prunksaal** (p63), before late-lunching at the city's premiere market, **Naschmarkt** (p88). After lunch take in some much-needed fresh air in the **Prater** (p79) and treat yourself to a ride on the **Riesenrad** (p80). In the evening head to the outskirts of the city and pick a **Heuriger** (wine tavern; p142) that takes your fancy.

On the morning of the third day take a tour of **Schloss Schönbrunn** (p99) and spend some time in its manicured gardens. Lunch at **Café Gloriette** (p142) before heading back to view Gustav Klimt's sumptuous Beethoven Frieze in the **Secession** (p72). If there's time, make for **Kahlenberg** (p103) to beat the setting sun and spend the final evening exploring Vienna's nightlife along the Gürtel and in and around the Naschmarkt.

One Week

With one week, the city and its surrounds are yours. On the first three days follow the Three Day itinerary (see p49), then spend a day cycling or boating along the Danube Valley via the picturesque towns of **Krems** (p206), **Dürnstein** (p208) and **Melk** (p209). The next day visit the **Neusiedler See** (p211), exploring its quaint wine villages. If your sixth day coincides with a Saturday, combine breakfast and a flea market at the **Naschmarkt** (p185), then cross town to the gardens and galleries of **Schloss Belvedere** (p86) or head to the Innere Stadt to the **Albertina** (p63). This is a city where 'macabre' and 'imperial' comfortably sit in the same sentence, so an afternoon trip to the **Kaisergruft** (p57) should follow. The evening could be spent appreciating the fine acoustics of the **Konzerthaus** (p168) or **Musikverein** (p168).

The seventh day is mop-up day: enjoy anything that takes your fancy. If you need some guidance, spend the day shopping along **Kärntner Strasse** (p57) and **Mariahilf** (p186), sunning yourself on the **Donauinsel** (Danube Island; p82) or **Alte Donau** (Old Danube; p82), or simply wandering through the atmospheric back alleys of the Innere Stadt.

ORGANISED TOURS

Vienna is a city easily attacked on your own, but if you'd prefer the hassle taken out of touring, or time is of the essence, the city has a tour to suit; choose from bus, boat, bicycle, horse-drawn carriage, or the traditional walking tour.

It's also possible to organise your own tram tour; trams 1 and 2, which circle the Innere Stadt along the Ringstrasse, are perfect self-guided tours of the Ringstrasse's architectural delights, and Do-It-Yourself Tram Tours (p53) provides a few ideas for exploring the outer suburbs on your own. For suggestions of walking and cycling tours of the city, see the Walking & Cycling Tours chapter (p106).

Bus Tours

Bus tours are good for covering a lot of ground and taking in the further-flung sights.

CITYRAMA Map pp254-5

☎ 534 13; www.cityrama.at; 01, Börsegasse 1; 1hr/2hr/all-day city tours adult €13/16/20, child €7/7/7, day-long excursions adult/child from €99/45; ☽ 10am-5pm; ⊕ U1, U2, U4 Karlsplatz; ▣ D, J, 1, 2, 62, 65

Cityrama offers tours lasting from an hour to day, taking in not only Vienna (bus times are the same as on the Hop on Hop off Vienna Line; see right) but attractions within a day's striking distance of the city, including Salzburg, Budapest and Prague. Some tours require an extra fee for admission into sights, such as training at the Spanish Riding School. All details are on the website.

HOP ON HOP OFF VIENNA LINE
Map pp254-5

☎ 712 46 83; www.viennasightseeingtours.com; 04, Graf Starhemberggasse 25; 1hr/2hr/all-day tickets adult €13/16/20, child €7/7/7; ☽ 10am-5pm; ⊕ U1, U2, U4 Karlsplatz; ▣ D, J, 1, 2, 62, 65

Like Cityrama, Vienna Line buses stop at 14 sights in Vienna. Tickets range from one hour to all day, and you can hop on and off the buses as many times as you wish.

Buses circle the Innere Stadt, with a detour to Stephansplatz, departing on the hour, every hour, Monday to Thursday, and every half-hour Friday to Sunday, from outside Staatsoper. Buses at 11am, 1pm, 3pm and 5pm continue to sights east of the Innere Stadt, such as UNO city and Prater, the 10.05am, 12.05pm, 2.05pm and 4.05pm take in Schönbrunn and Schloss Belvedere.

OLDTIMER BUS TOURS Map pp254-5

☎ 503 74 43 12; www.oldtimertours.at; 07, Seidengasse 32; tours adult/student/child €18/15/8; ☽ May–mid-Oct; ▣ 1, 2

Vintage open-top (closed if rainy) oldtimer coaches trundle around the city centre and occasionally up to the Wienerwald (Vienna Woods). Tours last an hour and leave from in front of the Hofburg at Heldenplatz daily at 10.15am, 11.45am, 1pm, 3pm, and 4.30pm.

REDBUS CITY TOURS Map pp254-5

☎ 512 48 63; www.redbuscitytours.at; 01, Führichgasse 12; tours from adult/child €13/6.50; ☽ 10am-7pm; ⊕ U1, U2, U4 Karlsplatz; ▣ D, J, 1, 2, 62, 65

Vienna's newest bus tour company, Redbus offers 1½-hour tours of the main sites in and around the Innere Stadt and a day tour of the city's big sites, including stops at Schönbrunn and Grinzing. Buses leave from outside the Albertina (p63).

REISEBUCHLADEN Map pp254-5

☎ 317 33 84; reisebuchladen@aon.at; 09, Kolingasse 6; tours €27; ⏱ 10am-6pm Mon-Fri, 9.30am-12.30pm Sat; ⓜ U2 Schottentor; ⓡ 37, 38, 40, 41, 42, 43, 44

This travel agency conducts alternative sightseeing tours, such as 'Traum und Wirklichkeit' (Dream and Reality), which concentrates on Red Vienna and *Jugendstil* architecture, and a Friedensreich Hundertwasser tour. The guide isn't afraid to reveal uncomplimentary details about Vienna. Schedules depend on demand; tours are in German unless there are enough English speakers.

VIENNA SIGHTSEEING TOURS
Map pp254-5

☎ 712 46 83; www.viennasightseeingtours.com; tours adult/child €35/15

Run by the same company that organises the Hop On Hop Off tours, Vienna Sightseeing Tours offers a wide variety of half- and full-day tours in English with free hotel pick up. Its website lists all the tours and times.

Boat Tours

DDSG BLUE DANUBE Map pp254-5

☎ 588 80; www.ddsg-blue-danube.at; 01, Schwedenbrücke; full tour adult/child €15.50/7.75, half tour €11.30/5.65, children under 10 free; tours 11am & 3pm May-Sep; ⓜ U1, U4 Schwedenplatz; ⓡ N, 1, 2, 21

DDSG Blue Danube's boats circumnavigate Leopoldstadt and Brigittenau districts using the Danube Canal and the Danube as their thoroughfare. It's more of a relaxing break than a huge sightseeing tour. The half tour (two hours) ends at Reichsbrücke, the full tour (3¼ hours) back at Schwedenbrücke.

Its 'Hundertwasser Tour' is similar to the one above, the biggest difference being the boat docks at the Hundertwasser Haus (p85). It departs at 10.15am and 2pm daily from Schwedenplatz from April to September, and only on Friday, Saturday and Sunday in October. The tour takes around 1½ hours and costs the same as the tour above. You can either board at the Schwedenplatz or at Reichsbrücke.

DONAU SCHIFFAHRT
PYRINGER- ZOPPER Map pp254-5

☎ 715 15 2520; www.donauschiffahrtwien.at; 01, Schwedenplatz; grand tour adult/child €15.50/7.75, small tour €11.10/5.55; tours 10.45am Apr-Oct, 10.45am & 2.45pm mid-Jun-early-Sep; ⓜ U1, U4 Schwedenplatz; ⓡ N, 1, 2, 21

Pyringer-Zopper offers almost identical Danube circuits to DDSG Blue Danube and departs from either Schwedenplatz or Reichsbrücke.

Guided Walking Tours
MUSIC MILE VIENNA

☎ 588 30; www.musikmeile.at; 06, Linke Wienzeile 6; booklets €7

Reminiscent of Hollywood's 'walk of fame', this trail of marble stars runs from Stephansdom to Theater an der Wien and commemorates some 70 musical geniuses related to Vienna in one way or another. The stars are embedded in the footpath, often adjacent to where the composer, singer or musician lived or worked, and booklets provide background information on the person. The booklets are available from the following locations between 10am and 7pm: The Change Group (Map pp254–5; 01, Stephansplatz); Wien-Ticket Pavillon (Map pp254–5; 01, Herbert-von-Karajan-Platz) and Theatershop, Theater an der Wien (Map pp254–5; 01, Linke Wienzeile 6).

VERLIEBT IN WIEN

☎ 889 28 06; www.verliebtinwien.at; adult/child €12/6

Margarete Kirschner offers various themed walks covering such topics as Medieval Vienna, Art Nouveau and Hundertwasser and Modern Architecture. Tours take around 1½ to two hours, leaving at 10am and 2.30pm daily from June to October outside the Tourist Info Wien office (p230). Book direct or try through your hotel.

VIENNA TOUR GUIDES

☎ 876 71 11; www.wienguide.at; adult/child €12/6

Vienna Tour Guides are a collection of highly knowledgeable guides who conduct over 60 different guided walking tours, some of which are in English. Everything from Art Nouveau architecture to Jewish traditions in Vienna is covered. The monthly

Wiener Spaziergänge (Vienna's Walking Tours) leaflet from tourist offices (p230) details all of these, gives the various departure points, and also indicates those tours conducted in English. Tours last about 1½ hours and some require a valid public transport pass and extra euros for entrance fees into sights.

Other Tours

FIAKER

20-min/40-min/1-hr tour €40/65/95

More of a tourist novelty than anything else, a *Fiaker* is a traditional-style open carriage drawn by a pair of horses. Drivers generally speak English and point out places of interest en route. Lines of horses, carriages and bowler-hatted drivers can be found at Stephansplatz, Albertinaplatz and Heldenplatz at the Hofburg.

OLD-TIMER TRAMS Map pp254-5

☎ 790 91 00; www.wiienerlinien.at; adult/child €15/5; ⊕ U1, U2, U3 Karlsplatz, 🚋 D, J, 1, 2, 62, 65

On weekends and holidays from mid-May to October trams from 1929 trundle through Vienna taking people on one-hour tours of the city. They depart from the Otto Wagner Stadtbahn Pavillons on Karlsplatz at 11.30am and 1.30pm on Saturday and 9.30am, 11.30am and 1.30pm on Sunday.

Backstreets of the Innere Stadt (p55)

PEDAL POWER Map pp258-9

☎ 729 72 34; www.pedalpower.at; 02, Ausstellungsstrasse 3; tours with own bike adult/child €19/10, incl bike hire adult/student/child €23/19/12; ⊕ U1 Praterstern, 🚋 0, 5, 21

Pedal Power conducts half-day bicycle tours in and around Vienna from May until September. Tours start at 10am daily and there are five tours on offer: Ringstrasse, Hundertwasser Haus and Innere Stadt; Klosterneuburg and the Danube Island; Classic Music Memorials and Zentralfriedhof; Donau Park and Lobau; and the Danube Island and the *Heurigen* of Stammersdorf. Child seats and helmets cost €4 extra apiece.

Pedal Power also handles day and evening **Segway tours** (www.citysegwaytours.com/vienna; tours €70) through the Prater, along the Ringstrasse and into the Innere Stadt. They look funny but function without a hitch.

INNERE STADT

Drinking p139 & p146; Eating p119; Shopping p179; Sleeping p193

The Innere Stadt – and Vienna for that matter – started life as a Roman camp centred on what is now Hoher Markt around 15 BC, and since then it has remained the geographical, historical, financial, religious and imperial heart of the city.

It is a timeless and magical place, and nothing in Vienna comes close to it. A quick stroll down its back alleys and cobblestoned cul-de-sacs on a cold winter evening as the fog settles, or at dusk on a balmy summer evening, transports even the most hardened traveller into another world: one of horse-drawn carriages and Mozart and Beethoven recitals, when an imperial family ruled over this regal city. Deservedly, the entire district was designated a Unesco World Heritage Site in 2001.

Highlights abound. The imperial Hofburg is located here, as is the city's Gothic symbol Stephansdom. Every street seems to contain a museum or palace, and while the architecture is predominantly baroque, there are remnants of the Middle Ages and testaments to Vienna's *Jugendstil* days. Quality restaurants, top-notch bars and fine shops crowd the district, which is to say nothing of some of the city's most salubrious coffee houses.

DO-IT-YOURSELF TRAM TOURS

Trams have been operating in Vienna for well over a century and are an integral part of everyday life. Known locally as *Bim* after the sound of their warning bell, these red and white metal caterpillars are a smooth, hassle-free way to explore the city and often connect the Innere Stadt with the city's farther-flung districts. There are plenty of bonuses for touring the city this way: a window seat is a given, trams return to their original destination so there's little chance of getting completely lost, you'll see a side to the city most visitors don't and you may get the chance to practice your German (starting a conversation on a tram is certainly easier for tourists than locals).

We've supplied five suggestions for self-guided tram tours, but with 32 tram lines crisscrossing Vienna, these are only the tip of the iceberg.

Trams 1 & 2 Circle the Innere Stadt in opposite directions along the Ringstrasse and provide a glimpse of some of the city's richest architecture; ticket inspectors are rife on these lines, so remember to stamp your ticket.

Tram 6: Westbahnhof in Rudolfsheim-Fünfhaus to the Zentralfriedhof in Simmering. Runs along the busy Gürtel in the west into the working neighbourhoods of Favoriten (p96), then continues on to the wide streets of Simmering (p96) and the gates of the Zentralfriedhof (p97) to the southeast.

Tram 41 Schottentor on the Ringstrasse to Pötzleinsdorf in Währing. Starts downtown and climbs slowly northwest towards the Wienerwald (Vienna Woods) via the affluent districts of Alsergrund (p92) and Währing (p102) and terminates near the Geymüllerschlössel (p103) and woods.

Tram 60 Hietzing U-Bahn station to Rodaun in Liesing. Begins near the western entrance of Schönbrunn (p99), cuts south past the villas and prime real estate of Hietzing (p97) and into suburban Liesing, with its houses and sections and handful of *Heurigen*.

Tram D Südbahnhof in Favoriten to Nussdorf in Döbling. One of Vienna's longest tram lines, passing by Schloss Belvedere (p86) and along the Ringstrasse from Schwarzenberplatz to Schottenring before cutting through the pretty district of Alsergrund (p92) and arriving in the northerly *Heurigen* neighbourhood of Nussdorf (p102).

Sights

INNERE STADT

Not only is it beautiful, it is also compact. At only 1.8km across at its widest point and 3.6 sq km in size, the Innere Stadt is easily manageable on foot. In fact, it's best attacked on foot: pedestrian zones, tiny cobblestone streets and a confusing one-way system make driving in the Innere Stadt hell.

STEPHANSPLATZ

Stephansplatz is the focal point of the Innere Stadt and a good place from which to begin exploring Vienna; from here, some of the district's major thoroughfares, namely Kärntner Strasse, Graben and Rotenturmstrasse, connect to other attractions.

Stephansdom, the city's glorious Gothic cathedral, dominates the square so completely that it's hard to notice anything else, but there are one or two notable sights to find. To the north of the cathedral is the **Erzbischöfliches Palais** (Map pp254–5; Archbishop's Palace) which was built in 1640 and now houses the Dom- & Diözesanmuseum. On the corner of Stephansplatz and Graben is the controversial **Haas Haus** (Map pp254–5), a modern edifice of glass and steel that some love while others hate. The views of the square from the DO & CO hotel

and restaurant (p119) inside Haas House are ones for the photo album. Throughout much of the year Stephansplatz is full to overflowing with street performers, tour groups, Mozart lookalikes, *Fiaker* and voyeurs, a stark change to the Innere Stadt's peaceful back streets only a few minutes' walk away in any direction.

STEPHANSDOM Map pp254-5

☎ 515 52 3520; www.stephanskirche.at; ⊕ 01, Stephansplatz; admission free; ⊗ 6am-10pm Mon-Sat, 7am-10pm Sun; ⊕ U1, U3 Stephansplatz

The most beloved and recognisable structure in Vienna is the Gothic masterpiece Stephansdom (St Stephen's Cathedral), or Steffl (little Stephen), as it's locally called. It is the geographical and emotional heart of the city and an unmissable sight.

A church has stood on this site since the 12th century, but little remains of the original structure aside from the **Riesentor** (Giant's Gate) and the **Heidentürme** (Towers of the Heathens). Both features are Romanesque in style; the Riesentor (rumour has it that the gate was named because a mammoth's tibia, which was mistaken for a giant's shin, once hung here) is the main western

IT'S FREE

- Innere Stadt (p52) – an open-air museum and deserved Unesco World Heritage site
- Municipal Museums (p88) – free entry all day Sunday
- Stephansdom (p53) – only entry to the nave is free, but what a nave!
- Museum für Angewandte Kunst (MAK; p78) opens its doors to the public for free on Saturdays
- Zentralfriedhof (p97) – one of Europe's finest cemeteries and burial place to some of Vienna's most celebrated burghers

Stephansdom (p53)

entrance, and is topped by a tympanum of lattice patterns and statues. Stephansdom's Gothic makeover began in 1359 at the behest of Habsburg Duke Rudolf IV; he earned himself the epithet of 'The Founder' by laying the foundation stone.

The dominating feature of the church is the skeletal **Südturm** (south tower). It stands 136.7m high and was completed in 1433 after 75 years of hard labour. Ascend the 343 steps to the top (9am-5.30pm; adult/concession €3/1) for panoramic views over the Innere Stadt's rooftops from the cramped viewing platform; it's a long way, but well worth the effort. It was to be matched by a companion tower on the north side, but the imperial purse withered and the Gothic style went out of fashion, so the half-completed tower was topped off with a Renaissance cupola in 1579. Austria's largest bell, weighing in at a hefty 21 tonnes, is the **Pummerin** (boomer bell) and was installed here in 1952. The north tower, accessible by lift, is open from 9am to 6pm April to October, until 6.30pm July and August, and from 8.30am to 7pm November to March (adult/child €4/1.50).

From the outside of the cathedral, the first thing that will strike you is the glorious **tiled roof**, with its dazzling row of chevrons on one end and the Austrian eagle on the other; a good perspective is gained from the northeast of Stephansplatz. The cathedral suffered severe damage during a fire in 1945, but donations flowed in from all over Austria and the cathedral was completely rebuilt and reopened in just three years. Before entering the cathedral, take a little time to circumnavigate the intricate exterior. Decorated tombstones, complete with skull and crossbones, dot the outer walls, and a fading Gothic fresco of the agony of the Crucifixion lines the eastern façade.

While the façade will impress, the interior will amaze. Taking centre stage is the magnificent Gothic **stone pulpit**, fashioned in 1515 by Anton Pilgram. The expressive faces of the four fathers of the church (Saints Augustine, Ambrose, Gregory and Jerome) are at the centre of the design, but the highlight is Pilgram himself peering out from a window directly below the platform. He also appears at the base of the organ loft on the northern wall, seemingly holding up the entire organ on his own narrow shoulders. Take a closer look at the pulpit's handrailing: salamanders and toads fight an eternal battle of good versus evil up and down its length. The baroque **high altar**, at the very far end of the nave, shows the stoning of St Stephen. The chancel to its left has the winged Wiener Neustadt altarpiece, dating from 1447; the right chancel has the Renaissance red marble tomb of Friedrich III. Under his guidance the city became a bishopric (and the church a cathedral) in 1469. Guided tours of the cathedral in English are at 3.45pm daily from April to October; otherwise, tours in German leave at 10.30am and 3pm Monday to Saturday and 3pm Sunday (adult/concessions/child €4/2.50/1.50). Evening tours at 7pm every Saturday from June to September are also offered, and include a climb to the top of the south tower (€10/4). Organ concerts are a special treat, and are held at 8pm every Wednesday from May to October. Much of the nave is closed to the public during mass, which is held up to seven times a day, and can only be visited with a tour from July to mid-October. At times visibility can be poor, so visiting early morning and late in the day can sometimes prove annoying.

Entrance to the cathedral's **Katakomben** (catacombs; tours adult/child €4/1.50;

PEACEFUL POCKETS

The Innere Stadt can seem crowded at the quietest of times, and finding an undisturbed spot an impossibility. Surprisingly, some of its more atmospheric corners are only a few minutes' walk from tourist central:

Blutgasse to Stubenbastei Directly east of Stephansplatz is an intertwining set of streets, many of which are laid in cobblestones. Sights are few, but that doesn't matter when you're wandering the Innere Stadt's remaining medieval quarter.

Heiligenkreuzerhof & Schönlaterngasse Northeast of Stephansplatz, twisting Schönlaterngasse (lane of the beautiful lanterns) is lined with tall baroque buildings and connects to Heiligenkreuzerhof, a quiet residential courtyard and site of the city's most authentic Christmas market (p188).

Ruprechtsplatz & Around North of Stephansplatz is the old Jewish quarter and oldest church, Ruprechtskirche (p66).

Maria am Gestade & Around North of Stephansplatz, this fine Gothic church proudly stands guard over a flight of steps leading to quiet Concordiaplatz.

Between Am Hof & Judenplatz A tight, interlocking collection of streets decorated with fancy façades is just northwest of Stephansplatz.

---

every 15-30min 10-11am, 1.30-4.30pm Mon-Sat, 1.30-4.30pm Sun), which are open daily but can only be visited with a tour guide, is near the lift to the north tower. They house the remains of countless plague victims, kept in a mass grave and a bone house. Also on display are rows of urns containing the internal organs of the Habsburgs. One of the many privileges of being a Habsburg was to be dismembered and dispersed after death: their hearts are in the Augustinerkirche in the Hofburg and the rest of their bits are in the Kaisergruft.

DOM- & DIÖZESANMUSEUM Map pp254-5

515 52 3689; 01, Stephansplatz 6; adult/concession/child €5/4/2.15; 10am-5pm Tue-Sun; U1, U3 Stephansplatz

The Cathedral and Diocesan Museum of Vienna is a treasure-trove of religious art pieces spanning a period of over 1000 years. While the collection is blessed with extraordinary articles – such as the earliest European portrait, that of Duke Rudolph IV (1360), and two Syrian glass vessels (1280-1310) thought to be among the oldest glass bottles in the world – after a while it all seems to blend into one. If you're into religious art, however, this must be on your itinerary.

EAST OF STEPHANSPLATZ

The area just east of Stephansplatz is the last bastion of medieval Vienna in the Innere Stadt. It's labyrinth of cobblestone alleys and little-used streets are a pleasure to wander and amazingly free of the human traffic that flows through much of the central city. Di-

rectly behind Stephansdom is arguably the most charming section; here the tight alleys of Blutgasse, Domgasse and Grünangergasse intertwine to create a mesmerising scene, although the reopening of Mozarthaus Vienna on Domgasse has begun to disturb the peace a little during the day.

To the northeast of Stephansplatz the streets are a little wider but no less appealing; Heiligenkreuzerhof, home of one of the city's most delightful Christmas markets (p188), and Schönlaterngasse rank high on the quaint scale. Further north, Fleischmarkt (once the site of a meat market), which runs parallel to the Danube Canal and crosses Rotenturmstrasse, is blessed with a cluster of **Art Nouveau buildings**. No 14, built by F Dehm and F Olbricht between 1889 and 1899, exhibits gold and stucco embellishments, while No 7 (Max Kropf; 1899) was the childhood home of Hollywood film director Billy Wilder from 1914 to 1924. Arthur Baron was responsible for Nos 1 and 3 (1910), now home to a bank and a Spar supermarket. Other notables include the **Greek Orthodox Church** and Griechenbeisl (p122).

A fine pastime in this area is hunting down peaceful inner courtyards; many of the streets between Singerstrasse and the Danube Canal are sprinkled with them.

MOZARTHAUS VIENNA Map pp254-5

512 17 91; 01, Domgasse 5; adult/concession €9/7; 10am-8pm; U1, U3 Stephansplatz, bus 1A

Given a thorough polishing for the Mozart anniversary in 2006, Mozarthaus Vienna, the residence where the great composer spent 2½ happy and productive years, is now the city's premiere Mozart attraction.

The exhibition concentrates on the life and times of Mozart in Vienna (a total of 10 years). The top floor deals with the society of the age, providing asides into prominent figures in the court and Mozart's life, such as the Freemasons to whom he dedicated a number of pieces. Mozart's vices – his womanising, gambling and ability to waste excessive amounts of money – are far from ignored, but come across as endearing rather than wayward. The second floor concentrates on Mozart's music, and his musical influences. It was here he penned *The Marriage of Figaro,* which didn't go down well in Vienna, but was enthusiastically received in Prague. A surreal holographic performance of scenes from *The Magic Flute* grab most people's attention in the last room.

The final floor is sparsely furnished in period pieces to represent Mozart's apartment, but as no records exist of the purpose the rooms served, the layout is an educated guess. An audio guide is included in the admission price, and is an invaluable companion.

FRANZISKANERKIRCHE Map pp254-5

☎ 512 45 7811; 01, Franziskanerplatz; admission free; ☽ 7.30-11.30am & 2.30-5.30pm; ◉ U1, U3 Stephansplatz

It's quite a surprise to walk through the front doors of this early 17th-century Franciscan church after eyeing up the plain Renaissance façade to find a baroque interior strewn with gold and marble and heavy, glittering chandeliers. The high altar is a particularly impressive piece in the form of a triumphal arch. The archaeological findings of a recent dig at the church can be viewed by appointment only. Choir recitals are a regular feature here.

HAUS DER MUSIK Map pp254-5

☎ 516 48-0; www.hdm.at; 01, Seilerstätte 30; adult/concession/children under 12 €10/8.50/5.50; ☽ 10am-10pm; ▤ 1, 2, bus 3A

The Haus der Musik (House of Music) rates among the best museums in the city. Spread over four floors (the fifth is a café and restaurant), it helps explain sound in an amusing and interactive way (in English and German) that is accessible to both children and adults.

The first floor is host to the historical archives of the Vienna Philharmonic where a shortened version of the world famous

New Year's concert can be heard and a bizarre interactive tool allows you to compose your own waltz with the roll of a dice. Things change quickly upon entering the second floor – its first room, the 'prenatal listening room', re-creates noises heard by babies in the womb. It's the perfect place to lie down and relax for a while. The following rooms delve into the mechanics of sound, and feature plenty of engaging instruments, interactive toys and touchscreens. Here you can test the limits of your hearing and play around with sampled sounds to record your own CD (€7.30).

Floor 3 covers Vienna's classical composers. Josef Haydn, Wolfgang Amadeus Mozart, Ludwig van Beethoven, Franz Schubert, Johann Strauss and Gustav Mahler all receive a room each and their lives and astounding musical talents are detailed in a thoughtful and informative manner. The floor is polished off with the 'virtual conductor': a video of the Vienna Philharmonic responds to a conducting baton and keeps time with your movements, showing how hard it is to conduct a full orchestra.

The final level deals with experimental and electronic music, which you can also modify yourself. Singing trees, sound sticks and beeping buttons are just some of the hands-on 'instruments' at your disposal.

The museum hosts the occasional children's program – see the website for details.

DOMINIKANERKIRCHE Map pp254-5

☎ 512 91 74; 01, Postgasse 4; admission free; ☽ daily; ◉ U3 Stubentor, ▤ 1, 2, bus 2A

Dominikanerkirche (Dominican Church) was built on the site of an earlier church and completed in 1634. The expansive interior is incredibly baroque, with white stucco, frescoes and even the imperial double-headed eagle on the ceiling. The major advantage of visiting the Dominikanerkirche is the chance to appreciate a sumptuous baroque church without the crowds. The Dominicans first came to Vienna in 1226 under the invitation of Leopold VI of Babenberg.

GREEK ORTHODOX CHURCH Map pp254-5

01, Fleischmarkt 13; admission free; ☽ 11am-3pm Sun-Fri; ◉ U1, U4 Schwedenplatz, ▤ N, 1, 2, 21

For some, the beauty of the Greek Orthodox Church on Fleischmarkt outshines many of its baroque counterparts. Built in 1861 by Vienna's Greek community, its interior is a glittering blaze of Byzantine design which has left no wall space untouched. The ceiling fresco depicting the prophets surrounded by swirls of gold is topped by a high alter of 13 panels and a doorway to the inner sanctum, each of which features elaborate gilding. Outside opening hours, the church's dark entranceway provides a taster of the rich church within. The church is easy to spot; look for the colourful brickwork façade next to Griechenbeisl.

KÄRNTNER STRASSE & AROUND

As the main connection between Stephansplatz and the Staatsoper (p169), Kärntner Strasse receives the most attention of any street in Vienna. Once lined with the finest establishments in the city, it was *the* place to shop, but standards have dropped and High Street names and souvenir shops have taken over. There are a few exceptions, such as J & L Lobmeyr at No 26 (p181), seller of exquisite Werkstätte pieces. It's still a pleasant street to stroll down (though with so many people, it's more of a weave), enjoying the diverse array of busker performances; harp players and puppeteers are the norm.

Nearby **Albertinaplatz** is the sight of the troubling work **Monument against War and Fascism** (Map pp254–5) by Alfred Hrdlicka, created in 1988. This series of pale blocklike sculptures commemorates Jews and other victims of war and fascism. The dark, squat shape wrapped in barbed wire represents a Jew scrubbing the floor; the greyish block originally came from the Mauthausen concentration camp. A few streets north is the large and unattractive **Neue Markt**, once the city's flour market now home to the Kaisergruft (Imperial Burial Vault). Its centre is thankfully saved by a replica of Georg Raphael Donner's beautiful **Providentia Fountain** (1739; Map pp254–5). The original figures proved too risqué for Maria Theresia and had to be removed in 1773 – since 1921 they have resided in the Baroque Museum in the Lower Belvedere.

KAISERGRUFT Map pp254-5

☎ 512 68 53; 01, Neuer Markt; adult/concession/ child €4/3/1.50; ☼ 10am-6pm; ◎ U1, U3 Stephansplatz, bus 2A

The Kaisergruft beneath the Kapuzinerkirche (Church of the Capuchin Friars) is the final resting place of most of the

Habsburg royal family (the hearts and organs reside in Augustinerkirche and Stephansdom respectively). Opened in 1633, it was instigated by Empress Anna (1585–1618), and her body and that of her husband, Emperor Matthias (1557–1619), were the first to be entombed. Since then, all but three of the Habsburg dynasty found their way here; the last Emperor, Karl I, was buried in exile in Madeira and Marie Antoinette (daughter to Maria Theresia) still lies in Paris. The remains of Duc de Reichstadt, son of Napoleon's second wife Marie Louise, were transferred to Paris as a publicity stunt by the Nazis in 1940. The last Habsburg to be buried in the crypt was Empress Zita, wife of Karl I, in 1989. Needless to say, she was given a right royal sendoff by the city and its citizens.

It's interesting to observe how fashions change through the ages even in death – tombs range from the unadorned to the ostentatious. By far the most elaborate caskets are those portraying 18th-century baroque pomp, such as the huge double sarcophagus containing Maria Theresia and Franz Stephan, with fine scenes engraved in the metal and plenty of angels and other ornamentation. The tomb of Charles VI is also striking and has been expertly restored. Both of these were the work of Balthasar Moll. Most visitors come to see the tombs of Franz Josef I and his much-adored wife Empress Elisabeth; both are constantly strewn with fresh flowers.

The only non-Habsburg of the 138 people buried here is the Countess Fuchs, a formative influence on the youthful Maria Theresia.

STAATSOPERMUSEUM Map pp254-5

☎ 514 44 2250; 01, Goethegasse 1; adult/ senior/child €3/2.50/2, with Staatsoper tour €6.50/5.50/3.50; ☼ 10am-6pm Tue-Sun; ◎ U1, U2, U4 Karlsplatz, ☒ D, J, 1, 2, 62, 65

This shrine to one of Vienna's greatest icons covers the last 50 years of the Staatsoper. Photos on the museum's façade show the damage the building suffered during the war, and the painstaking restoration which took 10 years to complete. Inside, the museum runs through five decades of highlights such as Karajan's eight-year reign as director and the performance of *Lulu*. Photos and articles abound, but unfortunately it's all quite static and will only impress opera fans.

A visit to this museum is best combined with a tour of the Staatsoper (p169).

THEATERMUSEUM Map pp254-5

☎ 525 24 610; www.theatermuseum.at in German; 01, Lobkowitzplatz 2; adult/concession/family €4.50/3.50/9; ☺ 10am-6pm Tue-Sun; ◉ U1, U2, U4 Karlsplatz, bus 3A

The baroque Lobkowitz palace, which houses the Theatermuseum (Theatre Museum), is as much a delight to visit as the museum itself. Built between 1691 and 1694, it was the first of its kind in Vienna, and gained its name from the noble family who occupied its esteemed halls from 1753 onwards. The Eroicasaal, with its frescoed ceiling, is a sight to behold, and Beethoven conducted the first performance of his Third Symphony in the banquet hall.

The palace has served time as the French embassy and the Czech embassy, and as a fashion museum during WWII, but since 1991 has housed a museum devoted to the history of Austria's theatre. On display are costumes, props and set designs mixed in with theatre memorabilia, such as Mahler's farewell message to the Vienna Opera Company. A small room hidden towards the back of the 1st floor contains an ensemble of puppets from puppeteer Richard Teschner. These works of intricate detail range from magicians to orang-utans and are vaguely reminiscent of Java's *Wayang Golek* wooden puppets. They are often used in performances; inquire at the ticket desk for times. The museum is included in the Gold and Silver tickets (p69).

GRABEN & KOHLMARKT

With Kärntner Strasse, Graben and Kohlmarkt make up Vienna's holy trinity of streets. These pedestrian arteries which connect the Hofburg with Stephansdom are rarely empty of people beating a well-trodden path between the two.

Graben, which runs northwest from the junction of Stock-im-Eisen-Platz and Kärntner Strasse, started life as a protective ditch (*Graben* means 'ditch') for the Roman encampment. Today it is lined with expensive shops and historical and *Jugendstil* buildings. Particularly impressive is the neo-Renaissance Equitable Palais (Map pp254–5) at No 3; duck inside to see the ornate inner courtyard tiled with Hungarian Zsolnay ceramics. Note the blackened and aged stump encased in glass

on the building's eastern corner; apprentice journeymen during the Middle Ages would hammer nails into the stump to ensure a safe homeward journey. Other buildings of note include the neoclassical Erste Österreichisches Sparkasse (Map pp254–5; 1836) on the corner of Tuchlauben, complete with a gilded bee symbolising thrift and industriousness, and the *Jugendstil* Grabenhof (Map pp254–5; 1876) at No 14, built by Otto Wagner using the plans of Otto Thienemann.

Two unmissable features at street level are the Pestsäule (Plague Column; Map pp254–5) and Adolf Loos' public toilets (Map pp254–5). The Pestsäule, near the junction of Graben and Habsburgergasse, commemorates the ending of the plague and was erected in 1692. Designed by Johann Bernhard Fischer von Erlach, it is one of the finest of its kind in Europe. The toilets, not far northwest of the statue, are an impressive and practical use of *Jugendstil* design.

Kohlmarkt received its name from the charcoal market that once existed here. The charcoal is long gone, replaced by luxury shops that rival the Graben establishments. Best of all though is the view along Kohlmarkt towards Michaelertor and the Hofburg, which is arguably one of the most arresting sights in Vienna.

Of particular note is the café Demel (p140), maker of fine cakes and server of great coffee at No 14. It ranks among the best *Kaffeehäuser* (coffee houses) in Vienna, but also attracts swarms of tourists. At No 9 is the Artaria House, home to the city's leading map maker and seller, Freytag & Berndt (p180). Its *Jugendstil* façade was created by Max Fabiani.

Separating Kohlmarkt from the Hofburg is Michaelerplatz. Ringed by gorgeous architecture and centred on Roman ruins (Map pp254–5; reputed to be a brothel for soldier R&R), this cobblestoned circle is unsurprisingly packed with snap-happy travellers, ticket touts and *Fiaker*. On hot summer days the throng of people and the smell of horse poo can be overwhelming, but at other times it rates as one of the prettiest squares in the city. To the west is the neobaroque Michaelertrakt and also Michaelertor, one of the Hofburg's main entrances. The building is lined by statues of Hercules in various acts of bashing some poor creature or another, and at its edges are evocative fountains to the Power of the Land and Power of the Sea. Turning in a clockwise direction from Michaelertor are Café Grien-steidl (p140), Loos Haus and Michaelerkirche.

The **Loos Haus** (Map pp254–5) deserves special mention. Designed by Adolf Loos, this modernist gem, built between 1909 and 1911, seriously put Franz Josef's nose out of joint. Its intentionally simple façade offended the emperor so deeply that he ordered the curtains pulled on all palace windows overlooking the building. Critics described it as a 'house without eyebrows', referring to its lack of window detail, and work had to be stopped until Loos agreed to add 10 window boxes. Today it is widely accepted as a work of genius, and houses a bank on the ground floor and temporary exhibition halls on the upper floors (open normal banking hours).

JÜDISCHES MUSEUM Map pp254-5

☎ 535 04 31; www.jmw.at; 01, Dorotheergasse 11; adult/concession €5/2.90; ☼ 10am-6pm Sun-Fri, to 8pm Thu; ◎ U1, U3 Stephansplatz

Vienna's Jüdisches Museum (Jewish Museum) was founded in 1895, making it the first of its kind in the world. Unfortunately during WWII the museum's original collection was pillaged and only half has since been recovered, but what can be seen today is a poignant reminder of the Jewish influence on the city.

Taking up three floors of Palais Eskeles, the museum uses holograms and an assortment of objects to document the history of the Jews in Vienna, from the first settlements at Judenplatz in the 13th century up to the present. The ground floor is filled with the Max Berger collection: a rich compilation of Judaica mainly dating from the Habsburg era. Temporary exhibitions are presented on the 1st floor, with the 2nd floor dividing its space between more temporary exhibitions and 21 holograms depicting the history of the Jewish people in Vienna.

An audio guide included in the price and free tours on Sunday are conducted at 11am, noon, 1pm, 2pm and 4pm. A combined ticket of €7/4 per adult/child allows entry to the museum, the Stadttempel (p52) and the Museum Judenplatz (p52).

PETERSKIRCHE Map pp254-5

☎ 533 64 33; 01, Petersplatz; admission free; ☼ 10am-1pm & 4-7pm; ◎ U1, U3 Stephansplatz, bus 1A, 2A, 3A

Peterskirche (St Peter's Church; 1733), on Petersplatz, is one of the finest baroque churches in Vienna, outshone only by Karlskirche (p89). It is said that Charlemagne

founded the first church that stood on this site, an event depicted in the exterior relief on the southeast side. A large majority of the church was completed by the celebrated baroque architect Johann Lukas von Hildebrandt, and the dome's fresco was painted by JM Rottmayr. The fresco's colours have dulled over the years, but still manage to impress.

BAWAG FOUNDATION Map pp254-5

☎ 532 26 55; www.bawag-foundation.at; 01, Tuchlauben 7A; admission free; ☼ 10am-6pm Mon-Sat; bus 1A, 2A, 3A

Well located in the very heart of the Innere Stadt is this gallery, financed by the Bawag Bank. It features contemporary artists from both the international and local scene and has a regular influx of temporary exhibitions on display. Works range from sculpture pieces to photo exhibitions and film.

MICHAELERKIRCHE Map pp254-5

☎ 533 80 00; www.michaelerkirche.at in German; 01, Michaelerplatz; admission free; ☼ 7am-10pm; ◎ U3 Herrengasse, bus 2A, 3A

Michaelerkirche is the oldest building on Michaelerplatz (as long as you discount the Roman ruins as buildings), and dates from the 13th century. Its rather dark interior

Night view of Peterskirche (this page)

won't hold your interest for long, but, depending on your tastes, tours of its morbid and slightly disturbing crypt will. The tour (in German) takes you past numerous coffins, some of which have rusted away to reveal their long-deceased occupants in all their deathly splendour, and piles of bones of those who could not afford proper burials. Tour guides like to spice things up by turning out the lights at the worst possible moment. Tours (adult/child €5/3) depart at 1pm and 3pm Monday to Friday from November to April, and at 11am, 2pm, 3pm and 4pm Monday to Friday, and 3pm and 4pm Saturday from May to October.

HOFBURG

Like Schloss Schönbrunn and Schloss Belvedere, the Hofburg (Imperial Palace; Map pp254–5) is an incredible show of imperial power and the depths of an imperial purse. This impressive repository of culture and heritage was the home to one the most powerful empires Europe has ever seen: the Habsburgs based themselves here for over six centuries, from the first emperor in 1279 (Rudolph I) to the last in 1918 (Charles I). In that time new sections were periodically added, resulting in the hotchpotch of styles and the massive dimensions seen today. The palace now houses the offices of the Austrian president and a mix of fine museums.

The Hofburg owes its size and architectural diversity to plain old one-upmanship. Habsburg rulers took a dislike to inhabiting their predecessor's quarters and would build themselves new, grandiose digs to show the rest of Europe their strength and prowess. The oldest part is the **Schweizerhof** (Swiss Courtyard), named after the Swiss guards who used to protect its precincts. Dating from the 13th century, this small courtyard gives access to the Burgkapelle (Royal Chapel) and the **Schatzkammer** (Imperial Treasury). Its Renaissance entrance, known as the Swiss Gate, dates from 1553. The buildings encircling the Schweizerhof are collectively known as the **Alte Burg** (Old Palace).

Adjoining the Schweizerhof is a much larger courtyard, **In der Burg**. It sees most of the human traffic entering the Hofburg due to its easy access to Michaelerplatz and Kohlmarkt to the northeast, and Heldenplatz to the southwest. The courtyard is centred on a large **monument to Emperor Franz**, the last in a long line of Holy Roman em-

perors, and is the main entrance to the **Kaiserappartements**.

To the southeast of the Schweizerhof is **Josefsplatz**, a small square named after Joseph II, which gained celluloid immortality in the film *The Third Man*. It was here, outside Palais Pallavicini, that Harry Lime faked his own death. The monument to Emperor Josef II (Map pp254–5) stands in the middle of the square. In close proximity to Josefsplatz are the Albertina, Augustinerkirche, Nationalbibliothek, Spanish Riding School and Lipizzaner Museum.

The most active phase of building was carried out from the second half of the 19th century to WWI, culminating in the **Neue Burg**. Plans called for the building of a further wing, the mirror image of this curving façade on Heldenplatz (Hero's Square), but the Habsburg era ended before it could be instigated. Facing each other with eternal stares on Heldenplatz are the **monuments to Prince Eugene of Savoy** (closest to the Neue Burg) and **Archduke Karl** (Charles of Austria). Anton Fernkorn, the sculptor of both, is rumoured to have gone mad over his failure to correctly balance the Prince Eugene statue; the steed's tail rests on the ground to provide stability. The Neue Burg houses the Museum für Völkerkunde and the three Neue Burg museums, and its balcony holds an infamous distinction: it was from here that Hitler addressed a rally during his triumphant 1938 visit to Vienna after the Anschluss.

The **Sisi Ticket** (adult/student/child €19.90/ 17/10) covers entrance to the Kaiserappartements, Hofmobiliendepot (p91), and also includes a Grand Tour of Schloss Schönbrunn (p99).

KAISERAPPARTEMENTS Map pp254-5
☎ 533 75 70; www.hofburg-wien.at; 01, Innerer Burghof, Kaisertor; adult/student/child €8.90/7/4.50; ☟ 9am-5pm; ◉ U3 Herrengasse, bus 2A, 3A

The Kaiserappartements (Imperial Apartments) were once the official living quarters of Franz Josef I and Empress Elisabeth (or Sisi as she was affectionately named). The rooms are as opulent as you might expect, with fine furniture, hanging tapestries and bulbous crystal chandeliers.

The first six rooms, known as the **Sisi Museum**, are devoted to Austria's most beloved empress. A reconstruction of her luxurious coach, which carried her on many a journey, is impressive, but it's the small details that steal the show: a reconstruction of the dress she wore on the eve of her wedding, her sunshade, fans and gloves. There's even a replica of her personal fitness room complete with rings and bars, testament to her obsession with keeping slim. Many of the empress's famous portraits are on show, as is her death mask, made after her assassination in Geneva in 1898.

The museum then leads into the Kaiser's rooms. The dining room has a table for 20 laid out in suitably elegant fashion, and the Audienzzimmer contains the high desk Franz Josef used to receive petitions, a ritual he only relinquished on his deathbed.

The adjoining **Hoftafel- und Tafelkammer** (Court Tableware and Silver Depot) collection is included in the entry price. Laying a table with some of this silver and porcelain would certainly impress the in-laws: the largest silver service here can take care of 140 dinner guests.

Audio guides are included in the price.

SCHATZKAMMER Map pp254-5

☎ 525 24-0; 01, Schweizerhof; adult/concession/family €8/6/16; ☉ 10am-6pm Wed-Mon; ⊖ U3 Herrengasse, bus 2A, 3A

The Schatzkammer (Imperial Treasury) is among the best of its kind in Europe. Containing secular and ecclesiastical treasures of priceless value and splendour, the sheer wealth exhibited in the collection of crown jewels is staggering: Room 7 alone has a 2860-carat Colombian emerald, a 416-carat balas ruby and a 492-carat aquamarine, probably enough to wipe the debt of a third-world country.

Room 11 holds the highlight of the Treasury, the imperial crown. Dating from the 10th century, it has eight gold plates and precious gems alternating with enamel plaques to show religious scenes. The private crown of Rudolf II (1602) is a more delicate piece, with gems interspersed by four beautifully engraved gold bas-reliefs, showing Rudolf in battle and at three of his coronations.

Room 5 contains mementos of Marie Louise, the second wife of Napoleon; the best piece here is the cradle donated by the city of Paris to their son. The golden bees around the sides are a standard motif of Napoleonic state artefacts. Room 8 has two unusual objects formerly owned by Ferdinand I: a 75cm-wide bowl carved from a single piece of agate, once thought to be the Holy Grail, and a narwhal tusk (243cm long), once claimed to have been a unicorn's horn.

The Sacred Treasury almost outshines the rest of the museum, with its collection of rare, and hard to believe, religious relics. Fragments of the True Cross, one of the nails from the Crucifixion, a thorn from Christ's crown and a piece of tablecloth from the Last Supper all vie for your attention – and belief. There are also some rather more worldly artefacts on display, like the extremely elaborate Column of the Virgin Mary made from gilded silver, which stands over 1m tall and is encased with 3700 precious stones – a modest conversation piece fit for any mantelpiece.

An audio guide is included in the price and the Schatzkammer is part of the Gold, Silver and Bronze discount tickets (p69). Allow anything from 30 minutes to two hours to get around.

Sights

INNERE STADT

Statue of Archduke Karl (Charles of Austria) in front of the Neue Burg wing of the Hofburg (opposite page)

SLOVENIA CLAIMS THE LIPIZZANER

As of 1 January 2007, Lipizzaner stallions will be travelling the length and breadth of the EU – on new 20-cent Slovenian coins.

The famous white steeds originally graced the Austrian five-schilling coin until it was dropped in 2002 in favour of other images for the euro. Now Slovenia has taken up the image and is fighting Austria to become the official keeper of the central stud book, a move which, if successful, would transfer the origin of the Lipizzaner horse to Slovenia. Naturally Austria isn't keen to hand over the book; the horses share a 400-year history with the country and are part of the national identity. Slovenia's case is strong, however, as the small village of Lipica, from which the Lipizzaner name originates, is located in Slovenia, and the village recently celebrated 425 years of Lipizzaner breeding.

Either way, the Lipizzaner will remain on the coin, in the Hofburg and in the hearts of all horse-admirers.

BURGKAPELLE Map pp254-5

☎ 533 99 27; 01, Schweizerhof; Guided tours €2; ☙ 11am-3pm Mon-Thu, 11am-1pm Fri Sep-Jun; ◎ U3 Herrengasse, bus 2A, 3A

The Burgkapelle (Royal Chapel) originally dates from the 13th century and received a Gothic make-over from 1447 to 1449, but much of this disappeared during the baroque fad. The vaulted wooden statutory survived and is testament to those Gothic days. This is where the Vienna Boys' Choir sings at Mass (p168) every Sunday at 9.15am between September and June. Unfortunately, you can only visit the chapel with a tour guide or during choir performances.

SPANISH RIDING SCHOOL Map pp254-5

☎ 533 90 31; www.srs.at; 01, Michaelerplatz 1; admission €20-130; ◎ U3 Herrengasse, bus 2A, 3A

The world famous Spanish Riding School (Spanische Hofreitschule) is a Viennese institution truly reminiscent of the imperial Habsburg era. This unequalled equestrian show is performed by Lipizzaner stallions, a crossbreeding of Spanish, Arab and Berber horses. The horses were first imported from Spain (hence 'Spanish') by Maximilian II in 1562, and in 1580 a stud was established at Lipizza (hence 'Lipizzaner'), now within Slovenia and known as Lipica.

A Lipizzaner performance is an absolute must for any hippophile (others may think it's a show with horses doing dog-tricks). These graceful stallions perform an equine ballet to a program of classical music while the audience cranes to see from pillared balconies and the chandeliers shimmer above. The mature stallions are all snow-white (though they are born dark and turn white at age four) and the riders wear traditional garb, from their leather boots up to their bicorn hats.

Reservations for performances require bookings months in advance. Tickets can be ordered on the website; this is also the best source of information for the complicated arrangement of performance times. Cancellations sometimes occur: ask at the office as unclaimed tickets are sold around two hours before performances.

Tickets to watch a training session (adult/concession/child €12/9/6) or workout (€6) can be bought at the visitors centre (☙ 9am-4pm Tue-Sat); training is from 10am to noon and the workout from 10am to 11am Tuesday to Saturday on selective days. Guided tours (adult/concession/child €15/12/8), which include the stables, are available in English, German and French and normally take place at 2pm, 3pm and 4pm Monday to Saturday and 10am, 11am, 1pm, 2pm and 3pm Sunday. If you only want to grab a few photos, you can try waiting to see them cross between the school and the *Stallburg* (stables), which usually happens on the half-hour.

LIPIZZANER MUSEUM Map pp254-5

☎ 525 24 583; www.lipizzaner.at; 01, Reitschulestrasse 2; adult/concession/family €5/3.60/10; ☙ 9am-6pm; ◎ U3 Herrengasse, bus 2A, 3A

An arm of the Spanish Riding School, the Lipizzaner Museum fills visitors in on the history and heritage of the famous white stallions. It also has bits and bobs on the tricks they perform at the nearby school and the stud farm where they're raised. There's English text, but the content is a little thin. Windows allow a view directly into the stallion stables, albeit obscured by thick glass and fine mesh; otherwise you'll have to do with the views on two large monitors. A combined ticket for the museum and a training session at the Spanish Riding School costs €15/9 per adult/child. The Lipizzaner Museum is also part of the Gold ticket. (p69).

NATIONALBIBLIOTHEK Map pp254-5

☎ 534 10-0; www.onb.ac.at; 01, Josefsplatz 1; adult/concession/family €5/3/9; ⏰ 10am-6pm, Tue-Sun, until 9pm Thu; Ⓜ U3 Herrengasse, bus 2A, 3A

The Nationalbibliothek (National Library) was once the imperial library and is now the largest library in Vienna. The real reason to visit these esteemed halls of knowledge is to gaze on the **Prunksaal** (Grand Hall). Commissioned by Charles VI, this baroque hall was the brainchild of Fischer von Erlach, who died the year the first brick was laid, and finished by his son Joseph in 1735. Holding some 200,000 volumes, the sheer size of the hall is breathtaking. Leather-bound scholarly tomes line the walls, and the upper storey of shelves is flanked by an elegantly curving wood balcony. Rare ancient volumes (mostly 15th-century) are stored within glass cabinets, with pages opened to beautifully drawn sections of text. A statue of Charles VI stands guard under the central dome, which itself has a fresco by Daniel Gran depicting the emperor's apotheosis.

AUGUSTINERKIRCHE Map pp254-5

☎ 533 70 99; 01, Augustinerstrasse 3; admission free; Ⓜ U1, U3 Herrengasse, bus 2A, 3A

The Augustinerkirche (Augustinian Church) is one of the older parts of the Hofburg, dating from the early 14th century. Although Gothic in style, the interior was converted to baroque in the 17th century, and then restored to its original appearance in 1784. It is here that the hearts of the Habsburgs rulers are kept in the Herzgrüftel (Little Heart Crypt); viewings are by appointment only. An impressive tomb to look for is that of Maria Theresia's daughter Archduchess Maria Christina, designed by Canova.

The church hosts regular evening classical music concerts, and the 11am Mass on Sunday is celebrated with a full choir and orchestra; the choir practices on a regular basis and times are posted on the church door.

ALBERTINA Map pp254-5

☎ 534 83 555; www.albertina.at; 01, Albertinaplatz 1; adult/senior/student/child €9/7.50/6.50/3.50; ⏰ 10am-6pm, until 9pm Wed; Ⓜ U1, U2, U4 Karlsplatz, bus 3A

Once used as the Habsburg's imperial apartments for guests, the Albertina now houses the greatest collection of graphic art in the world. The collection, founded in 1768 by Maria Theresia's son-in-law Duke Albert von Sachsen-Teschen, consists of an astonishing 1½ million prints and 50,000 drawings, including 145 Dürer drawings (the largest collection in the world), 43 by Raphael, 70 by Rembrandt and 150 by Schiele. There are loads more by Leonardo da Vinci, Michelangelo, Peter Paul Rubens, Michael Bruegel, Paul Cézanne, Pablo Picasso, Henri Matisse, Gustav Klimt and Oscar Kokoschka. The space itself, which re-opened in 2003 after extensive and lengthy renovations costing over €90 million, is certainly worthy of such a collection.

Because of the sheer number of prints and drawings in the Albertina's archive, only a small percentage can be displayed at any one time. Exhibitions, which normally follow a theme or artist, are therefore changed every three months and also feature works from other collections. Whatever's on show, it's sure to be worth the entrance fee. The Österreichische Filmmuseum (p172) is also within the Albertina.

NEUE BURG MUSEUMS Map pp254-5

☎ 525 24-0; 01, Heldenplatz; adult/concession/family €8/6/16; ⏰ 10am-6pm Wed-Mon; Ⓜ D, J, 1, 2, bus 2A

Instruments of all shapes and sizes are on display at the **Sammlung Alter Musikinstrumente** (Collection of Ancient Musical Instruments), the first of three-museums-in-one in the Neue Burg. The forward-thinking Archduke Ferdinand of Tyrol started the whole thing off by collecting rare instruments; it now it ranks among the finest Renaissance collections in the world. The instruments were designed more for show than for playing; horns shaped like serpents and violins with carved faces are some of the elaborate pieces on display. Note the baroque cabinet incorporating a keyboard from the early 17th century (in Saal XI) – it's beautiful, but a strange combination.

The admission price includes entry to two adjoining collections. The **Ephesus Museum** contains artefacts from Ephesus and Samothrace supposedly donated (some say 'lifted') by the Sultan in 1900 after a team of Austrian archaeologists excavated the famous site in Turkey. The highlight of the museum is a massive frieze honouring the defeat of the Parthians by Lucius Verus and his Roman army. Noted as one of the finest museums of its kind in the world, the **Hofjagd und Rüstkammer** (Arms and Armour) collection dates mostly from the 15th and 16th centuries and has some superb examples of ancient armour. Most look far too elaborate to actually wear into battle, or just plain impractical – the bizarre pumpkin-shaped helmet from the 15th century is just one example.

Audio guides are available for €2 and the three museums are included in the price of a Gold, Silver or Bronze ticket (p69).

MUSEUM FÜR VÖLKERKUNDE

Map pp254-5

☎ 534 30-0; www.ethno-museum.ac.at; 01, Heldenplatz; adult/concession/family €8/6/16; ☉ 10am-6pm Wed-Mon; 🚋 D, J, 1, 2, bus 2A

The Museum für Völkerkunde (Museum of Ethnology), with its wide-ranging collection of exhibits on non-European cultures, makes good use of the furthest reaches of the Neue Burg. Exhibits are divided into nationalities, and cover such countries as China, Japan and Korea, and also the Polynesian, Native American and Inuit cultures. The highlight of the museum is the centrepiece of the Central America section, an Aztec feather headdress once worn by Emperor Montezuma. Tours in German are normally available at 11am (extra €2) and temporary exhibitions are commonplace. Audio guides are also €2, but don't cover temporary exhibitions.

Note the museum is due to reopen sometime in spring 2007 after extensive renovations.

SCHMETTERLINGHAUS Map pp254-5

☎ 533 85 70; www.schmetterlinghaus.at; 01, Burggarten; adult/senior/student/child 3-6 €5/4.50/4/2.50; ☉ 10am-4.45pm Mon-Fri, 10am-6.15pm Sat & Sun Apr-Oct, 10am-3.45pm Nov-Mar; Ⓤ U1, U2, U4 Karlsplatz; 🚋 D, J, 1, 2, 62, 65

Sharing the Habsburg's personal *Jugendstil* glasshouse (1901) with the Palmenhaus (p155), the Schmetterlinghaus (butterfly house) is for the butterfly-mad only. There are hundreds of butterflies and the shop stocks a great range of butterfly paraphernalia, but the air is hot and unbearably humid, the species range fairly limited and it's quite a small display area. It's located in the Burggarten, directly behind the Neue Burg.

NORTH OF HOFBURG

Running north from Michaelerplatz to Schottentor, this quarter of the Innere Stadt is peppered with palaces and churches. **Herrengasse** (Lords' Lane) has the majority of the grand houses, including Palais Mollard (housing the Globenmuseum), Ferstal Harrach, and Kinsky.

Palais Ferstel (Map pp254–5) dates from 1860 and is better known for its occupants, the Café Central (p139) and the Freyung Passage, a highly ornate passageway lined with elegant shops. **Palais Harrach** (Map pp254–5) is connected by the Freyung Passage to Palais Ferstal but predates its neighbour by some 170 years. Its courtyard is filled with galleries, antique dealers and designer fashion.

Palais Kinsky (Map pp254–5), built by Hildebrandt in 1716, faces the world with its classic baroque façade. Restored to its former glory, the highlight of this superb palace is the stairway off to the left of the first inner courtyard; rising three storeys, its elegant banisters are graced with statues at every turn, and the ceiling fresco is a fanciful creation filled with podgy cherubs, bare-breasted beauties, and the occasional strongman. The palace now contains highbrow art shops and classy restaurants.

Backing onto the northern tip of the Hofburg and across the square from Minoritenkirche is the Bundeskanzleramt (Federal Chancellor's Office). It's notable mainly for its historical significance as a seat of power since the time of Maria Theresia. Prince Metternich had his offices here, and it is where Chancellor Dollfuss was murdered by the Nazis on 25 July 1934. In 2000 the square outside became the meeting point for demonstrations (every Thursday) against the inclusion of the FPÖ (Freedom Party) in the federal government.

At the northern end of Herrengasse is the open cobblestoned square **Freyung**. It's dominated by the substantial façade of the Schottenkirche, and on Fridays is transformed into a farmers' market, where organic produce from Lower Austria finds its way into the larders of discerning Viennese. Directly opposite the Universität Wien (p69) just north of Freyung is Mölker Bastei, one of the two remaining sections of the old city walls (Map pp254–5); the other can be seen in the foyer of Palais Coburg.

Am Hof, at the southern end of Freyung, was once a powerful stronghold of the Babenberg rulers (p39), who built a fortress here before moving to the Hofburg. Its history dates back to the Roman era and a few excavations can be seen at the **Feuerwehr Centrale** (Fire Brigade Centre; Map pp254–5; 01, Am Hof 9; currently closed due to conservation works). These days it's the largest square in the Innere Stadt, with little life and plenty of parked cars. There are a few buildings of note, such as the 16th-century **former civic armoury** (Map pp254–5) on the north side at No 10, with an elaborate façade. The former Jesuit monastery **Kirche Am Hof** (Map pp254–5; admission free; ⏱ 8am-noon, 4.30-6pm), on the southeast side, is even more impressive – the baroque façade was adapted from its fire-damaged Gothic predecessor and the hugely expansive nave is lined with white pillars and topped with gold badges.

Mariensäule (Mary's Column; Map pp254–5) in the centre of the square is dedicated to the Virgin Mary and was erected in 1667.

GLOBENMUSEUM Map pp254–5

☎ 534 10 710; www.onb.ac.at; 01, Herrengasse 9, 1st fl; adult/concession/family €3/2/5; ⏱ 10am-2pm Mon-Wed, Fri & Sat, 3-7pm Thu; ⊕ U3 Herrengasse, bus 2A, 3A

Part of the Nationalbibliothek (National Library) collection of museums is this small museum dedicated to cartography. Among the plethora of 19th-century globes and maps in the collection are a couple of gems a few centuries older. Look for the globe made for Emperor Karl V by Mercator in 1541 and a map of the world produced in 1551, also for Karl V.

The often-missed **Esperanto Museum** (☎ 534 10 730; www.onb.ac.at; 01, Herrengasse 9, ground floor; adult/child/family €2/1.50/3; ⏱ 10am-2pm Mon-Wed, Fri & Sat, 3-7pm Thu), devoted to the artificial language created by Dr Ludvik Zamenhof back in 1887, is also part of the library. The first book in Esperanto, written by Dr Zamenhof himself, is displayed in the museum.

Both are located in Palais Mollard, one of many palaces on Herrengasse.

KUNSTFORUM Map pp254–5

☎ 537 33 26; www.ba-ca-kunstforum.at; 01, Freyung 8; adult/concession/family €8.70/7.30/16; ⏱ 10am-7pm Sat-Thu, 10am-9pm Fri; ⊕ U3 Herrengasse, bus 2A, 3A

Often forgotten among the palaces and churches lining Freyung, the Kunstforum is a stalwart of the Vienna art scene and

hosts a number of temporary exhibitions throughout the year. The overall exhibit theme is not confined to one genre, but leaps and bounds between them with ease.

MINORITENKIRCHE Map pp254-5

☎ 533 41 62; 01, Minoritenplatz; admission free; ⏱ 3-6pm Sat, services Sun; ⊕ U3 Herrengasse

The Minoritenkirche (Minorite Church) is a 14th-century church that, like many in Austria, later received a baroque face-lift. If you think the tower looks a little short, you're right on the button: the top was 'shortened' by the Turks in 1529. The most noteworthy piece inside is a mosaic copy of da Vinci's *Last Supper,* commissioned by Napoleon.

The church often hosts classical concerts and choir recitals throughout the year; schedules are posted outside and tickets cost around €20.

PASQUALATI HAUS Map pp254-5

☎ 535 89 05; 01, Mölker Bastei 8; adult/child €2/1; ⏱ 10am-1pm & 2-6pm Tue-Sun; ⊕ U2 Schottentor, ⊕ 37, 38, 40, 41, 42, 43, 44

Beethoven made the 4th floor of this house his residence from 1804 to 1814 (he apparently occupied around 80 places in his 35 years in Vienna) and during that time composed Symphonies 4, 5 and 7 and the opera *Fidelio,* among other works. His two rooms (plus another two from a neighbouring apartment) have been converted into a museum, which is lightly filled with photos, articles and a handful of his personal belongings. The house is named after its longtime owner Josef Benedikt Freiherr von Pasqualati, and it is a municipal museum.

SCHOTTENKIRCHE Map pp254-5

☎ 534 98 600; 01, Freyung; museum adult/child €4/2; ⏱ 11am-5pm Thu-Sat; ⊕ U2 Schottentor, bus 1A

Freyung isn't particularly Scottish these days (the closest it comes is the Irish pub Molly Darcy's around the corner), but back in the 12th century it certainly was. At the time Schottenkirche (Church of the Scots; entrance free) was founded by Benedictine monks (the monks were probably actually from Ireland, then known as Scotia Maior), though the present façade dates from the 19th century. The interior is suitably elaborate, with a heavily frescoed ceiling and terracotta-red touches in every corner, but unfortunately outside of services the main nave is locked to visitors (it's still possible to peek through the gates). A small art and artefacts museum in the adjoining monastery displays religious pieces from the church and monastery, but of more interest is the church shop (☺10am-6pm Mon-Fri, 10am-5pm Sat, 10.30am-12.30pm Sun), which stocks homemade schnapps, honey and jams.

JEWISH QUARTER & AROUND

The old Jewish quarter, centred on Judenplatz, is reached from the northeast corner of Am Hof via a collection of tiny, cobblestoned streets, quiet corners and the Uhren Museum and Puppen & Spielzeug Museum. An attractive square lined with elaborate baroque and 19th-century buildings, Judenplatz was for centuries the heart of the Jewish ghetto; excavations in the late 20th century uncovered a medieval synagogue dating from 1420, which has subsequently been turned into the Museum Judenplatz. The focal point of the square is the Holocaust-Denkmal (Map pp254–5), a pale, bulky memorial to the 65,000 Austrian Jews who perished in the Holocaust. Designed by British sculptor Rachel Whiteread and unveiled in 2000, the 'nameless library' – a structure in the shape of a library where the spines of books face inwards – represents the untold stories of Holocaust victims and has the names of Austrian concentration camps written across its base. This powerful memorial has invoked criticism from Viennese residents who felt it would ruin business in the area, and from the Jewish community who claim it stands on a sacred site. On the north side of Judenplatz is the former Böhmische Hofkanzlei (Bohemian Court Chancery; Map pp254–5). Walk round to Wipplingerstrasse to see its striking façade by Fischer von Erlach.

Between Judenplatz and Schottenring is the Innere Stadt's least attractive corner; the solid buildings lack many of the delicate touches found throughout the rest of the district, and the streets are wide and impersonal. One exception is in and around Maria am Gestade (Map pp254–5), one of the city's most beautiful Gothic churches. Its interior is highlighted by a winged Gothic altar, and the church overlooks peaceful flights of steps.

Hoher Markt, Vienna's oldest square, is home to Roman ruins and the Ankeruhr (Anker Clock; Map pp254–5), an Art Nouveau masterpiece.

Created by Franz von Matsch in 1911, it's named after the Anker Insurance Co, which commissioned it. Over a 12-hour period, figures slowly pass across the clock face, indicating the time against a static measure showing the minutes. Figures represented range from Marcus Aurelius (the Roman emperor who died in Vienna in AD 180) to Josef Haydn, with Eugene of Savoy, Maria Theresia and others in between. Details of who's who are outlined on a plaque on the wall below. Tourists flock here at noon, when all the figures trundle past in succession and organ music from the appropriate period is piped out.

Judengasse leads from Hoher Markt to another of the city's calm, cobblestoned squares, Ruprechtsplatz. This area, dubbed 'The Bermuda Triangle' for its plethora of bars, is often ignored by tourists during the day and makes a welcome pit stop from the chaos that descends on much of the Innere Stadt; at night, its heaves with drunken revellers and is quite unappealing. A few steps north of Ruprechtsplatz is Ruprechtskirche (St Rupert's Church; Map pp254–5), the oldest church in Vienna. Records dating from 1137 first mention the church's existence, but some historians believe a few of the foundations date back to as early as 740. What is certain is that the lower levels of the tower date from the 11th century and the roof from the 15th. With its simple layout, ivy-clad walls and cobblestoned surrounds, it's more impressive from the outside, which is fortunate as it's rarely open to the public.

Nearby Seitenstrasse is home to the Stadttempel (City Synagogue) and its personal guard of police; just below on Morzinplatz is the Monument to the Victims of Fascism (1985; Map pp254–5) standing on the former site of the Gestapo headquarters. The monument features the Star of David and the pink triangle, representing the Jewish and homosexual victims of the Nazis.

MUSEUM JUDENPLATZ Map pp254-5

☎ 535 04 31; www.jmw.at; 01, Judenplatz 8; adult/concession €3/1.50; ☺10am-6pm Sun-Thu, 10am-2pm Fri; bus 2A, 3A

The main focus of the city's second museum is the excavated remains of a medieval synagogue that once stood on Judenplatz. Built around 1420, it didn't last long: Duke Albrecht V's 'hatred and misconception', as the museum puts it, led him to order its destruction in 1421. The basic outline of the synagogue can still be seen, lit with subdued lighting, and a small model of the building helps to complete the picture. Documents and artefacts dating from 1200 to 1400 are on display, and there is a short computer-graphics film on life in Jewish Vienna in the Middle Ages. Don't pass over the spacey interactive screens explaining Jewish culture at the bottom of the stairs as you walk in. A combined ticket for €7/4 per adult/child allows entry to the museum plus the Stadttempel and Jüdisches Museum.

UHREN MUSEUM Map pp254-5

☎ 533 22 65; 01, Schulhof 2; adult/child €4/2; 🕑 10am-6pm Tue-Sun; 🚇 U3 Herrengasse, bus 1A, 2A, 3A

Loudly ticking away behind the Kirche Am Hof is the municipal Uhren Museum (Clock Museum). Opened in 1921 in the Harfenhaus, one of Vienna's oldest buildings, its three floors are weighed down with an astounding 21,200 clocks and watches, ranging from the 15th century to a 1992 computer clock; it's collection of Biedermeier and belle époque models will, for most, steal the show. The peace and quiet is shattered at the striking of the hour, so those with sensitive ears should avoid these times. Unfortunately guided tours (3pm Thu, 10am and 11am Sun) are only in German.

PUPPEN & SPIELZEUG MUSEUM Map pp254-5

☎ 535 68 60; 01, Schulhof 4; adult/child €4.70/2.35; 🕑 10am-6pm Tue-Sun; 🚇 U3 Herrengasse, bus 1A, 2A, 3A

The Doll and Toy Museum, next door to the Uhren Museum, may sound like it's something for the kids, but in reality it's not. The collection is quite intriguing, with dolls from around the world, but there's no hands-on fun with the toys. Look for the *Kasperl* booth – the equivalent of Punch and Judy – which is a favourite with Viennese of all ages.

NEIDHART-FRESKEN Map pp254-5

☎ 535 90 65; 01, Tuchlauben 19; adult/child €2/1; 🕑 10am-1pm, 2-6pm Tue, 2-6pm Fri-Sun; bus 2A, 3A

An unassuming house on Tuchlauben hides quite a remarkable decoration: the oldest extant secular murals in Vienna. The small frescoes, dating from 1398, tell the story of the minstrel Neidhart von Reuental (1180-1240) and life in the Middle Ages, in lively and jolly scenes. The frescoes have lost some colour and are patchy in parts, but they are in superb condition considering their age. Neidhart is a municipal museum.

ARCHIV DES ÖSTERREICHISCHEN WIDERSTANDS Map pp254-5

☎ 228 94 69; www.doew.at; 01 Wipplingerstrasse 8; admission free; 🕑 9am-5pm Mon-Thu; bus 2A, 3A

Housed in the Altes Rathaus (Old City Hall), the Austrian Resistance Archive documents the little-known anti-fascist resistance force that operated during the Nazi regime; some 2700 resistance fighters were executed by the Nazis and thousands more sent to concentration camps. Surprisingly, the museum admits the Austrian Resistance did little to undermine the Nazi occupation, but

---

TOP SIGHTS: THE EXPERT VIEW

Sabina Egger, a native of Northern Germany but resident of Vienna since 1954, has been guiding tourists around the city for over 35 years. She knows the city inside out, and these are her must-sees:

- a walk through the Innere Stadt, exploring its **peaceful pockets** (p55)
- a trip to a **Heuriger** (p142), perhaps in Nussdorf, but not in Grinzing
- a visit to the **Wien Museum** (p88) for an overall picture of the city's history
- a trip to Otto Wagner's **Kirche am Steinhof** (p98)
- a tour through the **Kunsthistorisches Museum** (p73)
- a visit to the **Albertina** (p63), particularly if the temporary exhibition appeals

Kirche am Steinhof (p98)

Sights

INNERE STADT

points out that it did exist. The in-depth analysis of the Nazi doctrines on homosexuality, 'unworthy' citizens, concentration camps and forced labour is quite disturbing, as are many of the photos and memorabilia detailing the time before and after the Anschluss. The section on the Austrian Slovenes and their struggle in Carinthia during the war is poignant considering the flippant attitude Jörg Haider, the province's current governor, has towards them.

ROMAN RUINS Map pp254-5

☎ 535 56 06; 01, Hoher Markt 5; adult/concession €2/1; ⏰ 9am-1pm, 2-5pm Tue-Sun; bus 1A, 2A, 3A
Hiding under a nondescript Asian restaurant on Hoher Markt is a small expanse of Roman ruins dating from the 1st to the 5th century. The ruins are thought to be part of the officers' quarters of the Roman legion camp at Vindobona and consist of crumbled walls and tiled floors. There's a small but selective exhibit on artefacts found during the excavations. The ruins are part of the municipal museum group of Vienna.

STADTTEMPEL Map pp254-5

☎ 535 04 31; 01, Seitenstettengasse 4; adult/concession €2/1; tours ⏰ 11.30am & 2pm Mon-Thu; ⓤ U1, U4 Schwedenplatz, 🚋 N, 1, 2, 21, bus 2A
By the end of WWII Stadttempel was the only synagogue spared from destruction by the Nazis. Since then it has been the main place of worship for the ever-expanding Jewish community in Vienna. Built in 1824 by Josef Kornhäusel, the bland façade provides no hint of the exquisite Biedermeier interior within. Entrance is by guided tour only, which takes an hour; bring your passport as proof of identification. The Stadttempel is included in the combined ticket for the Jüdisches Museum and Museum Judenplatz.

RINGSTRASSE

Drinking p141 & p155; Eating p125; Shopping p184; Sleeping p196

The Ringstrasse, or Ring as it's known locally, is a wide, tree-lined boulevard encircling much of the Innere Stadt that follows the line of the old city walls. It's also the address of one momentous piece of architecture after the next; spend an hour or two strolling along its shaded pathways and

RINGSTRASSE TOP SIGHTS

- delight in the sheer extent of the **Kunsthistorisches Museum** (p73) collection
- explore the **MuseumsQuartier** (p75), one of the world's top exhibitor spaces
- spend hours discovering the likes of Schiele, Klimt and Kokoschka at the **Leopold Museum** (p76)
- wonder how Klimt's *Beethoven Frieze* was ever thought a temporary exhibition at the **Secession** (p72)
- gather ideas for home furnishings from the elaborate collection at **MAK** (p78)

you'll soon discover the architectural styles that dominated Europe's past.

The majestic architecture you see today is largely due to the efforts of Emperor Franz Josef I. The Ringstrasse originally began life as defensive walls in the 16th century, but by 1857 Franz Josef decided these military fortifications had become redundant and needed to be torn down. The exercise grounds, or *Glacis* as they were known, which separated the Innere Stadt from the suburbs, also needed to go; his idea was to replace them with grandiose public buildings that would better reflect the power and the wealth of the Habsburg empire. The Ringstrasse was laid out between 1858 and 1865, and in the decade that followed most of the impressive edifices that now line this thoroughfare were under construction. Franz Josef had extremely deep pockets to match his elaborate plans – consider this for an architectural shopping list: Staatsoper (built 1861-69; p169), Musikverein (1867-69; p168), MAK (1868-71), Akademie der bildenden Künste (1872-76), Naturhistorisches Museum (1872-81), Rathaus (1872-83), Kunsthistorisches Museum (1872-91), Parlament (1873-83), Universität Wien (1873-84), Burgtheater (1874-88; p170), Justizpalast (1875-81) and the Heldenplatz section of the Hofburg's Neue Burg (1881-1908).

World War I intervened and the empire was lost before Franz Josef's grand scheme was fully realised: a further wing of the Hofburg had been planned (which would have sat directly on the Ringstrasse, taking up what is now the Volksgarten), and the palace and the giant museums opposite were to be linked by a majestic walkway, rising in arches over the Ring. Nevertheless, what was achieved is quite beyond belief.

To fully appreciate the sheer scale of this endeavour, take a tour by foot of at least some of the Ringstrasse. The whole ring is about 5km long, but the grandest section, between the university and the opera, is less than 2km. Instead of walking, you can pedal along the bike path on either side of the Ringstrasse, or take tram No 1 (clockwise) or No 2 (anticlockwise). The sights of the Ringstrasse, set out below, are ordered for travel in an anticlockwise direction from the Schottenring U-Bahn stop on the Danube Canal to the Urania cinema and bar complex, once again on the banks of the Danube Canal.

While the MuseumsQuartier, Akademie der bildenden Künste and Secession do not lie directly on the Ringstrasse, we have included them in this section because they are easily accessible from the Ringstrasse.

DANUBE CANAL TO PARLAMENT

The first stretch of the Ringstrasse, from Schottenring – named after the same Benedictine monks who established Schottenkirche (see p65) in the 12th century – on the Danube Canal to the Votivkirche, is the least exciting. The only buildings to truly stand out are the **Börse Palais** (Map pp254–5) and **Rossauer Kaserne** (Map pp258–9). The Börse, an elegant building of red brick designed by Theophil Hansen, was completed in 1877; it houses the stock exchange. Just north of the Börse and one street off the Ringstrasse, the Rossauer Kaserne is a huge complex originally built as barracks after the 1848 revolution (p42). Also in red brick, it's a rather fanciful affair complete with turrets and massive entranceways.

Schottentor is dominated by the Votivkirche and the left flank of the **Universität Wien** (University of Vienna; Map pp254–5). Completed in 1884, the new university (the university actually dates back to 1365; the original building still exists at 01, Bäckerstrasse 20) is Italian Renaissance in style. It contains some beautiful rooms and a peaceful inner courtyard, but the highlight is the Grosser Festsaal, blessed with ceiling frescoes by Klimt. Unfortunately it's usually out of bounds to the public and only used for graduation ceremonies, but try your luck and sneak in anyway.

The Rathaus and Burgtheater square off across to Rathausplatz a little further to the south, followed by the Parlament and,

MUSEUM DISCOUNTS

In general, children up to the ages of 14 to 18 are charged the children's entrance fee, and concession prices cover senior citizens (over 65), students up to the age of 27 and disabled people. Family tickets usually mean two adults and two children; children under four normally enter free of charge.

The Vienna Card (€16.90 p225) is good value for weekend trippers; it includes three days' public transport and discounts on museums, shops and cafés.

If you plan to see more than one or two sights associated with the Kunsthistorisches Museum, consider purchasing a Gold, Silver or Bronze ticket. The Gold ticket (€23) allows entry to the Kunsthistorisches Museum, Schatzkammer and Neue Burg museums, as well the Lipizzaner Museum, Wagenburg in Schönbrunn and the Theatermuseum. The Silver ticket (€21) covers the Kunsthistorisches Museum, Schatzkammer, Neue Burg museums and the Theatermuseum, while the Bronze (€19) will get you into the Kunsthistorisches Museum, Schatzkammer and Neue Burg museums.

on the southern side of the Parlament, the German Renaissance **Justizpalast** (Palace of Justice; Map pp254–5), home of Austria's Supreme Court.

The **Volksgarten** (People's Garden; ☽ 6am-10pm Apr-Oct, 6am-8pm Nov-Mar) occupies a venerable position between the Burgtheater and Heldenplatz. It's attractively laid out, with a riot of rose bushes and several statues, including a monument to Empress Elisabeth in the northwest corner. In winter the roses are lovingly protected with hessian sacks, transforming them into rows of covered heads on poles. It's also home to the **Temple of Theseus** (Map pp254–5), an imitation of the one in Athens (commissioned by Napoleon), and the club **Volksgarten** (p165).

VOTIVKIRCHE Map pp254-5
09, Rooseveltplatz; admission free; ☽ 9am-1pm & 4-6.30pm Tue-Sat, 9am-1pm Sun; ⊙ U2 Schottentor, ⊞ 37, 38, 40, 41, 42, 43, 44
In 1853 Franz Josef I survived an assassination attempt when a knife-wielding Hungarian failed to find the emperor's neck through his collar – reports suggested that a metal button deflected the blade. The Votivkirche (Votive Church) was commissioned in thanks for his lucky escape; Heinrich von Ferstel designed this twin-towered Gothic

construction, which was completed in 1879. The interior, which is too bleak and spacious to be welcoming, is bedecked with frescoes and bulbous chandeliers. The tomb of Count Niklas Salm, one of the architects of the successful defence against the Turks in 1529, is in the Baptismal Chapel. Take note of the interesting stained-glass windows: one to the left of the altar tells of Nazism and the ravages of war.

RATHAUS Map pp254-5

☎ 525 50; www.wien.gv.at; 01, Rathausplatz; tours 1pm Mon, Wed, Fri; Ⓜ U2 Rathaus, 🚋 D, 1, 2

For sheer grandness, the Rathaus (City Hall) steals the Ringstrasse show. This neogothic structure, completed in 1883 by Friedrich von Schmidt, was modelled on Flemish city halls. Its main spire soars to 102m, that's if you include the pennant held by the knight at the top. You're free to wander through the seven inner courtyards, but you must join a guided tour to catch a glimpse of the interior, with its red carpets, gigantic mirrors, and frescoes (tours leave from the Rathaus information office on Friedrich-Schmidt-Platz). The largest of the courtyards sometimes hosts concerts.

Between the Rathaus and the Ringstrasse is the **Rathauspark**, with fountains, benches and several statues. It is split in two by Rathausplatz, which is lined with statues of notable people from Vienna's past. Rathausplatz is the sight of some of the city's most frequented events, including the Christkindlmarkt (Christmas Market; p188), Musikfilm Festival (p11) and the Wiener Eistraum (Vienna Ice Dream; p174).

PARLAMENT Map pp254-5

☎ 401 10 2577; www.parlament.gv.at; 01, Dr-Karl-Renner-Ring 3; tours adult/child €4/2; Ⓜ U2, U3 Volkstheater, 🚋 D, J, 1, 2, 46, 49

With its recent renovation now complete, the squat Parlament building opposite the Volksgarten once again strikes a governing pose over the Ringstrasse. Its neoclassical façade and Greek pillars, designed by Theophil Hansen in 1883, are in themselves quite striking, but the beautiful **Athena Fountain** (Map pp254–5), sculpted by Karl Kundmann, that guards the building steals the show with its gold-tipped spear and regal helm. Grecian architecture was chosen, as Greece was the home of democracy; Athena is the Greek goddess of wisdom. It was hoped that both qualities would be permanent features of Austrian politics. The four statues flanking Athena are of horse breaking (though some would say horse punching).

In general, guided tours (leaving from Gate 1) run at 10am, 11am, 2pm, 3pm and 4pm Monday to Friday year-round; on Saturday they leave at 10am, 11am, noon and 1pm. Tours are cancelled when the parliament is in session. The Parlament's **visitors centre** (admission free; ⏰ 9.30am-4.30pm Mon-Fri, 9.30am-2pm Sat), directly behind Athena, covers the history of Austrian politics and explains how parliament runs through the use of a multimedia show of video clips and interactive screens. A combined ticket for a tour of Parlament and entrance to Palais Epstein costs adult/child €7/3.

Façade of Rathaus (this page)

PARLAMENT TO SCHWARZENBERGPLATZ

Of all the Ringstrasse's sections, this is the most exceptional architecturally. The Naturhistorisches Museum and Kunsthistorisches Museum have full command of Maria-Theresien-Platz over which a **statue of Maria Theresia** (map pp254–5) gazes. Directly opposite is the austere Hofburg and its accompanying square, Heldenplatz.

Tucked behind the Hofburg, the **Burggarten** (Map pp254–5; ☾6am-10pm Apr-Oct, 6am-8pm Nov-Mar) is a leafy oasis from the hustle and bustle of the Ringstrasse and Innere Stadt. The marble **statue of Mozart** is the park's most famous tenant, but there's also a **statue of Franz Josef** in military garb. Lining the Innere Stadt border of the Burggarten is the Schmetterlinghaus and the ever-popular bar Palmenhaus (p155).

Further along the Ringstrasse are the celebrated Staatsoper (p169) and a string of luxury hotels.

PALAIS EPSTEIN Map pp254-5

☎ 401 10-0; www.palaisepstein.at in German; 01, Dr-Karl-Renner-Ring 1; admission to ground fl free, tours adult/concession/family €4/2/9; ☾10am-5pm Mon-Fri, 10am-1pm Sat; ☒ D, J, 1, 2, 46, 49, bus 48A

Designed by Parlament's architect Hansen, Palais Epstein started life as home to the prominent Jewish family Epstein before being sold off in 1873 due to financial problems. It later became the infamous Soviet Union headquarters during the 'four men in a jeep' period after WWII – nicknamed the 'Gateway to Siberia', around 1000 Austrians passed through its doorways on their deportation route to Siberia. Since undergoing extensive renovations in 2005, it has been used for parliamentary purposes and houses a small interactive display detailing the life of the Epstein family, Vienna's Jews in the late 19th century and the Soviet occupation of the palace. Its glass atrium rises an impressive four floors, but more inviting is the tour of its *bel étage* rooms; with its elaborate ceiling of gold lacework and circular frescoes (Hansen based it on detail in the Santa Maria dei Miracoli in Venice), the *Spielzimmer* (play room) is easily the highlight.

A ticket covering entrance to the palace and a tour of the Parlament costs adult/child €7/3.

NATURHISTORISCHES MUSEUM
Map pp254-5

☎ 521 77-0; www.nhm-wien.ac.at; 01, Burgring 7; adult/senior/concession €8/6/3.50; ☾9am-6.30pm Thu-Mon, 9am-9pm Wed; ⊙ U2, U3 Volkstheater, ☒ D, J, 1, 2

The Naturhistorisches Museum (Museum of Natural History) is the scientific counterpart of the Kunsthistorisches Museum (Museum of Art History) opposite. The building is a mirror image of the art history museum, and while some of the exhibits inside are quite extraordinary their actual presentation could do with a touch of modernisation (and the heating could be turned down). As you would expect in a natural history museum, there are exhibits on minerals, meteorites and assorted animal remains in jars. In the gemstone collection, the Colombian emerald, believed to be a present from the Aztec ruler Montezuma to the Spanish conquistador Hernán Cortés, is overshadowed by the bouquet of precious stones presented to Franz Stephan by Maria Theresia. It consists of a staggering 2102 diamonds and 761 other gems. Zoology and anthropology are covered in detail, including specimens of the extinct Moa and Dodo and the rare Komodo dragon. There's also a children's corner, some good dinosaur exhibits and a room with 3-D projections of microorganisms. The 25,000-year-old statuette *Venus of Willendorf* is here (see Dürnstein p208) – though she's a mere youngster compared to the 32,000 BC statuette *Fanny* from Stratzing (the oldest figurative sculpture in the world). Only photos of the statuette are on display; the real McCoy is in storage. Though seemingly inappropriately named, the nickname Fanny actually comes from her unusual pose, supposedly reminiscent of the Austrian ballerina Fanny Elssler.

AKADEMIE DER BILDENDEN KÜNSTE Map pp254-5

☎ 588 16-0; www.akademiegalerie.at in German; 01, Schillerplatz 3; adult/concession/child under 10 €7/4/free; ☾10am-6pm Tue-Sun; U1, U2, U4 Karlsplatz, ☒ D, J, 1, 2, 62, 65

The Akademie der bildenden Künste (Academy of Fine Arts) is largely passed over by most in favour of the bigger galleries, but is rewarding all the same. Its gallery concentrates on the classic Flemish,

HITLER IN VIENNA

Born in Braunau am Inn, Upper Austria, in 1889, with the name Adolf Schicklgruber (his father changed the family name when they moved to Germany in 1893), Adolf Hitler moved to Vienna when he was just 17. Six unsettled, unsuccessful, poverty-stricken years later he abandoned the city and moved to Munich to make a name for himself. He later wrote in *Mein Kampf* that his Vienna years were 'a time of the greatest transformation that I have ever been through. From a weak citizen of the world I became a fanatical anti-Semite'. Whether this had anything to do with being twice rejected by the Akademie der bildenden Künste (Academy of Fine Arts), who dismissed his work as 'inadequate', he did not say. Even though he was convinced that proper training would have made him into a very successful artist, these rejections caused Hitler to write to a friend that perhaps fate may have reserved for him 'some other purpose'.

Although Vienna would be happy for the world to forget about its association with Hitler, some tourists are retracing the Vienna footsteps of the infamous fascist. He spent several years living in a small, dimly lit **apartment** (Map pp262–3) at Stumpergasse 31, in the 6th district, and three years in the men's hostel **Meldenmannstrasse** (Map pp258–9) in Brigittenau. He was a regular visitor to the opera, and despite his penury, preferred to pay extra to stand in sections that were barred to women. **Café Sperl** (p141) is another address on the Hitler itinerary: here he would loudly express his views on race and other matters.

Hitler briefly returned to Vienna in 1938 at the head of the German army and was greeted by enthusiastic crowds in Heldenplatz. He left a day later.

Dutch and German painters, and includes some big names: Hieronymus Bosch, Rembrandt, Van Dyck, Rubens, Titian, Francesco Guardi, and Cranach the Elder all feature. The supreme highlight is Bosch's impressive and gruesome *Triptych of the Last Judgement* altarpiece (1504-08), with the banishment of Adam and Eve on the left panel and the horror of Hell in the middle and right panels. Many of the paintings are quite dark, which makes Rubens use of light and colour all that more striking. His *Bacchanal* (1611-15) is a genuine masterpiece; a stupefied Bacchus, full with wine and food, barely focuses on the viewer, while his playmates continue their revelry in the background. The building itself has an attractive façade and was designed by Hansen (of Parlament fame). It still operates as an art school, and is famous for turning down Adolf Hitler twice and accepting Egon Schiele (the latter however was happy to leave as quickly as possible). Directly in front of the academy a **statue of Schiller** takes pride of place on Schillerplatz.

Audio guides are available for an extra €2, and tours (€3), in German only, take place at 10.30am every Sunday.

SECESSION Map pp254-5

☎ 587 53 07; www.secession.at; 01, Friedrichstrasse 12; admission exhibition & frieze adult/concessions €6/3.50, exhibition only €4.50/3; ☼ 10am-6pm Tue-Sun, until 8pm Thu; ◎ U1, U2, U4 Karlsplatz
In 1897, 19 progressive artists broke away from the Künstlerhaus and the conservative artistic establishment it represented and formed the Vienna Secession (Sezession). Their aim was to present current trends in contemporary art and leave behind the historicism that was then in vogue in Vienna. Among their number were Klimt, Josef Hoffman, Kolo Moser and Joseph M Olbrich (a former student of Wagner). Olbrich was given the honour of designing the new exhibition centre of the Secessionists. It was erected just a year later and combined sparse functionality with stylistic motifs.

The building is certainly a move away from the Ringstrasse architectural throwbacks. Its most striking feature is a delicate golden dome rising from a turret on the roof that deserves better than the description 'golden cabbage' accorded it by some Viennese. Other features are the Medusa-like faces above the door with dangling serpents instead of earlobes, the minimalist stone owls gazing down from the walls and the vast ceramic pots supported by tortoises at the front. The motto above the entrance asserts: '*Der Zeit ihre Kunst, der Kunst ihre Freiheit*' (To each time its art, to art its freedom).

The 14th exhibition (1902) held in the building featured the famous *Beethoven Frieze* by Klimt. This 34m-long work was only supposed to be a temporary display, little more than an elaborate poster for the main exhibit, Max Klinger's Beethoven monument. Fortunately it was bought at the end of the exhibition by a private collector and transported – plaster, reeds, laths and all – in eight sections to the buyer's home. In 1973 the government purchased the frieze and spent 10 years restoring it to its original glory, and since 1983 it has been on display in the basement. The frieze has dense areas of activity punctuated by mostly open spaces, reminiscent of something plastic partially melted and stretched out over a fire. It features willowy women with bounteous hair who jostle for attention with a large gorilla, while slender figures float and a choir sings. Beethoven would no doubt be surprised to learn that it is based on his Ninth Symphony.

The small room you enter before viewing the frieze tells the story of the building. It served as a hospital during WWI and was torched by the retreating Germans during WWII (the gold dome survived the fire). The ground floor is still used as it was originally intended: presenting temporary exhibitions of contemporary art. It's an incredible achievement of modern functionality and a perfect compliment to the art: spacious, airy, bright and uninhibiting. It's amazing to think it was created over a century ago.

KUNSTHISTORISCHES MUSEUM

Ranking among the finest museums in Europe, if not the world, the **Kunsthistorisches Museum** (Museum of Art History; Map pp254–5; ☎ 525 24-0; www.khm.at; 01, Maria-Theresien-Platz; adult/concession/family €10/7.50/20; ❧ 10am-6pm Tue-Sun, until 9pm Thu; ◎ U2 Museumsquartier, ⊕ D, J, 1, 2) should not be missed. The Habsburgs were great collectors, and the huge extent of lands under their control led to many important works of art being funnelled back to Vienna.

The building itself is delightful and was designed to reflect the works it displays, with older architectural styles faithfully reproduced. No expense was spared in construction and all the marble here is genuine. Ceilings are superbly decorated with murals and stucco embellishments. Halfway up the stairway to the 1st floor you'll see Canova's sculpture *Theseus & the Minotaur*. On the walls above the arches are the portraits of some of the more important artists exhibited in the museum, such as Dürer, Rembrandt and Raphael. The murals between the arches were created by three artists, including a young Klimt (north wall), painted before he broke with classical tradition.

It's impossible to see the whole museum in one visit: after a while the paintings will all meld into one and lose their appeal. The best idea is to concentrate on specific areas. Temporary exhibitions (which may cost extra) sometimes cause reorganisation of rooms, and famous works are occasionally lent to other museums. Various guides and plans are for sale in the shops – you'll probably be able to make do with the *Kunsthistorisches Museum Vienna* booklet in English for €1.50, which includes a floor plan of the museum, and information on sister collections (the Schatzkammer and Sammlung Alter Musikinstrumente in the Hofburg and the Wagenburg in Schönbrunn). Guided tours in English are available on request but usually they're in German; they leave from the information desk at 3.30pm Tuesday, Friday, Saturday and Sunday (€2). If none are available, pick up an audio guide (€2). The museum is part of the Gold, Silver and Bronze discount ticket (p69), and a ticket covering it and the Leopold Museum is available for €17.

Ground Floor

The west wing (to your right as you enter) houses the Egyptian collection, including the burial chamber of Prince Kaninisut. Amid the many sarcophagi and statues in this section are the peculiar mummified remains of various animals (falcon, baboon, cat etc) and examples of the Egyptian *Book of the Dead* on papyrus.

Next come the Greek and Roman collections, including sculptures, urns, vases and Etruscan art. One of the most impressive pieces is the *Gemma Augustea* cameo (Room XV), made from onyx in AD 10, with delicately carved white figures on a bluish-brown background.

The east wing contains a collection of sculpture and decorative arts covering Austrian high baroque, Renaissance, mannerism and medieval art. There are some exquisite 17th-century ornaments and glassware and an assortment of unbelievably lavish clocks from the 16th and 17th centuries (Rooms XXXV and XXXVII). Unfortunately back in 2004 the prime piece in the collection, a saltcellar (1543) made in gold for Francis I of France by Benvenuto Cellini, was lifted and has yet to be reclaimed.

Kunsthistorisches Museum (p73)

First Floor

The Gemäldegalerie (picture gallery) on this floor is the most important part of the museum – you could lose yourself for hours wandering round whole rooms devoted to works by Bruegel, Dürer, Rubens, Rembrandt, Van Dyck, Cranach, Caravaggio, Canaletto, Titian and many others. Some rooms have information cards in English giving a critique of particular artists and their work.

EAST WING

The east wing is devoted to German, Dutch and Flemish paintings. Room X contains the collection of Pieter Bruegel the Elder's works, amassed by Rudolf II, which is unrivalled in the world. A familiar theme in the artist's work is nature, as in his cycle of seasonal scenes, three of which are shown here. *Hunters in the Snow* (1565) portrays winter; the hunters return towards a Dutch-looking frozen lake with frolicking skaters, beyond which rise some very un-Dutch mountains. The viewer's eye is drawn into the scene by the flow of movement – a device commonly exploited by Bruegel. This is also seen in the atmospheric *The Return of the Herd* (1565), illustrating a glowering autumnal day. Bruegel's peasant scenes are also excellent, such as *The Battle Between Carnival & Lent* (1559), where the centre and

foreground are dominated by carnival tomfoolery, with the dour, cowled and caped figures in religious processions pushed to the edges of the scene.

The next gallery (Room XI) shows Flemish baroque, in vogue some 80 years later, with warm, larger-than-life scenes such as *The King Drinks* by Jacob Jordaens (with the revellers raising their glasses to a motto in Latin that translates as 'None resembles a fool more than the drunkard') and *The Fishmarket* by Frans Snyders.

Albrecht Dürer (1471–1528) is represented in Room XIV. His brilliant use of colour is particularly shown in *The Holy Trinity Surrounded by All Saints,* originally an altarpiece. The *Martyrdom of 10,000 Christians* and *The Adoration of the Holy Trinity* are other fine works.

The paintings by the mannerist Giuseppe Arcimboldo in Room XIX use a device well explored by Salvador Dali: familiar objects are arranged to appear as something else. But Arcimboldo did it nearly 400 years earlier! His series of four composite pictures *Summer, Winter, Water* and *Fire* (1563–66) cleverly show faces composed of objects related to those particular themes.

Rubens (1577–1640) was appointed to the service of a Habsburg governor in Brussels, so it is not surprising that the museum has one of the best collections of his works in the world. He was a very influential figure because of his synthesis of northern and Italian traditions. His works can be seen in Rooms XIII and XIV. Try to spot the difference between those he painted completely himself (eg note the open brushwork and diaphanous quality of the fur in *Ildefonso Altar*) and those that he planned and finished off, but were mostly executed by his students (like the vivid but more rigid *Miracles of Ignatius Loyola*, a dramatic baroque picture displayed along with Rubens' initial study for the scene).

Rembrandt has several self-portraits in Room XXI. Vermeer's *The Allegory of Painting* (1665-66) is in Room XXII. It's a strangely static scene of an artist in his studio, but one that transcends the mundane by its composition and use of light.

WEST WING

Room I has some evocative works by Titian, of the Venetian school. He uses colour and broad brush strokes to create character and mood, rather than distinct outlines. In Room 2 is *The Three Philosophers* (1508), one of the few authenticated works by Giorgione.

In Room 4 is Raphael's harmonious and idealised portrait *Madonna in the Meadow* (1505). The triangular composition and the complementary colours are typical features of the Florentine High Renaissance. Compare this to Caravaggio's *Madonna of the Rosary* (1606) in Room V, an example of new realism in early baroque; note the dirty soles on the feet of the supplicants. Caravaggio emphasises movement in this picture by a subtle deployment of light and shadow.

Susanna at her Bath (1555) by Tintoretto can be found in Room III. It re-creates the Old Testament tale of Susanna being surprised at her ablutions by two old men. The picture successfully portrays both serenity and implicit menace. Tintoretto employs mannerist devices (contrasting light, extremes of facial features) to achieve his effect.

Room VII has paintings by Bernardo Bellotto (1721-80), Canaletto's nephew. He was commissioned by Maria Theresia to paint scenes of Vienna, and several are shown here. Note the way landmarks are sometimes compressed to create a more satisfying composition; the view from Schloss Belvedere is not a faithful reproduction. The pastoral view of Schönbrunn is in stark contrast to its urban situation today.

Room X has portraits of the Habsburgs. Juan Carreño's portrait of Charles II of Spain really shows the characteristic Habsburg features: a distended lower lip and jaw and a nose that would be more at home in an aviary. Most of the young women in Diego Velázquez's royal portraits are wearing dresses broad enough to fit around a horse, but the artist still manages to make the subjects come to life.

MUSEUMSQUARTIER

It may have only been operating since 2001, but the **MuseumsQuartier** (MQ; Museums Quarter; ☎ 523 58 81-17 30, within Austria 0820-600 600; www.mqw.at; 07, Museumsplatz 1; ⊙ information & ticket centre 10am-7pm), with its excellent museums, great cafés and warm public spaces, has already gained third spot on Vienna's most-visited list (after Schönbrunn and the Kunsthistorisches Museum).

The MQ lies within the confines of the former imperial stables, just behind the Kunsthistorisches and Naturhistorisches Museums. The stables, designed by Fischer von Erlach, housed a reputed 600 horses, and contained two rooms just for the emperor's personal stock – one for the white stallions, the other for the black. The construction of the new complex began in earnest in 1998 – after much controversy and toing and froing between its supporters and opposition – and was completed in 2001, to the tune of €145 million. It's now the eighth-largest cultural complex in the world, with over 60,000 sq metres of exhibition space, and houses the Leopold Museum, Museum moderner Kunst (MUMOK; Museum of Modern Art), Kunsthalle, Zoom, Architekturzentrum Wien, Tanzquartier Wien (p170) and a number of cafés. Towards the front of the complex is **Quartier 21**, a mall-like space with a cluster of shops and temporary exhibitions, and near its Mariahilfer Strasse entrance is **Dschungel Wien** (Map pp254–5; ☎ 522 07 20; www.dschungelwien.at; adult/child €8.50/7.50), a theatre for children.

MuseumQuartier's major open space, the rectangular Haupthof, is constantly used for happenings and hosts both a winter and summer program of events (see the website for details). It's particularly popular during the summer months when tourists and locals alike get to work on their tans.

If you plan to see a number of attractions in the MuseumsQuartier, consider purchasing one of the following: **MQ Kombi Ticket** (€25), includes entry into every museum except for Zoom (which only has a reduced ticket price), and a 30% discount on performances in the Tanzquartier Wien; **MQ Art Ticket** (€21.50), allows admission into the Leopold Museum, MUMOK, and Kunsthalle; **MQ Duo Ticket** (€16), covers admission into the Leopold Museum and MUMOK. The **MQ Family Ticket** (two adults & two children under 13; €29) provides access to MUMOK and the Leopold Museum.

ARCHITEKTURZENTRUM WIEN Map pp254-5

☎ 522 31 15; www.azw.at; 07, Museumsplatz 1; exhibitions adult/student €5/3.50; ⏱ 10am-7pm, until 9pm Wed; ⊙ U2 Museumsquartier, U2, U3 Volkstheater, ▣ 49, bus 2A, 48A

The Architekturzentrum Wien (Vienna Architecture Centre) takes up much of the MQ north of MUMOK, collectively encompassing three halls used for temporary exhibitions, a library and the café Una (p126). Exhibitions focus on international architectural developments and change on a regular basis. The extensive library is open to the public 10am to 5.30pm Monday, Wednesday and Friday and until 7pm on Saturday and Sunday. The centre also organises walking tours through Vienna on Sunday, covering various architectural themes, but they are in German only.

KUNSTHALLE Map pp254-5

☎ 521 89 33; www.kunsthallewien.at in German; 07, Museumsplatz 1; Hall 1 adult/concession €7.50/6, Hall 2 €6/4.50, combined ticket €10.50/8.50; ⏱ 10am-7pm Sat-Wed, until 9pm Thu & Fri; ⊙ U2 Museumsquartier, ⊙ U2, U3 Volkstheater, ▣ 49, bus 2A, 48A

Between the Leopold and MUMOK is the Kunsthalle (Art Hall), a collection of exhibition halls used to showcase local and international contemporary art. While it doesn't have the sheer impact of the Tate Modern in London or the Centre Pompidou in Paris, its high ceilings, open space and pure functionality have seen the venue rated among the top institutions for exhibitions in Europe. Programs, which run for three to six months, tend to focus on photography, video, film, installations and new media.

Guided tours in German leave at 4pm on Saturday and Sunday and cost €2.

LEOPOLD MUSEUM Map pp254-5

☎ 525 70-0; www.leopoldmuseum.org; 07, Museumsplatz 1; adult/seniors/students & children €9/7/5.50; ⏱ 10am-6pm Mon, Wed & Fri-Sun, until 9pm Thu; ⊙ U2 Museumsquartier, U2, U3 Volkstheater, bus 2A

The Leopold Museum easily steals the show in the MuseumsQuartier. The museum is named after Rudolf Leopold, a Viennese ophthalmologist who, on buying his first Egon Schiele (1890–1918) for a song as a young student in 1950, started to amass a huge private collection of mainly 19th-century and modernist Austrian artworks. In 1994 he sold the lot – 5266 paintings – to the Austrian government for €160 million (sold individually, the paintings would have made him €574 million), and the Leopold Museum was born.

The building is in complete contrast to the MUMOK, with a white, limestone exterior, open space (the 21m-high glass-covered atrium is lovely) and natural light flooding most rooms. Considering Rudolf Leopold's love of Schiele, it's no surprise the museum contains the largest collection of the painter's work in the world. Most are to be found on the top floor; look for *Selbstportrait mit Judenkirschen* (Self-Portrait with Winter Cherries) and *Kardinale und Nüne* (Cardinal and Nun), two masterpieces of the expressive artist. Gustav Klimt (1862–1918) is also represented; his *Tod und Leben* (Death and Life) on the ground floor is by far the most impressive. Simple, yet highly emotional sketches from both artists are displayed in the basement.

Other artists well represented include Albin Egger-Lienz (1868–1926), Richard Gerstl (1883–1908) and Austria's third greatest expressionist, Kokoschka (1886–1980). Egger-Lienz had a knack for capturing the essence of rural life; this is seen in his stark *Pietá,* considered by Leopold as his greatest work. Kokoschka had a long life in the painting arena, but his earlier works steal the show; his *Selbstportrait mit ein Hand* (Self-Portrait with One Hand) from 1918 is his most substantial piece. Works by Loos, Hoffmann, (Otto) Wagner, Waldmüller and Romako are also on display.

Audio guides in English and German are available for €3, as are guided tours in

German at 3pm on Saturday and Sunday. A joint ticket covering the Leopold and the Kunsthistorisches Museum costs €17. On the top floor is **Café Leopold** (p155).

MUMOK Map pp254-5

☎ 525 00-0; www.mumok.at; 07, Museumsplatz 1; adult/concession €8/6.50; ☯ 10am-6pm Tue-Sun, until 9pm Thu; ☺ U2 Museumsquartier, U2, U3 Volkstheater, 🚋 49, bus 2A, 48A

The dark basalt edifice that houses the Museum moderner Kunst (MUMOK; Museum of Modern Art) is something the Borg from Star Trek would be proud of: sheer grey walls, sharp corners and a powerful presence. The exterior will certainly impress, but as a whole MUMOK fails to please. Inside, many of the exhibition rooms on its five floors, which house Vienna's premiere collection of 20th-century art, are cramped and devoid of natural light – great for cave dwellers but not for viewing art. The exhibition is centred around fluxus, nouveau realism, pop art and photorealism, but expressionism, cubism, minimal art and Viennese Actionism (p28) are also represented. The best of the bunch is an extensive collection of pop art featuring the likes of Warhol, Jasper Johns and Rauschenberg. If you've never seen Viennese Actionism, this is your chance as MUMOK's basement holds the largest collection of such art. Actionism is a melting pot of animal sacrifice, bloody canvases, self-mutilation and defecation, and certainly not everyone's cup of tea. Other well-known artists represented throughout the museum include Picasso, Paul Klee, René Magritte, Max Ernst and Alberto Giacometti.

ZOOM Map pp254-5

☎ 524 79 08; www.kindermuseum.at in German; 07, Museumsplatz 1; adult/child €3.50/5; programs from 8am-4pm; ☺ U2 Museumsquartier, U2, U3 Volkstheater, bus 2A

Zoom children's museum is basically an arts and crafts session with a lot of playing thrown in. Children are guided through themed programs, and get the chance to make, break, draw, explore – basically to be creative. Topics range from animation to zoology and change throughout the year. Programs begin every 1½ to two hours from 8.30am to 4pm; there are normally four programs a day Monday to Friday and

Map of Europe at the children's museum Zoom (this page)

five on both Saturday and Sunday. Advance bookings for the more popular programs are highly recommended, but you can also just turn up and try your luck. Zoom is aimed at kids between the age of zero and 14 and most staff speak English.

SCHWARZENBERGPLATZ TO THE DANUBE CANAL

The Ringstrasse begins this section overlooking Schwarzenbergplatz. The square is dominated by a **statue of Karl von Schwarzenberg** (Map pp254–5), leader in the Battle of Leipzig (1813), from whom the square gained its name. A short distance behind it is the huge fountain **Hochstrahlbrunnen** (Map pp254–5) and behind it is the rather gaudy **Russen Heldendenkmal** (Russian Heroes' Monument; Map pp254–5). The fountain was commissioned in 1873 to commemorate Vienna's first water mains and the monument is a reminder that the Russians liberated the city at the end of WWII. The latter is certainly not in the hearts of many Viennese. **Palais Schwarzenberg** (Map pp262–3), co-created by Fischer von Erlach and Hildebrandt, takes up the rear; it's now a luxurious hotel enjoying a complete overhaul.

Closer to the Danube Canal and stretching from Johannesgasse to Weiskirchnerstrasse is the largest of the Ringstrasse parks, the **Stadtpark** (City Park). Opened in

1862, it is an enjoyable recreational spot, with winding paths and a pond – great for strolling or relaxing in the sun and a favourite lunchtime escape for Innere Stadt workers. Of the several statues within the park (including Schindler, Bruckner and Schubert), the most recognisable is the **Johann Strauss Denkmal** (Map pp254–5), a golden statue of Johann Strauss the Younger under a white arch. It's easily the most photographed statue in the city. The Kursalon (p168), in the southwest corner, hosts regular waltz concerts, and one of Vienna's finest restaurants, Steiereck im Stadtpark (p129), overlooks the Wien Fluss (Vienna River), which cuts through the park on its way to the Danube Canal.

Squeezed between the park and the canal are the MAK, Otto Wagner's celebrated Postsparkasse and the **former Kriegsministerium** (Imperial War Ministry; map pp254–5).

MUSEUM FÜR ANGEWANDTE KUNST
Map pp254-5

☎ 711 36-0; www.mak.at; 01, Stubenring 5; adult/concession €7.90/5.50; ⏱ 10am-6pm Wed-Sun, 10am-midnight Tue; Ⓜ U3 Stubentor, ⒯ 1, 2
The Museum für angewandte Kunst (Museum of Applied Arts), better known as the MAK, has an extensive collection of household items better described as art pieces. MAK shares it's home with the excellent, café Österreicher im MAK (p127), and the building – a High Renaissance construction dating from 1871 – offers some fine features in its own right, especially the ceilings.

Each exhibition room is devoted to a different style, eg Renaissance, baroque, oriental, historicism, empire, Art Deco and the distinctive metalwork of the Wiener Werkstätte. Contemporary artists were invited to present the rooms in ways they felt were appropriate, which has resulted in the creation of eye-catching and unique displays. For example, in the Biedermeier room, Jenny Holzer placed electronic signs near the ceiling so that 'they can be ignored' while Barbara Bloom's display of Art Nouveau chairs is back-lit and presented behind translucent white screens. This takes nothing away from the actual objects on display, but rather complements their beauty. The 20th-century design and architecture room is impressive; Frank Gehry's cardboard chair is a gem. The museum's

collections encompass tapestries, lace, furniture, glassware and ornaments. Klimt's *Stoclet Frieze* is upstairs.

The basement houses the Study Collection. Here exhibits are grouped according to the type of materials used: glass and ceramics, metal, wood and textiles. Actual objects range from ancient oriental statues to sofas (note the red-lips sofa). There are some particularly good porcelain and glassware pieces, with casts showing how they're made.

MAK is free on Saturdays and tours (€2) are available in German at 11am on Saturday and in English at noon on Sunday.

POSTSPARKASSE Map pp254-5

☎ 534 53 33088; www.ottowagner.at; 01, Georg Coch Platz 2; museum adult/child €5/3.50; ⏱ 8am-3pm Mon-Fri, until 5.30pm Thu, 8am-5pm Sat; Ⓜ U1, U4 Schwedenplatz, ⒯ N, 1, 2, 21
The celebrated Post Office Savings Bank building is the work of Wagner, who oversaw its construction between 1904 and 1906, and again from 1910 to 1912. The design and choice of materials were both innovative for the time; compare the modern appearance of the Postsparkasse with the austere and powerful former Kriegsministerium on the Ring opposite, which was built around the same period. The grey marble façade is held together by some 17,000 metal nails while the inside is filled with sci-fi aluminium heating ducts and naked stanchions – perhaps Terry Gilliam posted a letter here before directing *Brazil*.

The small museum at the back of the main savings hall hosts temporary exhibitions of a design nature, whether it be office buildings or kitchenware.

EAST OF THE DANUBE CANAL
Drinking p156; Eating p126

East of the Danube Canal is divided between four districts – Leopoldstadt, Brigittenau, Floridsdorf, and Donaustadt. Collectively, Leopoldstadt and Brigittenau create an island bordered by the canal to the west and the Danube to the east, while Floridsdorf and Donaustadt, locally known as *Transdanubia* (a Hungarian term for 'across the Danube'), make up all of Vienna that lies east of the Danube.

The area is one of the more spacious – and flat – in the city. It is home to the Prater, Vienna's large, central green oasis; the Donauinsel (Danube Island), a recreational playground with beaches, water sports, and kilometres of walking, cycling, and inline-skating tracks; and the Alte Donau (Old Danube), an arm of the Danube long ago cut off from the river. Much of its large expanse is residential sprawl, with wide streets and 1950s apartment blocks the norm. Leopoldstadt, the closest of the four districts to the Innere Stadt, is by far the most interesting historically and culturally; a home to European Jews for centuries, in recent years it has become one of the city's more ethnically-diverse districts.

LEOPOLDSTADT

Leopoldstadt started life as a walled Jewish ghetto in 1624 under the watchful eye of Ferdinand II but the district gained its name from Leopold I. The heavily anti-Semite Habsburg dispelled Jews from a ghetto in the area in 1670, destroyed their synagogue and replaced it with the Leopoldkirche (Map pp258–9). Long the scapegoats of the city, Jews had slowly been drifting back to the city after their expulsion in the 15th century (p45) and resettling the area. By the 18th and 19th centuries, the city was once again experiencing an influx of immigrant Jews, particularly from Eastern Europe. The overcrowding and poor conditions were some of the worst in the city, but it was nothing compared to the treatment the residents received under the Nazis, who expelled all Jews and left the district desolate. The beginning of the 21st century has seen a new influx, and Jews now mix with the immigrants from Turkey and the Balkans who have filled the floundering district over the past decades; Karmelitermarkt (p185), the district's busy food market, is the place to find kosher food, halal food and a healthy ethnic diversity.

Leopoldstadt's biggest attraction is its parks. Prater (www.wiener-prater.at) is a term commonly used to encompass two distinct areas of one of the city's favourite outdoor playgrounds: the Wurstelprater (Map pp258–9) and the green woodland park on its outskirts. The Wurstelprater, or Volksprater as it's also known, is a large amusement park with all sorts of funfair rides, ranging from modern big dippers to merry-go-rounds and test-your-strength machines that could eas-

EAST OF THE DANUBE CANAL TOP SIGHTS

- pump up the adrenaline levels on the rides at the **Wurstelprater** (left)
- stroll along the tree-shaded pathways of the **Prater** (left)
- take a ride on one of Vienna's icons, the **Riesenrad** (p80)
- skate, walk, cycle, or simply laze about on the **Donauinsel** (p82)
- enjoying the **Alte Donau** (p82) in all seasons, with sailing and swimming in summer and ice skating in winter

ily date from the early 20th century. Bumper cars, go-karts, haunted houses, games rooms and minigolf attractions abound, as do hot-dog and candy-floss stands. There's also a 4km Lilliputbahn (minirailway; joint tickets with the Riesenrad are available), which connects the park with Ernst Happel Stadium. Kids go bananas over the place and rides cost around €1 to €5. One of the most popular attractions, however, is free: colourful, bizarre, deformed statues of people and creatures in the centre of the park, on and around Rondeau and Calafattiplatz. The 60 sq km of woodland park may be more appealing. Formally the royal hunting grounds of Joseph II, the Prater was first opened to the public in 1766. Viennese flock here to walk, run, cycle, inline skate or simple soak up the sun in the park's open green fields or tree-shaded alleys. Even though the park attracts a multitude of people, it's still possible to find a private patch of green, particularly in its southwestern reaches. The Prater is home to the Riesenrad, the Planetarium, the Pratermuseum and Ernst-Happel-Stadion (p173). If you're hungry try Lusthaus (p128) or the Schweizerhaus (p127), which is legendary for its Czech beer and *Schwiensstelze* (pork hocks).

Augarten (Map pp258–9; ☺ 6am-dusk Apr-Oct, 6.30am-dusk Nov-Mar) park is more genteel than its bigger brother the Prater. It gained its present shape in 1712, making it the oldest baroque garden in Vienna, and opened its doors to the public in 1775. The park is dotted with open meadows and crisscrossed with tree-lined paths but its most captivating features are the austere *Flaktürme* (flak towers; Map pp258–9) in its northern and western corners. Other

JEWISH VIENNA

In the past few years Vienna has experienced an influx of Jewish immigrants, mostly from Russia, plus a smaller group from Iran. Their presence has strengthened the city's Jewish community enormously, and increased awareness of the role Jewish culture has played in Vienna's history.

Due to the destruction of many sights during WWII, not much remains of Jewish Vienna today. The **Jüdisches Museum** (p59) holds the largest collection of Jewish artefacts, while **Museum Judenplatz** (p66) highlights a medieval synagogue. **Stadttempel** (p68) is not only the main synagogue for the Jewish community, but one of the very few left standing after the war. **Leopoldstadt** (p79) is home to the most active Jewish community in the city, with kosher shops and a lively market.

The handful of old Jewish cemeteries are sad – yet enchanting – reminders of Vienna's once large Jewish community. The **Zentralfriedhof** (p97) is the principal cemetery, while **Währinger Friedhof** (Map pp258–9; 18, Semperstrasse; ☺ 10am-3pm Sun-Thu) and **Friedhof Floridsdorf** (Map pp252–3; ☎ 531 04 235; 21, Ruthnergasse 28; ☺ by appointment only) are smaller, neglected versions of their bigger cousin. **Friedhof Rossau** (Map pp258–9; 09, Seegasse 9-11; ☺ 7am-3pm Mon-Fri), dating from 1540, is well hidden behind a modern apartment block (built on the site of the old Jewish hospital) and displays the scars of Nazi desecration.

buildings of note are the Augarten baroque palace, home to the Vienna Boys' Choir, the nearby Saalgebäude, where the Wiener Porzellanmanufaktur Augarten is located, and the Atelier, housing the Gustinus Ambrosi-Museum. The park is also home to the outdoor cinema Kino Unter Sternen (p173) in July and August.

Exploring the district on foot turns up a few oddities. Hollandstrasse and Tempelgasse contain a handful of kosher shops, and the remains of the district's largest synagogue can also be seen on Tempelgasse. Otto Wagner's neglected **Schützenhaus** (Map pp258–9), a white- and blue-tiled house built in 1907, overlooks the canal and awaits its next reincarnation (rumours are that it will soon be a café). The canal itself is lined with small parks and many a canal-bridge underbelly is bombed with graffiti, a sight rarely seen in Vienna. See the Walking and Cycling Tours chapter (p113) for a suggested tour through the district.

RIESENRAD Map pp258-9

☎ 729 54 30; www.wienerriesenrad.com; 02, Prater 90; adult/child/family €7.50/3/19; ☺ 9am-midnight May-Sep, 10am-10pm Mar, Apr & Oct, 10am-8pm Nov-Feb; ⓞ U1 Praterstern, 🚊 0, 5, 21
Dominating the Prater is the Riesenrad (Ferris Wheel), one of Vienna's eternal symbols. Built in 1897 by Englishman Walter B Basset, the wheel rises to 65m and takes about 20 minutes to rotate its 430-tonne weight one complete circle. This gives you ample time to snap some fantastic shots of the city laid out in front of you. It survived bombing in 1945 and recently received

a make-over which included dramatic lighting and a café at its base. If you think you're experiencing déjà vu upon spotting the great wheel, you're not: it achieved celluloid fame in *The Third Man,* in the scene where Holly Martins finally confronts Harry Lime, and also featured in the James Bond flick *The Living Daylights.*

Admission includes entry into the Panorama, a collection of disused wheel-cabins filled with models depicting scenes from the city's history, including Roman Vienna and the Turkish invasions. Joint tickets for the Lilliputbahn (adult/child €8.50/3.50), Donauturm (p78; adult/child €9.70/5.10) and Schönbrunn Tiergarten (p102; adult/child €14.50/5.90) are also available.

PLANETARIUM Map pp258-9

☎ 729 54 94; www.planetarium-wien.at in German; 02, Oswald Thomas Platz 1; adult/child/family €8/6/21; ⓞ U1 Praterstern, 🚊 0, 5, 21
The Planetarium, Vienna's extraterrestrial and interstellar viewfinder, is located on the edge of the Wurstelprater behind the Riesenrad. Shows, normally at 9.30am, 11am, 3pm and 6pm or 7pm, change on a regular basis, but normally focus on our closest neighbours or star constellations and how Earth fits in. Be aware that all shows are in German only.

PRATERMUSEUM Map pp258-9

☎ 726 76 83; 02, Oswald-Thomas-Platz 1; adult/concession/child under 6 €2/1/free; ☺ 10am-1pm Tue-Thu, 2-6pm Fir-Sun; ⓞ U1 Praterstern, 🚊 0, 5, 21
Sharing the same building as the Planetarium is this municipal museum that

traces the history of the Wurstelprater and its woodland neighbour, the Grüner Prater. For all the life and splendour the Prater has seen, unfortunately its museum has only a rather dull mix of photos and stories mainly from the 19th century. The antique slot machines, some of which are still functioning, are the museum's saving grace.

ATELIER AUGARTEN/GUSTINUS AMBROSI-MUSEUM Map pp258-9

☎ 795 57 134; www.atelier-augarten.at in German; 02, Scherzergasse 1a; adult/concession €5/3.50; ☺ 10am-6pm Tue-Sun; ☒ N, 5

Sculptures by Austrian-born Gustinus Ambrosi (1893-1975) are the highlight of the works displayed at Atelier Augarten, in the western corner of Augarten park. Alongside his works of art are other European sculptures from the 20th and 21st centuries. The Atelier also regularly features temporary exhibits from international artists – check the program on the website.

Entry to the Atelier is included in the Schloss Belvedere ticket (p86).

WIENER PORZELLANMANUFAKTUR AUGARTEN Map pp258-9

☎ 211 24-0; www.augarten.at; 02, Obere Augartenstrasse 1, Schloss Augarten; tours €4; ☺ 9.30am-5pm Mon-Fri; bus 5A

Wiener Porzellanmanufaktur Augarten (Vienna's Porcelain Factory) is the second-oldest porcelain manufacturer in Europe, producing exquisite pieces featuring plenty of fanciful flourishes which are available at the shop (p179). Tours of the premises are also possible and explain the process of turning white kaolin, feldspar and quartz

Flakturm in Augarten (this page)

into delicate creations through the process of moulding, casting, luting, glazing and painting; tours generally last around an hour.

WIENER KRIMINALMUSEUM Map pp258-9

☎ 214 46 78; www.kriminalmuseum.at in German; 02, Grosse Sperlgasse 24; adult/concession/child €4.50/3.50/2.50; ☺ 10am-5pm Thu-Sun; ☒ N, 21, bus 5A

Adding to the Viennese obsession with death is the Wiener Kriminalmuseum (Vienna Crime Museum). It takes a prurient, tabloid-style look at crimes and criminals in Austria and dwells on murders in the last

FLAKTÜRME

It can be quite a shock – and a little unnerving – to walk around the corner and be confronted with a gigantic relic from WWII, a *Flakturm* (flak tower). Built from 1943 to 1944 as a defence against air attacks, these bare monolithic blocks stand like sleeping giants among the residential districts of Vienna. Apart from their air-defence capabilities, they were built to house up to 30,000 troops, had an underground hospital and munitions factory and could control their own water and power supplies. They were built to last too: with 5m-thick walls of reinforced concrete, they are almost impossible to pull down. So they remain standing as an uncomfortable reminder of the Nazi era, featureless but for four circular gun bases at the top corners (these protrusions are strangely reminiscent of Mickey Mouse's ears).

Six flak towers still exist; two in Augarten (p79), one just off Mariahilfer Strasse in Esterházypark (housing the Haus des Meeres, p90) and another behind the MuseumsQuartier in the Stiftskaserne (Map pp260–1). Of the last two in Arenbergpark (Map pp262–3), one is used by MAK for temporary exhibitions (€5.50; ☺ 11am-4pm Sun May-Nov); even if you're not interested in what's on show, it's worth paying the entrance fee just to see the inside of one of these WWII dinosaurs.

TOP PICKS FOR CHILDREN

- playgrounds, swimming areas, bicycle and inline skate hire plus miles of pathways are on **Donauinsel** (right)
- little tykes can learn how to behave like right royal princes and princesses at **Schönbrunn Kindermuseum** (p102)
- the kids will go crazy over **Wurstelprater** (p79), a fun park with amusement rides and silly games
- Vienna's premiere children's museum, **Zoom** (p77) is one big arts and crafts lesson
- a mini version of the Wurstelprater, with rides, games and playgrounds is the **Böhmische Prater** (p96)

If you read German, Falter's *Kind in Wien* book is the only resource you'll ever need for any aspect of your child's life in Vienna. It's available from book stores.

100 years or so with particularly grisly relish, though there are skulls of earlier criminals, and even an 18th-century head pickled in a jar. Displays include death masks of convicted murderers and weapons supposedly used to carry out the murders.

JOHANN STRAUSS RESIDENCE

Map pp254-5

☎ 214 01 21; 02, Praterstrasse 54; adult/concession €2/1; ◷ 2-6pm Tue-Thu, 10am-1pm Fri-Sun; ◎ U1 Nestroyplatz, bus 5A

Strauss the Younger called Praterstrasse 54 his residence from 1863 to 1878 and composed *the* waltz, 'The Blue Danube', under its high ceilings. Inside you'll find an above-average collection of Strauss and ballroom memorabilia, including his grand piano and oil paintings from his last apartment which was destroyed during WWII. The rooms are bedecked in period furniture from Strauss' era. The residence is a municipal museum.

FLORIDSDORF

Vienna's most northerly district is solidly working class with few attractions, aside from producing over 30% of the city's wines. The neighbourhoods of Strebersdorf and Stammersdorf hog the most attention, and are well known for their traditional *Heurigen* (p142). Just outside the city limits – but still with public transport connections to Floridsdorf – is **Bisamberg**, a rounded hill rising from the flat plain. It's crisscrossed with walking and cycling paths and covered in vineyards, making it a lovely days' outing for wine and nature enthusiasts.

DONAUSTADT

Donaustadt is the largest of Vienna's districts, covering more ground than the Innere Stadt and the districts inside the Gürtel combined. Its main feature, aside from block after block of bland residential houses, is water: most of the **Donauinsel** (Map pp252–3) and **Alte Donau** fall within its borders.

The svelte Donauinsel (Danube Island) stretches some 21½km from opposite Klosterneuburg in the north to the Nationalpark Donau-Auen in the south and splits the Danube in two, creating a separate arm from the main river known as the **Neue Donau** (New Danube). It was created in 1970 and is Vienna's prime aquatic playground, with long sections of beach (don't except much sand) perfect for swimming, boating and a little waterskiing. The tips of the island are designated FKK (*Freikörperkultur;* free body culture), zones reserved for nudist bathers who also enjoy dining, drinking, walking, biking and inline skating *au naturel;* it's quite a sight. Concrete paths run the entire length of the island, and there are bicycle and inline-skate rental stores. Restaurants and snack bars are dotted along the paths, but the highest concentration of bars – collectively known as Sunken City and Copa Cagrana – is near Reichsbrücke and the U1 Donauinsel stop. In late June the island hosts the **Donauinselfest** (Danube Island Festival; p10). For more information on outdoor activities and nightlife on the island, see the Entertainment chapter (p162).

Separated from the Neue Donau by a sliver of land is the Alte Donau, a landlocked arm of the Danube; a third of it lies in Floridsdorf. It carried the main flow of the river until 1875, when artificial flood precautions created the Danube's path seen today. Now the 160-hectare water expanse is a favourite of Viennese sailing and boating enthusiasts, and also attracts swimmers, walkers, fishermen and in winter (if it's cold enough), ice skaters. Alongside free access points to the Alte Donau are almost a dozen city-owned bathing complexes which are open (approximately) from May to September. The biggest of these is Strandbad Gänsehäufel (p176) complex, on an island jutting out into the Alte Donau. The island also has a nudist section, swimming pools and lake access.

At the southern extremes of Donaustadt is the Lobau, an area of dense scrub and woodland home to the western extension of the Nationalpark Donau-Auen, a couple of industrial sights and an abundance of small lakes. Any way you look at it, it's a bizarre combination. In summer, Vienna's alternative crowd flock to the Lobau for skinny-dipping.

Nationalpark Donau-Auen (www.donauauen .at) is the most easterly section of Vienna. Established in 1996, the park currently covers around 9300 hectares and runs in a thin strip on both sides of the Danube, extending from the edge of Vienna to the Slovakian border. About 60% is forested and approximately 25% is lakes and waterways. It was created to try to protect an environment that was threatened by the building of a hydroelectric power station in Hainburg. You'll find plentiful flora and fauna, including 700 species of fern and flowering plants, and a high density of kingfishers (feeding off the 50 species of fish).

DONAUTURM Map pp252-3

☎ 263 35 72; www.donauturm.at; 22, Donauturmstrasse 4; adult/concession/child €5.30/4.20/3.90; ⏲ 10am-11.30pm; Ⓜ U1 Kaisermühlen Vienna International Centre, bus 20B

At 252m, the Donauturm (Danube Tower) in Donaupark is Vienna's tallest structure – next highest is the newly constructed Millennium Tower at 202m. Its revolving restaurant at 170m allows fantastic panoramic views of the whole city and beyond – it's just a pity the food isn't that great. Tickets covering entrance to the Donauturm and Riesenrad cost €9.70/5.10 per adult/child. The adventurous might imagine bungee jumping off the side of the tower.

UNO CITY Map pp252-3

☎ 260 60 3328; www.unvienna.org; 22, Wagramer Strasse 5; adult/concession/child €5/3/2; ⏲ 11am & 2pm Mon-Fri; Ⓜ U1 Kaisermühlen Vienna International Centre

The UNO City, or Vienna International Centre as it is officially known, is home to a plethora of international organisations, but mainly houses the UN's third-largest office in the world. Guided tours take you through conference rooms and exhibitions on UN activities and add insight into what goes on behind normally closed doors. The City probably looked the picture of modernism way back in 1979 when it was built, but now looks quite out of date. It has extraterritorial status, so take your passport when visiting.

MINOPOLIS Map pp252-3

☎ 0810 970 270; www.minopolis.at in German; 22, Wagramerstrasse 2; adult/child Thu & Fri €4/8, Sat & Sun €6/12; h2-7pm Thu & Fri, 10am-7pm Sat & Sun; Ⓜ U1 Kaisermühlen Vienna International Centre

The newest edition to Vienna's attractions for kids, this city theme park offers children the chance to play grown-up for the day. The 6000 sq m park of streets, buildings, shops and cars includes 25 stations which provide information and activities on various occupations, such as journalist, fire fighter, and doctor. Children are given Eurolinos, the money of Minopolis, to spend or save as they see fit, and while its commercially-orientated entertainment, children seem to love it.

INSIDE THE GÜRTEL

Drinking p141 & p156; Eating p128; Shopping p186; Sleeping p198

The districts inside the Gürtel are a dense concentration of apartment blocks pockated by leafy parks and the occasional baroque palace. Many of Vienna's more-refined citizens call this area home, as do a large number of students, young go-getters and successful entrepreneurs. This mix of people creates a diverse atmosphere which is at times hard to fathom: one neighbourhood is the epitome of repose while the next noisy, with new bars and restaurants randomly appearing. While the area isn't overflowing with sights, its strange bedfellows make exploring these districts a life-sized treasure hunt: you never know what little gem you may find tucked away down one of the side streets or back alleys.

The Gürtel was originally the site of *Linienwall*, Vienna's first line of defence against invaders. These days, it still forms a kind of barrier, if an invisible one: many of the city's immigrants fail to penetrate the inner sanctum of the districts inside the

INSIDE THE GÜRTEL TOP SIGHTS

- admire the distinctive architecture of Friedensreich Hundertwasser at the **KunstHausWien** (opposite) and **Hundertwasser Haus** (opposite)
- marvel at the magnificent **Liechtenstein Museum** (p92) and its extensive private collection of art
- be overawed by the baroque splendour of **Schloss Belvedere** (p86)
- discover the often-forgotten military exploits of Austria at the **Heeresgeschichtliches Museum** (right) in the Arsenal
- make your stomach turn at the bizarre displays of the **Pathologisch-anatomische Bundesmuseum** (p94)

Gürtel and invariably settle in the poorer areas just outside the big road. Lined with excellent bars and an ever-decreasing array of sex shops and divey strip bars, the Gürtel is one of Vienna's few areas of true urban grit.

The Ringstrasse and the Gürtel cordon off seven of the city's districts, which together basically form a large 'U' around the Innere Stadt to the north, south and west. Running from east to west along the area's southern stretch are the districts of Landstrasse, Wieden and Margareten. Climbing north from Margareten to the Danube Canal are the districts Mariahilf, Neubau, Josefstadt and Alsergrund. The Wien Fluss, a shallow, channelled river that's either a trickle or in flood, flows from the Wienerwald to the Danube Canal, creating a border between Margareten and Mariahilf. Each district has one or two major roads connecting the Gürtel and the Ringstrasse. Their names often follow the district: eg Wiedner Hauptstrasse in Wieden, Margaretenstrasse in Margareten, Josefstädter Strasse in Josefstadt.

LANDSTRASSE

Landstrasse, the largest of the districts inside the Gürtel, is cordoned by the Danube Canal to the east and Wieden to the west (Prinz-Eugen-Strasse and Arsenalstrasse are the dividing lines). Its northerly reaches, near the Ringstrasse, are filled with 19th-century buildings and diplomatic staff, while its southern spread consists of modern apartment blocks and working-class neighbourhoods.

Landstrasse's 'Best in Show' is Schloss Belvedere, arguably the finest baroque palace in Europe, but the district has its fair share of tempting attractions. Within sight of the canal are two of Friedensreich Hundertwasser's creations, the Hundertwasser Haus and KunstHausWien, while the former army barracks Arsenal holds the enthralling Heeresgeschichtliches Museum. Not far from the Arsenal, and in sight of ugly Südbahnhof, is the **20er Haus** (Map pp262–3) – designed by Karl Schwanzer in 1962, this modern edifice once housed contemporary art now on display in MUMOK (p77). Back towards the Hundertwasser Haus is the **Wittgensteinhaus** (Map pp262–3; ☎ 713 31 64; 03, Kundmanngasse 19; ☺ 10am-noon, 3-4.30pm Mon-Thu; ⊙ U3 Rochusgasse), a work of Adolf Loos. Built in the late 1920s for philosopher Ludwig Wittgenstein, its severe lines and modern design feature both inside and out; it's now owned by the Bulgarian embassy and can be viewed via prior appointment only.

The major road **Rennweg** is worth a wander – see p90 for more details.

HEERESGESCHICHTLICHES MUSEUM

Map pp262-3

☎ 795 61-0; www.hgm.or.at; 03, Arsenal; adult/concession/child under 10/family €5.10/3.30/free/7.30; ☺ 9am-5pm Sat-Thu; ⎘ 18, bus 69A

In the wake of the 1848 rebellion, Franz Josef I decided his defences needed strengthening and ordered the Arsenal built – the large barracks and munitions depot was completed in neo-Byzantine style in 1856. Its handsome façade belied the true purpose of the building: it was a fortress built to quash any further uprisings. At the same time Franz Josef established the Heeresgeschichtliches Museum (Museum of Military History) within the Arsenal, making it the oldest public museum in Vienna.

It's not a modern museum as museums go, but it packs some punch. The first sign of this is the vaulted entrance hall, which is lined with life-size marble statues of pre-1848 Austrian military leaders. The second is the Ruhmes Halle (Hall of Fame) at the top of the stairs on the 1st floor. Its heavily frescoed ceiling is spectacular, and beautifully complemented by Moorish columns.

The museum is laid out chronologically, starting on the 1st floor with the Thirty Years' War (1618–48) and working its way through to the Hungarian Uprising and the Austro-Prussian War (ending in 1866). In between are the Napoleonic and Turkish Wars. Some of the booty from the Turkish invasions is impressive, but first prize goes to the Great Seal of Mustafa Pasha, which fell to Prince Eugene of Savoy in the Battle of Zenta in 1697.

The ground floor picks up where the 1st floor left off, with a show of the imperial army uniforms from 1867 onwards. However the room covering the assassination of Archduke Franz Ferdinand and his wife in Sarajevo in 1914 – which set off a chain of events culminating in WWI – steals the show. The car he was shot in (complete with bullet holes), the sofa he bled to death on and his rather grisly blood-stained coat are all on display. The next room moves onto the war itself; the star attraction here is a 1916 Haubitze, a colossal cannon of immense power. The eastern wing covers the Republic years after WWI up until the Anschluss in 1938. The excellent displays are peppered with propaganda posters and Nazi paraphernalia, plus video footage of Hitler's rhetoric speeches. The last room is devoted to Austria's navy when the Adriatic coastline fell within its territory.

The courtyard is filled with tanks frozen in motion; German and Allied forces tanks are equally represented.

HUNDERTWASSER HAUS Map pp262-3

03, Löwengasse/Kegelgasse; N
This residential block of flats was designed by Hundertwasser, Vienna's radical architect and lover of uneven surfaces. It is now one of Vienna's most prestigious addresses, even though it only provides rented accommodation and is owned by the city of

Façade of Hundertwasser Haus (this page)

Vienna. It's not possible to see inside, but you can visit the **Kalke Village** (Map pp262-3; 9am-5pm, until 7pm in summer), also the handiwork of Hundertwasser, created from an old Michelin factory. It contains overpriced cafés, souvenir shops and art shops, all in typical Hundertwasser fashion with colourful ceramics and a distinct absence of straight lines.

KUNSTHAUSWIEN Map pp258-9

712 04 91; www.kunsthauswien.com; 03, Untere Weissgerberstrasse 13; adult/concession €9/7, incl temporary exhibitions €12/9, children under 10 free; 10am-7pm; N, O
The KunstHausWien (Art House Vienna), with its bulging ceramics, lack of straight lines and colourful tilework, is another of Hundertwasser's inventive creations. The art house is something of a paean in honour of Hundertwasser, displaying his paintings, graphics, tapestry, philosophy, ecology and architecture. His vivid paintings are as distinctive as his diverse building projects. Hundertwasser's quotes are everywhere; some of his pronouncements are annoyingly didactic or smack of old hippydom ('each raindrop is a kiss from heaven'), but they're often thought-provoking. There are even a couple of films about him. The gallery also puts on quality temporary exhibitions featuring other artists. Be sure to wander to the rooftop where you'll find a shady patch of grass under the grove of trees.

Monday is half-price day (unless it's a holiday) and guided tours leave at noon on Sundays.

ST MARXER FRIEDHOF Map pp262-3

03, Leberstrasse 6-8; 7am-7pm Jun-Aug, 7am-6pm May & Sep, 7am-5pm Apr & Oct, 7am-dusk Nov-Mar; 71, bus 74A
Also known as the Biedermeier cemetery, after the period when all 6000 graves were laid out, St Marxer Friedhof (Cemetery of St Mark) is a pilgrimage site for Mozart aficionados. In December 1791 Mozart was buried in an unmarked grave with none of his family present. Over time the site was forgotten and his wife's search for the exact location went in vain. It did, however, bear one fruit: a poignant memorial (Mozartgrab) made from a broken pillar and a discarded stone angel was erected in the area where he was most likely buried. In

May the cemetery is blanketed in lilies and is a sight to behold.

STRASSENBAHNMUSEUM Map pp262-3

☎ 786 03 03; www.wiener-tramwaymuseum .org in German; 03, Erdbergstrasse 109; adult/child €3/free; ◷ 9am-4pm Sat & Sun May-Oct; ◉ U3 Schlachthausgasse, ◉ 18, bus 77A, 79A

With around 80 trams, the Strassenbahnmuseum is one of the largest of its kind in the world. Avid train- and tram-spotters will love it; the extensive collection ranges from an 1871 horse-drawn trolley to the latest Porsche-designed tram seen on Vienna's streets today, and a couple of buses are thrown in for good measure. Many of the shiny examples can be explored from the inside.

SCHLOSS BELVEDERE

Belvedere is considered one of the finest baroque palaces in the world. Designed by Hildebrandt, it was built for the brilliant military strategist Prince Eugene of Savoy, conqueror of the Turks in 1718 and hero to a nation. The Unteres (Lower) Belvedere was built first (1714-16), with an orangery attached, and was the prince's summer residence. Connected to it by a long, landscaped garden is the Oberes (Upper) Belvedere (1721-23), the venue for the prince's banquets and other big bashes.

Considered together, the Belvedere residences were at the time almost more magnificent than the imperial residence, the Hofburg. This irked the Habsburgs, especially as the prince was able to look down onto the city from the elevated vantage point of the Oberes Belvedere. It was therefore with some satisfaction that Maria Theresia was able to purchase the Belvedere after the prince's death. It then became a Habsburg residence, most recently occupied by the Archduke Franz Ferdinand who started a court there to rival his uncle's (Franz Josef I) in the Hofburg.

The Belvedere is now home to the **Österreichische Galerie** (Austrian Gallery), split between the Unteres Belvedere, which houses the baroque section, and the Oberes Belvedere, showcasing 19th- and 20th-century art. A **combined ticket** (adult/senior/student €9/7.50/6) allows entry to the Unteres and Oberes Belvedere, plus the Atelier Augarten/Gustinus Ambrosi-Museum (p81). Fortunately this ticket is valid for more than

one day. Regular children's events are held in both the Oberes and Unteres Belvedere, usually on a Sunday. Pick up information from the palace itself or check the website.

OBERES BELVEDERE Map pp262-3

☎ 795 57-0; www.belvedere.at; 03, Prinz-Eugen-Strasse 27; adult/senior/student/child/family €9/7.50/6/3/18; ◷ 10am-6pm Tue-Sun; ◉ D

The Oberes Belvedere is a must for all visitors to Vienna, firstly for the collection it houses (which is easily the more important of the two in the Belvedere) and secondly for the sublime baroque palace itself. It's a mix of styles that strangely works: the baroque interior provides a diverting setting for the drift into modern art. Appropriately, Herculean figures supporting columns greet you in the entrance lobby and exploits of Alexander the Great flank the stairs climbing from the entrance to the 1st floor.

The 1st floor has paintings from the turn of the 19th century, particularly the works of Hans Makart (1840–84) and Anton Romakos (1832–89); these artists both influenced the later Viennese Art Nouveau artists. While you can't take anything away from these 19th-century painters, the 20th-century section of this floor has the gallery's best exhibits. The works of Austrian artists on display are simply breathtaking, and only the Leopold Museum's collection comes anywhere close to matching it.

The two most noteworthy artists represented here are Klimt (1862–1918) and

Schiele (1890–1918). Klimt was one of the founders of the Secessionist Art Nouveau school. His later pictures employ a harmonious but ostentatious use of background colour (with much metallic gold and silver) to evoke or symbolise the emotions of the main figures. One of the best known but also one of the most intriguing works here is Klimt's *The Kiss* (1908). It shows a couple embracing, surrounded by the usual Klimt circles and rectangles. Some of Klimt's impressionist landscapes are also on display.

Schiele produced intense, melancholic works. Notice the hypnotic and bulging eyes on the portrait of his friend, *Eduard Kosmack* (1910). Schiele's bold, brooding colours and unforgiving outlines are in complete contrast to Klimt's golden tapestries and idealised forms. He lived with one of Klimt's models for a while – Schiele's portraits of her were very explicit, bordering on the pornographic. Schiele's last work is *The Family*. He added the child between the woman's legs when he found out his own wife was pregnant; however, she died of Egyptian flu before the child was born. Schiele died of the same illness before this painting was completely finished (look closely and you'll see the imprecision of the male's left hand).

Other artists represented include Herbert Boeckl, Anton Hanak, Arnulf Rainer and Fritz Wotruba. There are several examples of the output of the influential expressionist Kokoschka (1886–1980). A smattering of international artists is also on display, including such greats as Edvard Munch, Claude Monet, Vincent Van Gogh, Pierre-Auguste Renoir and Cézanne.

The top (2nd) floor has a concentration of 19th-century paintings from the romantic, classical and Biedermeier periods. In particular, this section has work by the Biedermeier painter Georg Waldmüller (1793-1865), showing to good effect his very precise portraits and rural scenes. Other artists represented include Friedrich von Amerling (1803-1887), Casper David Friedrich (1774-1840) and Moritz von Schwind (1804-1871).

Headphones with a commentary in English can be rented for €4; tours costs €3.

UNTERES BELVEDERE Map pp262-3
☎ 795 57-0; www.belvedere.at; 03, Rennweg 6; adult/senior/student €7/5/4; ⏰ 10am-6pm Tue-Sun; 🚋 71

The baroque section offers some good statuary, such as the originals from George Raphael Donner's (1693-1741) Neuer Markt fountain and the *Apotheosis of Prince Eugene*. Eugene was presumably suffering delusions of grandeur by this time, for he commissioned the latter work himself; the artist, not to be outdone, depicted himself at the prince's feet. Paintings include those of Maria Theresia and her husband, Franz Stephan. A room is devoted to the vibrant paintings by Franz Anton Maulbertsch (1724-96), and other notable Austrian baroque artists on display include Johann Michael Rottmayer (1654-1730) and 'Kremser' Schmidt (1718-1801).

The attached **Orangery** (Map pp262–3) houses a collection of Austrian medieval art, which is comprised of religious scenes, altarpieces and statues. There are several impressive works by Michael Pacher (1435-98), a Tirolean artist who was influenced by both early Low Countries art and the early Renaissance of northern Italy.

Sights

INSIDE THE GÜRTEL

STOLEN TREASURES

After the Anschluss in 1938 many Jewish families were forced to flee the country, at which time the Nazis seized their property. The Bloch-Bauer family was one such unfortunate family, and amongst their substantial fortune were five Klimt originals, including the *Portrait of Adele Bloch-Bauer I* (1907).

The stolen paintings hung in the Oberes Belvedere until early 2006 when a US Supreme Court ruled the Austrian government must return the paintings to their rightful owner, Adele Bloch's niece and heir Maria Altmann. Austria believed it was entitled to the paintings because Adele Bloch, who died in 1925, had specified they be donated to the national gallery; however, her husband, who died in exile in 1945, wanted them returned to his family.

The paintings arrived in the US to much joy, while Austria mourned the loss of part of its cultural heritage. The government however was offered the chance to buy the paintings, but the US$100 million price tag was regarded as too steep. The price tag was actually a bargain – the *Portrait of Adele Bloch-Bauer I* alone fetched US$135 million at auction, the highest price paid for a painting. It now hangs in the New York Neue Galerie, a museum devoted to German and Austrian art.

Sights

Belvedere Gardens (this page)

GARDENS
03, Rennweg/Prinz-Eugen-Strasse; 🚋 D, 71
The long garden between the two Belvederes was laid out in classical French style and has sphinxes and other mythical beasts along its borders. South of the Oberes Belvedere is a small **Alpine Garden** (Map pp262–3; adult/concession €4/3; 🕙 10am-6pm Apr-Jul), which has 3500 plant species and a bonsai section. North from here is the much larger **Botanic Gardens** (Map pp262–3; admission free; 🕙 9am to1 hr before dusk) belonging to the Vienna University.

WIEDEN
Wieden is a small district with a healthy sprinkling of sights. **Karlsplatz** hogs the limelight, not for its layout, which is a confusing clump of underground passageways and busy roads, but for its Wien Museum, the *Jugendstil* Stadtbahn Pavillons and stunning baroque Karlskirche. Forming a border between Wieden and its northern neighbour Mariahilf is the Naschmarkt, a market unrivalled in Vienna. It offers the most exotic variety of food in the city – stuffed peppers, Greek feta and Italian olives sit alongside Indian spices and Southeast Asian ingredients. The dining selection is grand and come Saturday morning the market is overflowing with Viennese enjoying a lazy breakfast.

In and around the junction of Schliefmühlgasse and Margaretenstrasse is a con-centration of bars and clubs that rank this area high on the list of destinations for a good night out.

WIEN MUSEUM Map pp254-5
☎ 505 87 47-0; www.wienmuseum.at; 04, Karlsplatz 5; adult/concession/child €6/4/3; 🕙 9am-6pm Tue-Sun; ⓞ U1, U2, U4 Karlsplatz, 🚋 D, J, 1, 2, 62, 65, bus 4A
The Wien Museum provides a snapshot of all that is on offer in the city. It also gives a detailed rundown on the development of Vienna from prehistory to the present day, and does a pretty good job of putting the city and its personalities in context, without needing words.

Exhibits occupy three floors. The ground floor covers the period from 5600 BC to the end of the Middle Ages, and features medieval helms with bizarre ornamentations (one with a dragon, another has a woman with fish for arms) and artefacts from Stephansdom. The 1st floor moves on to the Renaissance and baroque eras; both Turkish sieges are well represented, but the spoils of the second siege (1683), with its curved sabres and colourful banners, steal the show. The model of the Innere Stadt, capturing the city in its medieval heyday, is quite fascinating.

The second floor begins with the Biedermeier era and works its way through the 20th century. Biedermeier-painter Waldmüller is well represented, and Klimt's

Emilie Flöge (1902) hangs on the wall next to Schiele's *Arthur Roessler* (1910) and *Self Portrait* (1911). The reconstructed rooms from the homes of Adolf Loos and Franz Grillparzer are also worth a peek. The second model of the Innere Stadt shows the full impact of the Ringstrasse developments, and there are some good period photographs.

KARLSKIRCHE Map pp254-5

☎ 712 44 56; www.karlskirche.at in German; 04, Karlsplatz; adult/concession/child under 11 €6/4/free; ☉ 9am-noon, 1-5.30pm Mon-Sat, 1-5.30pm Sun; ☉ U1, U2, U4 Karlsplatz

At the southeast corner of Resselpark is Karlskirche (Church of St Charles Borromeo), the finest baroque church in Vienna. This imposing creation was built between 1716 and 1739, after a vow by Karl VI at the end of the 1713 plague. It was designed and commenced by Fischer von Erlach and completed by his son Joseph. Although predominantly baroque, it combines several architectural styles. The twin columns are modelled on Trajan's Column in Rome and show scenes from the life of St Charles Borromeo (who helped plague victims in Italy), to whom the church is dedicated. The huge oval dome reaches 72m; in combination with the church's large windows, the dome's height creates a bright, open nave. The admission fee includes entrance to Museo Borromeo and a small museum with a handful of religious art and clothing purportedly from the saint, but the highlight is the lift to the dome for a close-up view of the detailed frescoes by Johann Michael Rottmayr. The altar panel is by Sebastiano Ricci and shows the Assumption of the Virgin. In front of the church is a pond, complete with a Henry Moore sculpture from 1978.

KUNSTHALLE PROJECT SPACE
Map pp254-5

☎ 521 89 33; www.kunsthallewien.at; 04, Treitlstrasse 2; admission free; ☉ 4pm-midnight Tue-Sat, 1-7pm Sun & Mon; ☉ U1, U2, U4 Karlsplatz, ☒ D, J, 1, 2, 62, 65

Formerly the only home of contemporary art in Vienna, the Kunsthalle Project Space now plays second fiddle to the museums in the MuseumsQuartier (p75). It hosts temporary exhibitions of up-and-coming artists, which are often quite challenging. After the

exhibition enjoy some chill-out time at the Kunsthallencafé (p156) next door.

STADTBAHN PAVILLONS Map pp254-5

☎ 505 87 478 5177; 04, Karlsplatz; adult/concession €2/1; ☉ 9am-6pm Tue-Sun Apr-Oct; ☉ U1, U2, U4 Karlsplatz, ☒ D, J, 1, 2, 62, 65, bus 4A

Peeking above the Resselpark at Karlsplatz is two of Otto Wagner's finest designs, the Stadtbahn Pavillons. Built in 1898 during the creation of Vienna's first public transport system (1893–1902), of which Wagner was the overall designer, the pavilions are gorgeous examples of *Jugendstil*, with floral motifs and gold trim on a structure of steel and marble. The west pavilion now holds an exhibit on Wagner's most famous creations, the Kirche am Steinhof (p98) and Postsparkasse (p78), which any fan of *Jugendstil* will love, while the eastern pavilion is now home to Club U (p156). The pavilion is a municipal museum.

GENERALI FOUNDATION Map pp262-3

☎ 504 98 80; www.gfound.or.at; 04, Wiedner Hauptstrasse 15; adult/concession €6/4.50; ☉ 11am-6pm Tue-Sun, till 8pm Thu; ☒ 62, 65

The Generali Foundation is a fine gallery which picks and chooses exhibition pieces from its vast collection – numbering around 1400 – with the utmost care. The majority of its ensemble covers conceptual and performance art from the latter half of the 20th century, with names like Dan Graham and Gordon Matta-Clark popping up on a regular basis. The entrance to the exhibition hall is towards the back of a residential passageway. Guided tours, which take place at 6pm on Thursdays, cost €2.

SCHUBERT COMMEMORATIVE ROOMS Map pp260-1

☎ 581 67 30; 04, Kettenbrückengasse 6; adult/concession €2/1; ☉ 2-6pm Fri-Sun; ☉ U4 Kettenbrückengasse, bus 59A

Franz Schubert spent his dying days, from 1 September to 10 November 1828, in this, his brother's apartment. Even on his death bed (he either died of typhoid fever from drinking infected water, or syphilis) he still managed to compose a string of piano sonatas and his last work, *Der Hirt auf dem Felsen* (The Shepherd on the Rock). The apartment is fairly bereft of personal effects but does document his final days with a

STREETS TO EXPLORE

What attracts people to the districts inside the Gürtel are not only their major sights, but also the normal, everyday streets. **Rennweg**, which runs from Schwarzenbergplatz to the St Marxer Friedhof in **Landstrasse**, is dotted with intriguing sights. At No3 and No5 are houses designed by Otto Wagner; the former is in the mould of the Ringstrasse establishments while the latter is where Gustav Mahler lived from 1898 to 1909. Close by, and opposite the entrance to the Unteres Belvedere, is the **Gardekirche** (Map pp262–3); designed in 1763, it still retains a rococo interior and is frequented by Vienna's Polish community. On adjoining **Ungargasse** at No59 is the **Portois & Fix** (Map pp262–3) building designed by Max Fabiani and built in 1900; with its lime-green tiled façade and *Jugendstil* wrought-iron features, it's reminiscent of Otto Wagner's Majolikahaus (below).

Neubau is Vienna's quirky shopping district. A stroll down the likes of **Zollergasse**, **Kirchengasse**, **Neubaugasse** and **Lindengasse** turns up small shops selling anything from handmade T-shirts to Japanese porcelain and paintings. At Döblergasse 4, near the northern end of Kirchengasse, is the site of the **Otto Wagner Apartment** (Map pp260–1), where Otto Wagner spent his final years until his death in 1918.

Neubau's close neighbour, **Josefstadt**, has its fair share of window-shopping opportunities. Its main street, **Josefstädter Strasse**, hogs much of the shopping limelight, but a diversion down **Piaristengasse** and **Lange Gasse** brings just rewards in second-hand shops and antique stores. At No40 Strozzigasse is a fine example of folk art; the **Bäckerei & Konditorei** (Map pp258–9) sculptured façade features motifs of bakers busy at their profession.

few bits and pieces, and provides information on his funeral.

BESTATTUNGSMUSEUM Map pp262-3

☎ 501 95-0; www.bestattungwien.at in German; 04, Goldeggasse 19; adult/concession €4.50/2.50; ☽ by prior arrangement 7.30am-3.30pm Mon-Fri; ▣ D, bus 13A

The Bestattungsmuseum is devoted to the art of undertaking. By no means in the same gruesome league as the Pathologisch-anatomisches Bundesmuseum (p94) or the Josephinum (p94), it still never fails to intrigue. Displays include photos, documents and paraphernalia retelling the history of undertaking in this often macabre city. Donations are welcome.

MARIAHILF

Mariahilf is dominated by Mariahilfer Strasse, Vienna's equivalent to London's Oxford Street. The crowds are thickest on Saturday, when half the city it seems converges on the street to purchase the latest H&M wear. The rest of the district, which gradually slopes downhill to the Wien Fluss, is residential apartment blocks; the Esterházypark, with its flak tower housing the Haus des Meeres, is one of the few parks to break up the uniformity.

Overlooking the Naschmarkt is the celebrated Majolikahaus (Map pp260–1; 06, Linke Wienzeile 40; ◉ U4 Kettenbrückengasse), an Art Nouveau masterpiece created by Otto Wagner in 1899. So named for the ma-

jolica tiles used to create the flowing floral motifs on the façade, this attractive building outshines most others in the city. Next door at No 38 is another Wagner concoction; it features railings created from metal leaves and a brace of jester figures on the roof shouting to the heavens. The golden medallions on the façade are by Kolo Moser.

HAUS DES MEERES Map pp260-1

☎ 587 14 17; www.haus-des-meeres.at; 06, im Esterhazypark, Fritz-Grünbaumplatz 1; adult/concession/child 6-15/under 6 €9.80/7.50/4.60/3.10; ☽ 9am-6pm, till 9pm Thu; ◉ U3 Neubaugasse, bus 13A, 14A

The 'house of the seas' is a rather unspectacular collection of lizards, sharks, crocodiles and snakes, with a few fish and spiders thrown in. Saving graces include the shark and piranha feeding at 3pm Wednesday and Sunday, the reptile feeding at 10am Sunday and 7pm Thursday, and a glass tropical house filled with lithe monkeys and a small rainforest. It occupies the inside of a *Flakturm* (flak tower), giving you a chance to see the interior of one of these giant monoliths.

HAYDNHAUS Map pp260-1

☎ 596 13 07; 06, Haydngasse 19; adult/concession €2/1; ☽ 10am-1pm & 2-6pm Wed & Thu, 10am-1pm Fri-Sun; ◉ U3 Zieglergasse, bus 57A

Hayden bought this house in 1793 and, obviously thinking it too small, added an extra floor. He didn't move in until the end of 1796 and then spent the remainder of his years here, dying in 1809. Within that time he composed *The Creation* and *The Seasons*. There's not much to see except a smattering of period furniture and the odd piece of memorabilia. The museum also has rooms devoted to Brahms (who lived in Vienna from 1862 onwards), displaying some of his personal items. The Haydnhaus is a municipal museum.

NEUBAU

Neubau, to the north of Mariahilfer Strasse, is a vibrant district of selective shops, downbeat restaurants, and 'in' bars. The liveliest section backs onto the MuseumsQuartier (p75), between the district's namesake street Neubaugasse and Spittelberg. **Neubaugasse** is well known for its second-hand shops and unusual stores, making it a fine alternative to the generic nature of Mariahilfer Strasse. **Spittelberg**, a tiny quarter of cobblestone alleys lined with Biedermeier architecture, is a delight to explore; once a red-light district, it's now home to antique dealers and bars. At Christmas it is transformed into one of the city's best-patronised markets, with craft stalls aplenty and city workers sipping *Glühwein* (mulled wine)

At the western end of Neubau is the **Bücherei Wien** (Map pp260–1; ☎ 400 08 45 00; www.buechereien.wien.at; 07, Urban-Loritz-Platz; ⏱ 11am-7pm Mon-Fri, 11am-5pm Sat; ◎ U6 Burggasse-Stadthalle, ⌷ 6, 18), Vienna's main library. Straddling the U6 line, its pyramid-like steps lead up to the enormous main doors that are two-storeys tall. At the top of the library is the café Canetti (p142), which has far-reaching views to the south.

One of the few sights in the district is the Hofmobiliendepot, the storage warehouse for Habsburg furniture.

HOFMOBILIENDEPOT Map pp260-1
☎ 524 33 570; www.hofmobiliendepot.at; 07, Andreasgasse 7; adult/concession/child/family €6.90/4.50/3.50/14.90; ⏱ 10am-6pm Tue-Sun; ◎ U3 Zieglergasse

The Hofmobiliendepot is a storage space for furniture not displayed in the Hofburg, Schönbrunn, Schloss Belvedere and other Habsburg residences, plus a smattering of late-20th-century examples. Covering four floors, the collection is incredibly exten-

sive, and ranges from complete rooms to an assortment of various furniture pieces, such as mirrors, candleholders, dressers, desks, chairs, tables and the like. Standout one-offs include the cradle of Crown Prince Rudolf, with carved wooden sidings, mosaic inlays and a two-headed eagle figurine (the Habsburg symbol), as well as an ensemble of imperial thrones. The Egyptian Cabinet Room and Crown Prince Rudolph's Turkish Room/Opium Den are the height of decadence.

Biedermeier aficionados will love the second floor; here 15 rooms are beautifully laid out in the early 19th-century style, and a few dozen chairs from the era can be tested by visitors. In all, it's the most comprehensive collection of Biedermeier furniture in the world. The top floor displays *Jugendstil* furniture from the likes of Wagner, Loos and Hoffmann.

This, one of the more underrated museums in the city, is included in the Sisi Ticket (p60).

JOSEFSTADT

To the north of Neubau is Josefstadt; its close proximity to the University has traditionally attracted many students. Its main street, Josefstädter Strasse, is lined with shops, the majority of which are basically extensions of their owner's personality and ooze individual flair.

The end of Josefstadt towards the Innere Stadt is filled with Biedermeier architecture, while its Gürtel end is far more gritty and grotty. Here a string of bars fill the archways of the U6 line, and revellers can be seen wandering from one to the next almost every night of the week. In between, sights are few, but it's enjoyable exploring the back streets for second-hand clothes or that bargain antique piece (opposite).

MUSEUM FÜR VOLKSKUNDE Map pp258-9
☎ 406 89 05; www.volkskundemuseum.at in German; 08, Laudongasse 15-19; adult/child/family €5/2/9; ⏱ 10am-5pm Tue-Sun; ⌷ 5, 33, bus 13A

Housed in 17th-century Palais Schönborn, this folk-art museum gives a taster of 18th- and 19th-century rural dwelling, and is stocked with handcrafted sculptures, paintings and furniture from throughout Austria and its neighbouring countries. Many of the pieces have a religious or rural theme, and telltale floral motifs are everywhere. Temporary exhibitions regularly feature and tours in English take place at 3pm Sunday.

PIARISTENKIRCHE Map pp258-9

08, Jodok-Fink-Platz; admission free; ☼ 7-9am, 6-8pm Mon-Sat, 7am-1pm, 6-8pm Sun; ⊠ J, bus 13A

The Piaristenkirche (Church of the Piarist Order), or Maria Treu Church, is notable for two interior pieces: the ceiling frescoes and the organ. The stunning frescoes, completed by Franz Anton Maulbertsch in 1753, depict various stories from the bible, while the organ holds the distinction of being used by Anton Bruckner for his entry examination into the Music Academy. At the end of his exam one judge was heard to say 'he should be examining us!' In summer, two restaurants – including Il Sestante p134 – have outdoor seating on Jodok-Fink-Platz; it's quite a wonderful setting with the church as a backdrop.

ALSERGRUND

Alsergrund creates the northern border of the districts inside the Gürtel. Its quiet streets contain a surprising array of sites, the highlight of which is the handsome Palais Liechtenstein, housing the Liechtenstein Museum. Not far to the southwest is the expansive Alte AKH, once the city's main hospital; it's now a university campus sporting a shaded courtyard with a plethora of bars and the highly original Pathologisch-anatomische Bundesmuseum. The quickest route between the palace and the Alte AKH is the Strudlhofstiege, an impressive set of *Jugendstil* steps designed in 1910. Connected to AKH both physically and ideologically is the Josephinum, Vienna's museum of medial history. Closer to the Innere Stadt is the Sigmund Freud Museum, where Freud lived and worked for many years.

Dominating the Serviten quarter – a small confluence of cobblestone streets lined with bars, restaurants and shops a few blocks from the Ringstrasse – is the Serviten Kirche (Map pp258-9; 09, Servitengasse 9; U4 Rossauer Lände, ⊠ D), the only church outside the Innere Stadt to survive the second Turkish siege. Its baroque interior and oval nave were inspired by the Karlskirche, but unfortunately it's only open for Mass; outside of this you'll have to make do peer-

ing through iron railings. The adjoining monastery is an oasis of calm, in particular its inner courtyard. At the opposite end of Alsergrund on the banks of the Danube Canal is the Fernwärme (Map pp258-9; ☎ 313 26; 09, Spittelauer Lände 45; admission free; tours by appointment only; U4, U6 Spittelau, ⊠ D), a mundane waste incinerator transformed into an absorbing building by Hundertwasser in 1989. The façade, a visual bonanza featuring his trademark enthusiasm for colour, is highlighted by a smoke stack crowned with a massive golden bulb.

LIECHTENSTEIN MUSEUM Map pp258-9

☎ 319 57 670; www.liechtensteinmuseum.at; 09, Fürstengasse 1; adult/concession/child/family €10/8/5/20; ☼ 10am-5pm Mon-Fri; ⊠ D, bus 40A

Until 1938, the Royal family of Liechtenstein resided in Vienna, but after the Anschluss they made a hasty retreat to their small country squeezed between Austria and Switzerland. They didn't, however, manage to take everything with them, and it was only near the end of WWII that they transferred their collection of baroque masterpieces to Vaduz.

After many years collecting dust in depot vaults, this private collection of Prince Hans-Adam II of Liechtenstein is once again on display in Palais Liechtenstein. It's one of the largest private collections in the world, consisting of around 200 paintings and 50 sculptures, dating from 1500 to 1700.

The magnificent Palais Liechtenstein almost outshines the collection itself. Built between 1690 and 1712, it is a supreme example of audacious and extravagant baroque architecture that completely dazzles the eyes. Frescoes and ceiling paintings by the likes of Johann Michael Rottmayer and Marcantonio Franceschini decorate the halls and corridors. Its Herkulessaal (Hercules Hall) – so named for the Hercules motifs in its ceiling frescoes by renowned Roman painter Andrea Pozzo – is an absolute highlight, extending over two storeys. The neoclassical Gentlemen's Apartment Library, on the ground floor, contains an astounding 100,000 volumes and is not to be missed. The extensive gardens, originally baroque and transformed into an English landscape in the 19th century, are an exercise in manicured perfection.

The art collection, known as the Princely Collection, is displayed over two of the

SIGMUND FREUD

For many, Sigmund Freud (1856-1939), the father of psychoanalysis, is Vienna's most famous son. His writings not only influenced the intellectual thinkers of his day, but have formed the basis of psychological thought throughout the world – even nonpsychologists understand the term 'Freudian slip'.

Freud began his medical career as a Doctor of Medicine in 1881 and opened his first office as a neurologist in 1886. His first experiments in neurological disorders involved hypnotism, cocaine and electroconvulsive therapy, but he soon gave up the practice, moved his office to Alsergrund and commenced exploring the realm of psychoanalysis in earnest. He soon began using 'free association', the practice of having patients lie on a couch and talk about whatever came to mind.

It wasn't until 1896 that Freud coined the term 'psychoanalysis', and within four years he had enough material to publish his seminal work, *The Interpretation of Dreams* (1899). In it he proposed that the unconscious exists beyond the conscious, and went on to describe a method of connecting with it. Freud also stated that the unconscious was crucial for the brain's repression of memories – painful memories could not be banished from the mind but could leave a person's conscious.

Other famous theories dealt with sexual desire, in particular libido, sublimation, the Oedipus complex, penis envy, and the oral, anal and phallic stages of childhood. He believed that humans begin life 'polymorphously perverse' – a state in which almost anything can be sexually arousing. In *The Ego and The Id* (1923), Freud split the mind into the three categories of the ego, the superego and the *id*. The *id*, he said, contained our most primeval desires such as hunger, lust, and anger; the superego held our moral standards learned from parents and society; and the ego not only remembered, planned and was the main force in forming our personality, but it also played mediator between the others by using defence mechanisms.

Although many academics and physicians were hostile towards his published works, Freud was able to gather around him a core of pupils and followers. Among their number was the Swiss psychologist Carl Jung, who later severed his links with the group because of personal differences with Freud.

As a Viennese Jew, the arrival of the Nazis in 1938 meant it was time to leave. Freud was allowed to emigrate to London on 4 June, but not before he was forced to sign a statement which stated he had been treated fairly; this he did, after which he added the sentence 'I can heartily recommend the Gestapo to anyone'. He died in London on the 23 September 1939 from a lethal dose of morphine instigated at his request (he had been battling cancer of the mouth since 1923).

While many of Freud's ideas are as controversial today as they were in his time, there is no doubting his substantial contribution to psychology; 'free association' is still the common method of psychotherapy, and the concept of the unconscious is present in many schools of psychoanalytical thought.

palace's three floors and includes the likes of Rubens, Raphael, van Dyck and Rembrandt. Four galleries – one devoted to sculpture and the rest to paintings – are located on the ground floor. Gallery III contains celebrated Biedermeier works and the lion's share of highlights on this floor; Friedrich von Amerling's *Portrait of Maria Franziska of Liechtenstein at Age Two* (1836) is a sublime piece of art capturing the peaceful princess.

The big guns, however, are on the upper floor. Seven galleries intertwine to provide a trip through 200 years of art history, starting in 1500 with early Italian religious paintings in Gallery IV. Gallery V is dedicated to Renaissance portraits; Raphael's *Portrait of a Man* (1503) takes first prize for the intensity and depth of the subject's stare. Moving onto Gallery VI, you'll find Italian baroque paintings; Sebastiano Ricci and Pompeo Batoni both feature heavily here.

Leaving the Herkulessaal aside, the focal point of the upper floor is Gallery VII, home to Rubens' *Decius Mus* cycle (1618). Consisting of eight almost life-sized paintings, the cycle depicts the life and death of Decius Mus, a Roman leader who sacrificed himself so that his army would be victorious on the battlefield. The vivid paintings, a powerful display of art, detail and action, readily take hold of the viewer. Gallery VIII is devoted to Rubens, containing over 30 of his Flemish baroque paintings. Myths and legends are the subjects of many of his works, including his coy *Venus at a Mirror* (1613-14). More Rubens works are on display in Gallery IX – this time his portraits – which hang alongside works by Van Dyck and Fran Hals. The sheer exuberance and life captured by Rubens in his *Portrait of Clara Serena Rubens* (1616) is testament to the great artist's

VIENNA'S MACABRE SIDE

It's a well-known fact the Viennese have a morbid fascination with death. Funerals are big business in the city and for many it's a case of the bigger the better; *eine schöne Leich*, which literally means 'a beautiful corpse', is a must. Tombstones are often grandiose affairs, Sunday trips to the cemetery commonplace, songs performed in *Heurigen* often deal with the subject, and death masks were common in the 18th and 19th centuries. This fascination also stems to attractions, and Vienna is home to more than it's fair share of macabre sights:

Bestattungsmuseum (p90) The forerunner to *Six Feet Under;* a museum devoted to funerals and the undertaker's profession

Josephinum (below) Collection of wax cadavers in various states of dissection

Kaisergruft (p57) Final resting place of the Hofburg royalty, with tomb stones grandiose and plain

Michaelerkirche (p59) & **Stephansdom** (p53) Church crypts filled with coffins (some open) and plenty of bones

Pathologisch-anatomische Bundesmuseum (below) Various dead 'things' in jars of formaldehyde and abnormal human skeletons

Wiener Kriminalmuseum (p81) Vienna's criminal museum, concentrating on gruesome murders from the 19th and 20th centuries

talent. Gallery X is lined with Dutch stills and landscapes.

Audio guides are available for €1, and guided tours in German (€4) leave at 3pm Saturday and 11pm Sunday.

SIGMUND FREUD MUSEUM Map pp258-9

☎ 319 15 96; www.freud-museum.at; 09, Berggasse 19; adult/concession/child €8/6/3; ☽ 9am-6pm; 🚇 D

The apartment where Sigmund Freud lived and worked from 1891 till his forced departure from Vienna with the arrival of the Nazis in 1938 is now a museum devoted to the father of psychoanalysis. It contains a number of his possessions, and Freud's obsessions – travelling, smoking and antique collecting – are well represented; Egyptian and Buddhist statues are everywhere, and only a handful of his many portraits capture him without his trademark half-smoked cigar. Overly detailed notes (in English) illuminate the offerings and audio guides are available at the ticket desk, but neither offers any real insight into Freud's theories.

The newly opened second floor is used for temporary exhibitions.

JOSEPHINUM Map pp258-9

☎ 427 76 3401; 09, Währinger Strasse 25; adult/concession €2/1; ☽ 9am-3pm Mon-Fri, 10am-2pm 1st Sat every month; 🚇 37, 38, 40, 41, 42

The Josephinum, located on the 1st floor of the building, is also known as the Ges-

chichte der Medizin (Museum of Medical History).

The prime exhibits of the museum are the ceroplastic and wax specimen models of the human frame, created over 200 years ago by Felice Fontana and Paolo Mascagni. They were used in the Academy of Medico-Surgery, an institution instigated by Joseph II in 1785 to improve the skills of army surgeons who lacked medical qualifications. These models, showing the make-up of the body under the skin, were intended to give the students a three-dimensional understanding of the organs, bones, veins and muscles. Three rooms of this gory lot will make you feel like you've wandered onto the set of a tacky horror movie. If you can dismiss your queasiness, the models are quite intriguing and their level of detail is a testament to the skill of their creators.

The rest of the museum contains arcane medical instruments, photos of past practitioners, accounts of unpleasant-looking operations and ailments, and some texts (one book is thoughtfully left open on a page dealing with the dissection of eyeballs).

PATHOLOGISCH-ANATOMISCHE BUNDESMUSEUM Map pp258-9

☎ 406 86 72; www.narrenturm.at; 09, Spitalgasse 2; admission €2; ☽ 3-6pm Wed, 8-11am Thu, 10am-1pm 1st Sat in the month; 🚇 5, 33

Housed in the round Narrenturm (Fool's Tower), which served as an insane asylum from 1784 to 1866, the Pathologisch-anatomische Bundesmuseum (Pathological Anatomy Museum) is not for the weak of heart. Filled with medical oddities and abnormalities preserved in jars of formaldehyde, plus the odd wax model with one grisly disease or another, a visit to the museum can be a disturbing or fascinating experience depending on your view. Those suffering from a bad back should visit the top floor for some perspective, which contains a mass of deformed human skeletons. The Narrenturm is a bit hard to find inside the confusing layout; once inside the Altes AKH just consult a map.

SCHUBERT GEBURTSHAUS Map pp258-9
☎ 317 36 01; 09, Nussdorfer Strasse 54; adult/concession €2/1; ☉ 10am-1pm & 2-6pm Tue-Sun; ⊠ 37, 38

The house where Schubert was born in 1797 was known at that time as *Zum roten Krebsen* (The Red Crab), but Schubert probably didn't remember much of it as he and his family moved on when he was five. Like many of the city's municipal museums devoted to Vienna's musical sons, there's not a lot to see, but at least you can hear some music and catch the occasional concert. Bizarrely, a couple of rooms of the house are given over to Adalbert Stifter

FARMERS MARKETS

Bauern Märkte (Farmers Markets) are a well-established part of Vienna's scenery. During the week, farmers from Lower Austria descend on Vienna to sell their produce, which consists of homegrown seasonal fruits and vegetables, dried meats and sausages, bread, eggs, cheese, wine, schnapps, fruit juice, honey, marmalade and flowers. The atmosphere is bustling and energetic, with stall owners yelling out prices and shoppers constantly on the lookout for the freshest produce. The majority only come to town Friday afternoons and Saturday mornings, although some also set up shop Monday through Thursday; Saturday morning is the best time to enjoy the market vibe, while the end of a day (4-5pm Mon-Fri, 1-2pm Sat) is good for picking up bargains.

The city has 14 such markets, the bigger of which are at **Brunnenmarkt**, **Karmelitermarkt**, and **Naschmarkt** (p185). Smaller markets include **Rochusmarkt** (Map pp262–3; 03, Landstrasser Hauptstrasse) in Landstrasse, **Meidlinger Markt** (Map pp260–1; 12, Niederhofstrasse) in Meidling, **Viktor-Adler-Markt** (Map pp262–3; 10, Viktor-Adler-Platz) in Favoriten, **Hannovermarkt** (Map pp258–9; 20, Hannovergasse) in Brigittenau and **Floridsdorfer Markt** (Map pp252–3; 21, Pitkagasse) in Floridsdorf. **Freyungmarkt** (Map pp254–5; 01, Freyung; ☉ 8am-7.30pm Fri & Sat; ⊕ U2 Schottentor, bus 1A) is a sedate affair selling organic produce from farmers.

Stuffed peppers for sale at Naschmarkt (this page)

(1805-68) and his Biedermeier paintings. The two men had absolutely nothing to do with each other.

OUTSIDE THE GÜRTEL

Drinking p142 & p160; Eating p135; Shopping p190; Sleeping p201

Collectively, the 11 districts outside the Gürtel create a large swathe of suburbia that surrounds the city from the south, west and, to a lesser extent, the north. Each district has its own particular personality and in general is either working class or well-off.

Favoriten and Simmering, two of three districts making up Vienna's southern border, are thoroughly blue-collar and quite unappealing at first glance. Closer examination reveals large parks and the city's atmospheric Zentralfriedhof. Meidling, west of Favoriten, continues this trend but is more urban and has a strong ethnic make-up.

Liesing, in Vienna's southwestern corner, is a sprawling district with a grouping of *Heurigen* in its Mauer neighbourhood and easy access to the Wienerwald. To the north of Liesing is the city's most exclusive district, Hietzing; Schönbrunn, the glorious summer palace of the Habsburgs, is located here.

Continuing north, Penzing, Ottakring and Hernals stretch from close to the Gürtel to the Wienerwald. Fairly similar to each other, they encompass the spacious housing suburbs that penetrate the Wienerwald and the dense mix of Turk, Serb, Croat and African immigrant communities on the Gürtel. Rudolfsheim-Fünfhaus, a neighbourhood with a large migrant population, is squeezed between Penzing and the Gürtel.

To the north of Hernals are Währing and Döbling, two of Vienna's wealthier districts; the streets seem cleaner, the air fresher, and the atmosphere a little stuffier. The outer reaches of Döbling are covered in vineyards and *Heurigen*. Some are unashamedly touristy while others are traditional and *Gemütlch* (cosy).

Even though it falls outside the city limits, we've included Klosterneuburg in this section as it is close enough to enjoy as an afternoon outing from the city.

SOUTHERN VIENNA

With over 170,000 people, **Favoriten** is Vienna's largest district populationwise. Its working class atmosphere is vibrant and energetic,

even if its postwar housing is generally dull and featureless. The focal point of the district is **Reumannplatz** (Map pp262–3), a large square that sees an endless parade of nationalities and eager ice-cream lovers queuing at Tichy (p122), one of the city's best ice-cream parlours. The square is also home to the *Jugendstil* Amalienbad (p176); built from 1923 to 1926, it's worth taking a dip in this indoor pool just to see the colourful interior brightened with mosaics and tiles.

The **Böhmische Prater** (Map pp252–3; Bohemian Prater; 10, Laaer Wald), a tiny, old-fashioned version of the Wurstelprater (p79), is a short ride from Reumannplatz. Riding the merry-go-rounds and testing your strength on 'strongman' machines here is like stepping back to Victorian times, and a quaint reminder of how complicated entertainment has become these days. To get there take the 68A bus from U1 Reumannplatz stop to Urselbrunnengasse and walk to the junction of Urselbrunnengasse and Laaer Wald.

Near busy Triester Strasse, Vienna's main thoroughfare south, is the **Favoriten Water Tower** (Map pp252–3; ☎ 599 59 31006; 10, Windtenstrasse 3; ⓐ 65). Built in 1889, this tall tower is all that remains of a pumping station that brought water from the Alps to Vienna; its striking yellow- and red-brick façade is highly decorative and topped with turrets, and tours are occasionally offered. Just south of the tower is the **Wienerberg** (Map pp252–3), once the site of Europe's largest brickworks and now a public park. Unlike many of Vienna's parks, it's quite disorderly and basically left to the laws of nature.

Simmering is similar in look and feel to Favoriten. Its biggest drawcard is the Zentralfriedhof, an enormous cemetery on the southern outskirts of the city. Not far from the cemetery is the small, sad **Namenlosen Friedhof** (Cemetery of the Nameless; 11, Alberner Hafen; bus 6A). Unidentified bodies washed up on the shores of the Danube eventually make their way here; some may recognise it from the movie *Before Sunrise*. Bus 6A connects with tram 71 at the tram terminus, but it doesn't always go as far as the cemetery. Simmering is also home to the **Gasometer** (Map pp262–3; 10, Guglgasse 6-14; ☺ 10am-7.30pm Mon-Fri, 9am-5pm Sat; ⊚ U3 Gasometer), the collective name for four round, uniform, brownstone gas containers 75m-tall and each big enough to house the Riesenrad. They supplied gas to the city from 1899 to 1969 before being transformed into 615 apartments, a students' hostel, an event hall, a cinema and a shopping complex. Their arresting yellow- and brown-brickwork and arched windows are best admired from a distance.

ZENTRALFRIEDHOF Map pp252-3

☎ 760 41-0; 11, Simmeringer Hauptstrasse 232-244; admission free; ☺ information office 8am-3pm Mon-Fri, cemetery 7am-7pm May-Aug, 7am-6pm Mar, Apr, Sep & Oct, 8am-5pm Nov-Feb; ⛟ 6, 71

Opened in 1874, the Zentralfriedhof (Central Cemetery) has grown to become one of Europe's biggest cemeteries – larger than the Innere Stadt and, with 2½ million graves, far exceeding the population of Vienna itself. It contains the lion's share of tombs to Vienna's greats, including numerous famous composers – Beethoven, Schubert, Brahms, Schönberg and the whole Strauss clan are buried here. A monument to Mozart has also been erected, but he was actually buried in an unmarked mass grave in the St Marxer Friedhof (p85).

The cemetery has three gates. The first is opposite Schloss Concordia (p136) and leads to the old Jewish graves while the second, the main gate, directs you to the tombs of honour and the cemetery's church, Dr Karl Lueger Kirche. The third is closer to the Protestant and new Jewish graves. The information centre and map of the cemetery are at Gate Two.

The **Ehrengräber** (Tombs of Honour) are just beyond Gate Two and, besides the clump of famous composers, includes Hans Makart, sculptor Fritz Wotruba, architects Theophil Hansen and Adolf Loos, and *the* man of Austrian pop, Falco (Hans Hölzel).

Behind the Dr Karl Lueger Kirche, at the far end of the cemetery, are **simple plaques** devoted to those who fell in the world wars. These are in contrast to the ostentatious displays of wealth in the mausoleums of the rich. Most graves are neat, well tended and adorned with fresh flowers. For a further contrast, wander around the old **Jewish section**, where the tangle of broken headstones and undergrowth is a reminder that few relatives are around to maintain these graves.

WESTERN VIENNA

Western Vienna takes in the districts of Liesing, Hietzing, Penzing, Rudolfsheim-Fünfhaus, Ottakring, and Hernals. Here the Wienerwald ends and the city begins; from west to east the districts' structures change from spacious villas at the woods' edge to five-storey apartment blocks surrounding concrete parks near the Gürtel. In between are *Jugendstil* and Biedermeier delights, an imperial palace and ethnic diversity – a snapshot of Vienna, combining both past and future.

Much of the spread that is Liesing is of little interest to the average visitor, unless row after row of sectioned houses appeals. Its Mauer neighbourhood is a diamond in the rough, with vineyards and around a dozen quality *Heurigen*, and from here it's only a short walk to the Wienerwald and the wild Lainzer Tiergarten. Hietzing, a district which bettered itself on the back of imperialism, contains one of Vienna's prime attractions, the Hofburg summer palace Schönbrunn. Visitors should take a little time to explore the backstreets just to the west of the palace; Biedermeier and Modernist villas by Adolf Loos, Josef Hoffmann and Friedrich Ohmann are scattered throughout the area (particularly along Gloriettegasse and Lainzer Strasse).

To the north of Hietzing is Penzing, with two top attractions; Otto Wagner's gorgeous Kirche am Steinhof and the city's Technisches Museum. Ottakring is noted for its pockets of *Heurigen* and the **Jubiläumswarte** (Map pp252–3; 16, Pelzer Rennweg; bus 46B, 148), a tower rising above the Wienerwald's green canopy. The sweeping views from the uppermost platform take in most of Vienna, and on a windy day the climb to the top can be quite an adrenaline rush. Bus No 148 (from U4 Hütteldorf) terminates close to the tower; from bus No 46B, there's a short, sharp climb uphill.

For a suggested cycling tour through Hietzing and Liesing and a walking tour taking in Steinhof and the Jubiläumswarte, see p115.

HOFPAVILLON HIETZING Map pp260-1

☎ 877 15 71; 13, Schönbrunner Strasse; Ⓜ U4 Hietzing, 🚊 10, 58, 60, 61

Built between 1898 and 1899 by Otto Wagner as part of the public transport system, the Hofpavillon Hietzing was originally designed as a private station for the imperial court. The elaborate wood-panelled interior is suitably regal and was designed by Wagner in conjunction with Olbrich. Its white façade, decorated with wrought ironwork, is easily spotted just east of the U4 Hietzing stop. It is currently closed for renovation until further notice.

HIETZINGER FRIEDHOF Map pp260-1

☎ 877 31 07; 13, Maxingstrasse 15; admission free; ⏱ 8am-6pm May-Aug, 8am-5pm Mar, Apr, Sep & Oct, 9am-4pm Nov-Feb; bus 56B, 58B, 156B

Aficionados of Vienna's Secessionist movement will want to make the pilgrimage to the Hietzinger cemetery to pay homage to some of its greatest members. Klimt, Moser and Wagner are all buried here, although Wagner's haughty tomb won't impress many. Others buried in the cemetery include Engelbert Dollfuss, leader of the Austro-Fascists assassinated in 1934, and composer Alban Berg.

TECHNISCHES MUSEUM Map pp260-1

☎ 899 98-0; www.technischesmuseum.at; 14, Mariahilfer Strasse 212; adult/senior/child/family €8.50/7/5/17; ⏱ 9am-6pm Mon-Fri, 10am-6pm Sat & Sun; 🚊 52, 58

The Technisches Museum (Technical Museum) has been around since 1918, but thankfully enjoyed a well-deserved overhaul in the past few years. Covering four floors, it's a shrine to man's advances in the fields of science and technology. There are loads of hands-on displays and heavy industrial equipment, but even with all the updating the exhibits recently received, they still look and feel outdated.

The ground floor is devoted to Nature and Knowledge, while the second floor is given over to Heavy Industry and Energy.

Nature and Knowledge is filled with interactive scientific experiments with mostly German instructions. If you're into gazing at steam engines and mining models, then Heavy Industry is for you, but the museum's saving grace is its Energy section – it's full of fun and physical displays (the human-sized mouse wheel is particularly enjoyable). The top two floors host temporary exhibitions plus permanent displays on musical instruments and transport. The latter has some wonderfully restored old-timer trams and planes, but the museum unfortunately employs a 'look but don't touch' policy. While you won't be entertained for hours at the museum, your kids will be, and if you time it right, they can join in with the regular activities organised by the museum's staff. Das Mini, on the third floor, has loads of kids toys and activities and is specifically aimed at two- to six-year-olds.

From its vantage point on top of a grassy knoll, the museum looks down over Auer-Welsbach-Park towards the yellow of Schönbrunn.

KIRCHE AM STEINHOF Map pp252-3

☎ 910 60 11204; 14, Baumgartner Höhe 1; tours €4; ⏱ 3-4pm Sat; bus 47A, 48A

This distinctive Art Nouveau creation was the work of Wagner from 1904 to 1907; Moser chipped in with the mosaic windows. The roof is topped by a copper-covered dome that earned the nickname *Limoniberg* (lemon mountain) from its original golden colour. The design illustrates the victory of function over ornamentation prevalent in much of Wagner's work, even down to the sloping floor to allow good drainage. The church is on the grounds of the Psychiatric Hospital of the City of Vienna and is currently closed for renovation – phone ahead to check opening times.

ERNST FUCHS PRIVAT MUSEUM
Map pp252-3

☎ 914 85 75; www.ernstfuchs-zentrum.com; 14, Hüttelbergstrasse 26; adult/concession €11/6; ⏱ 10am-4pm Mon-Fri; bus 148, 152

About 2km north of the U4 Hütteldorf stop is this small museum, devoted to Ernst Fuchs' fantastical paintings, etchings and sculptures. The works have a, shall we say, drug-induced look about them and what may be more interesting to the visitor is the

Sights

OUTSIDE THE GÜRTEL

villa housing the collection. Built by Wagner in 1888, it was saved from ruin by Fuchs and restored to its former glory in 1972. In the gardens (visible from the road) are some interesting statues, ceramics and the ornate **Brunnenhaus** created by Fuchs, and at No 28 is another fine villa designed by Wagner.

LAINZER TIERGARTEN Map pp252-3
13, Hermesstrasse; 8am-dusk; bus 60B
At 25 sq km, the **Lainzer Tiergarten** (Lainzer Zoo) is the largest (and wildest) of Vienna's city parks. The 'zoo' refers to the plethora of wild boar, deer, woodpeckers and squirrels that freely roam the park, and the famous Lipizzaner horses which summer here. At 2pm every day the park's wild animals are fed by park staff; check the notice board at the park's gate for the location. Apart from the extensive walking possibilities through lush woodland, attractions of the park include the **Hermesvilla** and the Hubertus-Warte (508m), a viewing platform on top of Kaltbründlberg.

HERMESVILLA Map pp252-3
 804 13 24; 13, Lainzer Tiergarten; adult/child €5/2.50; 10am-6pm Tue-Sun late-Mar-Oct, 9am-4.30pm Tue-Sun Nov–mid-Mar; bus 60B
The Hermesvilla was commissioned by Franz Josef I and presented to his wife as a gift in an attempt to patch up their failing marriage. Built by Karl von Hasenauer between 1882 and 1886, with Klimt and Makart on board as interior decorators, the villa is suitably plush and has all the hallmarks of a mansion as opposed to a villa. Empress Elisabeth's bedroom is particularly over the top, with the walls and ceiling covered in motifs from Shakespeare's *A Midsummer Night's Dream*.

For all its opulence and comforts, the villa unfortunately did not have the desired effect: Elisabeth never really took to the place and rarely ventured back to Vienna. She did, however, name it after her favourite Greek God. Hermesvilla is a municipal museum.

KIRCHE ZUR HEILIGSTEN DREIFALTIGKEIT Map pp252-3
 888 50 03; 23, Georgsgasse/Rysergasse; admission free; 2-6pm Sat, 9am-5pm Sun; bus 60A
The stack of concrete blocks that form the Kirche zur Heiligsten Dreifaltigkeit (Holy Trinity Church) is an unusual work of art. An industrial piece with little warmth, some will find it exceptionally ugly while others will see it as a triumph of contemporary over conformity; however, there's no doubting its powerful presence. It's more commonly known as 'Wotrubakirche' after its architect Fritz Wotruba, who completed it in 1976.

SCHÖNBRUNN

Schloss Schönbrunn and its adjoining garden are second only to Versailles in a show of imperial wealth and might, but that wasn't the idea; this baroque palace is a much-diminished version of the grandiose imperial centrepiece that was originally planned.

The name comes from the Schöner Brunnen (Beautiful Fountain), which was built around a spring that Emperor Matthias (1557-1619) found while hunting. A pleasure palace was built here by Ferdinand II in 1637, but this was razed by the Turks in 1683. Soon after, Leopold I commissioned Fischer von Erlach to build a more luxurious summer palace. Fischer von Erlach came up with hugely ambitious plans for a palace that would dwarf Versailles to be built on the hill where the Gloriette now stands. The imperial purse felt the venture unworthy and a 'less elaborate' building was constructed. It was finished in 1700.

Maria Theresia, upon her accession to the throne in 1740, chose Schönbrunn as the base for her family and her court. The young architect Nikolaus Pacassi was commissioned to renovate and extend the palace to meet the new requirements, and work was carried out from 1744 to 1749. The interior was fitted out in rococo style, and the palace then had some 2000 rooms, as well as a chapel and a theatre. Like most imperial buildings associated with Maria Theresia, the exterior was painted her favourite colour: *Schönbrunngelb* (Schönbrunn yellow).

The Habsburgs were not the only famous residents of Schönbrunn. Napoleon took the palace as his own in 1805 and 1809. The last in the Habsburg line, Karl I, was also the last to leave when he abdicated in the Blue Chinese Salon in 1918. After that the palace became the property of the new republic. Bomb damage was suffered during WWII, and restoration

Sights OUTSIDE THE GÜRTEL

was completed in 1955. In 1992 the palace administration was transferred to private hands, whereupon further renovations commenced at a slow pace and admission prices soared.

If you plan to see quite a few sights at Schönbrunn, consider purchasing a Classic or Gold Pass. The **Classic Pass** (adult/concession/child/family €14.90/13/7.50/33) covers entry to the Grand Tour, Privy Garden, Gloriette, Maze and the **Schönbrunn bakery** (admission to bakery only €6.40; ☉ 10am-5pm), where you can see strudel made from scratch and get to taste the results. The **Gold Pass** (adult/concession/child €36/30/18) includes the Grand Tour, Privy Garden, Tiergarten, Palmenhaus, Wüstenhaus, Wagenburg, Gloriette, Maze and Schönbrunn bakery. Combining the Grand Tour, Hofmobiliendepot, and Kaiserappartements is the **Sisi Ticket** (adult/student/child €19.90/17/10). There is a separate combined-ticket for the Tiergarten, Palmenhaus and Wüstenhaus for adult/senior/student/child €16/13/7.50/6).

The palace can be reached by the U4 line; Schönbrunn is the closest stop, though Hietzing is better for the zoo and the western part of the gardens.

SCHLOSS SCHÖNBRUNN Map pp260-1

☎ 811 13-0; www.schoenbrunn.at; 13, Schloss Schönbrunn; Imperial Tour adult/concession/child €8/7.90/4.70, Grand Tour €11.50/10.20/6, with tour €14/12.70/7; ☉ 8.30am- 6pm Jul-Aug, 8.30am-5pm Apr-Jun & Sep-Oct, 8.30am-4.30pm Nov-Mar; ◉ U4 Schönbrunn, U4 Hietzing, bus 10A

The regal rooms of Schloss Schönbrunn (Schönbrunn Palace) are in a league of their own – the Kaiserappartements of the Hofburg hardly come close. The interior of the palace is a majestic mix of frescoed ceilings, crystal chandeliers and gilded ornaments. However, the endless stucco and gold twirls can seem overdone at times. Franz Josef I evidently thought so, too, for he had the rococo excesses stripped from his personal bedchamber in 1854.

Of the 1441 rooms within the palace, only 40 are open to the public. The full quota are viewed in the Grand Tour, which takes in the apartments of Franz Josef and Empress Elisabeth, the ceremonial and state rooms and the audience chambers of Maria Theresia and her husband Franz Stephan. The Imperial Tour excludes the chambers of Maria Theresia and Franz Stephan and

only visits 22 rooms. Both include an audio guide in English but only the Grand Tour is available with a guide. It may be worth opting for an audio guide either way, as you can set your own pace and won't be dragged along on someone else's schedule. Because of the popularity of the palace, tickets are stamped with a departure time, and there may be a time lag before you're allowed to set off in summer, so buy your ticket straight away and then explore the gardens.

Both tours start in the west wing at the bottom of the **Blauerstiege** (Blue Staircase) and climb to the private rooms of Franz Josef and Elisabeth. They're similar in style to the Hofburg and probably won't hold your interest for long, but the small **Breakfast Room** has fine views of the gardens and is decorated with embroideries made by Maria Theresia and her daughters.

The ceremonial and state rooms start with the **Spiegelsaal** (Hall of Mirrors) where Mozart (then six) played his first royal concert in the presence of Maria Theresia and the royal family in 1762. His father revealed in a letter that afterwards young Wolfgang leapt onto the lap of the empress and kissed her. The pinnacle of finery is reached in the **Grosse Galerie** (Great Gallery). Gilded scrolls, ceiling frescoes, chandeliers and huge crystal mirrors create the effect. Numerous sumptuous balls were held here, including one for the delegates at the Congress of Vienna (1814-15).

Near the Grosse Galerie is the **Round Chinese Room**, which is touched by governing genius. Maria Theresia held secret consultations here: a hidden doorway led to her adviser's apartments and a fully laden table could be drawn up through the floor so that dignitaries could dine without being disturbed by servants.

The Imperial Tour ends with the **Ceremonial Hall**, blessed with a fine set of paintings by Martin van Meytens of Joseph II's wedding to Isabella of Parma in 1760. The Grand Tour continues with the **Blue Chinese Room** where Karl I abdicated in 1918.

The next room of interest is the **Napoleon Room**, where he is thought to have slept. The stuffed crested lark here was the favourite childhood bird of Napoleon's son, Duc de Reichstadt, who died in this room.

Following on from the Napoleon Room is the **Porcelain Room** and the **Miniatures Room**, with drawings by members of the imperial family. Both are overshadowed by the **Millions Room**, named after the sum that Maria Theresia paid for the decorations, which are comprised of Persian miniatures set on rosewood panels and framed with gilded rocaille frames. The **Gobelin Salon** features Belgian tapestries from the 18th century.

While not joined to the main set of rooms, the **Bergl Rooms** are worth visiting to see paintings by Johann Wenzl Bergl (1718-89); his exotic depictions of flora and fauna attempt to bring the ambience of the gardens inside, with some success.

GARDENS

13, Schloss Schönbrunn; admission free; ☺ 6am-dusk Apr-Oct, 6.30am-dusk Nov-Mar; ◉ U4 Schönbrunn, U4 Hietzing, bus 10A

The beautifully tended formal gardens of the palace, arranged in the French style, are a symphony of colour in the summer and a combination of greys and browns in winter; both are appealing in their own right. The grounds, which were opened to the public by Joseph II in 1779, hide a number of attractions in the tree-lined avenues that were arranged according to a grid and star-shaped system between 1750 and 1755. From 1772 to 1780 Ferdinand Hetzendorf added some of the final touches to the park under the instructions of Joseph II: fake **Roman ruins** (Map pp260–1)

in 1778, the **Neptunbrunnen** (Neptune Fountain; Map pp260–1), a riotous ensemble from Greek mythology, in 1781, and the crowning glory, the **Gloriette** (Map pp260–1; rooftop access per adult/student/child €2/1.50/1; open Apr-Oct) in 1775. Standing tall on the hill overlooking the gardens, the view from the Gloriette, looking back towards the palace with Vienna shimmering in the distance, ranks among the best in Vienna. It's possible to venture onto its roof, but the view is only marginally superior. The original **Schöner Brunnen** (Map pp262–3), from which the palace gained its name, now pours through the stone pitcher of a nymph near the Roman ruins. The garden's 630m-long **Maze** (adult/student/child €2.90/2.40/1.70; open Apr-Oct) is a classic hedge design based on the original maze that occupied its place from 1720 to 1892; next door is the **Labyrinth**, a new playground with games, climbing equipment and a giant mirror kaleidoscope.

To the east of the palace is the **Privy Garden** (adult/student/child €2/1.50/0.90; ☺ 9am-6pm Jul & Aug, 9am-5pm Apr-Jun, Sep & Oct), a replica of the Baroque garden that occupied the space around 1750. Its colourful twirls of yellow and red sand, with Schönbrunn's west wing in the background, make for a lovely holiday snapshot.

Fiaker outside Schloss Schönbrunn (opposite page)

KINDERMUSEUM Map pp260-1

☎ 811 13 239; www.schoenbrunn.at/kinder in German; 13, Schloss Schönbrunn; adult/child/family €6.50/4.50/17; ☼ 10am-5pm Sat & Sun, school holidays 10am-5pm daily; ◉ U4 Schönbrunn, U4 Hietzing, bus 10A

Schönbrunn's Kindermuseum (Children's Museum) sticks to what it knows best: imperialism. Activities and displays help kids discover the day-to-day life of the Habsburg court, and once they've got an idea, they can don princely or princessly outfits and start ordering the serfs (parents) around. Other rooms devoted to toys, natural science and archaeology all help to keep them entertained. When guided tours are offered, they depart from the ticket desk at 11am, 2pm and 3.30pm (in English by appointment only).

WAGENBURG Map pp260-1

☎ 877 32 44; 13, Schloss Schönbrunn; adult/concession/family €4.50/3/9; ☼ 9am-6pm Apr-Oct, 10am-4pm Tue-Sun Nov-Mar; ◉ U4 Schönbrunn, bus 10A

The Wagenburg (Imperial Coach Collection) is *Pimp My Ride* imperial style. On display is a vast array of carriages, but nothing can compete with Emperor Franz Stephan's coronation carriage, with its ornate gold plating, Venetian glass panes and painted cherubs. The whole thing weighs an astonishing 4000kg. Also look for the dainty child's carriage built for Napoleon's son, with eagle-wing-shaped mudguards and bee motifs. Entry to the Wagenburg is included in the price of a Gold ticket (p69).

PALMENHAUS Map pp260-1

☎ 877 50 87406; 13, Maxingstrasse 13b; adult/senior/student/child under 5 €4/3.50/2.80/2; ☼ 9am-6pm May-Sep, 9.30am-5pm Oct-Apr; ◉ U4 Hietzing, 🚃 10, 58, 60, 61

If you think you're experiencing déjà vu on sighting the Palmenhaus (Palm House), you are: it was built in 1882 by Franz Segenschmid as a replica of the one in London's Kew Gardens. The glorious glass-and-iron construction still houses palms and hot-house plants and is particularly photogenic after a heavy fall of snow. The inside is a veritable jungle of tropical plants from around the world.

WÜSTENHAUS Map pp260-1

☎ 877 50 87; 13, Maxingstrasse 13b; adult/senior/student/child under 5 €4/3/2.50/2; ☼ 9am-6pm May-Sep, 9am-5pm Oct-Apr; ◉ U4 Hietzing, 🚃 10, 58, 60, 61

The small Wüstenhaus (Desert House) near the Palmenhaus makes good use of the once disused Sonnenuhrhaus (Sundial House) to re-create arid desert scenes. There are four sections – Northern Africa and the Middle East, Africa, the Americas, and Madagascar – with rare cacti and desert animals, such as the naked mole from East Africa, on display.

TIERGARTEN Map pp260-1

☎ 877 92 94; www.zoovienna.at; 13, Maxingstrasse 13b; adult/senior/student/child €12/10/5/4; ☼ 9am-6.30pm Apr-Sep, 9am-5.30pm Mar & Oct, 9am-5pm Feb, 9am-4.30pm Nov-Jan; ◉ U4 Hietzing, 🚃 10, 58, 60, 61

Founded in 1752 as a menagerie by Franz Stephan, Schönbrunn Tiergarten (Zoo) is the oldest zoo in the world. It houses some 750 animals of all shapes and sizes; the most recent arrivals to excite crowds were giant pandas in 2003, although lemurs, armadillos and baby Serbian tigers spurred plenty of interest in 2006. Thankfully most of the original cramped cages have been updated and improved, but the odd one still remains. The zoo's layout is reminiscent of a bicycle wheel, with pathways as spokes and an octagonal pavilion at its centre. The pavilion dates from 1759 and was used as the imperial breakfast room; it now houses a fine restaurant (so you can feel regal, too). Feeding times are staggered throughout the day – maps on display tell you who's dining when.

NORTHERN VIENNA

The affluent districts of Währing and Döbling reach well into the hills north of the city. Noble villas and leafy parks are the norm here, but most people venturing this far from the city centre will be looking for *Heurigen*. Four of the city's more popular wine villages – Neustift am Walde, Sievering, Grinzing, and Nussdorf – are all in this northern section. While many wine taverns in Grinzing and an ever-increasing number in Neustift am Walde cater to busloads of tour groups with unbearable folk music and tacky shows, it would be a shame to dismiss the entire region as a *Heurigen* no-go area. Nussdorf is particularly atmospheric, with a string of traditional *Heurigen* along its main street, Kahlenberger Strasse. Beethoven spent a good portion of his time in the area; nearby Pfarrplatz is the site of one of his many apartments (it's now a *Heuriger*, Mayer am Pfarrplatz p143), and only a few steps away on Probusgasse is the **Beethoven Apartment Heiligenstadt** (Map pp252–3; ☎ 370 54 08; 19, Probusgasse 6; adult/child €2/1; ⏰ 10am-1pm, 2-6pm Tue-Sun; 🚇 D, bus 38A), which is part of the city's municipal museums.

Architecture fans and socialists will also enjoy the trip north; opposite the U4 Heiligenstadt U-Bahn station is one of the crowning achievements of Red Vienna (p44), the **Karl-Marx-Hof** (Map pp252–3; 19, Heiligenstädter Strasse 82-92; 🚇 U4 Heiligenstadt, 🚇 D). Stretching for almost one kilometre along Heiligenstädter Stadt, this colossal housing project in pale pink and yellow was built by Karl Ehn, a student of Otto Wagner, between 1927 and 1930. It originally contained some 1600 flats, plus community facilities and inner courtyards. In 1934 was the centre of the Social Democratic resistance during the civil war. It received heavy bombardment by the Austro-Fascists to break the resistance and underwent a full restoration in 1989.

With its elevated position of 484m and extensive views across Vienna to the Lesser Carpathians hills of Slovakia, **Kahlenberg** (19, Höhenstrasse; bus 38A) is a magnet for visitors. At the summit is a small café and restaurant, the St Josef church, and sometime in the near future, a new hotel. A more peaceful spot with similar views is **Leopoldsberg** (19, Höhenstrasse; bus 38A), 1km further along the Höhenstrasse. Atop this peak is a small fortified church and café. A pleasant alternative to taking the bus back down from either is to set off by foot through the vineyards to Nussdorf; see p111 for more information.

GEYMÜLLERSCHLÖSSEL Map pp252-3
☎ 479 31 39; 18, Pötzleinsdorfer Strasse 102; €7.90; ⏰ 11am-4pm Sun May-Nov; 🚇 41, bus 41A
The Geymüllerschlössel, named after its first owner, the banker and merchant Johann Jakob Geymüller, is arguably the finest

example of Biedermeier architecture in Austria. Built around 1808 by an unknown architect, it is a mixture of Gothic, Indian and Arabic styles characteristic of the times. The interior, embellished with floral designs and graceful lines, is perfectly preserved. It houses MAK's (p78) collection of around 160 Viennese clocks dating from 1760 to the second half of the 19th century, and furniture from the period 1800 to 1840. It's a fair way out from the centre and best combined with a walk in the Wienerwald nearby.

EROICA HAUS Map pp258-9
☎ 369 14 24; 19, Döblinger Hauptstrasse 92; adult/concession €2/1; ⏰ 3-6pm Fri; 🚇 37, bus 10A, 39A
For the brief time Beethoven spent at Eroica Haus (the summer of 1803), his work production was grandiose: it was here that he wrote Symphony No 3, *Eroica*. The house is rather empty, however, and no personal effects of the great composer are present, but you can listen to *Eroica* and gaze at a few watercolours and maps. The Eroica Haus is a municipal museum.

KLOSTERNEUBURG
The small village of Klosterneuburg lies around 13km north of Vienna along the Danube. It's the easiest destination for a day trip out of the city and contains a huge Augustinian monastery and a progressive art museum. For the fit, the walk from Kahlenberg or Leopoldsberg through the woods and vineyards to the village is a real pleasure.

STIFT KLOSTERNEUBURG
☎ 02243-41 12 12; www.stift-klosterneuburg.at; Stiftplatz 1, Klosterneuburg; adult/seniors/students/children/family €7/6/5/4/14; ⏰ 9am-6pm; Schnellbahn S40, bus 239 (Klosterneuburg-Kierling stop) from 🚇 U4 Heiligenstadt)
This large Augustinian abbey dominates the small town of Klosterneuburg. Founded in 1114, the abbey's baroque face-lift didn't begin until 1730 and wasn't completed until 1842. The plans actually called for something far grander, but fortunately these were not realised, leaving large sections in their original medieval style. The abbey's museum is an eclectic mix

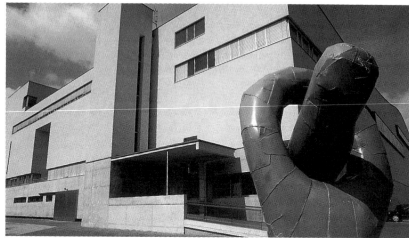

Sammlung Essl (this page)

of religious art from the Middle Ages to the present day. If you've ventured this far, however, you're better off including a guided tour on your itinerary, which takes in the cloister and the church (tours in English require advanced notice). The tour's highlight is the *Verdun Altar* in St Leopold's Chapel, an annexe of the church. Produced by Nicholas of Verdun in 1181, it is an unsurpassed example of medieval enamel work and is gloriously adorned with 51 enamelled panels showing biblical scenes.

SAMMLUNG ESSL

☎ 02243-370 50; www.sammlung-essl. at; Kunst Der Gegenwart, An der Donau-Au 1, Klosterneuburg; adult/seniors/child/family €7/5/3.50/14; ⏰ 10am-7pm Tue-Sun, until 9pm Wed; Schnellbahn S40, bus 239 (Weidling stop) from Ⓤ U4 Heiligenstadt)

This fine gallery is the brainchild of Agnes and Karlheinz Essl, collectors of contemporary art from the 20th and 21st centuries. They desired somewhere suitable to showcase their extensive collection, so they built the gallery. Expect to see a plethora of big names: Gerhard Richter, Hermann Nitsch, Georg Baselitz and Elke Krystufek are but a few of the artists on show. The construction itself is the work of Austrian architect Heinz Tesar and incorporates clean white lines, an abundance of natural light and plenty of open space. Entry is free from 7pm to 9pm on Wednesday.

Walking & Cycling Tours ∎

Walking & Cycling Tours

Vienna is easily explored with a combination of walking and cycling. The Innere Stadt, with its maze of narrow, cobblestone one-way streets and pedestrian zones, is best explored on foot, while its surrounding suburbs are generally flat. The only hills to speak of start in the outer districts which border the Wienerwald; here a little more exertion is required, particularly if you wish to tackle them by bike.

The Rathaus information office (p230) stocks a number of brochures detailing walks and cycle routes in the city; inquire directly or consult their website (www.wien.gv.at/english; search under 'Leisure', then 'Sport'). If you're planning to do a lot of cycling pick up a copy of Argus' comprehensive *Stadtplan Wien für RadfahrerInnen*, which maps out cycle paths in Vienna. Detailed information on mountain biking trails in the Wienerwald is available on www.mbike.at (in German).

Every city has its quirks, and Vienna is no exception. Viennese drivers are notoriously aggressive behind the wheel, often ignoring zebra crossings and yelling abuse at fellow drivers, pedestrians and cyclists with equal vigour; fortunately it's mostly hot air, and an exchange of blows is a very rare occurrence. Jaywalking is severely discouraged and an instant fine from the police will result if you're caught crossing a road within 25m of a zebra crossing or failing to wait for a green traffic light. Occasionally pedestrians and cyclists clash, particularly when the former wanders onto the latter's designated path; it's advisable to take stock of where you're standing or walking in case you're blocking a cycle path.

The first five tours below are walking tours, while the last two cycling. Of the walking tours, only Essential Vienna and Ottakring & the Wienerwald are unsuitable for cycling; the rest can be tackled with a combination of cycling and walking (each trail passes through a park where cycling is not permitted). If an organised tour is more your style, see p50 for details.

ESSENTIAL VIENNA

This walk takes you through some of the most well-trodden tourist trails in Vienna, but there's a reason why so many visitors flock to the area. Instantly recognisable sights – Gothic Stephansdom and the Hofburg, the Habsburg's winter palace – dominate this quarter of the Innere Stadt, while Kärntner Strasse, Graben and Kohlmarkt attract visitors by the bus load. The beauty of it all, however, is that you can duck down a cobblestoned side street and often have the city to yourself.

Start your walk at the **Staatsoper 1** (p169) and head north along **Kärntner Strasse 2** (p57), the Innere Stadt's main street. It soon becomes a pedestrian-only walkway of plush shops, cafés and street entertainers. Detour left down Marco-d'Aviano-Gasse to Neuer Markt and the **Kaisergruft 3** (p57), final resting place of the Habsburg family. Continue north on Seilergasse before ducking down Kärntner Durchgang past the **American Bar 4** (p155), designed by Adolf Loos in 1908, and left onto Kärntner Strasse once more. A little north the pedestrianised street opens out onto Stock-im-Eisen-Platz and eventually Stephansplatz; here the tall spire of Gothic **Stephansdom 5** (p53) commands the square. Before continuing with the walking tour, take a few moments to explore the hidden streets behind the cathedral for a taste of medieval Vienna; Blutgasse, Domgasse and Grünangergasse are particularly atmospheric and often bereft of people.

Take a peek inside the neo-Renaissance **Equitable Palais 6** (p58) and note the nail-studded stump on one of its outside corners before heading west on **Graben 7** (p58).

WALK FACTS

Start Staatsoper
Finish Staatsoper
Distance 2½km
Duration Straight walk – 1½ to 2 hours, with stops for sights – all day
Transport U1, U2 or U4 to Karlsbergplatz, or take tram D, J, 1, 2, 62 or 65

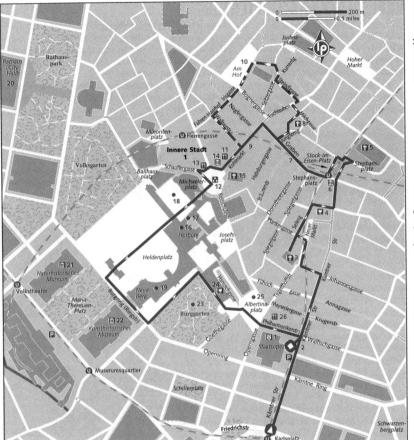

Wander down Graben and take a detour right onto Jungferngasse to admire **Peterskirche 8** (p59), one of the city's finest baroque churches. From here a couple of alternatives arise; either retrace your steps back to Graben and turn left onto **Kohlmarkt 9** or duck down Milchgasse and cross Tuchlauben onto Steindlgasse. Steindlgasse leads to a collection of quiet cobblestone streets and the spacious **Am Hof 10** (p64) square. From Am Hof cross onto Irisgasse which leads onto unhurried Fahren-Haarhof; at Wallnerstrasse turn left and you're soon on Kohlmarkt.

A coffee and cake break in **Demel 11** (p140) may be in order before heading to Michaelerplatz, and a menagerie of architectural delights: the **Roman Ruins 12** (p58), **Café Griensteidl 13** (p140), the unusual **Loos Haus 14** (p59), **Michaelerkirche 15** (p59), and Michaelertor, gateway to the **Hofburg 16** (p60).

A little time admiring the **Schweizertor 17** (Swiss Gate) and **In der Burg 18** (p60) is a rewarding experience, then push onto the impressive **Neue Burg 19** (p60) on Heldenplatz. The view from the square, taking in the **Rathaus 20** (City Hall; p70), **Naturhistorisches Museum 21** (p71) and **Kunsthistorisches Museum 22** (p73), is breathtaking. Exit Heldenplatz and turn left onto the Ringstrasse before ducking around behind the Neue Burg to the quiet **Burggarten 23** (p71) and its Victorian **Palmenhaus 24** (p155). Walk through the garden to **Albertinaplatz 25**, from where a quick stroll down Philharmonikerstrasse will bring you past **Café Sacher 26** (p140) and its celebrated *Sacher Torte* to near the walk's start.

KARLSPLATZ TO SCHOTTENTOR

Collectively, the architectural splendour stretching along the Ringstrasse from near Karlsplatz to Schottentor is a major drawcard for Vienna. It is simply astounding how so many visual delights can be crammed into such a small space. Add to that the hustle and bustle of the Naschmarkt, the art space of the MuseumsQuartier and the golden dome of the Secession, and you have a walk to thrill even the most jaded tourist.

Instead of following the tempting course of the Ringstrasse, head west from Karlsplatz along Friedrichstrasse to the **Secession 1** (p72) and admire its golden-leafed globe, before entering the tangle of the **Naschmarkt 2** (p185), Vienna's biggest, most colourful market. After

WALK FACTS

Start Karlsplatz
Finish Schottentor
Distance 3½km
Duration 2 hours
Transport U1, U2 or U4 to Karlsbergplatz, or take tram D, J, 1, 2, 62 or 65

a quick look around, retrace your steps to Secession and continue west, then north, west again, and then south around the perimeter of the **Akademie der bildenden Künste 3** (p71) and past Schillerplatz. Next, turn right onto Getreidemarkt heading northwest to the **MuseumsQuartier 4** (p75). Enter from Mariahilfer Strasse and walk directly to the main square; here you're confronted with the black-and-white twin buildings of the **Leopold Museum 5** (p76) and **Museum moderner Kunst 6** (MUMOK; p77). Exit via the central gates which lead onto Museumsplatz; cross the road to Maria-Theresien-Platz, where a proud statue of Maria Theresia resides over the **Naturhistorisches Museum 7** (p71) and the **Kunsthistorisches Museum 8** (p73).

From the square turn left onto leafy Ringstrasse. Just past regal frontage of **Palais Epstein 9** (p71) you'll soon see the Greek columns of the **Parlament 10** (p70), then the busts of great playwrights adorning the façade of the **Burgtheater 11** (p170) appear on your right. Towering above Rathausplatz directly opposite is the **Rathaus 12** (p70). Continue north along the Ringstrasse to the solid **Universität Wien 13** (p69) before veering right up one of the last remnants of the old city walls, Mölker Bastei, to reach **Pasqualati Haus 14** (p65), a former residence of Beethoven that's now a museum. Turn left up Schottengasse to Schottentor and the twin spires of the **Votivkirche 15** (p69), and finish with a bite to eat in **Café Stein 16** (p160).

LEOPOLDSTADT

The absolute delight of this walk is the understated charm of the Leopoldstadt district, with its mix of beautiful parks, lively markets and busy residential streets.

From Schwedenplatz head north across the Danube Canal (Donaukanal) on Taborstrasse, past the striking façade of the **Odeon 1** (p168) until Haidgasse, then turn left. Pass the quaint house hiding the **Weiner Kriminalmuseum 2** (p81) and head to **Karmelitermarkt 3** (p185), the district's central market. A detour to the canal brings Otto Wagner's **Schützenhaus 4** (p80) into

view; backtrack and head up Leopoldsgasse to the T-junction at Untere Augartenstrasse. Turn right and cross Obere Augartenstrasse, entering **Augarten 5** (p79) through the main gates. Directly in front of you is Augartenpalais, home to the **Wiener Porzellanmanufaktur 6** (p81), makers of fine porcelain crafts.

Circumnavigate the park, taking in the two towering **Flaktürme 7 & 8** (p81) before leaving by the gate from which you entered and heading southeast on Obere Augartenstrasse. At Castellezgasse turn left and head north. This street soon changes to Scherzergasse and ends at the front doors of the Atelier Augarten, home to the **Gustinus Ambrosi-Museum 9** (p81) and a small coffee house. Retrace your steps along Castellezgasse/Scherzergasse to Klanggasse, which soon merges with Heinestrasse. Continue directly to the Praterstern; from there make a beeline for the **Prater** (p79) and the fairground rides of the **Wurstelprater 10** (p79). Ride the **Riesenrad 11** (p80) before recharging your batteries at the **Schweizerhaus 12** (p127). Spend the rest of the day wandering around the Prater, or jump on the N Tram back to Schwedenplatz.

WALK FACTS

Start Schwedenplatz
Finish Prater
Distance 7½km
Duration 3 hours
Transport U1 or U4 to Schwedenplatz, or take tram N, 1, 2 or 21

STADTPARK TO KARLSPLATZ

This long walk connects some of Vienna's better- and lesser-known sights, following a path that winds its way through the diplomatic neighbourhood of Landstrasse.

Begin by paying homage to some of Vienna's great composers, who are honoured with statues in the **Stadtpark 1** (p77). At the northern end of the park join the Ringstrasse and head north, past **Museum für angewandte Kunst 2** (MAK; p78) and Wagner's celebrated **Postsparkasse 3** (p78), to the **Urania 4** (p155) on the banks of the Danube Canal. From Urania veer east on Uraniastrasse, which soon becomes Radetzkystrasse. Radetzkystrasse ends at Radetzkyplatz, where you'll find **Gasthaus Wild 5** (p128), a fine neo-*Beisl*. From here duck under the railway tracks and follow Löwengasse southeast until you hit Krieglergasse, at which point turn left and head directly towards the **KunstHausWien 6** (p85), one of

WALK FACTS

Start Stadtpark;
Finish Karlsplatz
Distance 6km
Duration 3 hours
Transport U4 to Stadtpark, or take tram 1 or 2

Hundertwasser's eye-catching creations. Then turn right along Untere Weissgerberstrasse past another of Hundertwasser's works, the **Hundertwasser Haus 7** (p85), and cut right at the

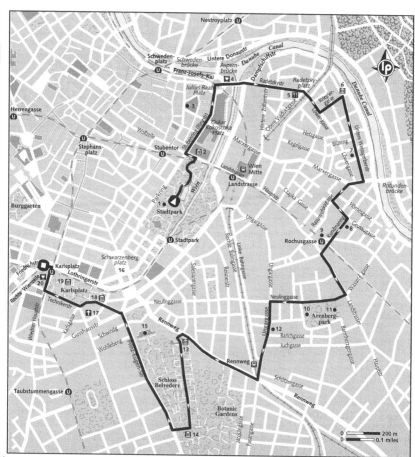

end of the street onto Rasumofskygasse. After a few blocks head left on Geusaugasse and then right on Kundmanngasse to pass the modernist **Wittgensteinhaus 8** (p84); if it's a Saturday stop in at the **Rochusmarkt 9** (p95) on nearby Rochusgasse.

From Rochusgasse turn left on Landstrasser Hauptstrasse; follow it until you hit Neulinggasse on your right, which leads to Arenbergpark, home to two of the six goliath **Flaktürme 10 & 11** (p81) in Vienna. One currently serves as a temporary exhibition space for MAK.

Continue west along Neulinggasse and take Ungargasse left; after a couple of blocks the rewarding sight of the Jugendstil **Portois & Fix 12** (p90) swings into view. At the end of Ungargasse turn right and head up Rennweg to the gates of the **Unteres Belvedere 13** (p87). Wander through the baroque palace's gardens to its second edifice, the **Oberes Belvedere 14** (p86), before leaving by the southern gate and heading north along Prinz-Eugen-Strasse past **Hotel im Palais Schwarzenberg 15**. At the southern end of **Schwarzenbergplatz 16** (p77) veer left onto Technikerstrasse, which leads onto Karlsplatz and its ring of attractions – **Karlskirche 17** (p89), **Wien Museum 18** (p88) and Wagner's **Stadtbahn Pavillons 19** (p89). At the far end of Karlsplatz is the **Kunsthallencafé 20** (p156), where a rejuvenating drink awaits.

KAHLENBERG TO NUSSDORF

This walk offers panoramic views of the city, vineyards and *Heurigen,* and a gentle descent to the wine village of Nussdorf. It's best appreciated in the afternoon at which time most *Heurigen* open for business.

After disembarking from bus 38A at **Kahlenberg 1** (p103), walk past **St Josef Kirche 2** and veer left to the beginning of Kahlenberger Strasse. Follow the windy street down to the small **Friedhof Kahlenberg 3** hidden amongst the trees and past row after row of wine vines. At the junction of Kahlenberger

WALK FACTS

Start Kahlenberg; **Finish** Nussdorf
Distance 3½km
Duration at least 4 hours with *Heurigen* stops
Transport U4 to Heiligenstadt then bus 38A

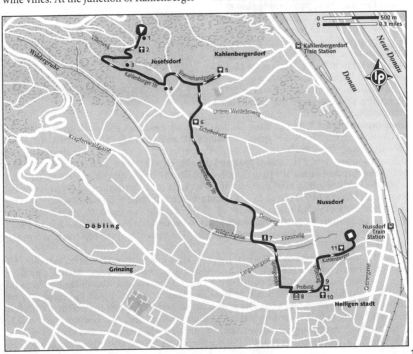

Strasse and Eisernenhandgasse, five minutes after the cemetery, stop to take in the **view 4** of Vienna over the vineyards of Kahlenberg, before turning left on Eisernenhandgasse and following it downhill to the secluded *Heurigen* **Hirt 5** (p143). After a quick stop to soak up the views of the Danube, and sample a little local wine, head back up the steep hill to Unterer Weisleitenweg, a dirt path that heads left through vineyards to Kahlenberger Strasse and **Sirbu 6** (p143), another of the area's quality *Heurigen*.

Continue the walk south on Kahlenberger Strasse; from here, the city is laid out in front of you to the right. After a while the road starts to feature houses, then makes a sharp right and crosses Frimmelgasse. Immediately after Frimmelgasse turn left and pass the **Beethoven Ruhe 7**, a memorial to the dead composer dating from 1863. Cross Schreiberbach, the small stream just south of the memorial, and head south on Springsiedel. At the end of the street the walk completes a dogleg: first left into Rudolf-Kassner-Gasse, then right into Ambrustergasse, and finally left into Probusgasse. Probusgasse is a picturesque, cobblestone street lined with immaculate town houses, including the **Beethoven Apartment Heiligenstadt 8** (p103) at No 6. At its far end is Pfarrplatz, a quiet square with the *Heuriger* **Mayer am Pfarrplatz 9** (p143) and the 17th-century **St Jakob Kirche 10** (☺ 1.30-4.30pm) with Roman foundations.

Take Eroicagasse (named after Beethoven's Third Symphony) north to Kahlenberger Strasse and head east; a string of pleasant *Heurigen* greet you along the way, including the inviting **Kierlinger 11** (19, Kahlenberger Strasse 20; ☺ 3.30pm-midnight), which consistently wins awards for its Rheinriesling and Weissburgunder. The walk finishes in Nussdorf at the D tram, accessible from Kahlenberger Strasse via Schätzgasse.

OTTAKRING & THE WIENERWALD

The green belt of the Wienerwald on the western edge of Vienna is inviting for both walkers and cyclists. This walk dips into the woods bordering Ottakring and passes by small pockets of vineyards. It's for those with a reasonable fitness level, and its best to bring water and snacks as refuelling stations only appear towards the end. Also, wear sturdy shoes.

From the U3 end station Ottakring catch bus 46B nine stops to **Feuerwache am Steinhof 1** at the corner of Johann-Straud-Strasse and Savoyenstrasse. If you're feeling energetic walk this section, but the stretch up Thaliastrasse and Johann-Straud-Strass passes by bland residential housing and will be of little interest to most. Quell the urge to head straight into the woods and instead enter **Erholungsgebiet Steinhof 2**, a large park filled with grassy meadows and small clumps of trees.

WALK FACTS

Start Johann-Straud-Strasse
Finish U3 Ottakring
Distance 7½km
Duration 4 hours
Transport U3 to Ottakring then bus 46B

At its southern edge is Otto Wagner's sublime **Kirche am Steinhof 3** (p98); to reach it, follow the path due south from the bus stop through the park until an opening in a wire fence. Pass through and veer left at the sealed road and the church will soon appear. Retrace your steps to the bus stop and follow the path directly opposite the Erholungsgebiet Steinhof entrance with white-yellow-white markings into the woods. It initially parallels Savoyenstrasse but soon turns left at a fork; keep to the path and you'll reach Johann-Straud-Strasse. Cross the street and follow the '4A' signs directly uphill; here the woods are thick and scrubby, and after 15 to 20 minutes you'll encounter Johann-Straud-Strasse again. Turn left and soon the **Jubiläumswarte 4** (p97) tower comes into sight. The views from the top reach to Slovakia and take in all of Vienna.

Head back along Johann-Straud-Strasse and after a few hundred metres take the '4A' path once more, but this time left into the woods and across the **Kreuzeichenwiese 5**, a pleasant meadow with picnic tables. The path follows Pelzer Rennweg and soon ducks back into the woods; at the first major junction turn right and keep to the right path indicated by a red arrow (a blue arrow points left). The path heads downhill through the prettiest stretch of the walk – here the trees are tall, mature, and uncrowded, and all sounds of the city fade. The Dornbach stream appears on your right and after a while a row of small houses on your left. When the houses end turn right (follow the '4A' sign) and cross the **stream 6**; after rain

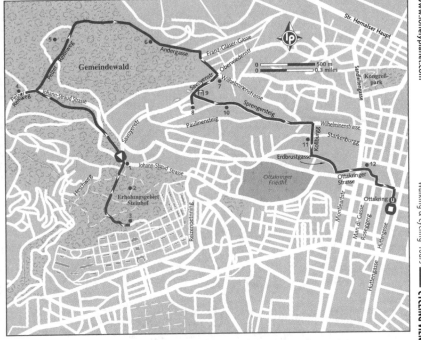

this section is slippery so care should be taken. Continue downhill through open woods and out onto Andergasse, then right up the never-ending stairs on Eselstiege.

At the top of Eselstiege is the welcoming sight of **Villa Aurora 7** (16, Wilhelminenstrasse 237; ☻ 10am-midnight), a charming wooden villa with a gorgeous garden, heavenly coffee with lashings of whipped cream, and a Vienna panorama. Pause here or continue up Savoyenstrasse to **Schloss Wilhelminenberg 8** (p202); if neither appeals turn left at the **Mausoleum 9** just before the Schloss and follow Sprengersteig down past vineyards and Vienna views to **Leitner 10** (16, Sprengersteig 68; ☻ 5-11pm Tue-Fri, 4-11pm Sat, 4-10pm Sun), a tiny *Heurigen* on the edge of suburbia. After refuelling, stick to Sprengersteig, which soon becomes Paulinensteig and eventually Wilhelminenstrasse. At Kollburggasse turn right and carry on downhill past early 20th-century **villas 11** at No 14 and 25 to Erdbrustgasse; turn left and follow the street to Ottakringer Strasse, where another left will bring you to tram J and busy Sandleitengasse. A string of **Stadt Heurigen 12** awaits you on the far side of Sandleitengasse, otherwise take the tram or walk down to U3 Ottakring.

CYCLING VIENNA'S PARKLANDS & WATERWAYS

This tour takes in Vienna's favourite park and its biggest waterways. With no strenuous hills – and for the most part following well-marked cycle lanes – it can be tackled by almost anyone at their own pace.

From Schwedenplatz head north along the western bank of the Danube Canal – not via the busy road, but down on the cycle and running path which hugs the canal. Glide past the **Summer Stage 1** (p128) near Rossauer Brücke, which, if it's summer, will be in full swing, and continue on your way until the **Fernwärme 2** (p92), the city's rubbish incinerator with a Hundertwasser make-over, comes into view. Just before the incinerator, take the cycle ramp on your left, which climbs above the canal and ducks behind the Fernwärme. The path then makes a right turn (follow the sign 'Donauinsel') and crosses over the canal via the Gürtelbrücke to Leipziger Strasse and the district of Brigittenau. Stick to

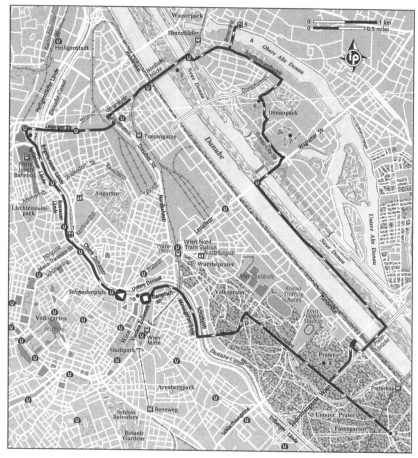

CYCLE FACTS

Start Schwedenplatz
Finish Schwedenplatz
Distance 23km
Duration 4 to 5 hours
Transport U1 or U4 to Schwedenplatz, or take tram N, 1, 2 or 21

Leipziger until it hits Universumstrasse, at which point turn left and continue until it ends at Winarskystrasse. Turn right onto Winarskystrasse and follow the path to Nordbahnbrücke, which spans the Danube (Donau), the Neue Donau (New Danube) and the **Donauinsel 3** (Danube Island; p82), a long island crisscrossed by paths and dotted with swimming areas.

At the eastern end of Nordbahnbrücke the path drops down onto Arbeiterstrand-badstrasse and the **Alte Donau 4** (Old Danube; p82). Stay on Arbeiterstrandbadstrasse until Birnersteig appears on your left: duck along this street to the northern side of the Alte Donau for a much-needed pit stop at **Strandgasthaus Birner 5** (p126), a tiny eatery overlooking the water. Back on Arbeiterstrandbadstrasse, continue along the cycle path until it cuts right into the Donaupark (don't take the first sign to the Donauturm along Donauturm-strasse, take the second), directly to the base of the **Donauturm 6** (p83). Turn left and follow the path in the direction of the **UNO City 7** (p83); your trail actually heads just west of the UNO building. At Leonard-Bernstein-Strasse turn left then right into Donau-City-Strasse, a street that slices between the high-rises of UNO City and Donau-City. You'll soon find yourself at Reichsbrücke; turn right and cross the Neue Donau to the Donauinsel. Follow the bicycle path down onto the island itself and head southeast on any path that appeals. This is a good place to stop and enjoy a refreshing dip.

Continue southeast until you hit Praterbrücke, and signs directing you to the **Prater 8** (p79), the city's favourite playground. Cross over the Danube once more and stick to the path leading into the Prater itself, which winds its way through the shipping centre Handelskai and onto Grünlandgasse before eventually hitting Hauptallee, the park's main thoroughfare. If you're peckish, turn left and stay on Hauptallee until you reach the **Lusthaus 9** (p128), a former hunting lodge. Back on Hauptallee, retrace your path northwest and continue until you reach the end station of the N Tram, and Rotunden Allee, a road off to the left leading to the Danube Canal. Cross over the canal on Rotundenbrücke and turn right until the **Urania 10** (p155) complex swings into view. This is your finishing point, and a perfect spot to reflect on the day's ride over a coffee or beer.

SOUTHWEST VIENNA CYCLING TOUR

This tour travels out of the city centre to noble **Hietzing** (p97) and passes through a diverse selection of districts. With only one hill to speak of, it can be completed using a **Vienna City Bike** (p219); there is a stand at Karlsplatz, the beginning of the ride, and four along the way (the furthest east is at Margaretengürtel U-Bahn station). If you'd prefer a better grade of bike, hire one at **Pedal Power** (p219) and cycle around the Ringstrasse to the start of the tour.

From in front of the **Staatsoper 1** (p169) follow Operngasse south into Margareten Strasse until Pilgramgasse; most of this

> ### CYCLE FACTS
> **Start** Karlsplatz
> **Finish** Karlsplatz
> **Distance** 21km
> **Duration** 4 to 5 hours

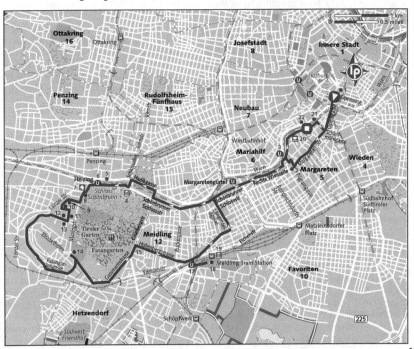

Schönbrunn gardens, featuring the Neptunbrunnen (Neptune fountain) and the Gloriette (p101)

stretch is blessed with a cycle path and passes through the urban districts of Wieden and Margareten. At Pilgramgasse, take stock of the tall turrets and glass conservatory of the neo-classical **Margaretenhof** (1884–85; 05, Margaretenplatz) 2 before turning right and following the road until the **Pilgramgasse U-Bahn station** 3. From the station a well-marked cycle path parallels the Wien Fluss all the way along Wienzeile to the gates of **Schönbrunn** 4 (p99). This section of the ride is bereft of sights but it's intriguing to see Vienna change from a city of tight streets and heavily urbanised neighbourhoods to wide boulevards and open spaces.

After a good 30 minutes cycling through the Vienna's urban spread, the majestic entrance to Schloss Schönbrunn, guarded by Schlossbrücke's lion statues, greet you. Continue west on Schönbrunner Strasse, passing the **Hofpavillon Hietzing** 5 (p98), to the **Hietzing U-Bahn station** 6 and take Hietzinger Hauptstrasse south past the Schönbrunn-yellow façade of **Parkhotel Schönbrunn** 7 (p201). Near the tall spire of **Maria Geburt Kirche** 8, turn left into Maxingstrasse and after two blocks right into Trauttmansdorfgasse.

Trauttmansdorfgasse is lined with well-preserved examples of **Biedermeier villas** 9 & 10 – Nos 40, 54 and 56 are highlights. About half way down Trauttmansdorfgasse take Woltergasse left and then Wattmanngasse right; at No 29 pause for the arresting sight of the **Lebkuchenhaus** (Gingerbread House) 11, so-called for its elaborate brown-tiled façade in majolica. At the end of Wattmanngasse take Gloriettegasse right for more sumptuous villas. Built in 1913–15 by Josef Hoffmann, the **Primavesi Villa** 12 at No 18 features two large triangular pediments with statues, and at No 21, **Villa Schopp** 13, designed by Friedrich Ohmann in 1902, is a classic piece of *Jugendstil* craftsmanship.

At the end of Gloriettegasse follow the relatively steep path left up Frank-Schalk-Platz and through the small wooded park to Pacassistrasse; from here it's an easy cruise downhill to busy Fasangartengasse. At Fasangartengasse turn left and after four blocks left again up Stranzenberg to Maxingstrasse and the **Hietzinger Friedhof** 14 (p98). From the cemetery backtrack on Maxingstrasse and cycle around the southern extremes of Schönbrunn, using the cycle path that follows Elisabethalle, Am Fasangarten and Gassmannstrasse. If you've hired a bike from Pedal Power, or somehow arranged a lock for your City Bike (bicycles are forbidden in Schönbrunn), stop at Schönbrunn's **Maria Theresia Gate** 15 and wander along to lovely **Café Gloriette** 16 (p142) for a coffee break.

Once refreshed, take the Hohenbergstrasse cycle path east to **Philadelphiabrücke U-Bahn station** 17, pass through the station and come out the other side at **Friedhof Meidling** 18 (12, Haidackergasse 6; ☻7am-6pm), a quiet cemetery overrun by wild – but cute – hamsters. Backtrack through the Philadelphiabrücke station and head east on Wilhelmstrasse past the **Schnappsmuseum** 19 (Map pp260–1; ☎ 815 73 00; 12, Wilhelmstrasse 19-21; admission €5; ☻9am-5.30pm Mon-Fri; U6 Philadelphiabrücke, ☒ 62) to Langenfeldgasse, which leads directly to the Wienzeile. From here it's a straight run back along the Wienzeile cycle path past **Café Rüdigerhof** 20 (p141) to the **Naschmarkt** 21 (p185). Admire the **Majolikahaus** 22 (p90) over well-earned refreshments, before taking Schleifmühlgasse to Operngasse and the cycle path back to Karlsplatz.

Eating ■

Eating

It's a fine thing, dining out in Vienna. The choice is extensive, the locations varied, and the cuisine global.

Beisln, a species unique to Vienna, are simple beer houses featuring wood-panelling, ceramic ovens, plain tables and hearty Viennese cuisine such as schnitzel and *Tafelspitz* (boiled beef, potatoes and horseradish sauce). The word *Beisln* originates from the Yiddish for 'little house', and they

serve Viennese from all classes of society. It's hard to find more traditional *Beisln* than Ubl (p130) and Quell (p136), and we've included a list of our favourites (see p135). *Heurigen*, informal wine taverns on the outskirts of the city, sport overflowing buffets of salads and pork, plus an endless supply of new wine; standout examples include Zawodsky (p144) and Göbel (p144). *Kaffeehäuser* (coffee houses) – esteemed cafés where pomp, ceremony and surly waiters are par for the course – serve full meals (typically Austrian cuisine) alongside rich, calorie-bomb cakes. Café Sperl (p141), Café Landtmann (p141) and Café Engländer (p140) are just a few esteemed choices. Vienna's *Würstelstand* (sausage stand; p14) fulfils the city's fast-food requirement; conveniently located on street corners and squares, these one-man stands provide ready-to-eat sausages with dark bread or hotdog buns (and for good measure, a beer). The dominance of this culinary institution is now under attack – from kebab stands.

Dining out in Vienna does have its downsides. Canine companions sometimes accompany their owners to restaurants, which raises questions of hygiene for some diners; however, this practice seems to be on the decline. Smoking in eateries is still commonplace and some smokers display scant regard for their fellow diners. If you find smoking bothersome, choose your table carefully or ask to be seated in the nonsmoking section.

The Innere Stadt hosts a wide range of superlative restaurants and cuisines. Many districts inside the Gürtel have a healthy sprinkling of fine eateries, but fewer options exist outside

Outdoor tables at Café Gloriette, Schönbrunn (p142)

the Gürtel and east of the Danube Canal. With fresh produce close at hand, the Naschmarkt (p185) has become a practical choice of location for many of Vienna's newer, and better, restaurants, while the MuseumsQuartier and its pretty neighbour Spittelberg contain their fair share of culinary highlights.

Most restaurants take reservations, and it's advisable in the more popular eateries to do so – if a restaurant consistently requires a reservation, we've said so in the review. Note that some close for a few weeks over the summer months, others for all of July and August. To be on the safe side, call ahead at this time.

Self-Catering

Vienna has plenty of supermarkets for the self-caterer. Billa, Spar and Merkur are the city's better varieties, usually containing well-stocked delis that make sandwiches to order - a quick and inexpensive way to enjoy lunch on the run. Hofer, Penny Markt and Zielpunkt are acknowledged as the cheapest, while Meinl am Graben (p181) is the cream of the crop, stocking a bonanza of gourmet delights.

In the Innere Stadt, there is an **Interspar supermarket** (Map pp254–5) on the corner of Rotenturmstrasse and Fleischmarkt, a **Billa supermarket** (Map pp254–5) on Singerstrasse and another in the basement of Ringstrassen Galerien (Map pp254–5). Otherwise ask a passer-by where the closest can be found.

Food markets abound. The best of the bunch are Naschmarkt, Brunnenmarkt, Freyung-markt and Karmelitermarkt. For information on these other markets see p185.

Outside of normal shopping hours it can be difficult to stock up on groceries. Westbahnhof has an Okay grocery store open 5.30am to 11pm daily, as does Südbahnhof. Petrol stations stock basic items but they're more expensive.

INNERE STADT

The Innere Stadt is tourist central, which means plenty of touristy restaurants; however, these are easy to spot, and therefore easy to avoid. What's left is a surprisingly large selection of fine restaurants for such a small space. The gastronomic range is quite diverse, but there's still plenty of Wiener schnitzel and *Schweinsbraten* if you so desire and while prices are a little higher than the rest of Vienna, a few budget options are hidden down the backstreets.

STEPHANSPLATZ

DO & CO STEPHANSPLATZ

Map pp254-5   International €€€
☎ 535 39 69; 01, Stephansplatz 12, Haas-Haus; mains €20-30; ⏱ noon-3pm, 6pm-midnight; ◉ U1, U3 Stephansplatz

DO & CO is still the darling of Vienna's prominent crowd (politicians, the business elite) despite a thorough renovation in 2005. Subtle lighting, pseudo lounge chairs and light-brown shades create a vaguely retro look, while the silver service and views of Stephansdom remain the same. The international menu heavily features Austrian favourites, but its highlight is the exceptional Thai cuisine.

EAST OF STEPHANSPLATZ

BEIM CZAAK Map pp254-5   Beisl €
☎ 513 72 15; 01, Postgasse 15; midday menus €6.50, mains €5.50-12.50; ⏱ 8.30am-midnight Mon-Fri, 1pm-midnight Sat; ◉ U1, U4 Schweden-platz, 🚊 N, 1, 2, 21

Beim Czaak is a polished *Beisl*, and one of only a handful left in the Innere Stadt. Meat dominates the menu, and hard choices need to be made between the likes of the *Waldvierteler Schnitzel* (with fried bacon, onions and mushrooms) and the *Haus Schnitzel* (weighted down with ham, cheese, mushrooms and onions – yum). Standard Viennese vegetarian, such as *Eiernockerl* (egg pasta) and *Spinatknödel* (spinach dumplings), are also options. In summer take advantage of the umbrella-shaded tables on the tiny square out front.

FIGLMÜLLER Map pp254-5   Beisl €€
☎ 512 61 77; 01, Wollzeile 5; mains €6.50-14; ⏱ 11am-10.30pm (closed Aug); bus 1A

Vienna, and the Viennese, would simply be a little less without Figlmüller. This famous *Beisl* has some of the biggest – and best – schnitzels in the business, and everyone knows it, including tour guides and hoteliers who direct tourists in their droves to

MENU DECODER

Useful phrases

Can you recommend a ...?	*Können Sie ... empfehlen?*
bar/pub	*eine Kneipe*
café	*ein Café*
restaurant	*ein Restaurant*
local speciality	*eine örtliche Spezialität*
A table for ..., please.	*Einen Tisch für ..., bitte.*
We have booked a table under the name ...	*Wir haben einen Tisch unter dem Namen ... reserviert.*
Do you have a menu in English?	*Haben sie eine Speisekarte in Englisch?*
I'm a vegetarian.	*Ich bin Vegetarier/Vegetarierin. (m/f)*
Is this dish spicy?	*Ist diese Speise scharf?*
What are the daily specials?	*Was sind die Tagesspezialitäten?*
I'd like the set menu, please.	*Ich hätte gerne das Tagesmenü, bitte.*
I'd like the bill, please.	*Ich würde gerne zahlen, bitte/Zahlen, bitte.*
Cheers!	*Prost!*
Bon appétit.	*Güten Appetit.*
Can I have some more ..., please.	*Bitte noch ein ...*
Is this chair/table free?	*Ist der Sessel/Tisch frei?*
Is service included in the bill?	*Ist die Bedienung inbegriffen?*

Basics

essen	to eat
trinken	to drink
das Frühstück	breakfast
das Mittagessen	lunch
das Abendessen	dinner
das Menü/Mittagsmenü	fixed-priced menu/midday menu
das Tagesmenü/die Tageskarte	menu of the day
die Speisekarte	menu
die Weinkarte	wine list

its front door. The rural decor is a little too contrived for some, and beer isn't served (only wine from the owner's own vineyard), but all in all it's an enjoyable experience.

IMMERVOLL

Map pp254-5   Austrian & International €€

☎ 513 52 88; 01, Weihburggasse 17; midday menus €7-9, mains €8-15; ☽ noon-midnight; ◉ U1, U3 Stephansplatz

Even though it changes daily, a menu strongly representing Austrian standards, and with a hint of Italian and Asian cuisine, consistently greets diners at this esteemed Innere Stadt eatery. Inside, the vaulted ceilings and subtle touches of interior design (by Hermann Czech, architect of nearby Kleines Café p141) create a surprisingly cosy space, but the best feature of all is the seating on Franziskanerplatz in summer.

Suppe & Vorspeise

Fritattensuppe	clear soup with chives and strips of pancake
Gemischter Salat	raw vegetables with tart wine or vinegar dressing
Griessnockerlsuppe	Clear beef soup with semolina dumplings
Kartoffel/Erdäpfel Salat	potato salad
Leberknödelsuppe	liver dumpling soup
Rindssuppe	clear beef soup

Soups & Starters

Hauptspeise/Hauptgerichte

Backhendl	fried breaded chicken
Bauernschmaus	platter of cold meats
Beuschel	chopped offal with sauce
Blunzengröstl	blood sausage with potatoes and onions fried in a pan
Erdäpfelgulasch	potato stew; sometimes includes meat
Grammelknödel	pork dumplings
Rindsgulasch	thick beef soup
Schweinsbraten	roast pork
Schinkenfleckerln	ovenbaked ham and noodle casserole
Semmelknödel	bread dumplings
Stelze	roast hock
Tafelspitz	boiled beef, potatoes and horseradish sauce
Tiroler Gröstl	potatoes, onions and flecks of meat fried in a pan
Wiener Schnitzel	breaded veal cutlets (sometimes with pork or turkey)
Zwiebelrostbraten	slices of roast beef smothered in gravy and fried onions

Mains

Nachspeise

Apfelstrudel	apple strudel
Germknödel	yeast dumplings with poppy seeds
Kaiserschmarrn	sweet pancake with raisins
Marillenknödel	apricot dumplings
Mohr im Hemd	chocolate pudding with whipped cream and chocolate sauce
Palatschinken	crepes
Topfenknödel	cheese dumplings

Desserts

HOTEL RIVIERA Map pp254-5   European €€

☎ 907 61 49; 01, Schönlaterngasse 13; midday menu €6, mains €10-15; ⏱ 10-2am Mon-Sat; Ⓜ U1, U4 Schwedenplatz, 🚊 N, 1, 2, 21

Neatly tucked away in the backstreets of the Innere Stadt is Riviera, a lovely little restaurant with plenty of charm and charisma. The menu is a creative blend of Italian and Austrian cuisine; homemade gnocchi with tomato-basil sauce or truffle oil and Parmesan sits alongside grilled zander with carrot strudel, as do traditional options such as schnitzel or *Tafelspitz*. Seasonal ingredients feature heavily, so expect a selection of *Eierschwammerl* (chanterelle mushrooms), apricot, asparagus or wild-game dishes throughout the year. Service is fresh and unpretentious, the decor plain and very creamy. In summer Riviera shares the square outside with Beim Czaak.

GRIECHENBEISL Map pp254-5　　Beisl €€

☎ 533 19 77; 01, Fleischmarkt 11; mains €11-24;
⏰ 11-1am; ⓤ U1, U4 Schwedenplatz, 🚊 N, 1, 2, 21
As the oldest guesthouse in Vienna (it
first opened its doors in 1447), and once
frequented by the likes of Ludwig van
Beethoven, Franz Schubert and Johannes
Brahms, Griechenbeisl is a firm fixture on
the tourist trail. It's still a lovely haunt, with
vaulted rooms, age-old wooden panelling
and a figure of Augustin trapped at the
bottom of a well stands just inside the front
door. Every classic Viennese dish is on the
menu, and in summer the plant-fringed
front garden is the best place to be.

NEU WIEN Map pp254-5　　Austrian €€

☎ 512 09 00; 01, Bäckerstrasse 5; mains €16-19,
menu €32; ⏰ 6pm-1am Mon-Sat; bus 1A, 2A, 3A
Neu Wien is a plush new restaurant on
the edge of the Innere Stadt's medieval
quarter, with the look and feel of a lounge
bar (low leather seats, well-stocked bar).
The cuisine harks back to the days of the
Habsburg empire, with the likes of roasted
fillet of zander, fillet of Alp ox, and proper
veal Wiener schnitzel filling the menu, but
there are a few unusual dishes too, like
mushroom *Gulasch* (goulash). After the
meal, head downstairs to KIK (Kultur im
Keller) for cabaret and live music.

EXPEDIT Map pp254-5　　Italian €€

☎ 512 33 13-0; 01, Wiesingerstrasse 6; mains €8-25;
⏰ noon-midnight Mon-Fri, 6-midnight Sat; 🚊 1, 2
Expedit has successfully moulded itself on a
Ligurian *Osteria* and become one of the most
popular Italian restaurants in town. Its warehouse décor, with shelves stocked full of oil,
pesto, olives and wine from Liguria, helps to
create a busy yet informal atmosphere and
a clean, smart look. Every day brings new,
seasonal dishes to the menu, but count on a
few divine vegetarian, meat and fish specialities. Reservations are recommended.

KÄRNTNER STRASSE, GRABEN & KOHLMARKT

TRZESNIEWSKI Map pp254-5　　Fast Food €

☎ 512 32 91; 01, Dorotheergasse 1; breads from
€3; ⏰ 8.30am-7.30pm Mon-Fri, 9am-5pm Sat;
ⓤ U1, U3 Stephansplatz
Possibly the finest sandwich shop in
Austria, Trzesniewski has been serving
spreads and breads to the entire spectrum
of Viennese (Kafka was a regular here) for
over 100 years. Choose from 21 delectably
thick spreads – paprika, tuna with egg,
salmon, and Swedish herring are but a few
examples – for your choice of bread, or
simply pick a selection from those waiting
ready-made. Plan on sampling a few; two

WE ALL SCREAM FOR ICE CREAM!

It's a sticky summer's day in the city – what's a visitor to do? Head for the nearest ice-cream parlour, as any hot-and-
bothered Viennese would. These places are our favourites:

Am Schwedenplatz (Map pp254-5; ☎ 533 19 96; 01, Franz-Josefs-Kai 17; ice cream from €1.70; ⏰ 10am-11pm
Mar-Sep; ⓤ U1, U4 Schwedenplatz, 🚊 N, 1, 2, 21) Over 75 years in the ice cream business; huge selection of ice
cream flavours, including those made without milk, with organic milk, and choices suitable for diabetics.

Eissalon Tuchlauben (Map pp254-5; ☎ 533 25 53; 01, Tuchlauben 15; ice cream from €1.70; ⏰ 10am-11.30pm
Mon-Sat, 11am-11.30pm Sun mid-Mar-Sep; bus 2A, 3A) Over 20 creamy ice-cream sorts that change with the
seasons, completely nonsmoking, and a constant queue for takeaways that moves quickly.

Gelateria Hoher Markt (Map pp254-5; ☎ 533 32 97-1; 01, Hoher Markt 4; ice cream from €1.70; ⏰ 7.30am-
11.30pm Mon-Sat, 10am-11.30pm Sun; bus 1A, 2A, 3A) Thirty varieties, an assortment of elaborate sundaes, outdoor
seating and picturesque surroundings.

Tichy (Map pp262-3; ☎ 604 44 46; 10, Reumannplatz 13; ice cream from €1.50; ⏰ 10am-11pm mid-Mar-Sep;
ⓤ U1 Reumannplatz) Ice-cream parlour of legendary status in Vienna. Pioneered the *Eismarillenknödel* (ball of
vanilla ice cream with apricot jam centre) and has three varieties of diabetic-friendly ice cream.

Zanoni Facincani (Map pp258-9; ☎ 406 82 31; 18, Währinger Gürtel 3; ice cream from €1.50; ⏰ 10am-11.30pm
mid-Feb–mid-Oct; ⓤ U6 Alserstrasse, 🚊 43) Authentic Italian ice cream, cheeky staff and over 40 flavours.

Zanoni Luciano (Map pp254-5; ☎ 512 79 79; 01, Lugeck 7; ice cream from €1.70; ⏰ 7am-midnight; bus 1A, 2A,
3A) One of the biggest and best-known ice cream parlours in the city; despite it's popularity its standard of delectable
ice cream (around 35 varieties) hasn't dropped.

bites and they're gone. This branch is one of seven in Vienna.

ROSENBERGER MARKT RESTAURANT
Map pp254-5   Viennese Buffet €

☎ 512 34 58; 01, Maysedergasse 2; meals around €10; ⊗ 10.30am-11pm; U1, ⊕ U2, U4 Karlsplatz, 🚋 D, J, 1, 2, 62, 65, bus 3A

Rosenberger provides a huge array of ready-made pasta meals, cooked meats, salads, freshly squeezed juices and desserts to the hungry mouths of the Innere Stadt. While the food is good and filling, the main reason for visiting is the low cost; watch out for extras like bread and butter which can push up the price. The seating area is enormous and the layouts, which range from a traditional Viennese coffee house to a *Heuriger* cellar, are kitsch but fun.

YOHM Map pp254-5   Asian €€

☎ 533 29 00; 01, Petersplatz 3; midday menu €16-20, mains €12-20; ⊗ noon-3pm & 6pm-midnight; ⊕ U1, U3 Stephansplatz, bus 2A

A typical scene in Yohm: black-clad waiters glide from table to table, refilling glasses with celebrated Austrian wines as diners enjoy views of Peterskirche with their contemporary Asian cuisine. Sushi looms large on the menu, but consider ordering one of the kitchen's more creative offerings, something like udon noodles with Scottish salmon or fried duck roll with fresh mint and plum sauce. For all its class, it's a wonder that meals are served with cheap wooden chopsticks.

MEINL AM GRABEN
Map pp254-5   International €€€

☎ 532 33 34; 01, Graben 19; mains from €30, 3-course set menu €34; ⊗ 8.30am-midnight Mon-Wed, 8am-midnight Thu & Fri, 9am-midnight Sat; ⊕ U1, U3 Stephansplatz, bus 1A, 2A, 3A

Ranked among the top five restaurants in the country, Meinl am Graben combines cuisine of superlative quality with an unrivalled wine list and views of the Graben. Head chef Joachim Gradwohl creates a daily menu of inviting dishes with delicate Mediterranean sauces and sweet aromas; the ingredients are the freshest of fresh, direct from the city's best gourmet supermarket just downstairs. The waiters professional to a fault, but the atmosphere is surprisingly relaxed and easy-going.

Würstelstand am Hoher Markt (p124)

HOFBURG

SOHO   Map pp254-5   International €

☎ 0676-309 51 61; 01, am Josefplatz 1; menu €4.90-5.40; ⊗ 9.30am-4pm Mon-Fri; ⊕ U1, U2, U4 Karlsplatz, 🚋 D, J, 1, 2, 62, 65

Soho is the Hofburg's canteen, with excellent food at canteen prices. Daily menus – one vegetarian, one meat – are invariably European based, but the occasional Asian dish sneaks in now and then. The simple wooden tables, splashes of colour and smattering of paintings combine to create an appealing look, and the service is welcoming and friendly. It's a little hard to find, however: follow your nose past the Schmetterlinghaus (p64) and it's directly west.

NORTH OF HOFBURG

SOUPKULTUR Map pp254-5   Soups & Salads €

☎ 532 46 28; 01, Wipplingerstrasse 32; soups around €5, salads around €7; ⊗ 11.30am-3.30pm Mon-Thu, 11.30am-3pm Fri; bus 1A, 3A

Soupkultur caters to office workers in search of a healthy bite on the run. Organic produce and aromatic spices are used to create eight different soups and six varieties of salads each week, which can range from red-lentil soup or traditional Hungarian goulash to Caesar salad or chicken and orange salad. There is a token seating area, but count on taking it away (a leafy park is just around the corner).

JEWISH QUARTER & AROUND
WÜRSTELSTAND AM HOHER MARKT
Map pp254-5   Sausage Stand €

01, Hoher Markt; sausages from €3; ⏱ 7am-4am; bus 1A, 2A, 3A

Würstelstand am Hoher Markt attracts people from all walks of life with its consistently good sausages, central location and long opening hours. Try the *Käsekrainer*, a hearty sausage infused with cheese; it can be a messy affair, but something you won't forget in a hurry. If you're feeling cocky, order it with *Eitrige mit an Buckl* (loosely translated, it's the equivalent of 'a hunchback full of pus') which will get you the sausage plus the highly prized end of the bread loaf – or an unintelligible Viennese insult.

MASCHU MASCHU
Map pp254-5   Oriental/Israeli €

☎ 533 29 04; 01, Rabensteig 8; mains €3-8; ⏱ 11.30am-midnight Sun-Wed, 11.30-4am Thu-Sat; ◎ U1, U4 Schwedenplatz, 🚊 N, 1, 2, 21

Speedy service, a relaxed atmosphere, and the freshest falafels, hummus and salads are the keys to Maschu Maschu's success. This branch on Rabensteig, with its meagre number of tables, is better used as a takeaway joint (grab the best pitta falafel

---

MENSEN

Mensen (university cafeterias) are open to the general public and provide the cheapest sit-down meal in the Innere Stadt. Normally they only open Monday to Friday and offer a limited range of two or three daily specials, including a vegetarian choice. The food won't win any awards, but it's filling and, to drive a point home, cheap. These are three of the bigger *Mensen*:

Universität Mensa (Map pp254-5; ☎ 406 45 94; 01, Universitätsstrasse 7; full meals around €8; ⏱ lunch Mon-Fri; ◎ U2 Schottentor, 🚊 37, 38, 40, 41, 42, 43, 44) Take the doorless, continuous lift to the 6th floor (which is worth the trip in itself).

Katholisches Studenthaus Mensa (Map pp254-5; ☎ 408 35 85; 01, Ebendorferstrasse 8; mains €3.50-5.50; ⏱ lunch Mon-Fri, closed Aug–mid-Sep; ◎ U2 Schottentor, 🚊 37, 38, 40, 41, 42, 43, 44)

Music Academy Mensa (Map pp254-5; ☎ 512 94 70; 01, Johannesgasse 8; mains €4-5; ⏱ lunch Mon-Fri, only to 1.30pm during summer holidays; 🚊 1, 2) You may be lucky enough to hear music students rehearsing one classical piece or another over lunch.

---

in Vienna and stroll the old Jewish quarter), while the Neubaugasse branch (Map pp260–1; ☎ 990 47 13; 07, Neubaugasse 20; mains €4-18; ⏱ 11am-midnight; ◎ U3 Neubaugasse) is a fully fledged restaurant with sunny streetside seating and a menu loaded with lamb cutlet dishes.

BODEGA MARQUÉS Map pp254-5   Spanish €€
☎ 533 91 70; 01, Parisergasse 1; tapas €3.50-15; ⏱ 5pm-1am Mon-Sat; bus 2A, 3A

Calamari specialities, *Gambas* (shrimps) and over 30 different tapas straight from Spain help make Bodega Marqués an excellent choice for dining in the Innere Stadt. The 120 varieties of wine also do their part, but the sheer volume of choice can be overwhelming. The vaulted ceilings and subdued lighting create a romantic atmosphere, except on Friday and Saturday nights when live flamenco music is featured.

EN Map pp254-5   Japanese €€
☎ 532 44 90; 01, Werdertorgasse 8; midday menus €8-9.50, mains €8-15; ⏱ 11.30am-2.30pm, 5.30-10.30pm Mon-Sat; bus 3A

A Tokyo chef and Hokkaido staff have banded together to create an exceptionally good Japanese restaurant in a quiet corner of the Innere Stadt. The 14 varieties of sushi (including octopus and sweet shrimp) are well above par; unlike many places in Vienna, EN is generous with the fresh fish and stingy on the rice. The wasabi is nicely sharp but not overpowering, the gyoza delightful, and some warm sake or *genmai-cha* (green tea with roasted rice) makes a perfect accompaniment. The atmosphere is suitably peaceful and respectful.

WRENKH Map pp254-5   Vegetarian €€
☎ 533 15 26; 01, Bauernmarkt 10; midday menus from €7.70, mains €10-18; ⏱ 11.30am-11.30pm Mon-Sat; ◎ U1, U3 Stephansplatz

Wrenkh has been leading the way in vegetarian cuisine for years but its owner, Christian Wrenkh, recently decided to introduce a handful of meat and fish dishes to the menu. The quality and presentation is still exquisite though, and everything is prepared with organic produce. Choose from the vibrant front section with its glass walls and chatty customers, or the quieter rear room with its intimate booths. Self service and takeaway is also available from noon to 4pm Monday to Friday.

Eating   INNERE STADT

A GOOD START TO THE DAY

The Viennese like a good weekend brunch, and can spend hours over coffee and croissants. The following places are all excellent for breakfast or brunch (as are many places on the Naschmarkt), whether your choice be hearty or healthy:

Breakfast Club (p131) Restaurant devoted to the first meal of the day, with ten choices and a separate menu aimed at children.

Das Möbel (p158) Huge breakfast buffet to set you going for the day, with breads, spreads, sheep's cheese, sausage, cereals, eggs, eight juices, 18 teas and the usual coffee selection.

Do-An (p129) Glass box on the Naschmarkt with an international array of breakfasts, easy-going air and plenty of passers-by; tables are hard to come by on sunny Saturday mornings.

Kent (p136) Turkish breakfasts in huge garden; of the six omelette choices, *Melemen* (omelette with tomato and paprika) comes out on top, but the *Kent Kahvalti* (sheep's cheese, sausage, tomatoes, eggs, olives, tea or coffee) is the definitive Turkish breakfast.

Mas! (p159) From 10am to 4pm Sunday Mas! puts on an all-you-can-eat Mexican buffet (€18) of cereals, omelettes, cheeses, sausage, fruits, cakes and coffee; sit back and enjoy it all day.

LIVINGSTONE   Map pp254-5   Californian €€
☎ 533 33 93; 01, Zelinkagasse 4; mains €14-19; ⏰ 5pm-4am; 🚋 1, 2, bus 3A

A creative menu and long hours (the kitchen closes at 3.30am) have helped keep Livingstone on Vienna's culinary short list for some time. Strips of marinated beef with ginger sits comfortably alongside Japanese soba noodles and the chilli-burger, and in between servings it's possible to nip in for a wee drab of whiskey at bar Planters next door.

ZUM SCHWARZEN KAMEEL

Map pp254-5   International €€
☎ 533 81 25; 01, Bognergasse 5; sandwiches around €3, soups €6, mains from €20; ⏰ 8.30am-midnight Mon-Sat; bus 1A, 2A

Zum Schwarzen Kameel is a strange combination of deli/sandwich shop and highbrow wine bar. The high-society set who frequents this place normally nibble on sandwiches at the bar while pondering which *Achterl* (glass of wine) to select from the lengthy list. Soups are available to go, while more substantial dishes are offered in the wood-panelled dining area upstairs.

RINGSTRASSE

There aren't a lot of eating options on the Ringstrasse – this prestigious street caters more to grand civic buildings, luxury hotels and expensive car dealerships – but the few choices available are of the highest standard.

The MuseumsQuartier is a tad more relaxed. Home to innovative cafés and hip restaurants, it attracts a younger crowd intent on lingering over coffee, food and conversation, and possibly engaging in a bit of talent spotting.

SCHOTTENTOR TO PARLAMENT

VESTIBÜL   Map pp254-5   International €€€
☎ 532 49 99; 01, Dr-Karl-Lueger-Ring 2; evening menus from €39, mains €16-24; ⏰ 11.30am-midnight Mon-Fri, 6pm-midnight Sat; 🚋 D, 1, 2

Vestibül takes pride of place in the southern wing of the Burgtheater. The interior is a heady mix of marble columns and chandeliers, and is topped off with a glorious sparkling mirrored bar. The menu features anything from good old Wiener schnitzel to octopus tartare with gherkin-mango salad, and it's hard to make a wine choice because the dozens on offer all look inviting. Reservations are recommended.

MUSEUMSQUARTIER

KANTINE   Map pp254-5   Café €
☎ 523 82 39; 07, Museumsplatz 1; daily menus €5.90-6.90, pitta breads €4.50-9; ⏰ 10am-midnight Sun-Wed, 10-2am Thu-Sat; 🚇 U2 Museumsquartier, U2, U3 Volkstheater

An upbeat café-bar housed in the former stables of the emperor's personal steeds, Kantine is the most laid-back spot to eat

Interior of Una (this page)

in the MuseumsQuartier. If the fresh daily menu – typically an Asian or Viennese dish with a vegetarian or fish choice thrown in – is sold out, meat- and salad-filled pitta breads will fill the gap. Grab a cocktail from the extensive list and make good use of the outdoor patio on MQ's main square.

HALLE Map pp254-5 International €

☎ 523 70 01; 07, Museumsplatz 1; midday menus €7, mains from €7; ☒ 10-2am; U2 Museums-quartier, Ⓜ U2, U3 Volkstheater

Managed by the owners of Motto (p131), Halle is the resident eatery of the Kun-sthalle. The interior has plenty of optical tricks, like cylindrical lamps and low tables, and the kitchen churns out antipastos, pastas, salads and Asian dishes to eager tourists and Vienna's 'see and be seen' crowd. On steamy summer days and it's usually a fight for an outside table between the Kunsthalle and MUMOK.

UNA Map pp254-5 Café €€

☎ 523 65 66; 07, Museumsplatz 1; mains €7-15; ☒ 9am-midnight Mon-Fri, 10am-midnight Sat, 10am-6pm Sun; Ⓜ U2 Museumsquartier, U2, U3 Volkstheater

Una resides in one of the original wings of the Habsburg imperial stables, and what

striking stables they are, with gorgeous Turkish tiles, arched ceilings and massive windows. The light menu features simple but carefully prepared fare, such as pasta dishes, vegetarian strudels, and seasonal specialities. The wine list is commendable and the atmosphere, and staff, refreshingly unpretentious.

EAST OF THE DANUBE CANAL

Leopoldstadt, Vienna's 2nd district, contains the lion's share of restaurants east of the Danube Canal. It's within easy striking distance by foot of the Innere Stadt, and has none of the pomp and ceremony of its larger and more illustrious neighbour. It's also a district slowly cultivating a cosmopolitan outlook, which is reflected in its restaurants. Across the Danube, options start to thin out, aside from the *Heurigen* neighbourhoods of Strebersdorf and Stammersdorf, but a few traditional *Gasthäuser* (guesthouses) line the banks of the Alte Donau.

CONTOR Map pp258-9 Spanish €€

☎ 219 63 16; 02, Leopoldgasse 51; tapas €4-8; ☒ 5pm-1am Mon-Thu, 5pm-2am Fri, 10am-2am Sat; bus 5A

Contor is a cosy and intimate tapas bar right on the Karmelitermarkt. Its delectable tapas are perfectly complimented by around 40 wines (from Spain, Italy and Austria), the freshest cheese from Lower Austria and the occasional impromptu guitar concert. Perfect for a romantic evening.

STRANDGASTHAUS BIRNER

Map pp252-3 Viennese €€

☎ 271 53 63; 21, An der Oberen Alten Donau 47; midday menus €5, mains €5-12; ☒ 9am-11pm Thu-Tue summer, 9am-10pm Thu-Tue winter; Ⓜ U6 Floridsdorf, Ⓡ 26

Like the Schweizerhaus (opposite), Strand-gasthaus Birner is a legend in Vienna. Its sun-drenched terrace overlooking the Alte Donau is one of the finest spots in summer, and the fish specialities from the kitchen irresistible; don't pass up a chance to try one of the sublime fish soups. Be aware that summer and winter opening times aren't date-specific but rather determined by the weather.

GESUNDES Map pp254-5   Organic/Vegetarian €
☎ 219 53 22; 02, Lilienbrunngasse 3; midday menus €7.60-9.60; ☻ 9am-3pm Mon-Sat; ⊙ U1, U4 Schwedenplatz, ⊠ N

Healthy food, a healthy ambience and a healthy attitude prevail at Gesundes, a tiny organic eatery and shop across the canal from the Innere Stadt. Vegetarian and vegan dishes are prepared using the principles of the five Chinese elements (wood, fire, earth, metal, water) to strike a balance of wellbeing in the body; the menu changes daily but expect lightly spiced earthy dishes (polenta, rice, potatoes, vegetables) complimented by freshly squeezed fruit juices. Cooking courses are also available (p128).

SCHWEIZERHAUS Map pp258-9   Austrian €€
☎ 728 01 52; 02, Strasse des Ersten Mai 116; mains €8-15; ☻ 11am-11pm Mon-Fri, 10am-11pm Sat & Sun mid-Mar–Oct; ⊙ U1 Praterstern, ⊠ 0, 5, 21

Every Viennese knows the Schweizerhaus. It's famous for its massive, tree-shaded

---

ÖSTERREICHER IM MAK

It's not unusual for a restaurant to be named after the head chef, but it is if the chef doesn't own the premises. So respected is the cooking of Helmut Österreicher that the newly renovated café of MAK renamed itself **Österreicher im MAK** (Map pp254–5; ☎ 714 01 21; 01, Stubenring 5; mains around €20; ☻ 10am-1am; ⊙ U3 Stubentor, ⊠ 1, 2) in fullest of confidence. Österreicher, arguably the top chef in the country, has been in the business for decades. He has worked at the Hotel Sacher, taken Steireck im Stadtpark (p129) to the top of Austria's restaurant scene, and collected numerous awards, including Gault Millau's 'Cook of the Decade' in 2001. Now, as resident head chef in Österreicher im MAK – a contemporary take on the traditional Viennese *Beisl* – he is using his exceptional culinary talents to bring Viennese cuisine to the fore; the restaurant uses solely Austrian products (aside from seafood) and creates both classical and modern Viennese dishes. He filled us in on his new restaurant and the city's dining scene.

Lonely Planet: Österreicher im MAK focuses on Viennese cuisine, why is this?
Österreicher: There is a 'Back to the Roots' trend in the city's dining scene and Viennese cuisine is very modern and in great demand. People are turning towards simplicity in their food, and are once again looking for indigenous dishes.

Lonely Planet: Your menu features both classical and modern Viennese cuisine – can you give a brief overview of the two?
Österreicher: Classical Viennese cuisine is dishes that are identical to the old recipes, not changed in any way, whereas modern Viennese cuisine integrates the spirit and style of classical Viennese but doesn't limit itself to regional products, creatively introducing new ones.

Lonely Planet: Austrian and Viennese food is often regarded as hefty portions of heavy food, yet MAK has gone for smaller servings with an emphasis on simplicity and taste. Why?
Österreicher: Austrian cuisine is no heavier – or lighter – than food from other countries. We try not to cook common servings because we want to give our guests the opportunity to try several courses. People are also going for smaller servings because of a higher awareness of health.

Lonely Planet: How important are seasonal ingredients in Austrian cooking?
Österreicher: Seasonal ingredients are essential in good home-style cooking – it is not possible without them. It is the clock inside of cooks, it is a matter of course!

Lonely Planet: How have you seen the Viennese dining experience change over the past five years? How have you seen the eating habits of the Viennese change?
Österreicher: The Viennese are now very open-minded and eager to try different styles of cuisine. Favourite restaurants often change, but there is a longing for traditional cuisine. Many Viennese are also very food health-conscious.

Lonely Planet: What do you see for the future of Viennese cuisine?
Österreicher: I see the future of Viennese cuisine as a flavourful high-class cuisine, a cuisine with plenty of regional influences from the former monarchy. When we keep cooking in our pure cultural style our cuisine will always endure.

Lonely Planet: What's your favourite Austrian dish? What do you like to cook at home?
Österreicher: It is Viennese onion roast (*Zwiebelrostbraten*)! I like to cook salads & vegetable dishes at home.

garden, which is constantly full, but it's more famous for what it serves: *Hintere Schweinsstelze* (roasted pork hocks). These gargantuan chunks of meat on the bone (€14.30 per kg, 750g minimum), best served with mustard and freshly grated horseradish, taste supremely better than they sound and are best shared between two. There are also chicken, beef and fish dishes, but vegetarians will have to stick to starters and salads. Wash it all down with draught Budweiser (the Czech stuff) direct from the barrel.

SCHÖNE PERLE Map pp258-9   Neo-Beisl €
☎ 243 35 93; 02, Grosse Pfarrgasse 2; midday menus €7, mains €7-11; 🕑 noon-midnight Mon-Fri, 11am-midnight Sat & Sun; bus 5A
Schöne Perle (beautiful pearl) has the look and feel of a well-designed student cafeteria, but the food is by no means as basic or as bland. Classic Austrian dishes, such as *Tafelspitz* and *Zwiebelrostbraten*, are mixed in with vegetarian and fish mains, and all are created with organic produce. Wines are from Austria, as are the large array of juices. Unusually for a Viennese restaurant, dogs are forbidden and kids welcome.

LUSTHAUS Map pp262-3   Austrian €€
☎ 728 95 65; 02, Freudenau 254; mains €8.70-18; 🕑 noon-11pm Mon-Fri, noon-6pm Sat & Sun May-Sep, noon-6pm Thu-Tue Nov-Mar; bus 77A
The Lusthaus is a former hunting lodge from the Habsburg days, with an abundance of 19th-century elegance. The menu is a mix of hearty Austrian specialities and lighter options; Wiener schnitzel is of course present, but so is *Steirischer Backhendlsalat* (Styrian chicken salad) and *Trüffel-Gnocchi* (truffle-gnocchi). Count on plenty of seasonal dishes too. The Lusthaus is in the heart of the Prater and best visited in combination with a long walk in the park.

INSIDE THE GÜRTEL

As with shops and bars, this is the area where Vienna's cuisine culture likes to experiment. It's been at the forefront of the city's eating scene for some years, and the trend continues unabated – Persian, Chinese, Japanese, Italian, French, Bohemian and, of course, a healthy dose of Austrian

are here to sample, scintillate and satisfy. Quality is generally high, as is the standard of service, and many places are relaxed, young and accommodating.

A major concentration of eateries is centred on the Naschmarkt, Vienna's premiere food market; the sights, smells and spices here are highly evocative – a perfect aperitif for dining out. **Summer Stage** (Map pp258-9; 09, Rossauer Lände; 🕑 5pm-1am May-Sep; 🚇 U4 Rossauer Lände), on the banks of the Danube Canal, is another spot for indecisive diners. Its diverse range of restaurants, which set up temporary stands over the summer months, and festive atmosphere (there's regular jazz and classical concerts in the evening) make it an appealing destination.

LANDSTRASSE

GASTHAUS WILD Map pp254-5   Neo-Beisl €€
☎ 920 94 77; 03, Radetzkyplatz 1; midday menus €7, mains €7-19; 🕑 10am-1am; 🚇 N, 0
Unassuming Radetzkyplatz is home to Gasthaus Wild, a former dive of a *Beisl* but now a sensational restaurant. Its dark, wood-panelled interior has been scrubbed and polished and the menu upgraded to not only include favourites like *Gulasch* and *Schnitzel mit Erdäpfelsalat* (schnitzel with potato salad), but also more imaginative dishes which change regularly. The ambience is relaxed, the staff welcoming and the wine selection good.

COOKING COURSES

Like something you've tried and want to reproduce it at home? Here's where you can learn a few cooking tips from old hands:

Babettes (p186; courses €100-120) Offers evening courses for a variety of cuisines including Viennese; the end result is a five-course meal.

Gesundes (p127; courses €48) Evening courses cover the five elements, vegetarian/vegan/microbiotic cuisine and all-round healthy cooking.

Kim Kocht (p135; courses €110) Try a 90-minute cooking course with Vienna's queen of organic Asian cuisine. Places are scarce so plan ahead.

Wrenkh (p124; courses from €75) Learn from Vienna's best vegetarian chef, including his tips on breakfasts.

STEIRERECK IM STADTPARK

Map pp254-5   Austrian €€€

☎ 713 31 68; 03, Steirereck im Stadtpark; mains €20-40, menus from €85; ⏱ noon-3pm, 7pm-midnight Mon-Fri; Ⓜ U3 Stubentor, ⓡ 1, 2

A gourmet restaurant of some repute, Steirereck im Stadtpark has been wowing diners for years and surprised many by moving to its current location in peaceful Stadtpark a couple of years ago. Lunch and dinner are a six-course affair (usually with two choices per course), with seasonal cuisine leading the way. An accompanying course of wine is an additional €50. Also of interest is the riverside Meierei (named after the nightclub formerly located here) milk bar; it lurks at the back of the restaurant and offers an amazing 150 cheeses and outstanding desserts.

WIEDEN

DO-AN Map pp254-5   Café €

☎ 585 82 53; 04, Naschmarkt 412; breakfast €4-6, salads €4.80-6.60; ⏱ 8am-10pm Mon-Sat; Ⓜ U4 Kettenbrückengasse

Do-An's menu is so successful it's hardly changed in the six years it's been open. Excellent Illy coffee is a perfect starter, followed by a range of simple sandwiches and salads, but you might be tempted to skip straight to one of the breakfasts from around the globe; the American reads more like a traditional English fry-up and the Continental is a nice, light starter of bread and spreads. Like Naschmarkt Deli (below), Do-An is a rectangular aquarium with huge glass walls and a steadfast following which enjoys the relaxed vibe and sunny corners.

NASCHMARKT DELI Map pp254-5 American €

☎ 585 08 23; 04, Naschmarkt 421; sandwiches €4-7, mains €6-9; ⏱ 8am-midnight Mon-Sat; Ⓜ U4 Kettenbrückengasse

One of Vienna's many eateries with bars, Naschmarkt Deli has cornered the Naschmarkt snack market. Sandwiches, falafel wraps, big baguettes and quick soups (lentil soup is a good bet) fill the menu, but the most space is left for a heady array of breakfasts. Come Saturday morning this glass box overflows with punters waiting expectantly for the Continental or English breakfast. Connoisseurs will note the latter is incomplete – no tomatoes, mushrooms, or baked beans. Shame.

MR LEE Map pp254-5   Asian €

☎ 581 45 60; 04, Naschmarkt 278; mains €6-10; ⏱ 10.30am-10.30pm Mon-Sat; Ⓜ U1, U2, U4 Karlsplatz

If the smells wafting from the door of this small Asian diner don't pull you inside, there's a good chance the smiling, friendly staff greeting passers-by will. The menu wanders across much of Asia, taking in Japanese sushi, Thai green curries and Chinese noodle dishes. Take a pew inside and watch the cooks prepare your meal in front of your eyes, or a table outside and enjoy the hustle and bustle of the Naschmarkt.

CHANG ASIAN NOODLES

Map pp262-3   Asian €

☎ 961 92 12; 04, Waaggasse 1; midday menus €5.70-6.90, mains €6.50-10; ⏱ 11.30am-3pm, 5.30-11pm Mon-Sat; ⓡ 62, 65

Chang is a small, well-established Asian diner a short walk from the Innere Stadt. The venue is bright, open, uncomplicated and highly relaxed, while the service is quick and attentive. Noodles (either fried or in a soup) are the mainstay of a menu spanning the Asian continent (at least from China to Singapore) – expect plenty of chicken, prawns (both baby and tiger) and vegetable choices. Everything is available for takeaway.

TOKO RI Map pp254-5   Japanese €

☎ 587 26 16; 04, Naschmarkt 261-263; midday box €7-9, sushi, sashimi & maki €5-9; ⏱ 11am-11pm Mon-Sat; Ⓜ U1, U2, U4 Karlsplatz

Toko Ri consistently delivers some of the best sushi in the city, despite the mounting competition. Fresh sushi, sashimi and *maki* (nori rolls) are the mainstay of the menu, but Korean dishes are also available. The buzzing surroundings of the Naschmarkt are also a big hit with diners, but if this doesn't suit, grab something to go.

INDIAN PAVILLON Map pp254-5   Indian €

☎ 587 85 61; 04, Naschmarkt 74-75; mains €7-13; ⏱ 11am-6.30pm Mon-Fri, 11am-5pm Sat; Ⓜ U1, U2, U4 Karlsplatz

Indian Pavillon is easily the smallest Indian in the city, but it's also the best. Using the freshest ingredients direct from the Naschmarkt, it whips up a storm of soups (the lentil soup is a must), lamb and chicken curries, biryanis, and *thali* (platters), all of

VIENNA'S BEST SCHNITZELS

- Figlmüller (p119) – central and touristy, but the schnitzels still wow the critics
- Gasthaus Wickerl (p135) – schnitzels like *Mutter* used to make, served in relaxed surroundings
- Schloss Concordia (p136) – quantity *and* quality – the biggest range in the city, and very, very good
- Zu den Zwei Liesln (p133) – gigantic schnitzels loved by high rollers and students alike
- Zum Alten Fassl (opposite) – touch of class, and a gorgeous garden to boot

which can be washed down with a cold Cobra beer. While the dishes have certainly been tempered for the Viennese palate, there's still enough bite to please. The handful of tables fill up quickly, so you may have to be happy with takeaway.

UBL Map pp260-1 Beisl €
☎ 587 64 37; 04, Pressgasse 26; mains around €10; ⏲ noon-2pm, 6pm-midnight; bus 59A
This much-loved *Beisl* is a favourite of the Wieden crowd. Its menu is heavily loaded with Viennese classics, such as *Schinken-fleckerl, Schweinsbraten* and four types of schnitzel, and is enhanced with seasonal cuisine throughout the year. You could do worse than finish the hefty meal off with a stomach-settling plum schnapps. The quiet, tree-shaded garden is wonderful in summer.

TANCREDI Map pp260-1 Neo-Beisl €€
☎ 941 00 48; 04, Grosse Neugasse 5; mains €7-16; ⏲ 11.30am-2.30pm, 6pm-midnight Tue-Fri, 6pm-midnight Sat; 🚋 62, 65
This former *Beisl* attracts a more affluent clientele with lovingly prepared regional and fish specialities, seasonal fare (the chef casually but confidently told us 'it's a mix of cuisines, but generally what's in season'), *bio* (organic) products and an extensive range of Austrian wines. The harmonious

surroundings are the icing on the cake: warm, pastel-yellow walls, stripped-back wooden floors, fittings from yesteryear and a tree-shaded garden that fills up quickly in summer. The entrance is on Rubengasse.

AROMAT Map pp260-1 International €€
☎ 913 24 53; 04, Margaretenstrasse 52; menus €7.50, mains €10-15; ⏲ 11am-10pm Tue-Sun, closed mid-Jul–Aug; bus 59A
Fusion cooking is the mainstay of this funky little eatery. A mixture of Upper Austrian and Vietnamese cuisine fills the menu, but that's as certain as anyone can be with a menu that changes daily with the whims of the chef. The food, which is always fresh, is cooked right in front of diners (the kitchen is open for all to see), and often caters for those with an intolerance to wheat and gluten. The charming surroundings feature simple Formica tables, 1950s fixtures, a blackboard menu, and one huge glass frontage. Personable staff help to create a convivial, bar-like atmosphere.

CHANG ASIAN DUCK Map pp262-3 Asian €€
☎ 208 70 93; 04, Waaggasse 3; mains €13-16, set menus €22-30; ⏲ 11.30am-3pm, 5.30-11pm Mon-Sat, 5.30-11pm Sun; 🚋 62,65
Chang Asian Duck is the classier brother of Chang Asian Noodles (p129), with soothing shades of red and brown, an intimate atmosphere, and a focus on floral art. The cuisine is wok-based, and as the name suggests, the speciality here is duck; duck breast in a tangy orange sauce and grilled-duck curry are both highlights, but the godly Beijing duck, which must be ordered two days in advance to allow proper marination, tops the bill. After the meal retire to the lounge bar downstairs for cocktails.

UMAR Map pp254-5 Fish €€
☎ 587 04 56; 04, Naschmarkt 76; midday menu €10-13, mains €8-35; ⏲ 10am-midnight Mon-Sat; 🚇 U1, U2, U4 Karlsplatz
Umar ranks as one of the best fish restaurants in the business, and puts nearby Nordsee (a German fast-food chain specialising in seafood) to shame. Importing its products direct from Italy and Turkey, it's able to offer the freshest fish around, which is usually served whole. Seafood is also available; it's hard to make a choice between mussels in white-wine sauce and

giant shrimps fried in herb butter. Seriously good wines from the Wachau (p205) round off the eating experience nicely.

MARGARETEN

BREAKFAST CLUB Map pp254-5 International €

☎ 581 26 92; 05, Schleifmühlgasse 12-14; breakfasts €5.50-6.50; ☺ 8am-2pm Mon-Fri, 6am-3pm Sat & Sun; bus 59A

Mix and match from an international range of ten breakfasts at this compact New York-style breakfast joint on lively Schleifmühlgasse. The Vienna Special of bread roll, honey, egg, seasonal fruit and *Melange* (milky coffee) is a fine choice, but is completely outdone by the BC Royal (salmon rolls, onions, hard boiled egg, toast and sekt). Kids will also love it: there's a small bar especially designed for the little ones, and a separate menu, too.

AMACORD Map pp254-5 Viennese & International €

☎ 587 47 09; 05, Rechte Wienzeile 15; breakfast €4.70-8, mains €6.40-13; ☺ 10am-2am; ⓜ U1, U2, U4 Karlsplatz, bus 59A

This small cellar café has been around for donkey's years. It's popularity stems from its convivial vibe, friendly staff, lovely vaulted ceilings, comfy surroundings and good, affordable food. Viennese classics are mixed in with a healthy range of Italian pastas, and the salad selection is extensive. However, some will find the smoke overpowering as the evening rolls on, and trying to find a seat on a Saturday morning is a fruitless enterprise.

ZUM ALTEN FASSL Map pp260-1 Beisl €€

☎ 544 42 98; 05, Ziegelofengasse 37; midday menus €5.70-7, mains €7-14; ☺ 11.30am-3pm, 5pm-midnight Mon-Fri, 5pm-midnight Sat, noon-3pm, 5pm-midnight Sun; bus 13A

With its private garden amid residential houses and polished wooden interior (typical of a well-kept *Beisl*), Zum Alten Fassl is worth the trip just for a drink. But it would be foolish to visit and not sample a menu loaded with Viennese favourites and regional specialities, like *Eierschwammerl* and *Blunzengröstl*. When it's in season, *Zanderfilet* (fillet of zander) is the chef's favourite, and shouldn't be missed. Round the evening off with unforgettable homemade *Topfen Palatschinken* (crepes with quark) smothered in vanilla sauce.

ZU DEN 3 BUCHTELN

Map pp260-1 Bohemian €€

☎ 587 83 65; 05, Wehrgasse 9; mains €8-13; ☺ 6pm-midnight Mon-Sat; bus 59A

Bohemian and Russian cuisine is Zu den 3 Buchteln's speciality. The thick, juicy goulash is excellent, but for something more unusual try the blood sausage with red cabbage and roast potatoes or the Russian blinis (buckwheat pancakes with egg, cream, red onions and trout caviar). Czech beer flows freely all night and the list of desserts is extensive.

ON Map pp260-1 Asian €€

☎ 585 49 00; 05, Wehrgasse 8; mains €9-14; ☺ 4.30pm-midnight Mon-Sat, noon-10pm Sun; bus 59A

With the look and feel of a *neo-Beisl* and creative, gluten-free Chinese cuisine, ON is onto a winner. The menu changes constantly with the whims of the head chef, but invariably a few vegetarian options sneak on and meat lovers should expect to make a choice between the likes of trout with ginger and garlic and *gan-bien* (fried) beef strips. The small, private garden is lovely in summer, but reservations are essential.

COLOMBO HOPPERS

Map pp260-1 Sri Lankan €€

☎ 545 43 08; 05, Schönbrunner Strasse 84; lunch buffet €7.60, mains €9-16; ☺ noon-2.30pm, 6-11pm Mon-Fri, noon-11pm Sat & Sun; bus 12A, 14A

Colombo Hoppers' appeal increased tenfold simply through the upgrading of their garden; instead of a few compromised tables, it now features neat cobblestones, shady trees, plenty of seating and a constant theatre of comings and goings from the nearby bike path. The Sri Lankan cuisine is meticulously prepared and presented, and the menu includes a high proportion of vegetarian dishes. Round off the evening's dining experience with a delightful almond-mango lassi.

MOTTO Map pp260-1 International €€

☎ 587 06 72; 05, Schönbrunner Strasse 30; mains €10-20; ☺ 6pm-4am; ⓜ U4 Pilgramgasse, bus 59A

A fusion of Asian, Austrian and Italian cuisine is the centrepiece of Motto's popularity. The likes of garlic chicken with mango, papaya, and tomato salsa, and grilled shrimps on Asian spinach salad certainly entice, but it's the fillet steaks (with chocolate-chilli sauce and mashed potatoes, no less) that win the day. Motto has been 'in' – particularly with the gay crowd – for years, so reservations are recommended. Entrance is through the forbidding chrome door on Rüdigergasse.

MARIAHILF

BAGEL STATION Map pp254-5   Fast Food €

☎ 208 08 94; 06, Capistrangasse 10; bagels €1.50-4; ⏱ 8am-8pm Mon-Fri, 9am-7pm Sat, 10am-6pm Sun; ⊕ U3 Neubaugasse

Over 20 varieties of freshly baked and filled bagels are available at these bright-orange bagel shops. At the bottom end of the price scale is the classic cream-cheese bagel, at the upper end the classic New Yorker, with smoked salmon, cream cheese, cress and capers. In between anything is possible, from chicken, salami, roast beef and Brie to fresh salad. Coffee-to-go is a given and, unusually for Vienna, is also available with soy milk. There's another shop handily located in Alsergrund (Map pp254–5; ☎ 276 30 88; 09, Währinger Strasse 2-4; ⏱ 8am-9pm Mon-Fri, 9am-8pm Sat, 10am-6pm Sun; ⊕ U2 Schottentor, ⊞ 37, 38, 40, 41, 42, 43, 44).

SAIGON Map pp254-5   Vietnamese €€

Map pp258-9; ☎ 585 63 95; 06, Getreidemarkt 7; midday menus €5-7, mains €7-16; ⏱ 11.30am-11pm Tue-Sun; ⊕ U1, U2, U4 Karlsplatz

Saigon was one of the original Asian restaurants in Vienna and it is a testament to the quality of the food that it has not only weathered the influx of Asian places in the city, but actually grown. The second Saigon is in Ottakring (Map pp258–9; ☎ 408 74 36; 16, Neulerchenfelder Strasse 37; ⏱ 11.30am-10.30pm; ⊕ U6 Josefstädterstrasse, ⊞ J). Both locations emphasise Vietnamese art and attentive service, and offer a selection of rice- and noodle-based dishes that seems unending. The duck is crispy and tender, the vegetables crunchy and fresh, and the noodle soups delicious – the *Pho Tai Bo* (beef noodle soup) is only more authentic in the motherland.

RA'MIEN Map pp254-5   Asian €€

☎ 585 47 98; 06, Gumpendorfer Strasse 9; mains €7-16; ⏱ 11am-midnight Tue-Sun, closed Aug; ⊕ U2 Museumsquartier, bus 57A

The designers of ra'mien went for a minimalist look, but somehow came out with a school cafeteria. Thankfully the chef's aren't

playing the game – the Asian fusion cuisine is a sheer delight. Choose from noodle soups and rice dishes during the day and a mixture of Thai, Japanese, Chinese and Vietnamese choices in the evening. ra'mien fills up quickly at night so it's best to book, but it should be no problem to wait for a table either; the lounge bar downstairs has regular DJs and stays open until at least 2am.

SHALIMAR map pp260-1   Indian €€

☎ 596 43 17; 06, Schmalzhofgasse 11; midday menu €5-6, mains €8-12; ⏱ 11.30am-2.30pm, 6-11.30pm; ⊕ U3 Zieglergasse

Shalimar is an Indian restaurant of some standing amongst the many in Mariahilfer. The food on offer crosses the entire subcontinent, but the speciality of the house is *Balti*, an Indian/Pakistani equivalent of wok cuisine cooked with generous portions of curry spice, onions, coriander and basil. In summer Shalimar's hidden garden – shaded by mature trees and guarded by pictures of Vishnu, Hanuman and Shiva – is a perfect antidote to Vienna's hot-and-bothered streets.

SHANGHAI TAN Map pp254-5   Chinese €€

☎ 585 49 88; 06, Gumpendorfer Strasse 9; dim sum €3.80-4.50, mains €8-12; ⏱ 6pm-2am Mon-Thu, 6pm-4am Fri & Sat; bus 57A

Tie Yang, owner of ra'mien, has created a slick, stylish Chinese restaurant in Shanghai Tan. The long list of dim sum is the menu's highlight, but a sprinkling of udon (thick noodles served in a soup) is also available. The devilishly dark and intimate interior is perfect for private liaisons, but sometimes makes it hard to see what you're eating. Downstairs is an opium den minus the opium – a chilled-out area with hidden corners and pillows for reclining.

PICCINI PICCOLO GOURMET

Map pp254-5   Italian €€

☎ 587 52 54; 06, Linke Wienzeile 4; mains €8-19; ⏱ 11am-7.30pm Mon-Fri, 9.30am-2pm Sat; ⊕ U1, U2, U4 Karlsplatz

'Gourmet' is a term all too frequently bantered around – these days gourmet pizzas, gourmet burgers, and even gourmet sandwiches are found on menus. But 'gourmet' fits perfectly to Piccini Piccolo. This is the finest antipasti restaurant in town, with around 40 different antipasti rolls, fish treats and stuffed vegetables to try. It also knows its *Brunello* from its *Vino Nobile,* which, with 60 varieties of wine available, is a good thing. Its shop next door has been selling imported Italian foods since 1856.

NEUBAU

ST JOSEF Map pp260-1   Organic/Vegetarian €
☎ 526 68 18; 07, Mondscheingasse 10; small/large menus €5.80/6.70; ☽ 8am-7.30pm Mon-Fri, 8am-4pm Sat; 🚊 49, bus 13A

This super-friendly restaurant produces wholly organic and vegetarian food for a throng of happy diners. The menu changes daily – when we visited, sweet potatoes, vegetarian strudel, lentils and salad were among the choices. *Dinkel* (spelt) is used in some dishes to cater for wheat-intolerant patrons, and drinks like guarana cola and cranberry ginkgo help to wash everything down. Take a seat upstairs, downstairs, outside on the wooden benches, or get something to go.

ZU DEN ZWEI LIESLN Map pp260-1   Beisl €
☎ 523 32 82; 07, Burggasse 63; mains €5-10; ☽ 11am-11pm; bus 48A

A classic *Beisl* of legendary status, Zu den Zwei Liesln has been serving celebrities, politicians, office workers and students for decades. Six varieties of schnitzel crowd the menu (the *Haus Schnitzel,* filled with Gorgonzola, ham and pepperoni, will never fail to please, or stuff), but there are other Viennese options, and even two vegetarian choices. The wood panelling, simple wooden chairs and chequered tablecloths create a quaint and cosy interior, but the tree-shaded inner courtyard is more inviting in summer.

GOLDMUND map pp254-5   Neo-Beisl €
☎ 522 56 82; 07, Zitterhofergasse 8; mains €6-10; ☽ 11.30am-3pm, 5.30pm-midnight Mon-Fri, 5.30pm-midnight Sat; ⓞ U2, U3 Volkstheater

Goldmund is one of the new breed of *Beisl* in the city. It's light, bright and breezy ambience extends to its cooking; plenty of basil and olive oil in dishes creates the flair and taste of the Mediterranean. Vegetarian dishes, such as tomatoes with mushrooms and basil pesto, are always available, and organic juices and select wines round things off nicely. Reservations aren't necessary but are advisable, particularly if you're set on a table outdoors in summer.

AMERLINGBEISL Map pp254-5   Beisl €
☎ 526 16 60; 07, Stiftgasse 8; midday menus from €5, mains €7-10; ☽ 9am-2am; U2, ⓞ U3 Volkstheater, bus 48A

Amerlingbeisl's solid Austrian fare (and sprinkling of Italian pasta dishes) won't set your tastebuds alight but when combined with the setting, this is a lovely place to dine. Situated in the pedestrian quarter of Spittelberg, an old-worldly spot of tight cobblestone streets and quirky shops, the inner courtyard of this *Beisl* is a lush oasis. On balmy summer nights the roof slides back to allow more fresh air to enter.

PODIUM Map pp260-1   International €€
☎ 522 15 87; 07, Westbahnstrasse 33; midday menus €6-7, mains €9-12; ☽ 11-1am Mon-Fri, 7pm-1am Sat; 🚊 49

This designer restaurant and bar in the fashionable Neubau district has you sit in the lollipop chairs near the floor-to-ceiling windows or nestle into one of the big, comfy couches to the rear. Podium offers a small but imaginative menu that on some days can range from hamburgers to pumpkin curry with basmati rice. The crowd, which often just drops in for a drink and a chat, is arty and cultured.

SCHON SCHÖN Map pp260-1   International €€
☎ 0699 1537 7701; 07, Lindengasse 53; mains €8-18; ☽ 11am-11pm Tue-Sat; ⓞ U3 Zieglergasse

Dining is a social experience at this new eatery in Neubau. With only one table (seating 24) it's hard to avoid your fellow diners, but it only helps the conversation to flow freely. The imaginative cuisine changes daily but invariably includes a handful of vegetarian and meat or fish dishes (grilled bass with zucchini risotto, and *Palatschinke* with vegetables on the day we visited) presented with a designer's touch. Clean white lines that prevail through the building, which includes a hairdresser and clothing shop.

GAUMENSPIEL Map pp260-1   International €€
☎ 526 11 08; 07, Zieglergasse 54; midday menus around €8, mains €10-18; ☽ 11.30am-2.30pm, 6pm-midnight Mon-Fri, 6pm-midnight Sat; 🚊 49, bus 48A

Gaumenspiel is an immaculate, modern *Beisl* with plenty going for it. The food is international with a heavy Mediterranean influence – try spinach dumplings with Parmesan and beetroot soup with Greek yoghurt – and cooked with professionalism and care. The service is attentive without being overbearing and the whole eating experience is focused on enjoyment. There's a sense of calm and informality about the menu written on chalkboards, the décor that's light in detail and the handful of streetside tables used in the summer. Reservations for dinner are recommended.

JOSEFSTADT

CAFÉ DER PROVINZ Map pp258-9 French €
☎ 944 22 72; 08, Maria Treu Gasse 3; crepes €3-4, galette €4-7; ⌚ 8am-11pm Mon-Fri, 9am-11pm Sat; ⓙ J, bus 13A

A charming little café near the Piaristenkirche (p92), Café der Provinz brings a touch of France to Vienna. Choose from sweet crepes, served with the likes of Nutella, chocolate, or honey, or sour *galettes* (buckwheat crepes, cooked on one side only) complemented by ham, cheese or egg. It's a sweet spot any time of the year – inside in winter it's warm and cosy and outside in summer the streetside seating is cool and breezy.

SIDE STEP Map pp258-9 Spanish €
☎ 0676 782 02 30; 08, Lange Gasse 52; tapas €3-7; ⌚ 6pm-2am Mon-Sat, 6pm-1am Sun; ⓤ U2 Rathaus, bus 13A

Forty tapas (both hot and cold) and 20 open wines make this slice of Spain in the heart of Josefstadt a real treat. The wine is attraction enough, but only the most stalwart dieter will be able to refuse the likes of balls of lamb in tomato sauce, shrimp with garlic sauce, or goat's cheese with homemade olive marmalade. The brick surroundings, easy-going air and excellent grappa are but icing on the cake.

IL SESTANTE map pp258-9 Italian €
☎ 402 98 94; 08, Piaristengasse 50; midday menus €6-7, mains €7-11; ⌚ 11.30am-11.30pm; bus 13A

Enjoy a slice of Italy in Vienna. Take a seat, order from a long list of mozzarella-based pizzas (including white pizzas – without tomato sauce), watch the skilled pizza-makers spin the base like plates, then sit back with a glass of Montepulciano d´Abruzzo and wait for it to arrive from the wood oven. Choose a table indoors near the animated waiters or one outside on pretty Jodok-Fink-Platz, with Piaristenkirche as a backdrop.

PARS Map pp258-9 Persian €€
☎ 405 82 45; 08, Lerchenfelder Strasse 148; midday menus €7.10, mains €9-14; ⌚ 11am-midnight Mon-Sat; ⓙ 46

Pars is heavily patronised by Vienna's Persian community, giving it a stamp of authenticity. Persian cuisine, such as *Schekampareh* (eggplant filled with meat), *Lubiapolo* (beans, lamb and rice) and a good selection of kebabs (shish, *Adana, Kubideh*), is complemented by over 30 varieties of quality Austrian wine. After the meal enjoy a puff on a hookah.

SAMRAT Map pp258-9 Indian €€
☎ 408 47 41; 08, Florianigasse 20; midday buffet €6.50, mains €9-14; ⌚ 11.30am-2.30pm, 6-11pm Mon-Sat; ⓤ U2 Rathaus

The inviting aromas wafting from Samrat's open doors is testament to the heady spices used in its Indian cuisine. The clay-oven baked curries are certainly tempered for the Viennese palate, but all in all they're very good. The Indian music and trappings from the subcontinent are suitably evocative.

KONOBA Map pp260-1 Dalmatian €€
☎ 929 41 11; 08, Lerchenfelder Strasse 66-68; mains €8-19; ⌚ 11am-2pm, 6pm-midnight Sun-Fri, 6pm-midnight Sat; ⓙ 46

Few restaurants in the city come close to Konoba's expertise with fish. The Dalmatian chefs know their product inside out and always manage to serve the catch fresh from the pan so that it's neither too dry nor too raw. Zander and *Goldbrasse* (sea bream) are often on the menu, but expect to find a healthy array of seasonal dishes too. The open-plan interior helps create a convivial atmosphere despite the stuffy crowd.

ALSERGRUND

WIENER DEEWAN Map pp258-9 Oriental €
☎ 925 11 85; 09, Liechtensteinstrasse 10; ⌚ 11am-11pm; ⓤ U2 Schottentor, ⓙ 37, 38, 40, 41, 42, 43, 44

Pakistani cuisine, cooked under the maxim 'good food, good mood', is one speciality of Der Wiener Deewan. The other is 'eat what you like, pay as you wish'. Two vegetarian and three meat dishes, accompanied by one dessert, are prepared daily and served in a buffet-style set-up; prices aren't set, and you can eat as much as you like. Most people are generous with their money, as the likes of the *Lamb Karah* (diced-lamb curry), *Tinda* (pumpkin curry) and dhal *Masur* (red lentil dhal) are excellent and full of subtle flavours. The atmosphere, like the staff, is very relaxed and unobtrusive.

VEGI RANT Map pp258-9   Vegetarian €€

☎ 407 82 87; 09, Währinger Strasse 57; midday menu €6.20-8.90, mains €6-8; ☽ 11.30am-6pm Mon-Fri; ⊙ U6 Währinger Strasse, ▣ 40, 41, 42
A well-established restaurant with a strong nutritional bent, Vegi Rant has daily menus for hungry souls wishing to avoid meat. The food is imaginative, light and tasty; as the menu changes on a weekly basis (but always consists of a soup, main and dessert), expect anything from *Linsengulasch* (lentil goulash) to *Topfenlaibchen* (tofu loaf). While you're there, stock up on natural remedies and all sorts of healthy goodies at the health food store next door.

GASTHAUS WICKERL Map pp258-9   Beisl €€

☎ 317 74 89; 09, Porzellangasse 24a; midday menu €5.80, mains €7-15; ☽ 9am-midnight Mon-Fri, from 10am Sat; ▣ D
Wickerl is a beautiful *Beisl* with an all-wood finish and a warm, welcoming environment. Seasonal fare, such as *Kürbiscremesuppe* (cream of pumpkin soup) and *Kürbisgulasch* (pumpkin goulash) in autumn, *Marillenknödel* in summer and *Spargel* (asparagus) in spring are mixed in with the usual Viennese suspects of *Tafelspitz, Zwiebelrostbraten* and veal and pork schnitzel. It's so good the city's top chefs dine here. If you can't make it to Alsergrund, stop in at Wickerl's small pavilion at Naschmarkt, Stand 525-529.

FLEIN Map pp258-9   Austrian €€

☎ 319 76 89; 09, Boltzmanngasse 2; mains €7-18; ☽ 11.30am-3pm, 5.30pm-midnight; ▣ 37, 38, 40, 41, 42
Every day brings a new menu to Flein, but it's safe to say it will always be from the creative school of cooking. When we visited, zucchini quiche and *Eierschwammerl* risotto satisfied the vegetarians, while grilled calamari and herbed lamb *Stelze* (hocks) pleased the meat eaters. The small garden, backing onto the French cultural institute, is peaceful and secluded despite

BEST BEISLN

- Beim Czaak (p119)
- Gasthaus Wickerl (left)
- Quell (p136)
- Ubl (p130)
- Zu den Zwei Liesln (p133)

busy Währinger Strasse being so close at hand. In summer, book ahead to secure a table.

STOMACH Map pp258-9   Austrian €€

☎ 310 20 99; 09, Seegasse 26; mains €10-17; ☽ 4pm-midnight Wed-Sat, 10am-10pm Sun; ⊙ U4 Rossauer Lände
Stomach has been serving seriously good food for years. The menu is filled with meat and vegetarian delights, such as Styrian roast beef, cream of pumpkin soup, and, when in season, wild boar and venison. The interior is authentically rural-Austrian, and the garden, all overgrown and uneven, has more character than some districts. The name 'Stomach' comes from the rearrangement of the word Tomaschek, the butcher's shop originally located here. Reservations are highly recommended.

KIM KOCHT Map pp258-9   Asian €€€

☎ 319 02 42; 09, Lustkandlgasse 6; set menus €42-59; ☽ 6pm-midnight Mon-Fri; ⊙ U6 Währinger Strasse, ▣ 40, 41, 42
Kim Kocht has been the talk of the town for years. Its Korean and Japanese cuisine is highly sought after in Vienna's culinary circles for its originality, quality and the creativity shown in presentation. The three- to five- course menus are constantly changing, but often feature fish as the main, and organic produce is always used. The restaurant only seats 25 and its popularity means reservations at least one month ahead are essential; if this doesn't suit stop in next door at the Shop & Studio (☎ 319 34 02; meals €3-6.50; ☽ 10.30am-midnight) for a quick snack of sushi, wok-vegetables or Thai noodles.

OUTSIDE THE GÜRTEL

This area of Vienna is by no means bereft of fine restaurants, but you're not as spoilt for choice as you are within the Gürtel's border. There are benefits to eating in the suburbs –

prices drop, authenticity increases, and as a tourist you'll be a rarity, which will mean either smiles or stares, but invariably some friendly service.

Worthy of special note is not one restaurant but an entire neighbourhood – 'Little Turkey' – which is centred on the bustling Brunnenmarkt (p185) in the 16th district. Here Turkish bakeries and restaurants flourish through the patronage of Vienna's Turkish community and the many Viennese who flock here to sample the excellent cuisine.

SIMMERING

SCHLOSS CONCORDIA (KLEINE OPER WIEN) Map pp252-3 Austrian €€

☎ 769 88 88; 11, Simmeringer Hauptstrasse 283; midday menu €7, mains €6-14; ⏰ 10am-1am; 🚊 71, 72
The gigantic stone Jesus that greets prospective diners to Schloss Concordia is a fitting welcome mat, what with the Zentralfriedhof directly opposite. It also sets the scene for inside; the bare wooden floors, gargantuan mirrors and stained-glass roof are suitably dated; when lit by candlelight in the evening it all creates a rather eerie picture. The overgrown garden at the rear only adds to the effect. The menu, which is crowded with schnitzels, will suit meat lovers; for a memorable experience, try *Degustationsmenü*, a hefty plate of different kinds of schnitzel. Thankfully there are a smattering of vegetarian options, too.

RUDOLFSHEIM-FÜNFHAUS

QUELL Map pp260-1 Beisl €

☎ 893 24 07; 15, Reindorfgasse 19; mains €5-11; ⏰ 11am-midnight Tue-Sun; bus 12A, 57A
Time stands still at Quell, a traditional *Beisl* in suburban Rudolfsheim-Fünfhaus. The panelled-wood interior looks untouched for years, the archaic wooden chandeliers and ceramic stoves wouldn't be out of place in the Museum für Volkskunde, and some guests look as though they've been frequenting the place since before the war. The menu is thoroughly Viennese, with *Schweinskotelett* (pork cutlets) and schnitzel featuring heavily, but there's also a surprising number of fish and vegetarian options. Genial staff and quiet streetside seating add to the ambience.

OTTAKRING

KENT Map pp258-9 Turkish €

☎ 405 91 73; 16, Brunnengasse 67; mains €3-9; ⏰ 6am-2am; Ⓜ U6 Josefstädterstrasse, 🚊 J
Kent means 'small town' in Turkish, an appropriate name considering the hordes that frequent this ever-expanding Turkish restaurant. But it's impossible to blame people; in summer the tree-shaded garden is one of the prettiest in the city and the food is consistently top-notch. The menu is extensive, but highlights that jump out include shish kebab, *Ispanakli Pide* (long Turkish pizza with sheep's cheese, egg and spinach) and *Büyük Meze Tabagi* (starter plate as big as a main with baked eggplant, carrots, zucchini, rice-filled vine leaves, green beans, hummus and other delights). The vegetarian and breakfast selections will please most, and everything is available for takeaway. For late-night desserts, try the bakery next door, which keeps practical opening times: 24-hours a day, seven days a week.

ETAP Map pp258-9 Turkish €

☎ 406 04 78; 16, Neulerchenfelder Strasse 13-15; midday menus €5-7, mains €3.50-11; ⏰ 5-2am Sun-Thu, 5-4am Fri & Sat; Ⓜ U6 Josefstädterstrasse, 🚊 J
Etap might not have Kent's garden or its popularity, but it certainly has its authenticity and heavenly Turkish cuisine. Its pan dishes, such as *Tavuk Sote* (roasted chicken with tomatoes, paprika, mushrooms and rice), arrive piping hot to the table, the wood grill adds a lovely flavour to the likes of the shish kebab, and the stuffed zucchini with yoghurt are hard to pass over. The open buffet (€9) on Friday and Saturday (from 6pm onwards) is a smorgasbord of Etap's best dishes; after 9pm live music accompanies the feast.

RESTAURANT WORLD

Map pp258-9 International €

☎ 06991 130 28 07; 16, Hofferplatz 5; midday menus from €4.80, mains €5-13; ⏰ 11am-3pm, 6-11pm Mon-Fri, 6-11pm Sat; 🚊 46
Restaurant World's menu is an inviting mix of Caribbean and Sri Lankan cuisine that includes spicy curries and filling noodle dishes. Vegetarian choices abound and vegans can dine here quite happily. The coconut bread will have you asking for the recipe, as will the mango lassi and mango cake. The restaurant owners are some of the most affable in the city, and children are more than welcome.

Drinking

Drinking

The pleasure of drinking in Vienna is variety. Wine, beer and coffee all have their special place in the hearts and minds of the Viennese, and exude a strong influence on the cultural make-up of the city.

Vienna has a strong claim to the 'Coffee Capital of the World' title. Its *Kaffeehäuser* (coffee houses) are as famous as the city's classical music heritage, and an attraction in their own right. The sheer number of coffee houses is staggering, but each has its own flair and flavour, and a trip to Vienna would be incomplete without sampling their unique ambience.

Wine is most beloved by the Viennese and outweighs beer in the consumption stakes. Seven sq km of vineyards lie within Vienna's borders, making it the world's largest wine-growing city. *Heurigen,* the city's equivalent of a wine taverns, are rustic establishments on the outskirts of the city where 'new' wine (normally only a year old) is served to eager patrons on warm summer evenings.

The bar scene, where much of the city's beer disappears down parched throats, is small but highly accommodating. Whether you're looking for a family-friendly microbrewery or grunged-up student hang-out, Vienna can supply. The distinction between bar and restaurant, and bar and club, is often blurred however. Don't dismiss a place because of the label above the door: many restaurants are just as good for a night out as the bars listed here.

While normal precautions should be taken when heading out for the night, it's good to remember Vienna is a very safe city. For information on the best sources for listings in the city, see the Entertainment chapter (p162).

COFFEE HOUSES

Vienna's coffee houses are legendary. As much a part of Viennese life as football is in Britain and BBQs are in Australia, they are places to halt a busy schedule, order a coffee, cake, or full meal, and replenish the system.

Coffee houses have for centuries graced Vienna's alleyways. Legend has it that coffee beans were left behind by the fleeing Turks in 1683, and by 1685 the first house opened, at 01, Rotenturmstrasse 14. However their popularity didn't take hold until the end of the 19th century; by this time there were a reputed 600 cafés in business. The tradition has waned over the years, but only slightly; the Viennese still love their coffee rituals and their coffee houses.

Café Hawelka (p140)

MORE THAN JUST COFFEE

Ordering with 'a coffee, please' won't go down well in most coffee houses. A quick glance at a menu will uncover an unfathomable list of coffee choices, and a little time studying the options is advisable. A good coffee house will serve the cup of java on a silver platter accompanied by a glass of water and a small sweet.

The general selection of coffee includes:

- *Brauner* – black but served with a tiny splash of milk; comes in *Gross* (large) or *Klein* (small)
- *Einspänner* – with whipped cream, served in a glass
- *Fiaker* – *Verlängerter* (see below) with rum and whipped cream
- *Kapuziner* – with a little milk and perhaps a sprinkling of grated chocolate
- *Maria Theresia* – with orange liqueur and whipped cream
- *Masagran* (or *Mazagran*) – cold coffee with ice and maraschino liqueur
- *Melange* – the Viennese classic; served with milk, and maybe whipped cream too, similar to the cappuccino
- *Mocca* (sometimes spelled *Mokka*) or *Schwarzer* – black coffee
- *Pharisäer* – strong *Mocca* topped with whipped cream, served with a glass of rum
- *Türkische* – comes in a copper pot with coffee grounds and sugar
- *Verlängerter* – *Brauner* weakened with hot water
- *Wiener Eiskaffee* – cold coffee with vanilla ice cream and whipped cream

The traditional coffee house comes in a number of guises; the grand affairs of the 19th-century – Café Central and Café Griensteidl – share the streets with *Jugendstil* delights, like Café Sperl, and post-WWII establishments, such as Café Prückel and Café Bräunerhof. *Konditoreien*, cake shops with seating and invariably an older clientele, are also commonplace; Aida is a classic example. Starbucks has recently had the gall to enter Vienna's already overcrowded coffee scene, but of the 35 planned sites, so far only seven have opened.

No matter the decor, the environment is the same – paused. Nothing moves fast in a coffee house, not even the clouds of smoke hanging in no-mans'-land. Patrons are encouraged to devour newspapers and magazines, including international titles, at their leisure, and pressure to order a second cup is non-existent. Waiters command their own genus; arrogant and scolding one minute (especially if your mobile phone goes off), courteous the next, they are annoyingly charming in their peculiar way of going about their business.

INNERE STADT

AIDA Map pp254-5

☎ 512 29 77; 01, Stock-im-Eisen-Platz 2; ⏰ 7am-8pm Mon-Sat, 9am-8pm Sun; ⓤ U1, U3 Stephansplatz
An icon of the *Konditorei* scene, Aida is a time warp for coffee lovers. Its pink and brown colour scheme – right down to the waitresses' socks – matches the 1950s retro

decor (all genuine of course) perfectly, and most of the clientele are well into retirement. Order a *Melange* and a slice of cake (there are almost 30 to choose from) and head upstairs to spy on the activity on Kärntner Strasse. Twenty-six such gems are scattered throughout Vienna.

CAFÉ BRÄUNERHOF Map pp254-5

☎ 512 38 93; 01, Stallburggasse 2; ⏰ 8am-9pm Mon-Fri, 8am-7pm Sat, 10am-7pm Sun; bus 2A, 3A
Bräunerhof is an authentic coffee house of some standing amongst *Kaffeehäuser* aficionados. It remains little changed from the days when Austria's seminal writer Thomas Bernhard frequented the premises; smoke-stained walls, tight tables, surly staff, and a huge newspaper selection. Classical music from the Bräunerhof features 3pm to 6pm on weekends and holidays.

CAFÉ CENTRAL Map pp254-5

☎ 533 37 6426; 01, Herrengasse 14; ⏰ 8am-10pm Mon-Sat, 8am-7pm Sun; ⓤ U3 Herrengasse
Grand Central has a rich history – Trotsky came here to play chess, and turn-of-the-century literary greats like Karl Kraus and Hermann Bahr regularly met for coffee. Its impressive interior of marble pillars, arched ceilings and glittering chandeliers now plays host to tourists rather than locals, but it's worth stopping in for a look. There's live classical music from 4pm to 7pm Monday to Saturday and noon to 5pm Sunday, and the plaster patron with the walrus mous-

Drinking

COFFEE HOUSES

tache near the door is a model of the poet Peter Altenberg.

CAFÉ ENGLÄNDER Map pp254-5

☎ 966 86 65; 01, Postgasse 2; 🕑 8am-1am Mon-Sat, 10-1am Sun; Ⓜ U3 Stubentor

Attracting the rich and the famous, Engländer is no classic *Kaffeehaus*, but rather a modern edifice with a discerning air and top wine and a contemporary take on Viennese cuisine. Its service and coffee are of the highest standard.

CAFÉ GRIENSTEIDL Map pp254-5

☎ 535 26 92; 01, Michaelerplatz 2; 🕑 8am-11.30pm; U3 Herrengasse, bus 2A, 3A

Griensteidl holds a prestigious position between the Hofburg and the Loos Haus, and was once the *Stammlokal* (local haunt) for Vienna's late-19th century literary set. It now caters mainly to tourists, but it still attracts with its *Jugendstil* lamps, wooden chairs and tables, and huge windows overlooking the comings and goings on Michaelerplatz.

CAFÉ HAWELKA Map pp254-5

☎ 512 82 30; 01, Dorotheergasse 6; 🕑 8am-2am Mon & Wed-Sat, 4pm-2am Sun; Ⓜ U1, U3 Stephansplatz

At first glance it's hard to see what all the fuss is about: dirty pictures, ripped posters, brown-stained walls, smoky air and cramped tables don't look too appealing. But a second glance explains it – the convivial vibe between friends and complete strangers. A traditional haunt for artists and writers, it attracts the gamut of Viennese society. You'll be constantly shunted up to accommodate new arrivals at the table. Be warned: the organising elderly Frau seizes any momentarily vacant chair (curtail your toilet visits!) to reassign elsewhere.

CAFÉ SACHER Map pp254-5

☎ 541 56-0; 01, Philharmonikerstrasse 4; Sacher Torte around €3; 🕑 8am-midnight; Ⓜ U1, U2, U4 Karlsplatz, 🚃 D, J, 1, 2, 62, 65

Sacher is the café every second tourist wants to visit. Why? Because of the celebrated *Sacher Torte*, a rich chocolate cake with apricot jam once favoured by Emperor Franz Josef. Truth be told, as cafés go Sacher doesn't rate highly for authenticity, but it pleases the masses with its opulent furnishings, battalion of waiters, and air of

nobility. The newly revamped section on Kärntner Strasse has at least brought some of the Sacher into the 21st century.

CAFÉ TIROLERHOF Map pp254-5

☎ 512 78 33; 01, Führichgasse 8; 🕑 7am-10pm Mon-Sat, 9.30am-8pm Sun; bus 3A

A lovingly renovated *Jugendstil* décor from the 1920s and homemade *Apfelstrudel* (apple strudel) help to make Tirolerhof an inviting Innere Stadt choice. Service is less tart than at other traditional coffee houses, and the location directly opposite the Albertina (p63) is a bonus.

DEMEL Map pp254-5

☎ 535 17 17; 01, Kohlmarkt 14; 🕑 10am-7pm; bus 2A, 3A

An elegant and regal café within sight of the Hofburg, Demel was once the talk of the town but now mainly caters to tourists. The quality of the cakes hasn't dropped however, and it wins marks for the sheer creativity of its sweets – its window displays an ever-changing array of edible art pieces (ballerinas and manicured bonsai for example). Demel's speciality is the *Ana Demel Torte*, a calorie-bomb of chocolate and nougat which rivals Café Sacher's *Torte*.

DIGLAS Map pp254-5

☎ 512 57 65; 01, Wollzeile 10; light meals €6-13; 🕑 7am-midnight; U1, U3 Stephansplatz, bus 1A

Diglas comes straight from the classic coffee house mould, with swanky red velvet booths, sharp-tongued waiters, extensive (and good) coffee range, and old dames dressed to the 9s. The reputation of Diglas' cakes precedes itself; some argue they're the best in town and the *Apfelstrudel* is unrivalled. Meals are delicate and more like snacks, but extend beyond the normal Viennese specialities to include a variety of Hungarian dishes. Live piano music fills Diglas from 8pm to 11pm every Tuesday, Friday and Saturday.

HAAS & HAAS Map pp254-5

☎ 512 26 66; 01, Stephansplatz 4; 🕑 8am-8pm Mon-Fri, 8am-6.30pm Sat; Ⓜ U1, U3 Stephansplatz, bus 1A

The fragrance of tea from around the world greets customers on entry to Haas & Hass, Vienna's prime teahouse. Green, herbal, aromatic, Assam, Ceylon, Darjeeling; the selection seems endless. The rear garden is a shaded retreat from the wind, rain, sun and tourist bustle, while the front parlour sports comfy cushioned booths and views of Stephansdom.

KLEINES CAFÉ Map pp254-5
01, Franziskanerplatz 3; ☽ 10am-2am Mon-Sat, 1pm-2am Sun; ⊕ U1, U3 Stephansplatz
Designed by architect Hermann Czech in the 1970s, the Kleines Café exudes a bohemian atmosphere reminiscent of Vienna's heady *Jugendstil* days. It's tiny inside, but the wonderful summer outdoor seating on Franziskanerplatz is arguably the best in the Innere Stadt.

RINGSTRASSE

CAFÉ LANDTMANN Map pp254-5
☎ 241 00; 01, Dr-Karl-Lueger-Ring 4; midday menus €9.60, mains €12-17; ☽ 7.30am-midnight; ⊕ U2 Schottentor, 🚋 37, 38, 40, 41, 42, 43, 44
Landtmann attracts both politicians and theatre-goers with its elegant interior and close proximity to the Burgtheater, Rathaus, and Parlament. The list of coffee specialities is formidable and the dessert menu features classics like the *Sacher Torte* and *Apfelstrudel*. There's a huge selection of Austrian and international papers, and live piano music from 8pm to 10pm on Sunday.

CAFÉ PRÜCKEL Map pp254-5
☎ 512 61 15; 01, Stubenring 24; ☽ 8.30am-10pm; ⊕ U3 Stubentor, 🚋 1, 2
Prückel's unique mould is a little different from other Viennese cafés: instead of a sumptuous interior, it features an intact 1950s design. Intimate booths, aloof waiters, strong coffee and diet-destroying cakes are all attractions, but the smoke can at times be bothersome; thankfully there's a nonsmoking room at the rear. Live piano music is offered 7pm to 10pm Monday, Wednesday and Friday.

X-CELSIOR CAFFÉ-BAR Map pp254-5
☎ 585 71 84; 01, Opernring 1; ☽ 7am-midnight; ⊕ U1, U2, U4 Karlsplatz, 🚋 D, J, 1, 2, 62, 65
Modern, styled, and devoid of *Melange* and strudel, X-Celsior is part of the new generation of cafés in Vienna. Espressos and cappuccino form the basis of the coffee menu at this Italian-chain café, and nibbles

like panini, ciabatta and bruschetta fill the menu. Its large bay windows overlook the Staatsoper and busy Karlsplatz.

INSIDE THE GÜRTEL

CAFÉ DRECHSLER Map pp254-5
☎ 587 85 80; 06, Linke Wienzeile 22; ⊕ U4 Kettenbrückengasse
Drechsler is closed for renovation but its reopening in the imminent future is eagerly awaited by insomniacs in search of breakfast or *Gulasch* (goulash) before sunrise.

CAFÉ FLORIANIHOF Map pp258-9
☎ 402 48 42; 08, Florianigasse 45; ☽ 8am-midnight Mon-Fri, 10am-8pm Sat & Sun; 🚋 5, 33
This child-friendly café in Josefstadt serves food heavily laden with organic produce and a remarkable array of fruit juices. Paintings by local artists add a splash of colour to the clean white walls, and in summer the streetside seating fills quickly. There's free internet access with the purchase of a drink.

CAFÉ HUMMEL Map pp258-9
☎ 405 53 14; 08, Josefstädter Strasse 66; ☽ 7am-12.30pm Mon-Sat, 8am-12.30pm Sun; 🚋 5, 33, J
Unpretentious and classic, Hummel is a large *Kaffeehaus* catering to a regular Josefstadt crowd. The coffee is rich, the cakes baked on the premises, and the waiters typically snobbish. In summer, it's easy to spend a few hours at Hummel's outdoor seating area, mulling over the international papers and watching the human traffic on Josefstädter Strasse.

CAFÉ RÜDIGERHOF Map pp258-9
☎ 586 31 38; 05, Hamburgerstrasse 20; ☽ 9am-2am; ⊕ U4 Kettenbrückengasse
Rüdigerhof's façade is a glorious example of *Jugendstil* architecture, and the furniture and fittings inside could be straight out of an *I Love Lucy* set. The atmosphere is homely and familiar and the terrace huge and shaded. On Saturday mornings it fills up quickly with Naschmarkt shoppers.

CAFÉ SPERL Map pp254-5
☎ 586 41 58; 06, Gumpendorfer Strasse 11; ☽ 7am-11pm Mon-Sat, 11am-8pm Sun (closed Sun in summer); bus 57A
With its gorgeous *Jugendstil* fittings, grand dimensions, cosy booths and unhurried air, Sperl is one of the finest coffee houses in

Vienna. And that's to say nothing of a menu that features *Sperl Torte* – a mouth-watering mix of almonds and chocolate cream.Grab a slice and a newspaper, order a strong coffee, and join the rest of the patrons people watching and day-dreaming.

CANETTI Map pp260-1

☎ 522 06 88; 07, Urban-Loritz-Platz 2A; ⏱ 9am-midnight Mon-Sat; Ⓜ U6 Burggasse/Stadthalle, 🚋 6, 18

Canetti is one of only a handful of eateries in Vienna with rooftop views. Perched on top of the Bücherei Wien (p91), its vantage point provides a sweeping vista of Vienna to the south. The Viennese dishes can be hit-or-miss unfortunately, but it's a fine place for a quiet coffee or something stronger.

OUTSIDE THE GÜRTEL

CAFÉ GLORIETTE Map pp260-1

☎ 879 13 11; 13, Gloriette; ⏱ 9am-1am; Ⓜ U4 Schönbrunn, Hietzing

Café Gloriette occupies the Gloriette, a neoclassical construction high on a hill behind Schloss Schönbrunn, built for the pleasure of Maria Theresia in 1775. With sweeping views of the Schloss, its magnificent gardens and the districts to the north, Gloriette has arguably one of the best vistas in all of Vienna. And it's a welcome pit stop after the short but sharp climb up the hill.

SCHAUKASTEN Map pp258-9

16, Brunnengasse, cnr Grundsteingasse; ⏱ 9am-6pm Mon-Fri, 9am-3pm Sat Apr-Oct; 🚋 J

A new concept on Brunnenmarkt, Schaukasten is a tiny container with excellent Italian coffee and a fresh menu daily. It's a delight to watch the market's comings and goings from one of the three small tables occupying the roof space, but if they're full, a pew at the ground-level bar is almost as good.

HEURINGEN

Like *Beisln* (beer houses) and *Kaffeehäuser*, *Heurigen* are an integral part of Vienna's cultural and culinary scene. These simple establishments date back to the Middle Ages, but it was Joseph II in 1784 who first officially granted producers the right to sell their wine directly from their own premises. It proved to be one of his more enduring

reforms and *Heurigen* have since become a permanent fixture in the city.

Heurigen can normally be identified by a *Busch'n* (green wreath or branch) hanging over the door. Decor is normally rustic, with basic wooden tables and benches, and a large garden or inner courtyard. Food is served buffet-style; roast pork, blood sausage, pickled vegetables, potato salad and strudel are the mainstay of *Heurigen* cuisine. Don't pass over the chance to try *Schwarz Wurzel Salat* (black root salad) and *Senf Gürke* (mustard gherkins) which taste spectacularly better than they sound. Wine, the most important feature of any *Heuriger*, is traditionally made by the owner and is usually only a year old, quite tart, and best when mixed with soda water. *Sturm* (literally 'storm' for its cloudy appearance and chaotic effects on drinkers), fermenting grape juice with a high alcohol content and deceptively sweet, nonlethal taste, is available from around early September to the middle of October. *Buschenshank* are a variation on *Heurigen* and only exist in the countryside bordering the city; open a few weeks of the year (normally in September), they are family-run and offer a small selection of food and wine. *Stadttheurigen* reside in the city's urban confluence and are either very basic affairs with tiny inner courtyards or multileveled cellars.

Heurigen are concentrated in and around Vienna's wine-growing regions. In the north, Grinzing has the largest concentration, but most cater to tour groups with kitsch live music and pseudo folk art and are often beyond the pale. Nearby Neustift am Walde is slowly going the way of Grinzing, while Sievering, squeezed between the two, still retains an air of authenticity. Old-worldy Nussdorf has a string of inviting *Heurigen* that cater to a healthy number of regulars, and elevated Kahlenberg is harder to get to but the views make it worth the effort.

Most *Heurigen* to the west in Ottakring are within the city's built-up area, but offer excellent views and peaceful gardens. Mauer, a small suburb in the southwest reaches of the city, contains a tiny pocket of traditional *Heurigen*; Maurer Lange Gasse is a good place to start hunting.

To the north across the Danube the neighbourhoods of Strebersdorf and Stammersdorf produce around 30% of the city's wine, making it Vienna's largest wine-growing district. The *Heurigen* here are far more traditional, and less frequented by tourists.

Radishes, Liptauer dip, bread and wine at Sirbu (this page)

KAHLENBERG

HIRT Map pp252-3

☎ 318 96 41; 19, Eisernenhandgasse 165; ☺ 3pm until late Wed-Fri, from noon Sat & Sun Apr-Oct, noon until late Fri-Sun Nov-Mar; bus 38A

Hidden among the vineyards on the eastern slopes of Kahlenberg, Hirt is a simple *Heuriger* with few frills. Basic wooden tables, a small buffet and marginal service all help to create a traditional atmosphere, while views of Kahlenbergerdorf and the 21st district across the Danube are a pleasure to enjoy over a few glasses of wine in the early evening. Hirt is best approached from the top of Kahlenberg; see the Walking & Cycling Tours chapter (p111).

SIRBU Map pp252-3

☎ 320 59 28; 19, Kahlenberger Strasse 210; ☺ 3pm-midnight Mon-Sat, mid-Apr–mid-Oct; bus 38A

Like Hirt, Sirbu has far-reaching views across Vienna's urban expanse from its quiet spot among the vineyards of Kahlenberg. Its wines have reached the pinnacle of Austrian success in recent years, and its garden is the perfect place to while away a sunny afternoon. Sirbu features in the Kahlenberg to Nussdorf walk (p111).

NUSSDORF

MAYER AM PFARRPLATZ Map pp252-3

☎ 370 12 87; 19, Pfarrplatz 2; ☺ 4pm-midnight Mon-Sat, from 11am Sun; bus 38A

Fifteen minutes' walk from U4 Heiligenstadt U-Bahn station, Mayer caters to tour groups but still manages to retain an air of authenticity, helped along by its peaceful ambience, vine-covered surrounds and history (Beethoven lived here in 1817). The huge shaded garden towards the rear includes a children's play area, and there's live music from 7pm to midnight daily.

GRINZING

REINPRECHT Map pp252-3

☎ 320 14 71; 19, Cobenzlgasse 22; ☺ 3.30pm-midnight mid-Feb–mid-Dec; bus 38A

Located in the heart of Grinzing, Reinprecht shines bright amongst the dull *Heurigen* in these parts. It still caters to the masses with its huge garden, enormous buffet and live music, but quality reigns throughout – it won the 2005 wine grower of the year award and features some of the best wine in the city. Check out the cork collection; at 3500 pieces, it's the largest in Europe.

WEINGUT AM REISENBERG Map pp252-3

☎ 320 93 93; 19, Oberer Reisenbergweg 15;
⏱ 5pm-midnight Mon-Fri, 1pm-midnight Sat & Sun
May-Sep, 6pm-midnight Wed-Sat Oct-Dec; bus 38A

A thoroughly modern premises with huge windows and a styled, brick interior, Weingut am Reisenberg is part of the new generation of *Heurigen*. Instead of the traditional Austrian buffet, Italian cuisine and vegetarian dishes are offered, and best enjoyed in its green garden overlooking the expanse of Vienna. It's a good 10-minute walk up a steep hill just north of Grinzing village, first up Cobenzlgasse and then Oberer Reisenbergweg; another 20 minutes further up Obere Reisenbergweg is Cobenzl, where you'll find a café and even better views of Vienna.

ZAWODSKY Map pp252-3

☎ 320 79 78; 19, Reinischgasse 3; ⏱ 5pm-midnight Mon & Wed-Fri, 2pm-midnight Sat & Sun Mar–mid-Sep; 🚋 38

Zawodsky is only a 15-minute walk from the touristy haunts of Grinzing, yet light years away in atmosphere. This stripped-back setup features picnic tables surrounded by apple trees and vineyards, and a small selection of hot and cold meats complemented by various salads. From Grinzing, walk up Strassergasse, take tiny Rosenweg on your left past the Maria Schmerzen Kirche and Reinischgasse appears on your right.

STAMMERSDORF & STREBERSDORF
ECKERT

☎ 292 25 96; 21, Strebersdorfer Strasse 158; ⏱ from 2pm daily every odd month; 🚋 26

Located in the heart of Strebersdorf, a 10-minute walk from the tram 26 terminus (walk north on Russberg Strasse and right at Strebersdorfer Platz), Eckert is a cross between a traditional establishment and an arts centre. Paintings by local artists adorn walls, live music features once a month (anything from jazz to rock and roll) and readings are common. Tours of the wine cellars are offered, and kids generally get the run of the place.

GÖBEL

One of the few highly original *Heurigen* in Vienna is Göbel (☎ 294 84 20; 21, Stammersdorfer Kellergasse 151; ⏱ changes with the seasons; bus 228, 233), the creation of owner Peter Göbel. Combining his significant talent at both wine making and architectural design, Peter has fashioned a *Heuriger* that not only delivers quality produce (80% of his wine is red, some of which are among the best in Vienna) but also provides a traditional atmosphere amongst stylishly clean lines and a strong natural-wood finish. Peter has been responsible for the family's wine making since 1991 and Göbel since 1996, but the business is in his blood, three generations in fact. We asked him for his learned opinion on Vienna's *Heuriger* scene.

'Viennese people like *Heurigen* because not much changes. The attraction will always be a garden, a courtyard, a food-buffet, and wine from a local vineyard. *Heurigen* to the Viennese means spare time, weekends, recreation, a family outing – or sometimes simply a quick stop for a glass of wine.

'With an increase in restaurant choice and open-air events in the city, the attraction of a traditional *Heuriger* has waned. Accordingly, the *Heuriger* culture has begun to adapt and now tries to go with the flow – food specials are offered, and information is available on the internet. Nevertheless, traditional establishments still exist, and variations on the old *Heuriger* theme continue to open.

'When you go to a *Heuriger*, my advice is to drink everything, particularly the mixed varieties. Vienna has the advantage of diverse soils and a microclimate, which means a lot of varieties coexist, and every wine maker has special rarities, so it's best to ask. Eat anything that looks great – that's the advantage of a buffet – and what you're not familiar with. This is half the adventure.

'My favourite wine from my own production is the Alte Reben Zweigelt. It corresponds with my idea of a Viennese wine – not international, very autonomous, at the beginning quite distant and complicated, but with time and understanding for its qualities, a very personal wine. I also enjoy Grüner Veltliner from the Wachau and Kamptal (the Danube Valley).

'To experience traditional *Heurigen*, either visit places recommended here or drive to one of the wine areas on the city border and drop into every place that has a *Busch'n* hanging from its door. At the latter you should have no expectations of quality, just take it as it comes.'

SCHMIDT

☎ 292 66 88; 21, Stammersdorfer Strasse 105;
☾ 3pm-midnight Thu-Sun, closed Jul; ⓔ 31, bus 30A

A well-established Stammersdorf *Heuriger*, Schmidt stocks wonderful Muskateller and Grüner Veltliner and offers wine tastings of local vintages. In November, around the birthday of St Martin, you can also sample the traditional *Martinigansl* (goose). Schmidt is a few minutes' walk northwest of the tram 31 terminus, and the same distance southeast of the bus 30A terminus.

WEINGUT SCHILLING

☎ 292 41 89; 21, Langenzersdorferstrasse 54;
☾ 4pm-midnight Mon-Fri, from 3pm Sat & Sun even months; ⓔ 26

With the spread of vineyards rising over Bisamberg hill in full view from its large garden, Schilling attracts many on warm evenings. It's reputation for quality wine also helps its popularity ranking and tours of the wine cellar are available for those who ask nicely. Schilling is a 15-minute walk from the final destination of tram 26; walk north along Russbergstrasse to Langenzersdorferstrasse and then west for a short distance.

WIENINGER

☎ 292 41 06; 21, Stammersdorfer Strasse 78;
☾ 3pm-midnight Wed-Fri, from noon Sat & Sun Mar–mid-Jul & mid-Aug-Dec; ⓔ 31, bus 30A

Bus 30A stops a few minutes' walk east of Wieninger, a family-run *Heuriger* in central Stammersdorf. The food buffet, which features organic produce and a healthy smattering of vegetarian options, is extensive, the wine from its own vineyard fruity and light, and the atmosphere local and relaxed. Cellar tours are also offered.

MAUER

ZAHEL Map pp252-3

☎ 889 13 18; 23, Maurer Hauptplatz 9; ☾ 3pm-midnight Tue-Sun; tram 60, bus 60A

One of the oldest *Heurigen* in Vienna, Zahel occupies a 250 year-old farmer's house on Maurer Hauptplatz. The buffet is laden with Viennese and seasonal cuisine and wine is for sale to take home. It sometimes closes for weeks at a time; if so, head two blocks south to Maurer Lange Gasse for more options.

STADTHEURIGEN

WEINSTUBE JOSEFSTADT Map pp258-9

☎ 406 46 28; 08, Piaristengasse 27; ☾ 4pm-midnight, closed Jan-Mar; bus 13A

Weinstube Josefstadt is one of the loveliest *Stadtheurigen* in the city. Its garden is a barely controlled green oasis amongst concrete residential blocks, and tables are squeezed in between the trees and shrubs. Food is typical, with a buffet-style selection and plenty of cheap meats (chicken wings go for only €1). The friendly, well-liquored locals come free of charge. The location is not well sign-posted; the only sign of its existence is a metal *Buschel* hanging from a doorway.

ESTERHÁZYKELLER Map pp254-5

☎ 533 34 82; 01, Haarhof 1; ☾ 11am-11pm Mon-Fri, 4-11pm Sat & Sun; ⓜ U3 Herrengasse, bus 1A

Esterházykeller is tucked away on a quiet courtyard just off Kohlmarkt. Its enormous cellar is a tad claustrophobic, but after a few glasses of excellent wine, direct from the Esterházy Palace cellar in Eisenstadt, no one seems to mind. The rustic decor, complete with medieval weaponry and farming tools, reeks of kitsch, but the individual wooden booths are its saving grace. Unlike most *Heurigen*, beer is offered.

ZWÖLF APOSTELKELLER Map pp254-5

☎ 512 67 77; 01, Sonnenfelsgasse 3; ☾ 4.30pm-midnight; U1, U3 Stephansplatz, bus 1A

Even though Zwölf Apostelkeller (Twelve Apostle Cellar) plays it up for the tourists, it still retains plenty of charm, dignity and authenticity. This is mostly due to the premises themselves: a vast, dimly lit multilevel cellar. The atmosphere is often lively and rowdy, helped along by traditional *Heuriger* music from 7pm Wednesday to Friday.

BARS & PUBS

It may not be massive, but Vienna has a kicking nightlife. Many locations feature DJs on a regular basis and begin to fill from around 9pm onwards; some go on until 4am or later depending on the day, while others start to peter out around 1am and are completely dead by 2am.

Concentrations of bars, pubs and clubs are spread throughout the city, and due to Vienna's compact size and its stellar public transport system, getting from one to the

Drinking

BARS & PUBS

AUSTRIAN WINE & BEER AT A GLANCE

A few of the main **wine** varieties in Austria:

Blauer Burgunder Austria's version of Pinot Noir; a complex and fruity red found near the Neusiedler See.

Blaufränkisch Dry, light-bodied red rich in tannin; grows best in middle- and southern-Burgenland.

Grüner Veltliner Austria's largest grape variety; a strong, fresh white with hints of citrus and pear.

Müller-Thurgau Mild and often flowery white found in Lower Austria and Burgenland.

Riesling/Rheinriesling Fruity white with strong acidity; predominantly produced in the Danube Valley.

St Laurent Dark, velvety red originating in the Bordeaux village of the same name.

Weissburgunder Mainly grown in Burgenland, this rich white has a slight almond taste and piquant acidity.

Welshriesling Fresh, fruity white with a touch of spice; planted mainly in Burgenland and Lower Austria.

Zweigelt Full-bodied red with intense cherry fruit aromas, found throughout Austria's wine-growing regions.

While wine is the chosen drink of the Viennese, **beer** features heavily in the city's cultural make-up. Gösser, Ottakring, Puntigamer, Stiegl, Wieselburger and Zipfer are typical labels. These are the main beer types you're likely to find:

Bockbier Strong lager beer (sometimes as high as 12% alcohol volume) only available around Christmas and Easter. Can be dangerous stuff.

Dunkel Thick dark beer with a very rich flavour.

G'mischt A mixture of *Helles* and *Dunkel*.

Helles Clear beer; light hops taste and very common.

Märzen Red-coloured beer with a strong malt taste.

Pils Pilsner beer; very crisp and strong, and often bitter.

Weizen Also known as Weissbier; full-bodied wheat beer, slightly sweet in taste. Can be light or dark, clear or cloudy, and is sometimes served with a slice of lemon.

Zwickel Unfiltered beer with a cloudy complexion; should always be drunk fresh.

next takes little effort. While the Innere Stadt never seems to empty of people, its scene is small and limited to a few select bars. The Bermuda Dreieck (Bermuda Triangle) in the old Jewish Quarter is rammed with places, but most are unbearable pick-up joints. Leopoldstadt is the new darling of Vienna's night owls; its bars and clubs ooze 'underground' and attract a motley crew of students, artists, and drunkards. Collectively, the Naschmarkt and its close neighbours Wieden and Mariahilf contain the largest consolidation of bars – Schleifmühlgasse in particular has some good pickings. Around Josefstädter Strasse U-Bahn station on the Gürtel is yet another area sporting a profusion of bars, some of which are leaders in the electronica scene while others host live acts and clouds of smoke.

With the advent of summer, many revellers descend on outdoor venues. The bars and shady courtyard at **Alte AKH** (Map pp258–9) attract plenty, as does the urban market square **Yppenplatz** (Map pp258–9)

in Ottakring. The reinvention of the Danube Canal as a bar strip has to date been a huge success; Summer Stage (p128) and Flex (p164) are long-established locations, but the likes of Strandbar Herrmann (p155) has added an entirely new dimension to the waterway. **Copa Kagrana** and **Sunken City** (Map pp252–3), near the Donauinsel U-Bahn station, are crowded with outdoor bars and clubs, but most are tacky and uninviting.

Getting home is hassle-free; night buses start when the U-Bahn and trams stop, and taxis are cheap and plentiful.

INNERE STADT

ALT WIEN Map pp254-5

☎ 512 52 22; 01, Bäckerstrasse 9; ⏰ 10am-2am Sun-Thu, 10am-4am Fri & Sat; Ⓤ U1, U3 Stephansplatz, bus 1A, 2A

Dark, Bohemian and full of character, Alt Wien is a classic dive attracting students

(Continued on page 155)

1 *Shop display at Art Up (p183)*
2 *Foyer of Staatsoper (p169)*
3 *Dorotheum auction house (p181)* 4 *Boutique shops along Kohlmarkt (p178)*
Previous page: *Prunksaal of the Nationalbibliothek (p63), Hofburg*

1 ...a Konditorei (p139)
...kstreets of the Innere
...(p55) 3 Melange at
...s Café (p141)

1 *Angel statue at Kirche* *Steinhof (p98)* 2 *Façade* *Hundertwasser Haus (p* 3 *Detail of the Stadtbah* *Pavillons (p89)* 4 *House* *Wagner at Linke Wienze* *38 (p90)*

värme incinerator (p92)
ikahaus (p90) by Otto
3 KunstHausWien

1 *Tanzcafé Jenseits (p15*
2 *Vineyards north of the*
Stadt (p111) 3 Sacher T◼
Café Sacher (p140)

1 *Neptune fountain and the Gloriette at Schönbrunn (p101)* 2 *Riesenrad (p80) in the Prater* 3 *Heuriger (p142) near the Wienerwald* 4 *Wall art at Kunsthallencafé (p156)*

(Continued from page 146)

and arty types. It's also a one-stop shop for a lowdown on events in the city – every available wall space is plastered with posters advertising shows, concerts and exhibitions. The goulash is legendary and perfectly complemented by dark bread and beer.

AMERICAN BAR Map pp254-5
☎ 512 32 83; 01, Kärntner Durchgang 10; ☉ noon-4am Sun-Wed, noon-5am Thu-Sat; ⓜ U1, U3 Stephansplatz

Designed by Adolf Loos in 1908 (it also goes by the name Loos-Bar), the American Bar is a tiny box with mirrored walls to trick the mind into thinking it's in a far bigger space. The cocktail list is lengthy and their mixing professional, which means the bar is often full to overflowing even on week nights.

FIRST FLOOR Map pp254-5
01, Seitenstettengasse 5; ☉ 7pm-4am Mon-Sat, 8pm-3am Sun; U1, U4 Schwedenplatz, ⓣ N, 1, 2, 21

First Floor is a true barfly haunt, with cocktails galore, classic jazz tunes, professional, laid-back bartenders and a huge aquarium (empty of fish). It's a grand place to get soddenly drunk with a best mate, or spend hours flirting with the opposite sex.

RINGSTRASSE

CAFÉ LEOPOLD Map pp254-5
☎ 523 67 32; 07, Museumsplatz 1; ☉ 10am-2am, till 4am Thu-Sat; ⓜ U2 MuseumsQuartier

The pick of the MuseumsQuartier bars, Café Leopold sits high at the top of the Leopold Museum (p76). Its design is sleek and smart – its conservatory overlooks the MQ's square – and the atmosphere is more club than bar (DJs feature Monday to Saturday). At times the air can become uncomfortably smoky.

STRANDBAR HERRMANN Map pp254-5
03, Herrmannpark; ☉ 10am-2am Apr-early Oct & Dec; ⓣ N, 1, 2

This newcomer on the banks of the canal made a huge splash in Vienna's bar scene in 2006. Its beach-bar design, complete with beach chairs, sand and an open-air outlook, attracts hordes of Viennese on hot summer evenings and at times its impossible to find a chair. Films occasionally feature, blankets are available on cooler

evenings, and *Glühwein* (mulled wine) is served in December.

PALMENHAUS Map pp254-5
☎ 533 10 33; 01, Burggarten; ☉ 10am-2am; ⓜ U1, U2, U4 Karlsplatz, bus 3A

Housed in a beautifully restored Victorian palm house, complete with high arched ceilings, glass walls and steel beams, Palmenhaus occupies one of the most attractive locations in Vienna. The crowd is generally well-to-do, but the ambience is relaxed and welcoming. The outdoor seating in summer is a must, and there are occasional club nights.

URANIA Map pp254-5
☎ 713 30 66; 01, Uraniastrasse 1; ☉ 9-2am Mon-Sat, 9am-midnight Sun; ⓣ 1, 2

Another addition to the canal's ever-increasing stock of bars, Urania occupies the first floor of a rejuvenated cinema and observatory complex. Its slick, clean decor, elevated position overlooking the canal and extensive cocktail selection are all big pluses.

VOLKSGARTEN PAVILLON Map pp254-5
☎ 532 09 07; 01, Burgring 1; ☉ 11-2am May–mid-Sep; ⓜ U2, U3 Volkstheater, Volkstheater trams

Volksgarten's second venue (after the club Volksgarten p165) is a lovely 1950s-style pavilion with views of Heldenplatz. On Tuesday nights its ever-popular garden is packed to the gunnels when it hosts 'Das Techno Cafe'; any other time entry is free.

Entrance to Urania bar & cinema complex (this page)

EAST OF THE DANUBE CANAL

A BAR SHABU Map pp258-9

02, Rotensterngasse 8; ⏳ 5pm-till late; bus 5A

A gorgeous little bar outfitted in '70s retro, Shabu welcomes all and sundry with an unaffected ambience and laid-back staff. Regular DJs provide an excellent backdrop of calming tunes, and the absinthe selection from around Europe is extensive. Don't miss the Japanese room, or should we say closet.

CABARET RENZ Map pp258-9

02, Zirkusgasse 50; ⏳ 8pm-late; Ⓤ U1 Praterstern, bus 5A

A former brothel turned bar/club, Cabaret Renz occupies an innocuous corner in residential Leopoldstadt. The velvet-clad club, which hosts clubbing on Friday and Saturday nights, attracts a 20-something crowd and the best local DJ talent, plus a few international acts. Renz's grungy, red bar next door is typically Viennese, with resident boozers, table football and plenty of heated chatter.

FLUC Map pp258-9

www.fluc.at in German; 02, Praterstern 5; ⏳ 6pm-4am; Ⓤ U1 Praterstern, 🚋 0, 5

Located on the wrong side of the tracks (Praterstern can be uncomfortable at times) and looking for all the world like a pre-fab schoolroom, Fluc is the closest Vienna's nightlife scene comes to anarchy – without the fear of physical violence. Black-clad students, smashed alcoholics, 30-something freelancers and the occasional TV celebrity all share the stripped-back venue without any hassle, and DJs or live acts play every night (electronica features heavily).

INSIDE THE GÜRTEL

Wieden

CAFÉ ANZENGRUBER Map pp254-5

☎ 587 82 97; 04, Schleifmühlgasse 19; ⏳ 5pm-2am Mon, 11am-2am Tue-Sat; bus 59A

This corner café attracts an arty crowd and many of Vienna's jazz musicians. Both the décor and atmosphere are laid-back, and the food, which has a distinct Croatian slant, is highly recommended. There's also a pool table.

CLUB U Map pp254-5

☎ 505 99 04; 04, Künstlerhauspassage; ⏳ 10pm-4am; Ⓤ U1, U2, U4 Karlsplatz

Club U occupies one of Otto Wagner's Stadtbahn Pavillons on Karlsplatz (p89). It's a small, student-infested bar/club with regular DJs and a wonderful outdoor seating area overlooking the pavilions and park.

KUNSTHALLENCAFÉ Map pp254-5

☎ 587 00 73; 04, Treitlstrasse 2; ⏳ 10am-2am; Ⓤ U1, U2, U4 Karlsplatz

The Kunsthallencafé carries plenty of 'cool' clout and attracts a relaxed, arty crowd with its DJs and close proximity to the Kunsthalle Project Space (p89). The big sofas go quickly, but there's plenty of small tables perfect for an intimate evening, and in summer the huge terrace (with more couches) is a big attraction. Thankfully, the building site surrounded this glass box has *finally* been cleared to let in the cityscape.

ORANGE ONE Map pp260-1

☎ 586 22 20; 04, Margaretenstrasse 26; ⏳ from 4pm; bus 59A

Once the haunt of down-and-outs and alcoholics, this former *Gasthaus* (guesthouse) received a complete make-over and reinvented itself as Orange One, a modern bar with a distinct retro feel and grown-up attitude. DJs play most nights and off-beat films are intermittently projected on the back wall. If smoke is a problem, it's best not to spend too much time here on winter nights.

SCHIKANEDER Map pp260-1

☎ 585 58 88; 04, Margareten Strasse 22-24; ⏳ 5.30pm-4am; bus 59A

Most of the colour in Schikaneder comes from the regularly projected movies splayed across one of its white walls – the students and arty crowd who frequent this grungy bar dress predominantly in black. But that's not to detract from the bar's atmosphere, which exudes energy well into the wee small hours of the morning. Schikaneder also hosts movies most nights (p172).

Mariahilf

BAR ITALIA LOUNGE Map pp254-5
☎ 585 28 38; 06, Mariahilfer Strasse 19-21; ◷ noon-2.30pm & 6.30pm-3am Mon-Fri, 6.30pm-3am Sat & Sun; ⊕ U2 Museumsquartier
One of a growing number of lounge bars in Vienna, Bar Italia caters to the trendy set with its slick decor and sharp service. The bar fills the ground floor, while downstairs is occupied by the lounge, where late-night revelry on the dance floor takes place.

CAFÉ SAVOY Map pp260-1
☎ 586 73 48; 06, Linke Wienzeile 36; 5pm-2am Mon-Fri, 9-2am Sat; ⊕ U4 Kettenbrückengasse
Café Savoy is an established gay haunt that has a more traditional café feel to it, except for the feathers everywhere. The clientele is generally very mixed on a Saturday – mainly due to the proximity of the Naschmarkt – but at other times it's filled with men of all ages.

CAFÉ WILLENDORF Map pp260-1
☎ 587 17 89; 06, Linke Wienzeile 102; ◷ 6pm-2am; ⊕ U4 Pilgramgasse, bus 13A
This is one of Vienna's seminal gay and lesbian bars. Housed in the pink Rosa Lila Villa (p226), it's a very popular place to meet for a chat, a drink or a meal. The lovely inner courtyard garden opens for the summer months.

ELEKTRO GÖNNER Map pp260-1
☎ 208 66 79; 06, Mariahilfer Strasse 101; ◷ 6pm-2am, till 4am Fri & Sat; ⊕ U3 Zieglergasse
Elektro Gönner is an unpretentious bar opened by architects (and attracting plenty from the profession). Much of the interior is uncomplicated and bare, aside from the occasional art installation in the back room, and the music diverse. The bar hides at the back of a courtyard off Mariahilfer Strasse.

www.lonelyplanet.com

FUTUREGARDEN BAR & ART CLUB
Map pp260-1
☎ 585 26 13; 06, Schadekgasse 6; ◷ 7pm-2am Mon-Sat, 9pm-2am Sun; ⊕ U3 Neubaugasse, bus 13A, 14A
With white walls, an open bar and basic furniture, it's hard to find a simpler place in Vienna. Its one piece of decoration – apart from the occasional art exhibition by local artists – is its rectangular disco 'ball', which swings from the ceiling. Futuregarden attracts a 30s crowd with a cool atmosphere and electric sounds.

MANGO BAR Map pp254-5
☎ 587 44 48; 06, Laimgrubengasse 3; ◷ 9pm-4am; ⊕ U4 Kettenbrückengasse, bus 57A
Mango attracts a young, often men-only gay crowd with good music, friendly staff and plenty of mirrors to check out yourself and others. It usually serves as a kick-start for a big night out on the town.

PHIL Map pp254-5
☎ 581 04 89; 06, Gumpendorfer Strasse 10-12; ◷ 10am-1am Tue-Sun, 5pm-1am Mon; bus 57A
A retro bar reminiscent of an East Berlin Lokal, Phil attracts a bohemian crowd happy to squat on kitsch furniture your Grandmother used to own. Half the establishment is store rather than bar; TVs from the '70s, DVDs, records and books are for sale, as is all the furniture. Staff are super friendly and the vibe is relaxed as can be.

TANZCAFÉ JENSEITS Map pp260-1
☎ 587 12 33; 06, Nelkengasse 3; ◷ 9pm-4am Mon-Sat; ⊕ U3 Neubaugasse, bus 13A, 14A
The red-velvet interior that might be out of a '70s bordello is a soothing backdrop for a night out at Jenseits. The tiny dance floor

Drinking

BARS & PUBS

fills to overflowing on Fridays and Saturdays with relaxed revellers slowing moving around each other to soul and funk.

TOP KINO BAR Map pp254-5

☎ 208 30 00; 06, Rahlgasse 1; ⏱ 10am-2am; ⊕ U2 Museumsquartier, bus 57A

Occupying the foyer of the cinema Top Kino (p172) is the Top Kino Bar, a pleasantly relaxed place that attracts a fashionable alternative crowd. The décor is highly retro, and there are tunes to match the furniture. Kozel, one of the Czech Republic's better Pilsners, is lined up against Austria's finest lagers.

Neubau

BLUE BOX Map pp260-1

☎ 523 26 82; 07, Richtergasse 8; ⏱ 6pm-2am Mon, 10-2am Tue-Thu & Sun, 10am-4am Fri & Sat; ⊕ U3 Neubaugasse, bus 13A

Don't let the smoke and the run-down appearance of Blue Box put you off. These trademarks, which seem to have been around for generations, are an integral part of the Blue Box experience. It's too small to afford dance-floor space, and most guests groove to the regular DJ beats in their seats. Superb breakfasts are available from 10am to 5pm Tuesday to Sunday.

MÖBEL Map pp254-5

☎ 524 94 97; 07, Burggasse 10; ⏱ 10am-1am; ⊕ U2, U3 Volkstheater, bus 48A

Das Möbel wins points for its furniture, consisting entirely of one-off pieces produced by local designers. Half the fun is choosing a spot that takes your fancy – whether it be a swinging chair or a surfboard bench. Light fittings, bags and various odds and ends complete the look, and everything is for sale.

EUROPA Map pp260-1

☎ 526 33 83; 07, Zollergasse 8; ⏱ 9am-5am; ⊕ U3 Neubaugasse, bus 13A

A long-standing fixture of the 7th district, Europa is a chilled spot any time day or night. During the sunny hours, join the relaxed set at a window table for coffee and food, and in the evening take a pew at the bar and enjoy the DJ's tunes. Its breakfast, served between 9am and 3pm on weekends, caters to a hungover clientele.

SHEBEEN Map pp260-1

☎ 524 79 00; 07, Lerchenfelder Strasse 45; ⏱ 5pm-2am Mon, 5pm-4am Tue-Fri, 1pm-4am Sat, 10am-2am Sun; ⏹ 46

Pub quizzes, darts, happy hours, live football, Guinness on tap, and locals wanting to practice their English – Shebeen is solidly un-Austrian, which is where the attraction for many lies. The dark wood-panelling and high ceilings are vaguely reminiscent of a Brit pub, while the boisterous clientele and lashings of beer are undisputedly Anglo-Saxon. The small garden is a blessing in summer.

SHULTZ Map pp260-1

☎ 522 91 20; 07, Siebensterngasse 31; ⏱ 9-2am Mon-Thu, 9am-3am Fri & Sat, 5pm-2am Sun; ⏹ 49

This lovely '60s-style bar mixes wonderful cocktails and attracts a laid-back and unpretentious crowd. During the day the glass walls allow daylight to flood the bar, while at night they provide ample room to watch the world roll on by outside.

WIRR Map pp260-1

☎ 929 40 50; www.wirr.at in German; 07, Burggasse 70; ⏱ 10am-2am Mon-Thu & Sun, 10-4am Fri & Sat; bus 48A

On weekends it's often hard to find a seat – particularly on the comfy sofas – at this colourful, alternative bar. Its rooms are spacious and open, the walls are covered in local artists' work, including a large (albeit bizarre) tie collection, and light snacks are available. Eclectic clubbings – which range from 60s pop to Balkan rhythms – are well attended in the downstairs club.

Josefstadt

B72 Map pp258-9

☎ 409 21 28; www.b72.at in German; 08, Hernalser Gürtel 72; ⏱ 8pm-4am; ⊕ U6 Alser Strasse, ⏹ 43, 44

Fringe live acts, alternative beats and album launches are the mainstay of B72's entertainment line-up, which collectively attracts a predominantly youthful crowd. Its tall glass walls and arched brick interior are typical of most bars along the Gürtel, as is the thick, smoky air and grungy appearance. Its name comes from its address, Bogen (arch) 72.

CHELSEA Map pp258-9

☎ 407 93 09; www.chelsea.co.at in German; 08, Lerchenfelder Gürtel 29-31; ⊗ 6pm-4am Mon-Sun; U6 Thaliastrasse, ⊛ 46

Chelsea is the old, ratty dog on the Gürtel and very much a favourite of the student/alternative scene. Posters and underground paraphernalia adorn walls, DJs spin loud sounds (usually indie, sometimes techno) when live acts aren't playing, and on weekends bouncers are required to control numbers. During football season, English premier league and Champions league football games are broadcast.on Sundays and some other times during the week.

FRAUENCAFÉ Map pp254-5

☎ 406 37 54; 08, Lange Gasse 8; ⊗ 6.30pm-2am Tue-Sat, ⊛ 46

A strictly women-only café/bar, Frauen-café has long been a favourite of Vienna's lesbian scene. It has a homely, relaxed feel and is located away from the hub of gay and lesbian bars around the Rosa Lila Villa.

MAS! Map pp258-9

☎ 403 83 24; 08, Laudongasse 36; ⊗ 6pm-2am Mon-Sat, 10am-2am Sun; ⊛ 5, 33

A designer bar specialising in cocktails and Mexican food, Mas! attracts an affluent and well-groomed set. Choose from a high, wobbly stool at the long, shimmering bar backed by an enormous light installation, or for a more intimate evening, a low, dimly lit table. Its Sunday brunch – a mix of Cajun, English and American breakfasts between 1am and 4pm – is legendary, and happy hour is from 6pm to 8pm daily.

RHIZ Map pp258-9

☎ 409 25 05; 08, Lerchenfelder Gürtel 37-38; ⊗ 6pm-4am Mon-Sat, 6pm-2am Sun; ⊚ U6 Josefstädter Strasse, ⊛ J, 33

Rhiz's decor of brick arches and glass walls is reminiscent of so many bars beneath the U6 line, but its status as a stalwart of the city's electronica scene gives it the edge over much of the competition. Black-clad boozers and an alternative set cram the interior during winter to hear DJs and live

VIENNA'S MICROBREWERIES

Venues where the beer is always fresh and the atmosphere boisterous, Vienna's microbreweries make for a hedonistic evening out. Most offer a healthy selection of beers brewed on the premises (and proudly display the shining, brass brewing equipment) that are perfectly complimented by traditional Austrian food. It's not the most salubrious combination, but it's definitely satisfying.

1516 Brewing Company (Map pp254-5; ☎ 961 15 16; www.1516brewingcompany.com; 01, Schwarzenberg-strasse 2; ⊗ 11am-2am; ⊛ D, 1, 2, bus 3A) Unfiltered beers and a few unusual varieties, such as Heidi's Blueberry Ale. Large choice of cigars and frequented by city workers and UN staff.

Fischer Bräu (Map pp258-9; ☎ 369 59 49; www.fischerbraeu.at in German; 19, Billrothstrasse 17; ⊗ 4pm-1am Mon-Sat, 11am-1am Sun; ⊛ 38, bus 35A) A new beer every four to six weeks, and a *Helles* lager all year round. Large garden and live jazz on Sundays.

Ottakringer Brauerei (Map pp252-3; ☎ 491 00-0; www.ottakringer.at in German; 16, Ottakringerstrasse 91; ⊛ J, 9, 44) Tours are available of Vienna's largest brewery; its shop (⊗ 9am-7pm Mon-Fri, 9am-6pm Sat) sells a vast array of Ottakring merchandise.

Salm Bräu (Map pp262-3; ☎ 799 59 92; www.salmbraeu.com; 03, Rennweg 8; ⊗ 11am-midnight; ⊛ 71) Brews its own *Helles, Pils, Märzen, G'mischt,* and *Weizen*. Hugely popular, and has happy hour from 3pm to 5pm Monday to Friday and noon to 4pm Saturday.

Siebensternbräu (Map pp254-5; ☎ 523 86 97; www.7stern.at; 07, Siebensterngasse 19; ⊗ 10am-midnight; ⊛ 49) Large brewery with all the main varieties, plus a hemp beer, chilli beer, and smoky beer (the malt is dried over an open fire).

Wiedner Bräu (Map pp262-3; ☎ 586 03 00; www.wieden-braeu.at in German; 04, Waaggasse 5; ⊗ 11.30am-1am Mon-Sat, 11.30am-midnight Sun; ⊛ 62, 65) *Helles, Märzen* and hemp beers all year round, plus a few seasonal choices, including a ginger beer. Happy hour 5.30pm to 7.30pm.

acts, while in summer the large outdoor seating area fills to overflowing. Staff couldn't be friendlier and there's internet access.

Alsergrund

CAFÉ BERG Map pp258-9

☎ 319 57 20; 09, Berggasse 8; ⊙ 10am-1am; ⊕ U2 Schottentor, ⛋ 37, 38, 40, 41, 42, 43, 44, bus 40A

Café Berg is Vienna's leading gay bar, although its welcoming to all walks of life. Its staff are some of the nicest in town, the layout sleek and smart and the vibe chilled. Its bookshop, Löwenherz (⊙ 10am-7pm Mon-Fri, 10am-5pm Sat), stocks a grand collection of gay magazines and books.

CAFÉ STEIN Map pp254-5

☎ 319 72 41; 09, Währinger Strasse 6-8; ⊙ 7am-1am Mon-Sat, 9am-1am Sun; ⊕ U2 Schottentor, ⛋ 37, 38, 40, 41, 42, 43, 44

During the day this three-level café is a popular haunt of students from the nearby university; come evening the clientele metamorphoses into city workers with a lot more money to spend. DJs control the decks in the evenings, and the all-day menu is extensive. During the summer there is outside seating, which enjoys superb views of the Votivkirche.

OUTSIDE THE GÜRTEL

BRUNNERS Map pp252-3

☎ 607 65 00; 22 fl, 10, Wienerbergstrasse 7; ⊙ 11am-2am Mon-Sat; ⛋ 65, bus 65A

Brunner's major attraction is its view; from its elevated position on the 22nd floor of Vienna's Twin Towers, the entire city is laid out in all its grandeur. The best time to visit is just before the sun sets over the Vienna Woods to the west, after which the fluorescent lighting system kicks in and spoils the scene somewhat.

LO:SCH Map pp260-1

☎ 895 99 79; 15, Fünfhausgasse 1; ⊙ 10pm-2am Fri & Sat; ⊕ U6 Gumpendorfer Strasse, bus 57A

This leather-fetish bar is normally strictly men only, but occasionally it hosts unisex parties on Saturday nights. Lo:sch sometimes opens during the week for special events.

SPARK Map pp258-9

☎ 968 57 02; www.spark.at; 18, Währinger Gürtel 107; ⊙ 6pm-2am Tue-Thu, 6pm-4am Fri, 7pm-4am Sat; ⊕ U6 Währinger Strasse, ⛋ 40, 41

This chilled bar is a bit of a trek for most, but with a 1970s retro décor, comfy couches, and a daily dose of DJs, it's worth the effort. Live concerts are held once a month, and absinthe fans will be in heaven; Spark stocks 25 different varieties.

Drinking

BARS & PUBS

Entertainment

Entertainment

There's no doubting Vienna's prowess as a classical music mecca, but an electronica centre, a jazz aficionado's haven, a fitness freak's playground? Vienna's entertainment scene is all this and more.

The city has come a long way from the days when a night out meant aperitifs at a stiff bar followed by a performance at the opera. Sure, it's still the place to do just that – the Staatsoper is one of the finest in Europe, the Vienna Philharmonic world renowned, the chorus of classical music concerts unceasing – but now options abound. Live music venues, like Porgy & Bess (p167) and Birdland (p166), attract superb jazz acts year round, while smaller locations cater to an array of local talent. The clubbing scene may be small, but quality over quantity, right? Homegrown DJs, such as Kruder & Dorfmeister and the Sofa Surfers, regularly perform alongside their international counterparts in clubs packed with revellers.

Those looking for fresh air and exercise won't come up short either. The old and new waterways of the Danube are literally made for swimming and boating, and the city is peppered with pools. Green parklands such as the Prater and the Donauinsel (Danube Island) provide plenty of space to stretch the legs, and the Wienerwald (Vienna Woods) on the city's western fringes is a beautiful area to enjoy on foot or by bicycle.

Vienna's weekly rag *Falter* (www.falter.at) is the best entertainment information source; it lists music concerts from every genre, cinema schedules, clubbings, theatre performances, children's events, and sporting fixtures. Both the paper and its virtual version are in German, but they shouldn't take much time to decipher. *City* (www.city-online.at, in German), another weekly events paper in German, is thin on news and topical chat but has basic listings. Local radio station FM4 (103.8FM; fm4.orf.at, in German) provides the lowdown on events in English at various times throughout the day. The tourist office produces a monthly listing of events covering theatre, concerts, film festivals, spectator sports, exhibitions and more; also see its seasonal magazine, *Vienna Scene*.

Vienna is one of the safest cities in the world, so if you have the urge to walk home after a night out don't think twice about it. There are a few places to avoid however; see the Directory chapter (p229) for details.

Dusk view of the Burgtheater (p170)

Tickets & Reservations

BUNDESTHEATERKASSEN Map pp254-5

☎ 514 44-7880; www.bundestheater.at; 01, Hanuschgasse 3; ☟ 8am-6pm Mon-Fri, 9am-noon Sat & Sun; ◉ U1, U2, U4 Karlsplatz, ⓡ D, J, 1, 2, 62, 65

The state ticket office only sells tickets to federal venues: Akademietheater, Burgtheater, Schauspielhaus, Staatsoper and Volksoper. The office charges no commission, and tickets for the Staatsoper and Volksoper are available here one month prior to the performance date. Credit cards are accepted and credit-card purchases can also be made by telephone. Alternatively, tickets for these federal venues can be booked over the internet.

JIRSA THEATER KARTEN BÜRO

Map pp260-1

☎ 400 600; viennaticket.at; 08, Lerchenfelder Strasse 12; ☟ 9.30am-5.30pm Mon, Thu & Fri, 9.30am-1pm Tue & Wed; ⓡ 46, bus 13A

Jirsa is one of the larger ticketing offices in the city (there are around 20 in total). Tickets for a range of performances and venues are sold here, but you might be charged commission (some places add 20% to 30%).

WIEN-TICKET PAVILLON

Map pp254-5

☎ 588 85; www.wien-ticket.at in German; 01, Herbert-von-Karajan-Platz; ☟ 10am-7pm; ◉ U1, U2, U4 Karlsplatz, ⓡ D, J, 1, 2, 62, 65

This ticket booth, housed in the hut by the Staatsoper, is linked to the city government

and charges anything from no commission up to a 6% levy. Tickets for all venues are sold here.

WEBSITES

Austria Ticket Online (www.austriaticket.at in German) Extensive online ticketing agent, covering the whole entertainment spectrum.

ClubTicket (www.clubticket.at in German) Another comprehensive online ticket agent, also with last-minute deals.

CLUBS

The Viennese aren't known for their tarantism ways, which means the clubbing scene in Vienna is relatively small. Small doesn't mean dire though; clubs invariably feature excellent DJs and also a variety of music genres, which means that you'll always find something to fit your tastes. As most local folk detest queuing, crowded dance floors and hefty entry prices, clubs are generally quite intimate, and massive, bombastic venues are rare creatures. Entry prices can and do vary wildly – from nothing to €20 – and depend on who's on the decks.

The dividing line between a club and bar in Vienna is often quite blurred and hard to pick. Most contemporary bars tend to feature DJs on a regular basis and some, such as Europa (p158), Tanzcafé Jenseits (p157), Café Leopold (p155) and Wirr (p158) have small, but well-used dance floors.

AUX GAZELLES Map pp254-5

☎ 585 66 45; www.auxgazelles.at; 06, Rahlgasse 5; Club Bar ☟ 10pm-4am Thu-Sat; ◉ U2 Museumsquartier, bus 57A

Aux Gazelles' club bar is beautifully Moorish and suitably filled with beautiful people. The music is an eclectic mix of smooth ethnic sounds, and there are plenty of dim corners and low, comfy couches to escape to if so desired. The rest of this gigantic club venue features a restaurant, bar, deli, and there's even a hammam (oriental steam bath). Aux Gazelles is one of the few clubs in town where a dress code is enforced.

TOP FIVE CLUBS

- Flex (p164) – outstanding sound system, top-rate DJs, and no dress code
- Roxy (p165) – progressive sounds, intimate dance floor, and not big enough to lose your friends
- Künstlerhauspassage (p165) – caters to the alternative set with techno DJs and fringe live acts
- Goodmann (p164) – opens its doors as others clubs wind down, and there's food!
- Passage (p165) – Vienna's club of the moment for the well-dressed crowd and after-work clubbers

VIENNA'S ELECTRONIC HEARTBEAT

For such a small city, Vienna has an impressive history in the dance music genre. At the forefront of house and techno tunes since the late 1980s/early 1990s, and linked to seminal centres like Detroit and New York, the city's smooth Downtempo sound and harder Techno beats reached heavenly heights and wowed clubbers worldwide in the mid 1990s. Inevitably, the sweet harmonies and catchy licks were ruthlessly commercialised, and by the end of the 1990s were splayed across the mainstream. Static years followed, but the scene is once more on the move. We asked Sebastian Schlachter-Delgado (www.myspace.com/schlachterdelgado),a well-known DJ who is one of FM4's (fm4.orf.at) resident electronica experts and coproducer of the station's *La Boum De Luxe* show (9.30pm–6am Friday), for his thoughts on Vienna's electronic heartbeat:

Lonely Planet: What is Viennese electronica? How would you class it?

Sebastian: Viennese Electronica was up until now known for two distinct styles, downtempo and techno. Downtempo is laid-back, more mellow, while techno/electro is quite avant-garde, more experimental and serious. Nowadays however the music styles are more and more mixed together. Thanks to the internet, musicians from all over the world and from different genres get together and this symbiosis creates new styles. At the moment a lot of cosmic, electro, disco, dub – but also funk, soul and ambient – is heard in Viennese studios. So you can't really say anymore which styles are typically Viennese.

Lonely Planet: Who are the current movers and shakers in the Viennese scene?

Sebastian: Cheap Records (www.cheap.at) and its founders Patrick Pulsinger and Erdem Tunakan are always worth looking out for. They released 'Waiting for my Love', a single by my band Twinnie. DJ Glow, with his Trust Records label (www.trust.at), is known worldwide for his constant electro movement. Kruder & Dorfmeister's label G-Stone Records (www.g-stoned.com) and artists like Megablast & Makossa and Stereotype are big names in the business, as is Mego Records, which produces experimental electronica. The Sofa Surfers is a name to look out for, as is the Vienna Scientists, but the latter produces more house compilations. The drum n bass scene is also quite big in Vienna.

Lonely Planet: Which bars and clubs regularly host electronica evenings?

Sebastian: Flex, rhiz, Künstlerhauspassage, Roxy, Fluc, Cabaret Renz, WUK, Elektrogönner. For the bigger parties that attract around 2000 people, and plenty of kids, check flyers around town. Flyers are also good for tracking down one-off parties as people are constantly looking for new locations to host an event.

Lonely Planet: Are there any particular nights people should attend to get a taste of Viennese electronica?

Sebastian: 'Dub Club' on Monday and 'Crazy' on Tuesday at Flex are good, as is 'Techno Cafe' at the Volksgarten Pavillon Tuesday evenings over summer. 'Icke Micke' is an excellent event that also attracts newer and more unknown artists and features plenty of techno and electro. During summer it's usually based at Künstlerhauspassage and in winter at Club Camera on Neubaugasse.

Lonely Planet: Who are your personal Austrian-based favourites?

Sebastian: I'm a fan of Gerhard Potuznik, Patrick Pulsinger and Erdem Tunakan. Christopher Just, I-Wolf, G Rizo, Microthol and all acts on Trust Records and Cheap Records too. Also Stereotype and Megablast & Makossa. It's difficult to just mention a few, there's a lot of great musicians in Vienna.

BACH Map pp254–5

☎ 0676-844 260 214; www.bach.co.at in German; 16, Bachgasse 21; ⏰ 9pm-3am Thu-Sat; 🚋 9, 46 An underground club of sorts, Bach features techno DJs and regular live acts from across Europe. The crowd leans towards the grungy side, and is genuine and relaxed, and the dance floor small and intimate. Bach is in the far-flung reaches of Ottakring.

FLEX Map pp254-5

☎ 533 75 25; www.flex.at in German; 01, Donaukanal, Augartenbrücke; ⏰ 6pm-4am; Ⓤ U2, U4 Schottenring, 🚋 1, 2, 31 Flex has been attracting a more mainstream crowd in recent times, but it still manages to retain a semblance of its former edgi-

ness, and the title of best club in town. The sound system is without equal in Vienna (some would say Europe), entry price generally reasonable and dress code unheard of. The monthly DJ line-up features local legends and international names, and live acts are commonplace. 'Dub Club' on Monday (the night to catch G-Stone DJs) and 'London Calling' (alternative and indie) on Wednesday are among the most popular nights. In summer the picnic tables lining the canal overflow with happy partygoers.

GOODMANN Map pp254-5

☎ 967 44 15; www.goodmann.at; 04, Rechte Wienzeile 23; ⏰ 4am-10am Mon-Sat; Ⓤ U4 Kettenbrückengasse, bus 59A

A tiny club attracting clubbers who don't want the night to end, Goodmann serves food upstairs (until 8am) and hides its night owls, who are an eclectic mix of old and young (but always in a merry state), downstairs.

KÜNSTLERHAUSPASSAGE Map pp254-5

☎ 01, Karlsplatz 5; ⏰ 9pm-late Thu-Sun Jun-Sep; ⊕ U1, U2, U4 Karlsplatz, 🚋 D, J, 1, 2, 62, 65

A glass box beneath the Künstlerhaus, Künstlerhauspassage is a refuge for Vienna's art scene. Spoken word performances, films, live music and DJs take turns entertaining a thoroughly alternative crowd; 'Icke Micke', every Friday night from August to September, tops the bill with progressive techno and electronica from the next big names in the DJ business. The adjoining outdoor ampitheatre is a perfect escape from the sweaty dance floor.

PASSAGE Map pp254-5

☎ 961 88 00; www.sunshie.at; 01, Babenberger Passage, Burgring 1; ⏰ 8pm-4am Tue-Thu, 10pm-6am Fri & Sat; 🚋 D, J, 1, 2

Passage is the closest Vienna comes to a megaclub. Its sleek interior, soothing colours and sweaty atmosphere attract the beautiful people of the city, their entourage of oglers and barflies. The music is loud (noise from the Ringstrasse traffic directly overhead is easily drowned out) and fairly mainstream, with R'n'B, hip-hop and house nights; 'Disco Fever Tuesdays' draws some of the biggest crowds. Expect lines and black-clad, muscle-bound doormen after 10pm (11pm on Friday and Saturday).

ROXY Map pp254-5

☎ 961 88 00; www.roxyclub.at; 04, Operngasse 24; ⏰ 11pm-late Thu-Sat; ⊕ U1, U2, U4 Karlsplatz, bus 59A

A seminal club for years, Roxy still manages to run with the clubbing pack, and sometimes lead the way. DJs from Vienna's electronica scene regularly guest on the turntables and most nights it's hard to find a space on the small dance floor. Expect a crowded, but very good, night out here.

TITANIC Map pp254-5

☎ 587 47 58; www.titanicbar.at in German; 06, Theobaldgasse 11; ⏰ 10pm-6am Tue-Sat; ⊕ U2 Museumsquartier, bus 57A

This club is old skool, with door check and bouncers (dress reasonably conservative), but once past these party poopers it's time to whoop it up. Two large dance floors soon fill with revellers either looking to pull or dance the night away to mainstream club sounds, R'n'B and '80s classics. Fun, but not to everyone's taste.

U4 Map pp254-5

☎ 817 11 92; www.u4club.at; 12, Schönbrunner Strasse 222; ⏰ 10pm-until late; ⊕ U4 Meidling Hauptstrasse, bus 10A

U4 was the birthplace of techno clubbings in Vienna way back when, and its longevity is a testament to its ability to roll with the times. A fairly young, studenty crowd are its current regulars, and while the music isn't as cutting edge as it used to be, it still manages to please the masses.

VOLKSGARTEN Map pp254-5

☎ 532 42 41; www.volksgarten.at in German; 01, Burgring 1; ⏰ 8pm-2am Mon-Wed, 9.30am-late Thu-Sat; ⊕ U2, U3 Volkstheater, 🚋 D, J, 1, 2

A hugely popular club superbly located near the Hofburg, Volksgarten serves a clientele eager to see and be seen. The long cocktail bar is perfect for people-watching and the music is an every rotating mix of hip-hop, house, salsa and reggae, but is hardly ever challenging. Opening hours are not fixed, and dress well to glide past the bouncers.

WHY NOT? Map pp254-5

☎ 535 11 58; www.why-not.at; 01, Tiefer Graben 22; ⏰ 10pm-6am Fri & Sat; bus 1A, 3A

Why Not? is one of the few clubs focusing its attention solely on the gay scene. The small club quickly fills up with mainly young guys out for as much fun as possible.

LIVE MUSIC

Formerly the end of the line for bands touring Europe, Vienna is now a crossroads for those heading to Eastern Europe. Big-name and new bands regularly perform on the city's stages and the yearly repertoire is a healthy mix of jazz, rock (both alternative and mainstream) and world music. Posters and flyers advertising future concerts are plastered across the city, making lining up concerts a simple task. International names often sell out, but you should be able to pick up a scalped ticket on the day.

Venues are invariably small and the crowds fairly subdued, making it easy to push your way to the front and not end the night bruised and winded. Concerts can cost as little as €5 for local performers (sometimes free) or €50 for an internationally acclaimed act. In general however, most will set you back €15 to €25.

Bars and clubs, in particular Flex (p164), rhiz (p159), Chelsea (p159) and B72 (p158), also regularly host touring bands. Festivals such as the Donauinsel Fest and Jazz Fest Wien are also excellent places to catch local and international talent (see p9).

ARENA Map pp262-3

☎ 798 85 95; www.arena.co.at in German; 03, Baumgasse 80; 2pm-late summer, from 4pm winter; U3 Erdberg

A former slaughterhouse turned music and film venue, Arena is one of the city's quirkier places to see live acts. Hard rock, rock, metal, reggae and soul (along with cinema) can be seen on its outdoor stage from May to September; over winter bands are presented in one of its two indoor halls. 'Iceberg', a particularly popular German-British 1970s new-wave bash, is held here once a month.

BIRDLAND Map pp254-5

☎ 219 63 93; www.birdland.at in German; 03, Am Stadtpark 1; 6pm-2am Tue-Sat; U3, U4 Landstrasse/Wien Mitte

With Birdland, world-renowned jazz musician and local boy Joe Zawinul has created a top-notch bar for discerning jazz fans. The acoustics and ambience are excellent, but then again, with the entry price rarely dropping below €30, they should be. Acts have included The Temptations, Hot Chocolate and Earth, Wind & Fire; quality on most nights is pretty much a given. It's situated below the Hilton Vienna.

CAFÉ CARINA Map pp258-9

☎ 406 43 22; www.café-carina.at in German; 08, Josefstädter Strasse 84; 5pm-2am; U6 Josefstädter Strasse, J, 33

Small, smoky, and pleasantly dingy, Carina is a muso's and drinker's bar. Local bands perform most nights, only a few feet from a normally enthusiastic audience, and the music is invariably folk, jazz or country.

CAFÉ CONCERTO Map pp258-9

☎ 406 47 95; www.caféconcerto.at; 16, Lerchenfelder Gürtel 53; 7pm-4am Tue-Sat; U6 Josefstädter Strasse, J, 33

Concerto is another of the bars on the Gürtel that hosts local live acts. Jazz features heavily on the program (which is also peppered with DJs) and both the cellar and ground-level bar are used for concerts, although the acoustics of the former may leave a little to be desired. Entry is often free.

JAZZLAND Map pp254-5

☎ 533 25 75; www.jazzland.at in German; 01, Franz-Josefs-Kai 29; 7.30pm-2am Mon-Sat; U1, U4 Schwedenplatz, N, 1, 2, 21

Jazzland has been an institution of Vienna's jazz scene for over 30 years. The music covers the whole jazz spectrum, and the brick venue features a grand mixture of local and international acts.

METROPOL Map pp258-9

☎ 407 77 40; www.wiener-metropol.at in German; 17, Hernalser Hauptstrasse 55; box office 10am-6pm Mon-Sat; 43

The Metropol is a bit of a musical chameleon: one week might see performances by international acts, the next kitsch musicals, cabaret and folk music. There's plenty of tables and bar stools so there should be no problem procuring a ticket.

MILES SMILES Map pp258-9

☎ 405 95 17; 08, Lange Gasse 51; 8pm-2am Sun-Thu, 8pm-4am Fri & Sat; J, bus 13A

One of two bars in town named after legend Miles Davis, Miles Smiles is for the discerning jazz fan who likes to see the whites of the artist's eyes. Live acts are irregular but always enthralling, and the atmosphere enthusiastic and energetic.

PLANET MUSIC Map pp258-9

☎ 332 46 41-0; www.planet.tt in German; 20, Adalbert-Stifter-Strasse 73; N, 31, 33

This dark and divey venue sticks to a program of band contests and international acts sliding off the popularity wagon, but every now and then something intriguing turns up. The acoustics aren't bad and the beer is cheap, but it's located a bit out of the centre.

PORGY & BESS Map pp254-5

☎ 512 88 11; www.porgy.at; 01, Riemergasse 11; ⊙ 8pm-4am Mon-Sat, 7pm-4am Sun; ⊚ U3 Stubentor, bus 1A

Quality is the cornerstone of Porgy & Bess' continuing popularity. Its program is loaded with modern jazz acts from around the globe, DJs fill spots on weekends, and jam sessions take place after 11pm on Fridays. The interior is dim and the vibe velvety and very grown-up.

REIGEN Map pp260-1

☎ 894 00 94; www.reigen.at in German; 14, Hadikgasse 62; ⊙ 6pm-4am; ⊚ U4 Heitzing, 🚋 60

Reigen's tiny stage is the setting for jazz, blues, and world music. While most acts won't ring many bells, the likes of Living Colour have made appearances here in recent times. If the music doesn't suit there's an amazing number of bars to escape to.

STADTHALLE Map pp260-1

☎ 981 00-0; www.stadthalle.com in German; 15, Vogelweidplatz 15; ⊚ U6 Burggasse/Stadthalle, 🚋 6, 18, bus 48A

Stadthalle is the largest concert venue in the city and usually caters to large, mainstream rock bands and local heroes. Check the posters around town for upcoming shows or check the website.

SZENE WIEN Map pp260-1

☎ 749 33 41; www.szenewien.com; 11, Hauffgasse 26; ⊚ U3 Zipperstrasse

Szene Wien tops the list of Vienna's small concert venues. Intimate and friendly, it's a superb place to catch international bands without fighting off the crowds. Concerts cover the music spectrum; rock, reggae, funk, jazz and world music have all been heard within these walls.

WUK Map pp258-9

☎ 40 121-0; www.wuk.at; 09, Währinger Strasse 59; ⊚ U6 Währinger Strasse, 🚋 40, 41, 41

WUK (Werkstätten- und Kulturhaus; Workshop and Culture House) is many things to many people. Basically a space for art (government subsidised but free to pursue an independent course), it hosts a huge array of events in its concert hall. International and local rock acts vie with clubbing nights, classical concerts, film evenings, theatre and even children's shows. Wom-

en's groups, temporary exhibitions and practical skills workshops are also on site, along with a smoky café with a fabulous cobbled courtyard.

OPERA & CLASSICAL MUSIC

Vienna is the world capital of opera and classical music. The rich musical legacy that flows through the city is evident everywhere: the plethora of monuments to its greatest composers and its princely music venues easily outnumber those of some countries, let alone other capital cities. A quick walk down Kärntner Strasse from the Staatsoper to Stephansplatz will turn up more Mozart lookalikes than you care to shake a baton at.

With such presence in the city, it should be no problem to catch a concert on your visit. The only stumbling block might be in obtaining tickets in the more salubrious venues, such as the Staatsoper and Musikverein; with these, it's advisable to book well ahead. Otherwise just turn up and enjoy.

Churches and coffee houses make fine venues to enjoy classical music. Augustinkirche (p63), Minoritenkirche (p65) and Burgkapelle (p62) are just some of the city's churches complementing Mass on Sunday morning with a full choir and orchestra, and some have regular evening concerts. Coffee houses featuring live music are mentioned throughout the Drinking chapter (p138), otherwise pick up the handy *Wiener Konzert Cafés* (Vienna's Concert Cafés) brochure from the tourist office.

Festivals (p9) such as the KlangBogen Festival and Vienna Festival are highlights on the music calendar, and the Rathausplatz plays host to a film festival of opera and classical concerts in July and August.

Ticket costs vary greatly. Standing room tickets can go for as little as €2, whereas a prime spot at a gala performance in the Staatsoper will set you back €254. Most venues produce a handy map of the seating layout, which is invaluable in choosing the perfect seat to match your budget.

HOFBURG Map pp254-5

☎ 587 25 52; www.hofburgorchester.at; 01, Heldenplatz; tickets €35-47; U3 Herrengasse, 🚋 D, J, 1, 2

The Neue Hofburg's concert halls, the sumptuous Festsaal and Redoutensaal, are

www.lonelyplanet.com

VIENNA BOYS' CHOIR

As with Manner Schnitten, Stephansdom, Lipizzaner stallions, and sausage stands, Vienna wouldn't be Vienna without the Vienna Boys' Choir (Wiener Sängerknaben; www.wsk.at). Now consisting of four separate choirs who share the demanding tour schedule, the original choir was instigated by Maximilian I in 1498. Over the ensuing centuries its ranks have included the likes of Haydn and Schubert.

Catching the choir in concert takes some organisation. Tickets (€5 to €29) for their Sunday performances at 9.15am (September to June) in the Burgkapelle (Royal Chapel) in the Hofburg (p62) should be booked around eight weeks in advance (☎ 533 99 27; www.bmbwk.gv.at/hmk in German). Otherwise try your luck for a last-minute ticket at the Burgkapelle box office from 11am to 1pm and 3pm to 5pm Friday for the following Sunday or immediately before Mass between 8.15am and 8.45am. Standing room is free, and you need to queue by 8.30am to find a place inside the open doors, but you can get a flavour of what's going on from the TV in the foyer.

The choir also sings a mixed program of music in the Musikverein at 4pm on Friday in May, June, September and October. Tickets range from €36 to €63, and can be purchased from Reisebüro Mondial (Map pp254–5; ☎ 588 04 141, www.mondial.at; 04, Operngasse 20b) and hotels in Vienna.

regularly used for Strauss and Mozart concerts, featuring the Hofburg Orchestra and soloists from the Staatsoper and Volksoper. Performances start at 8.30pm and tickets are available from travel agents, hotels and Mozart lookalikes. It's open-plan seating, so get in early to secure a good seat.

KAMMEROPER Map pp254-5

☎ 512 01 00-77; www.wienerkammeroper.at; 01, Fleischmarkt 24; tickets €5-48; box office ☺ noon-6pm Mon-Fri; U1, ⊕ U4 Schwedenplatz, ⊛ N, 1, 2, 21

The Kammeroper ranks as Vienna's third opera house after the Staatsoper and Volksoper. Its small venue is perfect for the unusual and quirky opera productions and over summer the entire company is transported to the Schlosstheater Schönbrunn to continue performances in more opulent surroundings. Students receive 30% discount, children under 14 receive 50% discount.

KONZERTHAUS Map pp254-5

☎ 242 002; www.konzerthaus.at; 03, Lothringerstrasse 20; tickets €10-100; box office ☺ 9am-7.45pm Mon-Fri, 9am-1pm Sat; ⊕ U4 Stadtpark, bus 4A

The Konzerthaus is a major venue in classical music circles, but throughout the year ethnic music, rock, pop or jazz can also be heard in its hallowed halls. Up to three simultaneous performances, in the Grosser Saal, the Mozart Saal and the Schubert Saal, can be staged; this massive complex also features another four concert halls. Students can pick up tickets for €12 30 minutes before performances; children receive 50% discount.

KURSALON Map pp254-5

☎ 512 57 90; www.strauss-konzerte.at; tickets €38-90; 01, Johannesgasse 33; ⊕ U4 Stadtpark, ⊛ 1, 2

Fans of the Strauss family will love the performances at Kursalon, which are devoted solely to the famous dynasty. The repertoire of ballet and operetta is held in the refurbished Renaissance building at either 8pm or 8.30pm, or otherwise stop by for coffee, cake and quartet waltz performance in the garden during the day.

MUSIKVEREIN Map pp254-5

☎ 505 81 90; www.musikverein.at; 01, Bösendorferstrasse 12; tours adult/child €5/3.50, tickets €4-85; box office ☺ 9am-8pm Mon-Fri, 9am-1pm Sat; ⊕ U1, U2, U4 Karlsplatz, ⊛ D, J, 1, 2, 62, 65

The Musikverein holds the proud title of the best acoustics of any concert hall in Austria, which the Vienna Philharmonic Orchestra makes excellent use of. The interior is suitably lavish and can be visited on the occasional guided tour. Standing-room tickets in the main hall cost €4 to €6; there are no student tickets. Smaller-scale performances are held in the Brahms Saal. The Musikverein closes in July and August.

ODEON Map pp254-5

☎ 216 51 27; www.odeon-theater.at; 02, Taborstrasse 10; tickets €15-40; box office ☺ 10am-6pm Mon-Fri; ⊕ U1, U4 Schwedenplatz, ⊛ N, 1, 2, 21

This oft-forgotten performance venue looks suitably grand from the outside but unfortunately doesn't quite live up to expectations inside. Anything from classical concerts to raves are held within its walls.

Entertainment

OPERA & CLASSICAL MUSIC

ORANGERY Map pp260-1

☎ 812 50 04; www.imagevienna.com; 13, Schloss Schönbrunn; tickets €39-55; box office ⏰ 8.30am-7pm; Ⓜ U4 Schönbrunn, bus 10A
Schönbrunn's lovely former imperial greenhouse is the location for year-round Mozart and Strauss concerts. Performances last around two hours and begin at 8.30pm daily.

PALAIS PALFFY Map pp254-5

☎ 512 56 81; www.palais-palffy.at; 01, Josefsplatz 6; tickets €36-43; box office ⏰ 1hr before performances; Ⓜ U3 Herrengasse
Another Mozart and Strauss performance venue, this time in Palais Palffy's stunning baroque Figarosaal (Figaro Hall). Mozart himself performed here as a child in 1762, and although the music isn't of the same quality as that of the Philharmonic, it's lively and enthusiastic. Performances start at 8pm daily.

RAIMUND THEATER Map pp260-1

☎ 599 77; www.musicalvienna.at in German; 06, Wallgasse 18-20; tickets €10-95; box office ⏰ 10am-1pm & 2-6pm; Ⓜ U6 Gumpendorfer Strasse, Ⓣ 6, 18
The Raimund Theater hosts big, Broadway-style musicals these days, but when it opened its doors in 1893 it produced only spoken dramas. With a seating capacity of more than 1000, obtaining a ticket won't be a problem.

STAATSOPER Map pp254-5

☎ 514 44-2250; www.wiener-staatsoper.at; 01, Opernring 2; tours adult/senior/child €5/4/2, tour plus Opera Museum €6.50/5.50/3.50; tickets €2-254; box office ⏰ 9am until 2hr before performance Mon-Fri, 9am-noon Sat; Ⓜ U1, U2, U3 Karlsplatz, Ⓣ D, J, 1, 2, 62, 65
The Staatsoper is the premiere opera and classical music venue in Vienna. Built between 1861 and 1869 by August Siccardsburg and Eduard van der Null, it initially revolted the Viennese public and Habsburg royalty and quickly earned the nickname 'stone turtle'. Both architects took it the worst possible way: van der Null hung himself and Siccardsburg died of a heart attack two months later. Neither saw the Staatsoper's first staged production. This shocked Franz Josef to such an extent that he kept his official comments from then on to: 'It was very nice. I enjoyed it very much.'

Façade detail of Staatsoper (this page)

Productions are lavish affairs and should not be missed. The Viennese take their opera very seriously and dress up accordingly. Wander around the foyer and refreshment rooms in the interval to fully appreciate the gold and crystal interior. Opera is not performed here in July and August (tours however still take place), but its repertoire still includes more than 70 different productions.

Tickets can be purchased up to one month in advance. Standing-room tickets, which go for €2 to €3.50, can only be purchased 80 minutes before performances begin and any unsold tickets are available for €30 one day before a performance (call ☎ 514 44 2950 for more information). Tour information is available on ☎ 514 44 2606.

THEATER AN DER WIEN Map pp254-5

☎ 588 30 265; www.musicalvienna.at in German; 06, Linke Wienzeile 6; tickets €23-95; box office ⏰ 10am-7pm; Ⓜ U1, U2, U4 Karlsplatz
The Theater an der Wien has hosted some monumental premiere performances, such as Beethoven's *Fidelo*, Mozart's *Die Zauberflöte* and Strauss Jnr's *Die Fledermaus*. These days the theatre is more attuned to popular culture and features musicals such as *Elisabeth* and *Mozart*. Discounts include two-for-one on Tuesdays between 2pm and 6pm, €11 tickets for students on sale 30 minutes before shows, and €2.50 standing tickets available one hour before performances.

VOLKSOPER Map pp258-9

☎ 514 44 3670; www.volksoper.at; 09, Währinger Strasse 78; tickets €2-70; box office ☷ 8am-6pm Mon-Fri, 9am-noon Sat & Sun; ☉ U6 Währinger Strasse, ⊞ 40, 41, 42

The Volksoper (People's Opera) features plenty of kitsch operettas, dance performances, musicals and a handful of operas. Standing tickets go for as little as €1 and, like many venues, there are a plethora of discounts and reduced tickets 30 minutes before performances. The Volksoper closes from July to mid-August.

THEATRE & DANCE

Theatre in Vienna started over 200 years ago with the creation of the Burgtheater, the oldest theatre in the German-speaking world. Today some 50 theatres are thriving in this theatre-loving city, but invariably performances are in German; theatre in English is reserved for the International Theatre and Vienna's English Theatre.

Contemporary dance is centred at Tanzquartier Wien, where it's going from strength to strength. ImPulsTanz (p11), a quality dance festival from mid-July to mid-August, is about the only other option for catching dance performances in Vienna. Traditional ballet features at both the Staatsoper and the Volksoper during the opera season.

BURGTHEATER Map pp254-5

☎ 514 44 4140; www.burgtheater.at; 01, Dr-Karl-Lueger-Ring; tours adult/child €4.50/2, tickets €4-48; box office ☷ 8am-6pm Mon-Fri, 9am-noon Sat & Sun; ⊞ D, 1, 2

The Burgtheater (National Theatre), one of the prime theatre venues in the German-speaking world. Built in Renaissance style to designs by Gottfried Semper and Karl von Hasenauer, it had to be rebuilt after sustaining severe damage in WWII. The grand interior has stairway frescoes painted by the Klimt brothers, Gustav and Ernst. Tours of the theatre are conducted daily at 2pm and 3pm in July and August and at 3pm daily for the remainder of the year. The Burgtheater also runs the small theatre Kasino am Schwarzenbergplatz (Map pp254–5; 03, Schwarzenbergplatz 1; ⊞ D, 1, 2, 71) theatre and the 500-seater Akademietheater (Map pp254–5; 03, Lisztstrasse 1; ☉ U4 Stadtpark, bus 4A), which was built between 1911 and 1913.

Tickets at the Burgtheater and Akademietheater sell for 50% of their face-value price an hour before performances, and students can purchase tickets for €7 half an hour before performances. Standing places are €1.50.

INTERNATIONAL THEATRE Map pp258-9

☎ 319 62 72; www.internationaltheatre.at; 09, Porzellangasse 8; tickets €20-24; box office ☷ 11am-3pm Mon-Fri, 11am-2pm Sat, 6-7.30pm on performance days; ⊞ D

The small International Theatre, with its entrance on Müllnergasse, has a mainly American company who live locally. Discounted tickets are available to students and senior citizens (€14). It closes for around five weeks at the beginning of August, and has a linked venue, Fundus, at 09, Müllnergasse 6A.

MARIONETTENTHEATER Map pp258-9

☎ 817 32 47; www.marionettentheater.at; 13, Schloss Schönbrunn; tickets full performances adult/child €9-28/6-19, short performances €7/5; box office ☷ 2-5pm Thu-Mon; ☉ U4 Schönbrunn, bus 10A

This small theatre in Schloss Schönbrunn puts on marionette performances of the much-loved productions The Magic Flute (2½ hours) and Aladdin (1¼ hours). The theatre also offers 30-minute shows that might be better suited to children.

SCHAUSPIELHAUS Map pp258-9

☎ 317 01 01-18; www.schauspielhaus.at; 09, Porzellangasse 19; tickets €20; box office ☷ from 4pm Mon-Fri, from 5pm Sat & Sun; ⊞ D

The Schauspielhaus pushes the boundaries of theatre in Vienna with unconventional productions, ranging from ethnic dance performances to political satires. Whatever the theme, you can guarantee it will be thought-provoking. Students and seniors receive a 50% discount.

TANZQUARTIER WIEN Map pp254-5

☎ 581 35 91; www.tqw.at; 07, Museumsplatz 1; tickets €11-18; box office ☷ 1 hr before performances; ☉ U2 Museumsquartier, U2, U3 Volkstheater, bus 2A

Tanzquartier Wien, located in the Museums-Quartier, is Vienna's first dance institution. It hosts an array of local and international performances with a strong experimental nature. Performances normally start at 8.30pm.

THEATER IN DER JOSEFSTADT

Map pp258-9

☎ 427 00 300; www.josefstadt.org in German; 08, Josefstädter Strasse 26; tickets €5-63; ☻ box office 10am-performance time Mon-Fri, 1pm-performance time Sat & Sun; ⓙ J, bus 13A

Theater in der Josefstadt is another theatre in the Volkstheater mould, with an ornate interior and traditional German productions. One hour before performances tickets are available to students and school children for €5; persons with disabilities, and children can purchase tickets for €12 at any time.

VIENNA'S ENGLISH THEATRE Map pp258-9

☎ 402 12 60-0; www.englishtheatre.at; 08, Josefs-gasse 12; tickets €19.50-38; box office ☻ 10am-7.30pm Mon-Fri, 5-7.30pm Sat & Sun (when performances scheduled); Ⓜ U2 Rathaus, ⓙ J

Founded in 1963, Vienna's English Theatre is the oldest foreign-language theatre in Vienna (with the occasional show in French or Italian). Productions range from time-less pieces, such as Shakespeare, through to contemporary works. Students, children and people with disabilities receive 20% discount on all tickets; standby tickets for €9 go on sale 15 minutes before showtime.

VOLKSTHEATER Map pp254-5

☎ 523 05 89-77; www.volkstheater.at in German; 07, Neustiftgasse 1; tickets €7.50-40; box office ☻ 10am-performance Mon-Sat Sep-Jun; Ⓜ U2, U3 Volkstheater, ⓙ 49

With a seating capacity close to 1000, the Volkstheater is one of Vienna's largest theatres. Built in 1889, it's no surprise that the interior is suitably grand. Only German-language shows are produced, and unsold tickets go on sale one hour before perform-ances start for €3.60, but only to students.

CINEMA

The Viennese love their *Kino* (cinema) and attend in droves. Both independent art-house films and Hollywood blockbusters are well patronised and unlike Austrian TV, where 99% of movies are dubbed in German, many cinema screenings are sub-titled to retain as much of a film's original ambience. The weekly *Falter* (www.falter.at, in German) and daily *Der Standard* (http://derstandard.at, in German) papers are the best sources for listings: *OF* or *OV* following a film title means it will screen in the origi-nal language; *OmU* indicates the film is in the original language with German subtitles; and *OmenglU* and *OmeU* signifies it's in the original language with English subtitles. Monday is known as *Kinomontag*, when all cinema seats go for around €6; a normal screening costs anything from €7 to €10.

ARTIS INTERNATIONAL Map pp254-5

☎ 535 65 70; www.cineplexx.at in German; 01, Schultergasse 5; bus 1A, 2A, 3A

Artis has six small cinemas in the heart of the Innere Stadt. It only shows English-language films, invariably straight from Hollywood.

BREITENSEER LICHTSPIELE Map pp260-1

☎ 982 21 73; www.bsl.at.tf in German; 14, Breiten-seer Strasse 21; Ⓜ U3 Hütteldorfer Strasse, ⓙ 10

This delightful Art Nouveau cinema is an ab-solute gem. Opened in 1909, it still retains its original wooden seats and carries the atmosphere of a bygone era in cinema his-tory. Films are usually in English with Ger-man subtitles, and some are quite risqué.

BURG KINO Map pp254-5

☎ 587 84 06; www.burgkino.at; 01, Opernring 19; Ⓜ U1, U2, U4 Karlsplatz, ⓙ D, J, 1, 2, 62, 65

The Burg Kino is a central cinema that shows only English-language films. It has regular screenings of the *The Third Man*, Orson Welles' timeless classic set in post-WWII Vienna, at 11pm Friday and Saturday, 3pm Sunday and 4.30pm Tuesday. Cinemas here range from small to extra large.

THE VIENNALE

Vienna's annual international film festival, the Vien-nale, is the highlight of the city's celluloid calendar. By no means as prestigious as Cannes or Berlin, it still at-tracts top-quality films from all over the world and is geared to the viewer rather than the filmmakers. For two weeks from mid-October city cinemas continu-ously play screenings that could broadly be described as fringe, ranging from documentaries to short and feature films. Tickets for the more popular screenings and most evening screenings can be hard to come by. Tickets can be bought two weeks before the festival starts from a number of stands around town. To get a jump on fellow festivalgoers, call ☎ 526 59 47 or check www.viennale.at.

CINEMAGIC Map pp254-5

☎ 586 43 03; www.cinemagic.at in German; 01, Friedrichstrasse 4; admission €4.70; ⊚ U1, U2, U4 Karlsplatz, ⓘ D, J, 1, 2, 62, 65

An initiative of the City of Vienna aimed at entertainment for children, Cinemagic is a cinema totally devoted to the little 'uns. Films come from around the globe and screen every Saturday and Sunday afternoon. In mid-November the cinema, along with three others, hosts a Children's Film Festival (www .kinderfilmfestival.at, in German) showcasing international children's films.

DE FRANCE Map pp254-5

☎ 317 52 36; www.defrance.at in German; 01, Schottenring 5; ⊚ U2 Schottentor, ⓘ 37, 38, 40, 41, 42, 43, 44

De France screens films in their original language, with subtitles, in its two small cinemas. The schedule includes a healthy dose of English-language films.

ENGLISH CINEMA HAYDN Map pp260-1

☎ 587 22 62; www.haydnkino.at; 06, Mariahilfer Strasse 57; ⊚ U3 Neubaugasse, bus 13A

The Haydn is a comfortable cinema screening only mainstream Hollywood-style films in their original language in three cinemas.

FILMCASINO Map pp260-1

☎ 587 90 62; www.filmcasino.at in German; 05, Margaretenstrasse 78; ⊚ U4 Pilgramgasse, bus 13A, 59A

An art-house cinema of some distinction, the Filmcasino screens an excellent mix of Asian and European docos and avant-garde short films, along with independent feature-length films from around the world. Its '50s-style foyer is particularly impressive.

GARTENBAUKINO Map pp254-5

☎ 512 23 54; www.gartenbaukino.at in German; 01, Parkring 12; ⊚ U3 Stubentor, U4 Stadpark, ⓘ 1, 2

Fortunately the interior of the Gartenbaukino has survived since the 1960s, making a trip to the flicks here all the more appealing. The actual cinema seats a whopping 750 people, which is often packed during Viennale screenings. Its regular screening schedule is full to overflowing with art-house films, normally with subtitles.

ÖSTERREICHISCHE FILMMUSEUM Map pp254-5

☎ 533 70 54; www.filmmuseum.at; 01, Augustinerstrasse 1; ⓒ Sep-Jun; ⊚ U1, U2, U4 Karlsplatz, ⓘ D, J, 1, 2, 62, 65

After a much-needed overhaul that did away with the original arse-numbing seats, the Filmmuseum is now a pleasure to visit. The range of films on show is quite extensive; each month features a retrospective on a group of directors or a certain theme from around the world. Tickets costs €9.50; with a year's membership (€12) this drops to €5.50.

SCHIKANEDER Map pp260-1

☎ 585 28 67; www.schikaneder.at; 04, Margaretenstrasse 24; bus 59A

Located next to the bar of the same name, Schikaneder is the darling of Vienna's alternative cinema scene. The film subject range is quite broad but also highly selective, and art house through and through. Schikaneder only seats 80 and all screenings are €6.

TOP KINO Map pp254-5

☎ 208 30 00; www.topkino.at in German; 06, Rahlgasse 1; ⊚ U2 Museumsquartier, bus 57A

Part of the restaurant, club and bar arrangement Top Kino, (p158), this cinema offers an ever-changing array of European films and documentaries, generally in their original language with German subtitles. The sloping theatre is good for all cinemagoers.

VOTIVKINO Map pp258-9

☎ 317 35 71; www.votivkino.at in German; 09, Währinger Strasse 12; ⓘ 37, 38, 40, 41, 42

Built in 1912, the Votiv is one of the oldest cinemas in Vienna. It's been extensively updated since then and is now among the best cinemas in the city. Its three screens feature a mix of Hollywood's more quirky ventures and art-house films in their original language. The 11am Tuesday screenings is reserved for mothers, fathers and babies.

WATCHING SPORT

The only spectator sport of note to gain regular – albeit small – audiences is football. Vienna is home to two of the Bundesliga's bigger teams, Rapid Vienna and Austria Memphis, whose rivalry is similar to England's Arsenal and Tottenham Hotspur. It may be hard to purchase a ticket

OPEN-AIR CINEMA

Open-air cinema is a growing phenomenon in Vienna. The city hosts at least seven such cinemas across town, the biggest of which is the Musikfilm Festival (p11) on Rathausplatz; Arena (p166) also hosts such a cinema in the summer months. **Kino Unter Sternen** (Cinema Under the Stars; Map pp258–9 ☎ 0800-664 040; www.kinountersternen.at in German; 02, Augarten; ⓤ 31, bus 5A) is a highly popular outdoor cinema (when the weather holds) in the shadow of one of Augarten's Flaktürme that shows films from mid-July to mid-August. The selection is an eclectic mix of classics, and films in English are often shown. **Krieau** (Map pp252–3; ☎ 524 68 02; www.krieau .com in German; 02, Nordportalstrasse 247; ⓤ 21, bus 80B) features more mainstream films and runs from July to August

for the local derby, but at any other time it won't be a problem. Austria, along with Switzerland, is hosting the 2008 European Championship, at which time the city will be in serious party-mode.

The Stadthalle (p167) is a major player in hosting sporting events. Tennis tournaments (including the Austrian Open), horse shows and ice-hockey games are just some of the diverse events held here. The swimming pool here is a major venue for aquatic events like races, water polo and synchronised swimming.

FOOTBALL

AUSTRIA MEMPHIS FRANZ-HORR-STADION Map pp252-3

☎ 688 01 50; www.fk-austria.at; 10, Fischhofgasse 12; ⓤ 67, bus 15A

The home ground of Austria Magna is currently waiting to be finished, but there are still plenty of seats available to catch a game.

ERNST-HAPPEL-STADION Map pp262-3

☎ 728 08 54; 02, Meiereistrasse 7; ⓤ 21, bus 80B

With a seating capacity nearing 50,000, the Ernst-Happel stadium is the largest sporting venue in Vienna and preferred venue for international games.

RAPID VIENNA GERHARD-HANAPPI-STADION Map pp252-3

☎ 914 55 19; www.skrapid.at in German; 14, Keisslergasse 6; ⓤ U4 Hütteldorf, bus 147

Hanappi stadium is the home ground for SK Rapid, Vienna's team of the working class. Of the city's two national league teams, Rapid has been the more successful internationally, fighting their way through to the European Cup finals on two occasions.

HORSE RACING

FREUDENAU Map pp252-3

☎ 728 95 31; www.freudenau.at in German; 02, Rennbahnstrasse 65; ☯ Mar-Nov; bus 77A

In the southern extremes of the Prater is Freudenau, Vienna's premiere horse-racing track and one of Europe's oldest. Bus 77A doesn't always go as far as the track so you might have to walk from Lusthaus (p128).

KRIEAU Map pp252-3

☎ 728 00 46; www.krieau.at in German; 02, Nordportalstrasse 274; ⓤ 21, bus 80B

Sidling up to the Ernst-Happel-Stadion in the Prater is Krieau, the track where Vienna's trotting meets are held. It's normally only open on Saturday afternoons from September to June. Tickets start at €5.

OUTDOOR ACTIVITIES

Vienna is a superb city for outdoor activities. The Wienerwald (Vienna Woods) to the west is crisscrossed with hiking and cycling trails, while the Donau, Alte Donau, Donauinsel (Danube Island) and Lobau to the east provide ample opportunities for boating and swimming (plus cycling and inline skating), and the city itself has hundreds of kilometres of designated cycle paths and is dotted with green parks, some big (the Prater), some small (Stadtpark).

The city's website, www.wien.gv.at, has a rundown on the main outdoor activities available in Vienna, as does *Sports & Nature in Vienna*, a brochure produced by the Vienna tourist board. It can also be downloaded from their website www.wien.info.

BOATING

The Alte Donau is the main boating and sailing centre in Vienna, but the Neue Donau, a long stretch of water separated from the Danube by the Donauinsel, also provides opportunities for boating, windsurfing and water-skiing.

SAILING SCHOOL HOFBAUER

Map pp252-3

☎ 204 34 35; www.hofbauer.at in German; 22, An der Obere Alte Donau 191; ⏰ Apr-Oct; ⊚ U1 Alte Donau

Hofbauer rents sailing boats (from €12.50 per hour) and windsurfers (€11 per hour) on the eastern bank of the Alte Donau and can provide lessons (in English) for those wishing to learn or brush up on their skills. Pedal boats are also available for hire.

CYCLING

Vienna's layout and well-marked cycle lanes make cycling a pleasant and popular activity, especially along the banks of the Danube, in the Prater and around the Ringstrasse. The extensive Wienerwald is popular for mountain biking. The Directory chapter (p219) has information on bicycle hire and taking bicycles on public transport, and the Walking & Cycling Tours chapter (p106) provides two cycletour suggestions and information on where to pick up maps and which internet sites to hit.

GOLF

Golf clubs in and around Vienna number over a dozen.

GOLF CLUB WIEN Map pp252-3

☎ 728 95 64; www.gcwien.at in German; 02, Freudenau 65A; green fees €70; bus 77A

This 18-hole course in the Prater cuts through part of the Freudenau race course. It belongs to Golf Club Vienna, the oldest club in the country. Only members of a golf club may play here.

HIKING

Hiking is a popular Viennese pastime. Many head for the rolling hills and marked trails of the Wienerwald (p210), but the likes of the Prater (p79), with its small woods and lengthy trails, and the Lainzer Tiergarten (see p99) animal reserve, a wild park located in the west of Vienna, attract plenty of locals looking for fresh air and exercise.

The Walking & Cycling Tours chapter (p112) has a coupe of suggestions for walks in the Wienerwald.

ICE SKATING

Most Viennese have ice skates collecting dust in the back of the wardrobe which are dragged out at least once over winter. Along with specialised ice-skating rinks, a number of outdoor basketball courts are turned into rinks during winter. For as little as €1 you can spend the whole day gliding around one of these temporary rinks; 08, Buchfeldgasse 7A (Map pp254–5), 16, Gallitzinstrasse 4 (Map pp252–3) and 19, Osterleitengasse 14 (Map pp258–9). When it's cold enough, the Alte Donau is transformed into an ice-skater's paradise, with miles of natural ice.

WIENER EISLAUFVEREIN Map pp254-5

☎ 713 63 53; www.wev.or.at in German; 03, Lothringerstrasse 22; adult/child €6/5, boot rental €5.50; ⏰ 9am-8pm Mon, Sat & Sun, 9am-9pm Tue-Fri Nov–mid-Mar; ⊚ U4 Stadtpark

At 6000 sq metres, the Wiener Eislaufverein is the world's largest open-air skating rink. It's close to the Ringstrasse and Stadtpark. Remember to bring mittens and a hat.

WIENER EISTRAUM Map pp254-5

☎ 409 00 40; www.wienereistraum.at in German; 01, Rathausplatz; adult/child from €3.50/2.50, boot rental €6/3.80; ⏰ 9am-11pm late-Jan–early Mar; ⊚ U2 Rathaus, ⓣ D, 1, 2

Rathausplatz is transformed into two ice rinks in the heart of winter. It's a bit of a mecca for the city's ice-skaters, and the rinks are complemented by food stands, special events, punch bars and a path that zigzags through the nearby park.

INLINE SKATING

With wide, smooth tar-sealed paths, the Donauinsel and Prater are just made for inline skating. Skates can be rented from a number of places on the island, particularly around the Copa Cagrana area. If you'd like to hook up with like-minded skaters, roll along to Heldenplatz at 9pm on Friday from May to September and join the Friday Night Skating (wien.gruene.at/skater) team on a tour of the city. Participation is free.

SKIING

Yes, there is skiing in Vienna. Only a handful of places offer skiing within the city limits, but if you've come this far and want

Sailing boats docked at Alte Donau (p173)

to go skiing you're much better off heading west and taking advantage of Austria's stunning Alps.

SKIANLAGE DOLLWIESE Map pp252-3
☎ 812 12 01; 13, Ghelengasse 44; 10 lift rides €4; ✆ noon-dusk Mon-Fri, 10am-dusk Sat & Sun Dec-Mar; bus 54B, 55B
Edging up to the Lainzer Tiergarten is Dollwiese, supposedly one of Austria's oldest ski slopes. At only 400m long, it's quite short.

SKIANLAGE HOHE WAND Map pp252-3
☎ 979 10 57; 14, Mauerbachstrasse 172-174; day pass adult/child €13/6; ✆ 9am-9.30pm Mon-Fri, 9am-10pm Sat & Sun Dec-Mar; bus 249, 250, 449
The Hohe Wand ski slopes can be used only when there is enough natural snow on the ground to bond with daily layerings of artificial snow. It's quite a way from the city centre, in the Wienerwald.

HEALTH & FITNESS
Like any city, Vienna has plenty of gyms and places to work up a sweat outdoors.

CLIMBING
A few climbing walls are scattered throughout its districts. Most are indoors.

KLETTERANLAGE FLAKTURM
Map pp260-1
☎ 585 47 48; 06, Esterhazypark; 2hr for around €12; ✆ 2pm-dusk Mon-Fri, 1pm-dusk Sat & Sun Apr-Oct; ⓤ U3 Neubaugasse, bus 13A, 14A
The stark outside walls of the Flakturm (flak tower) in Esterházypark are used for climbing exercises organised by the Österreichischer Alpenverein. Twenty routes (gradients four to eight) climb to a maximum height of 34m.

GYMS
Most large hotels have their own fitness centre for guests, but there are plenty of independent centres that provide day passes to visitors.

CLUB DANUBE Map pp262-3
☎ 798 84 00; www.clubdanube.at in German; 03, Franzosengraben; 2-hr/day card €14/19; ✆ 7.30am-10pm Mon-Fri, 7.30am-9pm Sat & Sun; ⓤ U3 Erdberg
Club Danube has a range of sports and activities alongside its well-appointed gym. There are nine such Club Danube gyms in the city; this one is in the same building as the Erdberg U-Bahn station.

SWIMMING
Swimming is easily the favoured summer pastime of the Viennese. The Donauinsel, Alte Donau and Lobau are often swamped with citizens eager to cool off on steamy hot summer days. Topless sunbathing is quite the norm, as is nude sunbathing but only in designated areas; much of Lobau and both tips of the Donauinsel are FKK (*Freikörperkultur;* free body culture) areas.

Alongside the natural swimming areas are a large number of swimming pools owned and run by the city which open 9am to 8pm Monday to Friday and 8am to 8pm on weekends mid-May to the beginning of September. Entry, including locker rental, costs €4/2 per adult/child, €3.50 for both

175

after noon and €2.50 for both after 4pm. Amalienbad, Krapfenwaldbad, Strandbad Alte Donau, and Strandbad Gänsehäufel all fall within this category. For a full list of pools call ☎ 60112 8044 between 7.30am and 3.30pm Monday to Friday, or log on to www.wien.at/baeder.

AMALIENBAD Map pp262-3
☎ 607 47 47; 10, Reumannplatz 23;
Ⓤ U1 Reumannplatz
This stunning *Jugendstil* bath-house has a range of facilities, including a solarium, steam room, massage, cosmetic treatments and a restaurant. There are separate saunas for men and women, and a unisex one.

KRAPFENWALDBAD Map pp252-3
☎ 320 15 01; 19, Krapfenwaldgasse 65-73; bus 38A
With its elevated position on the edge of the Wienerwald, Krapfenwaldbad has the best views of the city. Many who frequent the baths aren't too interested in the city-scape (or the two small pools) however, but rather their fellow bathers. Even though there are plenty of grassy areas, it's often full to overflowing.

STRANDBAD ALTE DONAU Map pp252-3
☎ 263 65 38; 22, Arbeiterstrandbadstrasse 91;
Ⓤ U1 Alte Donau, bus 91A
This bathing area makes great use of the Alte Donau during the summer months. It's a favourite of the working class and gets extremely crowded on weekends during summer. Facilities include a restaurant, beach volleyball court, playing field, slides and plenty of tree shade.

Swimming pool at Amalienbad (this page)

STRANDBAD GÄNSEHÄUFEL Map pp252-3
☎ 269 90 16; 22, Moissigasse 21; bus 90A, 91A, 92A
Gänsehäufel occupies half an island in the Alte Donau. It does get crowded in summer, but there's normally enough space to escape the mob. There's a swimming pool and FKK area.

THERMALBAD OBERLAA Map pp252-3
☎ 6800 996 00; www.oberlaa.at in German; 10, Kurbadstrasse 14; day card €18; thermal bath
🕑 8.45am-10pm Mon-Sat, 7.45am-10pm Sun; 🚋 67
In the southern reaches of Vienna is Ober-laa, a large thermal complex with both indoor and outdoor pools. It often stages concerts and theatrical performances and runs a wellness centre.

Shopping ■

Shopping

Shopping in Vienna can be a schizophrenic experience. First, there's the glitz. The Innere Stadt's grand baroque and Secessionist edifices house a dazzling array of high-end retailers – from chains like Prada, Cartier, Chanel, Swarovski and all the usual luxury suspects to homegrown upmarket heavyweights like Augarten and J&L Lobmeyr. Wandering the streets around Graben and Kohlmarkt will afford you some sumptuous window shopping, whether or not you can afford the delights on offer.

The riches of history are also up for sale, most notably in the remarkable Dorotheum auction house (see p181). The streets surrounding the Dorotheum and down to Albertinaplatz are filled with galleries selling all manner of opulent stuff – period and contemporary art from all over Europe; antique guns, porcelain, armour – like a random museum with price tags.

At the other end of the spectrum are Vienna's idiosyncratic *Altwaren* (old wares) shops, filled with secondhand odds and ends, where you may find the odd treasure amongst the dross. Reigning supreme in the bric-a-brac stakes is the famous *Flohmarkt* (see p185), a huge flea market crammed with bargain hunters on Saturdays, where the dusty contents of suburban attics mix with genuinely valuable and beautiful old pieces to make for a very enjoyable – and quintessentially Viennese – shopping experience.

In between, Vienna has its due share of global High Street names and chain stores, and in some areas, like along Kärntner Strasse and Mariahilfer Strasse, it seems not much besides. Little gems do exist, but you need to explore the hidden alleyways and backstreets to find them; a bit of legwork can bring great rewards. Local specialities include porcelain, ceramics, handmade dolls, wrought-iron work and leather goods, and many shops sell collectables such as stamps *Briefmarken* (stamps) and *Münze* (coins).

In the tiny Innere Stadt Hoher Markt, Bauernmarkt and around you'll find designer fashion and small boutiques, more and more of which are now selling locally designed clothes and accessories – as evidenced by outlets like designers' cooperative Art Up (p183), Vienna has a healthy local design scene. Outside the Ring, your best bets for a pleasant afternoon's shopping

Shoppers and tourists in the mall on Graben (p180)

are Mariahilf and Neubau – particularly Neubaugasse and Westbahnstrasse – and Josefstädter Strasse, where you'll find plenty of quirky one-offs and interesting boutiques.

Many of Vienna's finest shops are listed in the free *Shopping, Wining & Dining* booklet, produced by the tourist office and also available online at http://info.wien.at. *Best of Vienna*, a quarterly magazine (in German), has a large and typically idiosyncratic section devoted to shopping. For special reductions, look out for *Aktion* signs.

If you plan to do a bit of shopping, consider purchasing the Vienna Card (see the Directory chapter, p225, for more details).

TOP SHOPPING STRIPS

- Josefstädter Strasse – an old-fashioned shopping street filled with idiosyncratic shops selling anything from *Altwaren* to gemstones
- Kohlmarkt – a river of high-end glitz, flowing into a magnificent Hofburg view
- Kärntner Strasse – a bit more middlebrow than in its heyday, but still the Innere Stadt's main shopping street and a real crowd-puller
- Neubaugasse – a second-hand hunter's paradise and lined with unusual shops
- Mariahilfer Strasse – Vienna's largest shopping street, with plenty of High Street names and masses of people

Opening Hours

Most shops are open between 9am and 6pm on Monday to Friday and until 5pm on Saturday. Some have extended hours on Thursday or Friday till around 7.30pm. Although officially shops aren't permitted to trade on Sundays, you will find the odd renegade establishment open.

Consumer Taxes

Mehrwertsteuer (MWST; value-added tax) is set at 20% for most goods. Prices are displayed inclusive of all taxes, even (usually) service charges in hotels and restaurants.

All non-EU visitors are entitled to a refund of the MWST on purchases over €75. To claim the tax, a tax-refund cheque must be filled out by the shop at the time of purchase (you'll need to show your passport), which must then be stamped by border officials when you leave the EU. Vienna airport has a counter for payment of instant refunds. Counters are also at Westbahnhof, Südbahnhof and at major border crossings. The refund is best claimed upon departing the EU, as otherwise you'll have to track down an international refund office or make a claim by post. After a handling fee is deducted, refunds normally amount to 13% of the purchase price.

Bargaining

Bargaining is a no-no in shops, although you can certainly haggle when buying second-hand. It's a must at the *Flohmarkt* (see p185).

INNERE STADT

STEPHANSPLATZ

AUGARTEN WIEN
Map pp254-5 Glassware & Porcelain
☎ 512 14 94; www.augarten.at; 01, Stock-im-Eisen-Platz 3; ☷ 10am-6.30pm Mon-Fri, 10am-6pm Sat; U1, U3 Stephansplatz
Wiener Porzellanmanufaktur Augarten makes Vienna's finest porcelain; the most delicate of ornaments, vases and dinnerware with traditional hand-painted designs are available at a number of outlets around town. Beautiful, quality stuff (though perhaps a touch old-fashioned to some tastes)

with prices to match, starting at around €70 for a small vase. Tours of the factory (Map pp258–9) are available; ask at the shop or see the website for details.

MANNER Map pp254-5 Food
☎ 513 70 18; www.manner.com; 01, Stephansplatz 7; 10am-9pm Mon-Sat; ⊙ U1, U3 Stephansplatz
Even Manner – Vienna's favourite sweet since 1898, a glorious concoction of wafers and hazelnut cream – has its own concept store now, decked out in the biscuit's signature peachy pink. Here you can buy not only the product itself in every imaginable variety and packaging combination, but also Manner T-shirts, Manner bath towels, Manner toy trucks – you name it.

MADE IN VIENNA

- Art Up (p183) – the best in local fashion and design
- Vienna Bag (below) – chic and durable carry-alls
- Perzy Snow Globes (p187) – the original and the best
- Augarten Wien (p179) – traditional porcelain designs and super-high quality (beware of the miniature poodles though)
- Woka (right) – Wiener Werkstätte design at its most shining

Contemporary design on display at Art Up (p183)

EAST OF STEPHANSPLATZ

BRITISH BOOKSHOP Map pp254-5   Books

☎ 512 19 45-0; www.britishbookshop.at; 01, Weihburggasse 24; ⏰ 9.30am-6.30pm Mon-Fri, 9.30am-6pm Sat; 🚊 1, 2

The British Bookshop has the largest selection of English reference and teaching books in Vienna. There's also a well-ordered and extensive fiction section, children's books and a few DVDs. There's a second outlet in Neubau called **British Bookshop II** (Map pp254–5; ☎ 522 67 30; 07, Mariahilfer Strasse 4; 🚇 U2 Museumsquartier).

VIENNA BAG Map pp254-5   Accessories

☎ 513 11 84; 01, www.vienna-bag.com; Bäckerstrasse 7; ⏰ 10.30am-6pm Mon-Fri, 10.30am-5pm Sat

Vienna Bag have been making their funky and practical handbags and satchels since 2001. In both black and brightly coloured varieties, they're strong, lightweight and washable as well as chic.

WOKA Map pp254-5   Lighting

☎ 513 29 12; www.woka.at; 01, Singerstrasse 16; ⏰ 10am-6pm Mon-Fri, 10am-5pm Sat; 🚇 U1, U3 Karlsplatz

This is a great place to come to get a feel for the Wiener Werkstätte aesthetic and Bauhaus, Art Deco and Secessionist design, with its accurate reproductions of lamps designed by the likes of Adolf Loos, Kolo Moser and Josef Hoffmann. The collection on show is quite remarkable and well worth a look.

KÄRNTNER STRASSE, GRABEN & KOHLMARKT

ALTMANN & KÜHNE

Map pp254-5   Confectionery

☎ 533 09 27; 01, Graben 30; ⏰ 9am-6.30pm Mon-Fri, 10am-5pm Sat; 🚇 U1, U3 Stephansplatz

This charming small shop has a touch of the old world about it, partly due to the handmade packaging of their chocolates and sweets, designed by Wiener Werkstätte in 1928. Altmann & Kühne have been producing hand-made bonbons for more than 100 years using a well-kept secret recipe.

BERNSTEINZIMMER Map pp254-5   Jewellery

☎ 512 67 85; www.bernstein.co.at; 01, Seilergasse 19; ⏰ 10am-1pm & 2-6.30pm Mon-Fri, 10am-1pm Sat; 🚇 U1, U3 Stephansplatz

The 'Amber Room', named for the famous room of amber in Berlin's Schloss Charlottenburg which was lost after WWII, does its best to approximate the idea. Oversized beads, carved animals, cigarette holders – simply amber in all shapes & sizes, most of which is sourced from Poland. A must for amber freaks.

DOUGLAS Map pp254-5   Cosmetics

☎ 533 09 78; 01, Graben 29; ⏰ 9am-7pm Mon-Fri, 9am-6pm Sat; 🚇 U1, U3 Stephansplatz

Perfume, cosmetics and skin care from all the big European names, as well as professional-standard own-brand make-up brushes and accessories, are available here and at other Douglas branches throughout the city.

FREYTAG & BERNDT Map pp254-5 Books & Maps

☎ 533 86 85; www.freytagberndt.at; 01, Kohlmarkt 9; ⏰ 9am-7pm Mon-Fri, 9am-6pm Sat; 🚇 U3 Herrengasse, bus 2A, 3A

There is no better place for maps and travel guides than Freytag & Berndt. There's an exhaustive collection of guides and maps to Vienna and Austria (including some superbly detailed walking maps) and guides to Europe and the world (many in English).

J & L LOBMEYR
Map pp254-5   Glassware & Porcelain

☎ 512 05 08; www.lobmeyr.at; 01, Kärntner Strasse 26; ⊙ U1, U3 Stephansplatz

One of Vienna's most lavish retail experiences; the fine glassware and porcelain on display here glitters from the lights of the chandelier-festooned atrium. The firm has been in business since the beginning of the 19th century when it exclusively supplied the imperial court; these days, production is more focused towards Werkstätte pieces. Even if you're not in the market for a chandelier, you can sweep up the beautifully ornate wrought-iron staircase to the museum/showroom, with its somewhat cluttered collection of Biedermeier pieces and some Loos-designed sets and art-glass vases thrown in.

MEINL AM GRABEN
Map pp254-5 Food & Wine

☎ 532 33 34; www.meinlamgraben.at; 01, Graben 19; ⊙ 8am-7.30pm Mon-Wed, 8am-8pm Thu-Fri, 9am-6pm Sat; bus 1A, 2A, 3A

The most prestigious providore in Vienna, Meinl stocks quality foodstuffs from all over Europe. Most of the ground floor is given over to chocolates and confectionery; upstairs are impressive cheese and cold meats counters. The wine shop has premium European wines and a good stock of Austrian fruit liqueurs; Meinl's **Weinbar** (⊙ 11am-midnight Mon-Sat) in the cellar has a great selection of wines by the glass and a chilled, classy atmosphere. There's also a sushi bar and restaurant.

MÜHLBAUER
Map pp254-5   Accessories

☎ 512 22 41; www.muehlbauer.at; 01, Seilergasse 10; ⊙ 10am-6.30pm Mon-Fri, 10am-6pm Sat; ⊙ U1, U3 Stephansplatz

Adorning Viennese heads since 1903, Mühlbauer embodies the spirit of fun that hat-wearing in the 21st century should be all about: cool without being unapproachable, glamorous without being stuffy. Cloches, pillboxes, caps and even bonnets – designs nod to the traditional but with colours and detailing that are oh-so now (see the current collection on their website). There's a range of hats for men, too.

ALTWAREN AUCTIONS

Although you may never dream of dropping into Sotheby's for a quick browse, when in Vienna it seems perfectly natural to inspect what's on offer at the **Dorotheum** (Map p254–5; ☎ 515 60-0; www.dorotheum.com; 01, Dorotheergasse 17; ⊙ 10am-6pm Mon-Fri, 9am-5pm Sat; bus 2A, 3A). Amongst the largest auction houses in Europe, this is the apex of Vienna's *Altwaren*-consumer culture, the Flohmarkt's wealthy uncle. Something between a museum and the fanciest car-boot sale you ever saw, the rooms are filled with everything from antique toys and tableware to autographs, antique guns and Old Masters paintings.

The stock changes weekly, and not everything is priced sky-high – there are also affordable household ornaments up for grabs. On the 2nd floor is the Freier Verkauf section, a massive antique gallery where you can buy on the spot at marked prices.

Auction proceedings are fun to watch even if you don't intend to buy, and scheduled dates for auctions and viewings are available online (or at the ground-floor reception). If you lack the confidence to bid, you can commission an agent to do it for you. The hammer price usually excludes VAT; you'll have to pay this but you may be able to claim it back later.

OBERLAA
Map pp254-5   Confectionery

☎ 513 29 36; www.oberlaa-wien.at; 01, Neuer Markt 16, ⊙ 8am-8pm daily; ⊙ U1, U3 Stephansplatz

Oberlaa sells some of the most beautifully packaged chocolates in Vienna (in the face of some pretty stiff competition). Even more exquisite are their 'LaaKronen' – brightly coloured macaroons, in flavours like pistachio, lemon and strawberry, available singly or in gorgeous boxed sets. There are five other branches around town.

OPERN CONFISERIE
Map pp254-5 Confectionery

☎ 512 19 10; 01, Kärntner Strasse 47; ⊙ 9am-7pm Mon-Sat, 11am-6pm Sun; ⊙ U1, U2, U4 Karlsplatz, ⊙ D, J, 1, 2, 62, 65

An old-fashioned confectionery store in the midst of buzzing Kärntner Strasse, with a dizzying array of handmade truffles, many-shaped marzipan, and brightly coloured fruit *gelées*. Look out for Austrian-made Bachhalm handmade chocolate bars, with chunky ingredients – from standards like pistachio to more challenging taste concepts such as rose petal and shitake mushroom.

Shopping

INNERE STADT

ÖSTERREICHISCHE WERKSTÄTTEN

Map pp254-5   Glassware & Porcelain

☎ 512 24 18; www.austrianarts.com; 01, Kärntner Strasse 6; ☯ 10am-6:30pm Mon-Fri, 10am-6pm Sat; ⊙ U1, U3 Stephansplatz

Overcome your first impressions of this place – the ground floor is mostly high-end tourist tat – and go upstairs where you'll find the good stuff. Established in 1945, Österreichische Werkstätten is dedicated to selling work made by Austrian companies and designed by Austrian designers. Look out for Kisslinger, a family glassware company since 1946, with Klimt- and Hundertwasser-styled designs; Peter Wolfe's more traditional Tirol-style designed glassware; and of course the world-renowned Reidel wine glasses. The 'museum' downstairs is mostly a showroom for replica Hoffman and *Jugendstil* vases and glassware.

PALMERS Map pp254-5   Clothing

☎ 512 93 41; 01, Kärntner Strasse 4; ☯ 9.30am-7pm Mon-Fri, 9.30am-6pm Sat; ⊙ U1, U3 Stephansplatz

As Marks & Spencers' undies are to British women, so Palmers' are to Austrian women. Their own-brand underwear is reasonably priced, well-made and sexy. They've branched out into undies for men, too.

R HORNS Map pp254-5   Accessories

☎ 513 82 94; www.rhorns.com; 01, Bräunerstrasse 7; ☯ 10am-6.30pm Mon-Fri, 10am-5pm Sat; bus 2A, 3A

The leathergoods at this classy store follow the philosophy of the Wiener Werkstätte, with classic, elegant styles, immaculately finished. Most items are in calfskin with dark green moiré lining. Handbags, wallets, briefcases and accessories come at a price, but these are long-term investments, not faddish fashion pieces.

WOLFORD Map pp254-5   Fashion

☎ 512 87 31; 01, Kärntner Strasse 29; http://wolford.com; ☯ 9.30am-7pm Mon-Fri, to 9pm Thu, 9.30am-6pm Sat; ⊙ U1, U3 Stephansplatz

Perhaps the best-known Austrian brand in the fashion world, Wolford (founded in 1949) is renowned for high-quality hosiery. Here you'll find a huge range – including

---

VIENNA'S BEST CHOCOLATE & CAKES

- Café Sacher (p140) – their eponymous cake graces thousands of tourists' 'must-do in Vienna' lists
- Demel (p140) – a famed *Konditorei* with a *Jugendstil* interior and a peekable cake-designing studio out back
- Aida (p139) – magnificent retro interiors and fabulous cakes and sweets
- Oberlaa (p181) – gloriously packaged chocolates and biscuits
- Altmann & Kühne (p180) – world-famous bonbons made using a hundred-year-old recipe

fishnets in all colours of the rainbow and imaginatively patterned tights, stay-ups, stockings and knee-highs – as well as body stockings and swimwear. There are a number of Wolford branches scattered around town.

NORTH OF HOFBURG

KAUFHAUS SCHIEPEK Map pp254-5 Jewellery

☎ 533 15 75; 01, Teinfaltstrasse 3; ☯ 10.30am-6.30pm Mon-Fri, 10am-5pm Sat; bus 1A

This quirky and truly original shop stocks jars and jars of multicoloured baubles. Stock up on beads that look like liquorice allsorts and make your own crazy masterpiece, or buy one of their wacky plastic numbers featuring big plastic lobsters or birds' heads.

LODEN-PLANKL Map pp254-5   Clothing

☎ 533 80 32; www.plankl.at; 01, Michaelerplatz 6; ☯ 10am-6pm Mon-Sat; ⊙ U3 Herrengasse, bus 2A, 3A

Want to kit yourself out Von Trapp family-style? This 180-year-old institution is the place to come. Embroidered dirndls and blouses, capes, high-collared jackets and deer suede coats are all handmade (which is reflected in their prices), and modern variations are available as well as the traditional designs – though you're likely to find more nostalgic charm in the trad stuff. Christopher Plummer wannabes from around the world come to Loden-Plankl to buy the coats made from loden (a traditional fabric made from boiled and combed wool).

SHIPPING Map pp254-5 Toys

☎ 533 15 75; 01, Teinfaltstrasse 4; ☺ 1-6.30pm Mon-Fri, 10am-5pm Sat; bus 1A

An explosion of colour in the sedate backstreets behind the Burgtheater, this shop specialises in toys for adults – tacky-groovy plastic food-serving sets in bright colours, fake plastic food and lots of other useless but fun objets d'kitsch.

XOCOLAT Map pp254-5 Confectionery

☎ 535 43 63; www.xocolat.at; 01, Freyung 2; ☺ 10am-6pm Mon-Fri, 10am-5pm Sat, noon-5pm Sun; ⊕ U3 Herrengasse, bus 1A

An aromatic, chocolate-lovers' paradise, and a good reason to visit the magnificent Freyung Passage, this upscale *Konditorei* offers 40-odd varieties of beautifully decorated handmade chocolates, some of which qualify as tiny edible works of art. Too good to eat, and too good not to.

JEWISH QUARTER & AROUND

ART UP Map pp254-5 Fashion & Accessories

☎ 535 50 97; www.artup.at; 01, Bauernmarkt 8; ☺ 11.30am-6.30pm Mon-Fri, 11am-5pm Sat; ⊕ U1, U3 Stephansplatz

The best place to come if you want to take the temperature of Vienna's contemporary design scene, Art Up works on a cooperative model allowing the designers who stock their work here to get a foothold in the fashion world – around 35 of them at the time of research. The model makes for an eclectic collection – elegant fashion pieces rub alongside quirky accessories (Astroturf tie or handbag, anyone?) as well as ceramics and bigger art pieces. It's a testament to the liveliness of the fashion and design scenes in Vienna, given new vigour by students coming out of the city's fashion schools and driven by a burgeoning confidence in the quality of homegrown talent.

BLACK MARKET Map pp254-5 Music

☎ 533 76 17-0; 01, Gonzagagasse 9; ☺ midday-7pm Mon-Fri, 11am-6pm Sat; tram 1, 2, bus 2A

Black Market is Vienna's house, techno and electronic music specialist. The vinyl selection is enormous and the staff highly knowledgeable. You'll also find a small lounge with coffee, and cooler-than-cool T-shirts and sweats.

JUST LOOKING, THANKS

Vienna is a browser's dream; a city full of precious items in lavish outlets, and with a real respect for the art of browsing – you'll never be hurried along or frowned upon for just looking. These are our favourites, for a variety of reasons:

- J&L Lobmeyr (p181) – a glittering palace of wantful goods
- Dorotheum (p181) – what can we say – you could amuse yourself here for days
- Lichterloh (p186) – one of the coolest furniture shops you'll ever see
- Freyung Passage – come to this sumptuous shopping arcade to buy chocolates from Xocolat (left), but also to marvel at the Art Nouveau carved friezes, marble statuary and fountain
- Prachner im MQ (p184) – the collection of Austrian and Viennese art and architecture books here will inspire and inform your sightseeing

SHAKESPEARE & CO Map pp254-5 Books

☎ 535 50 53; www.shakespeare.co.at; 01, Sterngasse 2; ☺ 9am-8pm Mon-Fri, 9am-7pm Sat; bus 2A, 3A

This beautifully cluttered bookshop in a charming area just off Judengasse stocks Vienna's best collection of literary and hard-to-find titles in English – history,

Kaufhaus Schiepek (opposite page)

culture, classic and modern fiction – with a wide range of titles about Austria and by Austrian writers displayed separately. The personalised and friendly service makes this the best place in town to come for your train and plane reading needs.

SONG Map pp254-5   Fashion & Accessories

☎ 532 28 58; 01, Landskrongasse 2; ◷ 10am-6.30pm Mon-Fri, 10am-6pm Sat; ◉ U1, U3 Stephansplatz, bus 1A

Song stocks the latest and most cutting-edge gear from top international designers like Martin Margiela, Balenciaga and Walter van Beirendonck – lots of asymmetrics and unexpected fabrics.

UNGER UND KLEIN Map pp254-5   Wine

☎ 532 13 23; www.ungerundklein.at; 01, Gölsdorfgasse 2; ◷ 3pm-midnight Mon-Fri, 5-midnight Sat; ▣ 1, 2, bus 2A, 3A

Unger und Klein's small but knowledgeable wine collection spans the globe, but the majority of its labels come from Europe. The best of Austrian wines – expensive boutique varieties to bargain-bin bottles – is available. It's also a small, laid-back wine bar, with a reasonable selection of wines by the glass, which gets crowded on Friday and Saturday evenings.

WEIN & CO Map pp254-5   Wine

☎ 535 09 16; www.weinco.at in German; 01, Jasomirgottstrasse 3-5; ◷ 10am-midnight Mon-Sat, 11am-midnight Sun; ◉ U1, U3 Stephansplatz

With a wide selection of quality European and New World wines, and a huge variety of local bottles, Wein & Co is probably your best bet for wine shopping – you should be able to pick up a bargain, as the specials

TOP FIVE TOURIST TAT

Like any long-established tourist hot-spot, Vienna does a great line in rubbish souvenirs. These are our favourites:

- Mozart in every imaginable incarnation – keyrings, mousepads, tissues, chocolate balls
- wedding-cakey, sickly sweet porcelain figurines
- Klimt-printed everything
- little pottery cottages
- inexplicable miniature shoes.

here are always great. You can also buy cigars, and the wine bar has a terrace with a view of Stephansdom (try 'Happy Sunday' when all glasses are half-price 11am to 4pm). Five other Wein & Co shops are scattered around town.

RINGSTRASSE
PARLAMENT TO SCHWARZENBERGPLATZ

SPIELZUNG Map pp254-5   Toys

☎ 512 56 10; 01, Ringstrasse Galerien, Kärntner Ring 5-13; ◷ 10am-7pm Mon-Fri, 10am-6pm Sat; ◉ U2, U4 Karlsplatz, ▣ D, J, 1, 2, 62, 65

Beautifully wrought models – circuses, carousels, the Riesenrad – and slightly spooky handmade dolls are the mainstays of this famous shop, in Vienna for 40 years. Prepare to be enchanted and bemused by the huge array of dollhouse accessories – tiny plastic meals for dolls include tiny eggs in tiny eggcups and a tiny roast chicken meal complete with tiny carrots.

MUSEUMSQUARTIER

LOMOSHOP Map pp254-5   Photography

☎ 523 70 16; 07, Museumsplatz 1; ◷ 11am-7pm Mon-Sun; U2, U3 Volkstheater, bus 48A

The Lomographic Society's (www.lomography.com) first ever Lomography shop is in MuseumsQuartier. Lomo is a worldwide cult and the Lomoshop is considered its heart. There's all manner of Lomo cameras, gadgets and accessories for sale; an original Russian-made Lomo will set you back around €150, and you can get single-use disposable Lomo cameras for €12. There's also a wall full of Lomo photos on display, for inspiration.

PRACHNER IM MQ Map pp254-5   Books

☎ 512 85 88-0; www.prachner.at; 07, Museumsplatz 1; ◷ 10am-7pm Mon-Sat, 1-7pm Sun; ◉ U2, U3 Volkstheater, bus 48A

A must for coffee-table connoisseurs, this luxuriously airy and browse-friendly space hosts a serious collection of books on art, photography, fashion and design theory, including a great range on the history of Austrian and Viennese art and design.

MARKETS

With globalisation storming the world, multinational chain stores gobbling up local shops and independent retailers being forced into early retirement, it's refreshing to know that in Vienna the traditional market is still alive and kicking. Almost every district has at least one market selling fresh produce from Monday to Saturday, many reflecting the ethnic diversity of their neighbourhood. Some host *Bauernmärkte* (farmers markets) on Saturday mornings, where growers from the surrounding countryside travel to the big city to sell their wares –fresh vegetables, tree-ripened fruit, cured hams, free-range eggs, home-made schnapps and cut flowers.

The best of the bunch:

Naschmarkt (Map pp254–5; 06, Linke & Rechte Wienzeile; ☺ 6am-6.30pm Mon-Fri, 6am-5pm Sat; ⊕ U1, U2, U4 Karlsplatz, U4 Kettenbrückengasse) *The* market in Vienna. This massive market extends for more than 500m along Linke Wienzeile between the U4 stops of Kettenbrückengasse and Karlsplatz. The western end near Kettengasse is more fun, with all sorts of meats, fruit and vegetables (this is the place for that hard-to-find exotic variety), spices, wines, cheeses and olives, Indian and Middle Eastern specialities and fabulous kebab and falafel stands. (Check out the vinegar and oil place, with 24 varieties of fruit and veg-flavoured vinegar, 11 balsamics and over 20 types of flavoured oil.) The market peters out at the eastern end to stalls selling Indian fabrics and jewellery and trashy trinkets – suddenly you'll feel like you're in a Nepali tourist town.

Brunnenmarkt (Map pp258–9; 16, Brunnengasse; ☺ 6am-6.30pm Mon-Fri, 6am-2pm Sat; ⊕ U6 Josefstädter Strasse, tram J) Brunnenmarkt is the largest street-market in Vienna and reflects the neighbourhood's ethnic make-up – most stallholders are of Turkish or Balkan descent. The majority of produce sold is vegetables and fruit, but there are a few places selling unbelievably tacky clothes – this is the place to pick up that Hulk Hogan T-shirt you've always wanted. The kebab houses here are truly superb (see Kent, p136, and Etap, p136). On Saturday nearby Yppenplatz features the best *Bauernmarkt* in the city.

Flohmarkt (Map pp260–1; 05, Kettenbrückengasse; ☺ dawn-4pm Sat; ⊕ U4 Kettenbrückengasse) One of the best flea markets in Europe, this Vienna institution should not be missed. It's tacked onto the southwestern end of the Naschmarkt on Saturdays, and half of Vienna seems to converge here, either flogging or pawing through tonnes of antiques, *Altwaren* and just plain junk. It stretches for several blocks of stands hawking books, clothes, records, ancient electrical goods, old postcards, ornaments, carpets…you name it. It's very atmospheric – more like the markets of Eastern Europe – with goods piled up in apparent chaos on the walkway. Try to get there early, as it gets more and more crammed as the morning wears on. Stallholders know the value of their goods (and the fact this is a tourist attraction), so they'll quote high. Haggle!

Karmelitermarkt (Map pp258–9; 02, Im Werd; ☺ 6am-6.30pm Mon-Fri, 6am-2pm Sat; bus 5A) A market with a long tradition, the Karmelitermarkt reflects the ethnic diversity of its neighbourhood; you're sure to see Hasidic Jews on bikes shopping for kosher goods here. Set in a square with architecturally picturesque surrounds, the market is quiet during weekdays but has a good range of authentic ethnic places to eat; fruit and vegetable stalls share the marketplace with butchers selling kosher and halal meats. On Saturday the square features a *Bauern-markt*.

Freyungmarkt (Map pp254–5; 01, Freyung; ☺ 8am-7.30pm Fri & Sat; ⊕ U2 Schottentor, bus 1A) The Freyung market exclusively sells organic produce from farmers. The atmosphere here is quite sedate compared to the markets mentioned above.

Flohmarkt at Naschmarkt (this page)

INSIDE THE GÜRTEL
WIEDEN
BABETTES Map pp260-1   Food & Books
☎ 585 51 65; 04 Schleifmühlgasse 17; ⏰ 10am-7pm Mon-Fri, 10am-5pm Sat; bus 59A

Babettes is a unique concept in Vienna. Part eatery, part cookbook and spice store, it caters to a growing market of Viennese willing to experiment with what they cook at home. With more than a thousand cookbooks from around the world, you should be able to find something to match your tastes. Cooking courses are also available.

BOBBY'S FOOD STORE Map pp260-1   Food
☎ 586 75 34; 04, Schleifmühlgasse 8; ⏰ 10am-6.30pm Mon-Fri, 10am-6pm Sat; 🚋 62, 65, bus 59A

Craving Vegemite or Marmite? Salt-and-vinegar crisps? Heinz Spotted Dick? Bobby's is a one-stop food store for brands from the US, UK and beyond that are hard to find anywhere else in Vienna.

CLOTHING SIZES
Measurements approximate only, try before you buy

Women's Clothing					
Aus/UK	8	10	12	14	16	18
Europe	36	38	40	42	44	46
Japan	5	7	9	11	13	15
USA	6	8	10	12	14	16
Women's Shoes					
Aus/USA	5	6	7	8	9	10
Europe	35	36	37	38	39	40
France only	35	36	38	39	40	42
Japan	22	23	24	25	26	27
UK	3½	4½	5½	6½	7½	8½
Men's Clothing					
Aus	92	96	100	104	108	112
Europe	46	48	50	52	54	56
Japan	S		M	M		L
UK/USA	35	36	37	38	39	40
Men's Shirts (Collar Sizes)					
Aus/Japan	38	39	40	41	42	43
Europe	38	39	40	41	42	43
UK/USA	15	15½	16	16½	17	17½
Men's Shoes					
Aus/UK	7	8	9	10	11	12
Europe	41	42	43	44½	46	47
Japan	26	27	27½	28	29	30
USA	7½	8½	9½	10½	11½	12½

FLO VINTAGE MODE Map pp260-1   Fashion
☎ 586 07 73; 04, Schleifmühlgasse 15a; ⏰ 10am-6.30pm Mon-Fri, 10am-3.30pm Sat; bus 59A

In a city this enamoured with the glamorous past, it's no less than shocking that there's only one true vintage clothing store in town. The clothes here are fastidiously and beautifully displayed, from pearl-embroidered Art Nouveau masterpieces to 1950s and '60s New Look pieces and designer wear of the '70s and '80s (alphabetised Armani-Zegna). Prices are high, and so is quality.

MARIAHILF
EWA'S FASHION LOUNGE
Map pp260-1   Fashion
06, Schadekgasse 3; www.hotkultur.at in German; ⏰ 11am-7pm & 9pm-4am; 🚇 U3 Neubaugasse, bus 13A

Junky, but funky – Ewa's is a club by night, a trashy retro clothing shop by day. A DJ spins discs as you pause between racks and sit at the bar for a drink. The clothes are from the polyester and frayed cuff school of secondhand, but the vodka is cheap and the ambience is…interesting.

LICHTERLOH Map pp254-5   Furniture
☎ 581 83 06; www.lichterloh.com; 06, Gumpendorferstrasse 15-17; ⏰ 11am-6.30pm Mon-Fri, 11am-4pm Sat; bus 57A

This massive, ultra-cool space is filled with iconic furniture from the 1900s to 1970s, by names such as Eames, Thonet and Mies Van Der Rohe. Even if you're not planning to lug home a slick Danish sideboard, it's worth a look at this veritable gallery of modern furniture design. There's also some more transportable antique kitsch and glassware.

MÖRTZ Map pp254-5   Shoes
☎ 587 57 87; 06, Windmühlgasse 9; ⏰ 8.30am-1pm & 2-6pm Mon-Fri, 8.30am-noon Sat; bus 57A

On any given weekend, elderly ladies and gents of the city can be seen riding buses and trams to the Wienerwald (Vienna Woods) for a bit of *Wandern* (hiking). Their boots look as though they've survived both world wars and they'd easily survive another couple – they're probably from Mörtz. Here you can find superb handmade hiking boots sturdy enough for any hike you care to undertake, and they're comfortable to boot.

PARK
Map pp260-1   Fashion

☎ 526 44 14; www.park.co.at; 07, Mondscheingasse 20; ☷ 10am-7pm Mon-Fri, 10am-6pm Sat;
🚃 49, bus 13A

A serious designer store in a stark all-white
480 sq metre space, Park stocks fashion
books and magazines as well as cutting
edge fashion from designers such as Hussein Chalayan and Raf Simons. They also
sell the fantastic artist-designed 2k tees
(www.2ktshirts.com) from Japan.

PHILI'S – WITH LOVE
Map pp260-1   Fashion & Accessories

☎ 504 50 16-00; www.phili-s.com; 06, Gumpendorferstrasse 71; ☷ 9am-6.30pm Mon-Fri, 9am-
4pm Sat; ◉ U4 Pilgramgasse, bus 57A

A shop for girly girls – think frilly pink umbrellas, glam-and-glitter jewellery, flowery
hoodies, trainers and boots. Even tomboys
might be swayed by the super-cute novelty
totes and handbags from cult Danish label
Apfelsina and a range of other carefully
chosen bits and bobs by hip labels from
around the world.

PICCINI PICCOLO GOURMET
Map pp254-5   Food & Wine

☎ 587 52 54; 06, Linke Wienzeile 4; ☷ 9am-
6.30pm Mon-Fri, 8.30am-2pm Sat; ◉ U1, U2, U4
Karlsplatz

Piccini stocks only the finest and freshest
goods from Italy, all of which are handled
with love and care – wines, multitudes of
varieties of dried pasta, 20-odd different
types of salami, olives and oil. It's also a
superb restaurant (see p132).

SNOW GLOBES

There are many impersonators but only one true
snow-globe original – the Perzy Snow Globe. Back
in 1900 in his workshop in Vienna, Erwin Perzy I had
the idea of designing a globe containing a church
and filled with liquid and rice, which, when shaken,
produced the effect of snow falling. It became an
instant hit, even with Emperor Franz Josef.

More than a hundred years on the company is
still going strong, and is still in family hands; Erwin
Perzy III, the grandson of the snow-globe creator,
is the current head of the company. Their products
have travelled the globe, and have landed in some
illustrious paws – a Perzy snow globe was produced
for Bill Clinton's inauguration and contains the actual confetti from the event. One-off pieces have also
been produced for the films *Citizen Kane*, *Heidi* and
True Lies.

In a world of cheap-and-cheerful products,
churned out in their thousands by automated production lines, its surprising, and refreshing, to learn
that every snow globe is still handmade. Their factory
contains the small Perzy Snow Globe Museum (Map
pp258–9; ☎ 486 43 41; www.viennasnowglobe
.at; 17, Schumanngasse 87; ☷ 9am-3pm Mon-Thu;
🚃 9, 42), which stocks their snow globes and can be
visited by appointment.

POLYKLAMOTT
Map pp260-1   Clothing

☎ 969 03 37; 06, Hofmühlgasse 6; ☷ 11am-
7.30pm Mon-Fri, 11am-5pm Sat; ◉ U4 Pilgramgasse, bus 13A

This low-key secondhand shop is filled with
eminently rummagable racks of reasonably priced gear for men and women. Their
own-brand retro satchels round out the

Shu! (p188)

CHRISTMAS MARKETS

From around the middle of November, *Christkindlmärkte* (Christmas markets) start to pop up all over Vienna. Ranging from kitsch to quaint in style and atmosphere, they all have a few things in common: plenty of people, loads of Christmas gifts to purchase, mugs of *Glühwein* (mulled wine) and hotplates loaded with *Kartoffelpuffer* (hot potato patties) and *Maroni* (roasted chestnuts). Most close a day or two before Christmas day.

Some of the best include:

Alte AKH (Map pp258–9; 🚊 43, 44) A favourite of students, this small market occupies a corner of the Alte AKH's largest courtyard. There are farm animals and a horse-drawn sleigh for the kids.

Freyung (Map pp254–5; Ⓜ U2 Schottentor, bus 1A) Freyung's stalls devote themselves to Austrian arts and crafts, and the entire market attempts, with some success, to emit an old-worldy feel.

Heiligenkreuzerhof (Map pp254–5; Ⓜ U1, U4 Schwedenplatz, Schwedenplatz trams) This often-forgotten market is arguably the most authentic and quaint of all the *Christkindlmärkte*. It's off Schönlaterngasse, hidden within a residential courtyard.

Karlsplatz (Map pp254–5; Ⓜ U1, U2 U4 Karlsplatz) The Karlsplatz market mainly has stalls selling arty gifts and is situated close to the Karlskirche. People flock here to crowd around flaming metal barrels, clutching their cup of *Glühwein*.

Rathausplatz (Map pp254–5; 🚊 1, 2) This is easily the biggest and most touristy Christmas market in Vienna, held on the square in front of the Rathaus (City Hall). Most of the Christmas gifts on sale are kitschy beyond belief, but the atmosphere is lively and the *Glühwein* just keeps on flowing.

Schönbrunn (Map pp260–1; Ⓜ U4 Schönbrunn, bus 10A) Directly in front of the palace, the circle of stalls are generally quite upmarket, but there's loads of events for the kids and daily classical concerts at 6pm (more on weekends).

Spittelberg (Map pp254–5; Ⓜ U2, U3 Volkstheater, tram 49, bus 48A) Occupying the charming cobblestoned streets of the Spittelberg quarter, this market is traditionally the most beloved of the Viennese. Stalls sell quality arts and crafts, but not at the cheapest prices. No matter what the temperature, you'll find people crowded around *Glühwein* stalls, especially outside Lux and Plutzerbräu.

---

selection, and the automatic clothes dispenser – all items in the Automat are €5 – is open for business 24 hours a day.

RAVE UP Map pp260-1   Music
☎ 596 96 50; 06, www.rave-up.at; Hofmühlgasse 1; ◷ 10am-6.30pm Mon-Fri, 10am-5pm Sat; Ⓜ U4 Pilgramgasse, bus 13A
Friendly staff, loads of new vinyl and a massive collection makes a trip to Rave Up a real pleasure. The store specialises in indie and alternative imports from the UK and US, but you'll find plenty of electronica, hip-hop and retro tunes, and you can listen before you buy, too.

SHU! Map pp260-1   Shoes
☎ 523 14 49; 07, Neubaugasse 34; ◷ midday-6.30pm Tue-Fri, midday-5pm Sat; 🚊 49, bus 13A
Shoe fanatics flock to this store in droves, for the latest styles by Camper, Vic Matie, Gidigio and more at easy-on-the-wallet prices. In this spot for eight years, Shu! stocks men's and women's shoes.

THALIA Map pp254-5   Books
☎ 595 45 50; www.thalia.at; 06, Mariahilfer Strasse 99; ◷ 9.30am-7pm Mon-Wed, 9.30am-8pm Thu-Fri, 9.30am-6pm Sat; Ⓜ U3 Zieglergasse
Vienna's biggest bookshop, spread over four floors including a café, Thalia has an 'International Bookshop' at the back of the ground floor with lots of bestsellers in English and a small selection of books in Spanish, French, Italian and Russian.

NEUBAU

MÖBEL Map pp254-5   Furniture & Accessories
☎ 524 94 97; 07, Burggasse 10; ◷ 10-1am; Ⓜ U2, U3 Volkstheater, bus 48A
Das Möbel is more of a bar than a shop (see p158), but it showcases some of the funkiest and most original furniture in Vienna. Local artists and designers fill the place

with their latest creations, and it's all for sale. The bags hanging just inside the door, also locally designed and produced, are truly special creations.

EVA BLUT Map pp260-1 Fashion & Accessories
☎ 524 05 95; www.evablut.org; 07, Schotten-feldgasse 41-43/28a; ⊙ by appointment only; 🚋 49

Eva Blut's transformable clothing is mul-tiskilled: a jacket might become a bag, trousers turn into overalls. The result is an edgy, asymmetrical look with a Japanese aesthetic and a very urban manifesto. You'll have to phone ahead to make an appointment.

LOLLIPOP Map pp260-1 Confectionery
☎ 526 33 38; 07, Burggasse 57; ⊙ 7.30am-8pm Mon-Fri, 8am-8pm Sat, 10am-8pm Sun; bus 13A, 48A

An old-fashioned neighbourhood confec-tioners with a selection of traditional and newfangled sweets, Lollipop is sure to have something to please even the fussiest sweet-tooth.

ORATOR Map pp260-1 Photography
☎ 526 10 10-23; www.orator.at; 07, Westbahn-strasse 23; ⊙ 9am-7pm Mon-Fri, 10am-1pm Sat; 🚋 5, 49

Orator is one of a handful of specialist photography shops at the western end of Westbahnstrasse. The range of digital and SLR cameras and lenses is quite impressive, and the second-hand stock is worth brows-ing through. A technician is available to do repairs on Tuesdays and Thursdays.

SUBSTANCE Map pp260-1 Music
☎ 523 67 57; 07, Westbahnstrasse 16; ⊙ 11am-7.30pm Mon-Fri, 10am-6pm Sat; 🚋 49, bus 13A

Substance stocks the weird, the wild, the wicked and the wonderful – electronica, indie rock, world music, new and second-hand LPs and a small collection of music books and cult novels, mostly in English. It's a good place to find out about upcom-ing gigs.

WESC Map pp260-1 Fashion
☎ 526 54 84; www.wesc.com; 07, Westbahn-strasse 12; ⊙ 11am-6pm Mon, 11am-7pm Tue-Fri, 10am-4pm Sat; 🚋 49, bus 13A

This concept store is the Vienna home of the über-hip Swedish streetwear label

WeAretheSuperlativeConspiracy. The com-pany grew out of skateboard culture, and the lines of hoodies, tees, parkas and pants follow that aesthetic of simply cut, cool but durable design. Check the website for their latest collection.

JOSEFSTADT
K&K SCHMUCKHANDELS
Map pp254-5 Jewellery
☎ 408 99 53; 08, Josefstädterstrasse 5; ⊙ 10am-6pm Mon-Fri, 10am-2pm Sat; 🚋 J, bus 13A

When you enter this shop you'll feel like you've been immersed in a giant treasure chest, with strings of semiprecious stones heaped over every surface, as well as chi-noiserie, polished coral, shell and wooden beads. Bangles, bracelets, necklaces and earrings are on display, or you can get the trinket of your dreams custom-made from the gems of your choice.

Design furniture at Möbel (opposite page)

KUNSTHANDEL MARTINA MEIDERLE

Map pp254-5   Furniture & Jewellery

☎ 405 74 10; www.meiderle.at; 08, Josefstädterstrasse 14; ⊙ 10am-1pm & 3-6pm Mon-Fri, 10am-1pm Sat; ⊛ J, bus 13A

This is the place for high-quality, highly polished furniture, ornaments, lighting and art mainly from the Art Deco and Bauhaus periods. If you simply must have that Josef Hoffman sideboard, shipping can be arranged. You'll also find some Jakob Bengal costume jewellery here.

SZAAL

Map pp258-9   Furniture

☎ 406 63 30; www.szaal.at; 08, Josefstädter Strasse 74; ⊙ 10am-6pm Mon-Fri, 10am-noon Sat; ⊕ U6 Josefstädter Strasse, ⊛ J, 33

Szaal is a specialist in Biedermeier and baroque furniture, dating from around 1700 to 1840. You'll also find a few pieces from the late-19th and 20th centuries. Shipping can be arranged.

TEUCHTLER

Map pp254-5   Music

☎ 586 21 33; 08, Windmühlgasse 10; ⊙ 1-6pm Mon-Fri, 10am-1pm Sat; bus 57A

This is where you might just find that LP you've been searching the world for. Founded in 1948 and now run by the third generation of the family, this truly amazing record shop is a Vienna institution. The walls are lined with shelves of tightly-packed vinyl – around 500,000 according to the owners' best guess. They buy and exchange records and CDs, including rare and deleted titles.

LEOPOLDSTADT

NAGY STRICKDESIGN

Map pp258-9   Fashion

☎ 925 13 74; www.nagy-strickdesign.at; 02, Krummbaumgasse 2-4; ⊙ 11am-1pm & 2-6pm Tue-Fri, 11am-1pm Sat; bus 5A

The stripy cotton and viscose knitwear here is both classic and up-to-the-minute, with flattering shapes and vivid colours, and designs for hot and cold weather. There are also linen pants and skirts in a refreshing range of bright colours and casual styles.

OUTSIDE THE GÜRTEL

OTTAKRING

STAUD

Map pp258-9   Food

☎ 406 88 05-21; 16, Yppenplatz; ⊙ 8am-12.30pm Tue-Thu, 3.30-6pm Fri, 8am-12.30pm Sat; ⊕ U6 Josefstädter Strasse, ⊛ J, 44

The family business Staud has been making jams and pickled vegetables and fruit for more than 30 years. Prices are more than you'd pay in supermarkets for other brands, but the quality is by far the best in Vienna. Saturday morning is a great time to visit, when the nearby Brunnenmarkt (see p185) is in full swing.

Sleeping

Sleeping

Vienna's sleeping options cover the full spectrum, from youth hostels and student residences to luxury establishments like the Hotel Imperial and Hotel Sacher, where chandeliers, antique furniture and original 19th-century oil paintings are the norm rather than the exception. In between are homely *Pensionen* (guesthouses) and less ostentatious hotels, plus a small but smart range of apartments for longer-term rentals.

Standards remain high, and generally so do prices; bargains exist, but they're few and far between. As a rule, budget doubles are available for under €80 a night, midrange from €80 to €200, and top end anything above that (and the sky's the limit in this city). Breakfast is invariably included in the price – normally a Continental buffet – but parking isn't (anything between €6 and €26 per 24 hours).

The Innere Stadt is first to fill up, so booking well ahead is advised. District's one to nine are the next to go, with the outer districts (outside the Gürtel) mopping up the leftovers. If you arrive without accommodation, head for the Tourist Info Wien (p231) which books rooms for a small fee.

Accommodation Styles

HOTELS & PENSIONEN

As hotels and *Pensionen* make up the bulk of accommodation options in Vienna, a huge variation in styles and tastes exist.

PRICE GUIDE

Each sleeping option has been given a price ranking, indicating the room price at double occupancy.

€€€	over €200 a night
€€	€80-200 a night
€	under €80 a night

Leaving aside the city's luxury hotels, which are in a league of their own, hotels tend to be larger than *Pensionen*, have more facilities (on-site parking, bars and restaurants) and come with more extras (room service, laundry service etc). *Pensionen* are often located in apartment blocks, and can be far more personable and less standardised, with larger rooms. Prices start from around €50 to €60 for a basic double room with shared bath and top out at approximately €200 to €250 for an upmarket en-suite double in a four-star hotel. On average, expect to pay €100 to €150 for a decent double room in a hotel or *Pension*.

Note that many of the older hotels and *Pensionen* have a range of rooms and facilities, the cheapest of which share a toilet and shower with other guests.

HOSTELS & STUDENT RESIDENCES

Vienna has a smattering of *Jugendherberge,* private hostels or hostels affiliated with Hostelling International (HI). In the former, no membership is required. Dorm beds, singles and doubles are generally available in both; expect to pay around €18 for a dorm bed and €25 to €35 for a double room in high season.

Austria has two HI-affiliated youth-hostel organisations: **Österreichischer Jugendherbergsverband** (ÖJHN; Map pp258–9; ☎ 533 53 53; www.oejhv.or.at; 01, Schottenring 28; 🕙 9am-5pm Mon-Thu, 9am-3pm Fri; 🚇 U2, U4 Schottenring, 🚊 1, 2) and **Österreichischer Jugendherbergswerk** (ÖJHW; Map pp254–5; ☎ 533 18 33; www.jungehotels.at; 01, Helferstorferstrasse 4; 🕙 9.30am-6pm Mon-Fri; 🚊 1, 2). Either can provide information on all of Vienna's HI hostels.

For information on student residences, refer to the box (opposite).

LONGER-TERM RENTALS

Viennese looking for apartments rely on word of mouth or turn to *Bazar* magazine. It's *the* magazine if you're looking to buy, sell or rent anything, including apartments or rooms. The time scale of places on offer may range from indefinite rental to occupation of a flat for a month or so while the resident is on holiday. *Falter, Kurier* and *Standard* also carry accommodation ads.

A couple of short-term apartment rentals are listed in this chapter.

STUDENT RESIDENCES

When university students take their summer break from July to September, their student accommodation becomes available to tourists. The majority are outside the Innere Stadt, but are still reasonably convenient for the centre, and the rooms are perfectly OK but nothing fancy; expect single beds (perhaps placed together in doubles), a work desk and a wardrobe. Cheaper places have institutional-style shared facilities, while pricier places offer private shower and toilet, and the price includes breakfast. These are some of the better options:

Hotel Academia (Map pp260–1; ☎ 401 76; www.academia-hotels.co.at; 08, Pfeilgasse 3a; s/d €50/66; ☒ J, 46; ☐) Massive 498-bed student residence (with a lift, thankfully) with spacious rooms with en suite but no TV. There's a coffee bar on site.

Accordia (Map pp254–5; ☎ 212 16 68; www.albertina-hotels.at; 02, Grosse Schiffgasse 12; s/d €56/84; bus 5A) Modern, multifloor high-rise; pluses include private bathrooms, a bike storage room and the Innere Stadt only a short walk across the Danube Canal.

Avis (Map pp258–9; ☎ 408 96 60; www.academia-hotels.co.at; 08, Pfeilgasse 4; s/d €50/66; ☒ J, 46; ☐) Directly opposite Academia but more residential than its larger neighbour. Also has a garden.

Kolping Wien-Zentral (Map pp254–5; ☎ 587 56 31; www.wien-zentral.kolping.at; 06, Gumpendorfer Strasse 39; s/d from €45/70; ☺ U4 Kettenbrückengasse) Bold, brash and colourful student residence that also offers hotel-style accommodation year-round. Rooms come with shower and toilet but are a tad soulless. Enter via Stiegengasse.

INNERE STADT

The Innere Stadt is Vienna's prime accommodation location, with easy access to the lion's share of the city's attractions, and an excellent selection of restaurants, bars and music venues. Comparatively, prices tend to outdo the rest of Vienna (except the Ringstrasse) and reservations are well advised.

STEPHANSPLATZ

HOTEL AM STEPHANSPLATZ

Map pp254-5   Hotel €€

☎ 534 05-0; www.hotelamstephansplatz.at; 01, Stephansplatz 9; s/d from €140/205; ☺ U1, U3 Stephansplatz; ☐ ☒

Hotel am Stephansplatz occupies the perfect position in Vienna, overlooking the Gothic spires of Stephansdom, but its interior almost tops its location. The entire hotel is a model of eco-friendly design – all building materials used, right down to the glue, was subject to environmental restrictions, and the breakfast is a compilation of organic produce. Rooms are filled with modern furniture and warmed with earthy colours while the bedding is a treat – thick, snug and *über* skin-friendly. Room 702 steals the show; a rooftop suite with balcony views across Stephansplatz to the hallowed doors of Stephansdom.

EAST OF STEPHANSPLATZ

PENSION RIEDL   Map pp254-5   Pension €

☎ 512 77 79 ; www.pensionriedl.at; 01, Georg-Coch-Platz 3; s/d from €44/69; ☒ 1, 2

Pension Riedl is a traditional pension on the fringes of the Innere Stadt with a warm welcome and a homely atmosphere. Rooms are generally large and bedecked with mismatched furniture (bathrooms are on the small side); Nos 6 and 7 have tiny balconies overlooking Georg-Coch-Platz (and Otto Wagner's celebrated Postsparkasse) while the balcony in No 8 enjoys the peace of the inner courtyard. The pension's apartment, with its long balcony, enormous rooms, cosy ambience and kitchen, is a fine choice.

HOTEL-PENSION SUZANNE

Map pp254-5   Pension €€

☎ 513 25 07; www.pension-suzanne.at; 01, Walfischgasse 4; s/d €77/96; ☺ U1, U2, U4 Karlsplatz, ☒ D, J, 1, 2, 62, 65

More a *Pension* than a hotel, Suzanne is a solid accommodation option in the very centre of Vienna. Its 1950s facade belies rooms filled with attractive antique furniture in a multitude of hues and finished in polished wood, which help to distract from the room's small size, while bathrooms are thoroughly modern affairs. Extras that add charm include stacks of information on classical concerts, umbrellas to borrow on rainy days and unusually friendly and helpful staff.

APPARTEMENTS RIEMERGASSE

Map pp254-5   Apartments €€

☎ 512 72 20; www.riemergasse.at; 01, Riemergasse 8; apt per night/month from €93/2233; ⊕ U3 Stubentor, 🚃 1, 2

Riemergasse is an excellent option for travellers requiring a few home comforts while they're away. Studios are a little poky but include a kitchenette, while larger apartments are quite sizable and come with full cooking facilities; fittings in all apartments are more modern than most Viennese enjoy. Views from some of the top-floor apartments catch the spire of Stephansdom, but generally you'll be staring into the neighbours across the way. Breakfast is available for an extra €5.

HOTEL KAISERIN ELISABETH

Map pp254-5   Hotel €€

☎ 515 26; www.kaiserinelisabeth.at; 01, Weihburggasse 3; s/d €109/187; ⊕ U1, U3 Stephansplatz

It may look plain from the outside, but inside Kaiserin Elisabeth is a delight, with 19th-century imperial-style luxury balanced with modern comforts. Rooms contain splashes of stately design, with chandeliers, oriental carpets, wooden floors and antique pieces. Bathrooms are tiled in light colours and the superior variety sport double sinks and a separate shower and bath. Portraits of a forever-youthful Sisi line the hallways and common rooms, but she never set foot inside, although Wolfgang Amadeus Mozart, Oskar Kokoschka and Otto Wagner all did.

HOLMANN BELETAGE

Map pp254-5   Pension €€

☎ 961 19 60; www.hollmann-beletage.at 01, Köllnerhofgasse 6; r from €130; ⊕ U1, U4 Schwedenplatz; 🖵

A minimalist establishment of sorts, Hollmann Beletage is a *Pension* for guests with an eye for style, a penchant for clean lines and a desire for privacy. Rooms are slick units, with natural wood floors, bare walls, simple, classic furniture and designer lamps and door handles. Space is utilised to the max; bathrooms and cupboards are cleverly hidden behind tall double doors, creating a Tardis-like effect. The reception, with its open fireplace, sofas and footstools, library and CD collection, moonlights as a guest lounge. Advance booking is advisable.

KÖNIG VON UNGARN Map pp254-5 Hotel €€

☎ 515 84-0; www.kvu.at; 01, Schulerstrasse 10; s/d €142/203; ⊕ U1, U3 Stephansplatz

The 'King of Hungary' is a quality hotel balancing class and informality. The wonderful inner courtyard, with its pyramid skylight, wood panelling and leather furniture, will easily impress, as will the service, where breakfast is from 6am to noon (at which time the bar opens) and little acts of decadence, such as gold-plated, free-standing ashtrays, are everywhere (even in the lift). Rooms can be a little poky, but each is individually furnished with antiques and range in style from rather plain to downright extravagant: the best face Domgasse.

KÄRNTNER STRASSE, GRABEN & KOHLMARKT

PENSION AM OPERNECK

Map pp254-5   Pension €

☎ 512 93 10; 01 Kärntner Strasse 47; s/d €53/75; U1, U2, U4 Karlsplatz, 🚃 D, J, 1, 2, 62, 65

It's hard to beat Am Operneck on two very important points – location and price. Directly across from the famous Sacher, its front doors open out onto Kärntner Strasse, the busiest street in the city. Its rooms are similar to its owner – fading after years of use but still going strong and easily making guests feel comfortable and at home. As there are only six rooms (all of which are quite large), it's essential to book well ahead.

PENSION NOSSEK Map pp254-5 Pension €€

☎ 533 70 41-0; www.pension-nossek.at in German; 01, Graben 17; s/d from €58/110; ⊕ U1, U3 Stephansplatz

When it comes to real estate, it's all about location, location, location. And with a front door facing the Graben, and Stephansdom within sight, Nossek has oodles of all three.

TOP CLASSIC PENSIONEN

Stay in any of these to sample some traditional Viennese hospitality:

- Pension am Operneck (above)
- Pension Carantania (p199)
- Pension Kraml (p199)
- Pension Nossek (above)
- Pension Riedl (p193)

Service is professional, polite, a little stiff but typically Viennese; rooms are spotless, highly adequate, generally spacious and enhanced with baroque-style furnishings; views are either of the pedestrian street below or the quiet inner courtyard. Nossek is on the fourth floor, but fortunately there's a lift.

HOTEL WANDL Map pp254-5   Hotel €€

☎ 534 55-0; www.hotel-wandl.com; 01, Petersplatz 9; s/d from €60/110; Ⓜ U1, U3 Stephansplatz

A family-run hotel since 1854, Wandl attracts visitors to Vienna with its superb location and wide choice of accommodation options. Many of the rooms are arranged around pretty inner courtyards and range from quite plush affairs with ornamental carpets and fancy furniture (one features historical frescoes) to stripped-back digs (but still highly adequate) with shared facilities. Period furniture, antique pieces and helpful staff fill the reception, but note that tour groups do the same on a regular basis over the summer months.

PENSION PERTSCHY Map pp254-5   Pension €€

☎ 534 49-0; www.pertschy.com; 01, Habsburgergasse 5; s/d from €90/133; U1, U3 Stephansplatz; 🖥 🕭

It's hard to find fault with Pension Pertschy. It's quiet yet cental location, just off the Graben, is hard to beat, staff are exceedingly able, willing and friendly, and children are welcomed with gusto (toys for toddlers and high chairs for tots are available). Rooms are not only spacious but also filled with a potpourri of period pieces and a rainbow of colours; you'll find one bedecked in subtle hues of pink while its neighbour is awash in yellow. A little gem in the Innere Stadt.

AVIANO Map pp254-5   Pension €€

☎ 512 83 30; www.pertschy.com; 01, Marco-d'Aviano-Gasse 1; s/d €95/136; Ⓜ U1, U3 Stephansplatz

Like its sister pension Pertschy, Aviano earns its points for a supremely central position, high standards, and all-round value for money. Its standard rooms are small without being claustrophobic while its superior variety are exceedingly large, easily accommodating a sofa and accompanying chairs; corner rooms have a charming alcove overlooking Vienna's main pedestrian street. Furniture isn't particularly modern, but quite comfortable all the same. The

breakfast room is sunny and bright, and in summer utilises a small balcony on the inner courtyard.

HOTEL SACHER Map pp254-5   Hotel €€€

☎ 514 56-0; www.sacher.com; 01, Philharmonikerstrasse 4; s/d from €242/357; Ⓜ U1, U2, U4 Karlsplatz, 🚋 D, J, 1, 2, 62, 65; 🖥 🕭

Walking into the Sacher is like turning back the clocks 100 years. The reception, with its dark-wood panelling, deep red shades and heavy gold chandelier, is reminiscent of an expensive *fin-de-siècle* bordello. The smallest rooms are surprisingly large, with beds the size of small ships, while suites are truly palatial. All are fashioned with baroque furnishings and genuine 19th-century oil paintings (the hotel has the largest private oil painting collection in Austria); bathrooms are entirely modern and include bathtubs. The top floor is a high-tech spa complex, with herbal sauna, ice fountain and fitness room.

NORTH OF HOFBURG

STYLE HOTEL Map pp254-5   Hotel €€€

☎ 22 780-0; www.stylehotel.at; 01, Herrengasse 12; r from €250; Ⓜ U3 Herrengasse; 🖥 🕭

The name is naff, but there's no denying Style Hotel is a top contender for the title

Double room at Pension Pertschy (this page)

'most fashionable hotel address' in Vienna. The contemporary interior, with overtones of Art Nouveau/Art Deco, has been meticulously designed; even the empty spaces look perfectly planned. Rooms have also been carefully designed, but with comfort in mind – here you'll find dark woods, deep reds, smooth, clean lines, beds with six pillows, and complimentary Pringles. The basement contains the fitness room where an enormous safe door is the only reminder of the building's former tenants.

JEWISH QUARTER & AROUND

SCHWEIZER PENSION Map pp254-5 Pension €
☎ 533 81 56; www.schweizerpension.com; 01, Heinrichsgasse 2; s/d from €36/58; 🚇 1, 2
Rooms at this pleasant little *Pension* are super clean and, while not flushed with the most up-to-date amenities, everything you find inside – from big, comfy beds to ornamental ceramic stoves – has a cosy, homely feel to it. The feeling of wellbeing extends to the rest of the pension; Schweizer uses energy-saving light bulbs, equips rooms with wind-up clocks, and serves bio-breakfasts. As one of the cheapest options in the city centre, the 11 rooms fill up quickly, so book ahead.

TOP LUXURY HOTELS

Magnificently opulent, these hotels are institutions in a city filled with stand-out luxury options:

Grand Hotel (Map pp254–5; ☎ 515 80-8; www.grandhotelwien.com; 01, Kärntner Ring 9; s/d from €320/390) –Vienna's original luxury hotel

Hotel Bristol (Map pp254–5; www.westin.com/bristol; 01, Kärntner Ring 1; r from €405) – old-world extravagance and state-of-the-art amenities

Hotel Imperial (see opposite) – when royalty visit Vienna, this is where they stay

Hotel Sacher (see p195) – baroque gem with modern conveniences

Palais Coburg (Map pp254–5; ☎ 518 18-0; www.palais-coburg.com; ste from €810) – glorious hotel with banquet rooms to rival Schönbrunn

To read extensive reviews of Vienna's luxury hotels or to book accommodation go to www.lonelyplanet.com

HOTEL ORIENT Map pp254-5   Love Hotel €€
☎ 533 73 07; www.hotelorient.at in German; 01, Tiefer Graben 30; r per hr €57-85, overnight €160; 🚇 U1, U3 Stephansplatz
The Orient is a hotel that thrives on discreet, and not so discreet, *liaisons à deux*, and provides a playpen for the sexually adventurous. Rooms are rented by the hour (overnighting is only possible on Saturday and Sunday) – take your pick from, among others, the 'Oriental suite', the 'Roman suite' and the 'Kaiser suite'. Each has its own individual flair, character, cosy nooks and well-placed mirrors. Even if it's not your kind of thing, it's worth stopping by to gaze at the *fin-de-siècle* hallway and façade (scenes from *The Third Man* were shot here).

HOTEL AMADEUS Map pp254-5   Hotel €€
☎ 533 87 38; www.hotel-amadeus.at; 01, Wildpretmarkt 5; s/d €90/168; 🚇 U1, U2 Stephansplatz
With a pleasing interior of red and white and blood-red paisley carpeting (it looks better than it sounds) throughout, Amadeus is certainly easy on the eye. The foyer looks like a 19th-century living room, with chandeliers, period furniture and a handful of po-faced portraits, and while rooms don't quite match it for style, grace and space, they still do a good job of creating a comfortable atmosphere. Bathrooms are bright, white, spotless and fitted with modern trappings.

RINGSTRASSE

The Innere Stadt may have some beautiful hotels, but the Ringstrasse outguns it with the big boys in town – this is home to the Imperial, the Grand, the Bristol. Luxury is the mainstay here, where 'If you have to ask, you can't afford it' truly applies, but hidden amongst the grandeur are one or two options catering to most budgets.

PARLAMENT TO SCHWARZENBERGPLATZ

MERIDIEN Map pp254-5   Hotel €€€
☎ 588 900; www.lemeridien.com; 01, Opernring 13; s/d from €305/345; 🚇 U1, U2, U4 Karlsplatz; 🚋 D, J, 1, 2, 62, 65; 🖥 ♿
With its sleek rooms, cutting-edge interior, contemporary art themes and hi-tech

Lobby of Meridien (opposite page)

extras, Le Meridien has set the standard for designer hotels in Vienna. The lobby, a metrosexual's haven, is a vibrant space of contemporary art installations and plenty of comings and goings, while the basement showcases local artists on a regular basis. Rooms are the epitome of Le Meridien's ART+TECH motto, featuring designer furniture, Vienna-motif glass headboards, mammoth plasma TVs and freestanding power showers. Thankfully there are also personal touches, like real coffee, ironing equipment and copies of *Henry Moore's Sheep Sketchbook* (Why? Why not?). Service is young and fresh, but always professional and helpful.

HOTEL IMPERIAL Map pp254-5   Hotel €€€

☎ 501 10-333; www.luxurycollection.com/imperial; 01 Kärntner Ring 16; s/d from €469/563, royal ste from €2500; Ⓤ U2, U4 Karlsplatz, Ⓡ D, J, 1, 2, 62, 65; ▣ ♿

The Imperial – a name that makes most Viennese nod in awe and respect. This former palace, with all the glory and majesty of the Habsburg era, gives any respectable classical museum a run for its money. The Fürsten Stiege, cloaked in rich red carpet, is a flamboyant opening, leading from the reception to the Royal suite. Suites are filled with 19th century paintings and genuine antique furniture (and come with butler service), while 4th and 5th floor rooms in Biedermeier style are far cosier and may come with balcony. Oh, and the service is world class; the morning papers are even ironed.

SCHWARZENBERGPLATZ TO THE DANUBE CANAL
HOTEL AM SCHUBERTRING

Map pp254-5   Hotel €€

☎ 717 02-0; www.schubertring.at; 01, Schubertring 11; s/d from €99/128; Ⓤ U4 Stadtpark, Ⓡ 1, 2

Of the highly sought after hotels on the Ringstrasse, Am Schubertring is the only option available to the average-Joe. Rooms are either Biedermeier or Art Nouveau; the former are characterised by floral designs and graceful lines and may look disturbingly similar to your Granny's flat, while the latter are more dynamic, with flowing lines and little flourishes. All are in very good condition. Staff are friendly while keeping a healthy professional distance and the hotel spreads itself across the upper floors of two buildings.

Sleeping

RINGSTRASSE

RADISSON SAS PALAIS HOTEL

Map pp254-5 · · · · · · · · · · · · · · · Hotel €€€

☎ 515 17-0; www.radissonsas.com; 01, Parkring 16; r from €220; ⓡ 1, 2; ▣ ⓖ

A combination of two former *fin-de-siècle* palaces, Palais Leitenberger and Palais Henckel von Donnersmarck, the Radisson is a beautiful hotel on busy Ringstrasse. Rooms come in a variety of styles and colours – entire wings are decorated in vibrant floral patterns of green, red and yellow, while others are more reserved, with dark woods and light brown tones. All are clothed with understated furnishings and period pieces, and the best face the green of Stadtpark. The reception is lit by a high, glass skylight and perfect for a rejuvenating *Melange*.

INSIDE THE GÜRTEL

Depending on your perspective, staying inside the Gürtel (in the 3rd to 9th districts) is more preferable to overnighting in the Innere Stadt. It's less trampled by the tourist trail so advanced bookings are less of a problem, the big tourist attractions are still within easy striking distance, bars and restaurants abound, and the price could be more to your liking.

TOP DESIGN HOTELS

In a city noted for its architecture, it's no surprise that Vienna boasts a fine collection of design hotels, the pick of which are listed here:

Das Triest (right) –the hotel that planted the designer hotel seed in Vienna

Das Tyrol (opposite) – a lovely combination of art, comfort, and champagne

DO & CO (Map pp254–5; ☎ 241 88; www.doco .com; 01, Stephansplatz 12; r from €310) – the new kid on the block, with view of Stephansdom

Le Meridien (p196) – leading the way in interior design in the city

Style Hotel (p195) – Art Nouveau and Art Deco touches adorn this hotel that resides in a former bank

To read extensive reviews of Vienna's designer hotels or to book accommodation go to www .lonelyplanet.com

LANDSTRASSE

HOTEL HILTON Map pp254-5 · · · · · Hotel €€€

☎ 71 700-00; www.hilton.com; 03, Am Stadtpark 3; s/d €195/235; ⓔ U3, U4 Landstrasse/Wien Mitte; ▣ ⓖ

The Hilton Vienna is the city's, if not the country's, foremost business hotel, which recently enjoyed a €61 million makeover. Rooms (all 15 floors of them) employ a combination of light-browns and creams which go easy on the eye, and management go the extra mile to add personal touches to each and every one; bathrooms sport yellow rubber duckies and cotton buds (Q-Tips), while wooden clothes hangers and sewing kits hide behind wardrobe doors. Business facilities are top notch and an extensive fitness centre hides in the basement.

WIEDEN

DAS TRIEST Map pp262-3 · · · · · · · · Hotel €€€

☎ 589 18-0; www.dastriest.at; 04, Wiedner Hauptstrasse 12; s/d €200/258; ⓡ 62, 65; ▣ ⓖ

Designed by Sir Terence Conran, Das Triest is a symbiosis of history and modern design. The 300-year-old building once used as stables has been transformed into a cutting edge hotel, with an overall nautical theme; portholes replace spyholes and windows, and stairwell railings would be just at home on the Queen Mary 2. Rooms are stylish in their simplicity and bathed in pastel warmth, while little touches, such as fresh flowers, folded toilet rolls and more towels than you'll ever need, polish the scene off. Staff are highly professional while retaining an air of informality.

MARIAHILF

WESTEND CITY HOSTEL

Map pp260-1 · · · · · · · · · · · · · · · · Hostel €

☎ 597 67 29; www.westendhostel.at; 06, Fügergasse 3; s/d €47/56, 4-/6-/12-bed dm €17.50/19.50/21; ⓔ U3, U6 Westbahnhof; ▣

Westend, a no-party, no-fuss independent hostel, is suited to backpackers and adventurous families looking to pay the bare minimum for a bed. Dorm rooms are basic, with wooden bunks filling almost every available space and lacking colour, but each has an attached bathroom and lockers for every guest. Staff are knowledgeable and affable, and will arrange packed lunches on request.

PENSION KRAML Map pp260-1   Pension €

☎ 587 85 88; www.pensionkraml.at; 06, Brau-ergasse 5; s/d from €30/50, apt from €95; Ⓜ U4 Pilgramgasse, bus 13A, 57A

A cosy pension in a quiet neighbourhood, Kraml is family-run and from the 'Old-Skool' of hospitality, where politeness is paramount and the comfort of guests a top priority. Rooms are surprisingly large, accommodating twin beds, bed-side tables and a solid wardrobe, while leaving plenty of room for a close waltz. Furniture and fittings, including those in the bathroom, are a little dated but by no means past their used-by dates.

TYROL Map pp254-5   Hotel €€

☎ 587 54 15; www.das-tyrol.at; 06, Mariahilfer-strasse 15; s/d from €109/149; Ⓜ U2 Museums-quartier

Since its recent makeover, Das Tyrol ranks among the top design-hotels in the city. Each floor is devoted to a theme, but not always a serious one; the third floor is given over to Donald Duck and his love, Daisy. The cosy rooms are a subdued mix of greens and yellows and spacious enough to fit a small couch and desk, while bathrooms are a spotless combination of white-and-black tiling. Try for a corner room, which enjoy a small balcony overlooking busy Mariahilferstrasse. Breakfast – served with champagne – will keep you going for most of the day.

NEUBAU
JUGENDHERBERGE MYRTHENGASSE

Map pp260-1   Hostel €

☎ 523 63 16; hostel@chello.at; 07, Myrthengasse 7; dm €17, tw €50; bus 48A; ▢

This well-organised HI hostel on a quiet side street has all the trappings you'd expect. Its rooms are simple affairs, with bunk beds and en-suite bathrooms, but there's a secluded inner courtyard to escape to if need be. Self-service meals (Monday to Friday) are available and knowledgeable staff are happy to take telephone reservations.

PENSION CARANTANIA

Map pp260-1   Pension €

☎ 526 73 40; www.carantania.at; in German; 07, Kandlgasse 35; s/d €65/95; Ⓜ U6 Burggasse-Stadthalle

Carantania is a tiny, family-run pension of only six rooms with plenty of warmth

and cosy corners. Its sizable rooms are flooded with natural light and filled with a hotchpotch of furniture – some of which looks antique, some of which could do with repair – while bathrooms are the only modern corner of the pension. The reception area is pleasantly cluttered with plants, brochures and books, and the breakfast room is big enough for a banquet.

HOTEL FÜRSTENHOF Map pp260-1   Hotel €€

☎ 523 32 67; www.hotel-fuerstenhof.com; 07, Neubaugürtel 4; s/d from €69/110; Ⓜ U3, U6 Westbahnhof

This family-run affair overflowing with personality has been the choice of touring alternative bands (see the reception for proof) and knowledgeable visitors for years. Rooms don't come with a lot of extras but they're in excellent condition; blood-red carpets, full-length curtains and deep colours create a warm feel and furniture is simple yet highly functional. Bathrooms are big, bright, modern, and spotlessly clean. The house dates from 1906, so ceilings are higher than normal and the lift is a museum piece (the motor thankfully isn't).

ALTSTADT Map pp260-1   Pension €€

☎ 522 66 66; www.altstadt.at; 07, Kirchengasse 41; s/d from €109/129; bus 13A, 48A; ▢

Charming, tasteful, quirky, arty, welcoming – Altstadt is arguably the finest pension in Vienna. Each room is individually decorated, but they all have one thing in common; tasteful modern décor that's not overcooked, and the right consistency of art, practicality, comfort, and above all, warmth. Add to this brew high ceilings, plenty of space and natural light, and you have a room you'll find hard to vacate, even for the excellent breakfast. Staff are genuinely affable and the art work is from the owner's personal collection.

HOTEL AM SCHOTTENFELD

Map pp260-1   Hotel €€

☎ 526 51 81; www.falkensteiner.com; 07, Schottenfeldgasse 74; s/d €129/164; bus 48A; ▢ ♿

Am Schottenfeld is a business hotel in suburbia with a difference. Its interior sports a contemporary design and a clash of garish colours which may or may not appeal, depending on your tastes. Rooms

TOP CHEAP SLEEPS

- Jugendherberge Myrthengasse (p199) – quality HI hostel near the centre
- Schlossherberge am Wilhelminenberg (p202) – HI hostel with fabulous views of the city from the Wienerwald (Vienna Woods)
- Schweizer Pension (p196) – the best bargain in the Innere Stadt
- Westend City Hostel (p198) – simple and straight-forward hostel with plenty of amenities
- Wombat's (opposite) – Vienna's colourful party hostel, and a taste of Down Under

are another story altogether, with soft greys, greens and creams, and plenty of natural wood. The best rooms are saved for last; *Dach* (rooftop) suites come complete with sizable balconies and are awash with natural light. Service is sharp and snappy and there's a fitness room, sauna, steam room and solarium.

K+K MARIA THERESIA Map pp254-5 Hotel €€€
☎ 521 23; www.kkhotels.com; 07, Kirchberggasse 6; s/d €175/230; ⓜ U2, U3 Volkstheater; 🖥 ♿
The interior of this smart business hotel is clean and functional with touches of personality, like oriental carpets and a half-circle bar made for barflies. Rooms are filled to overflowing with modern furnishings, including a desk for working, and a smattering of individual affects, such as chocolates on pillows and flowers in vases, help liven up the scene. The big, bright and airy top-floor suites are the hotel's highlight.

JOSEFSTADT

PENSION WILD Map pp254-5   Pension €
☎ 406 51 74; www.pension-wild.com; 08, Lange Gasse 10; s/d from €37/45; 🚋 46
Wild is one of the very few openly gay-friendly pensions in Vienna, but the warm welcome extends to all walks of life. The top-floor Luxury rooms are simple yet appealing, with plenty of light-wood furniture and private bathrooms, the latter a big advantage over Wild's other two categories, Standard and Comfort. All however are spotlessly clean and kitchens are available for guests to use and abuse. Note that 'Wild' is the family name, not a description.

LEVANTE LAUDON Map pp258-9 Apartments €€
☎ 407 13 70; www.thelevante.com; 08, Laudongasse 8; apt per day/week from €130/840; 🚋 43, 44
Stay as long as a year or as little as a day at the Levante Laudon, an apartment building catering to short-term rentals. Apartments come in two varieties – Superior and Standard. Stylish touches, like freestanding sinks, make-up mirrors, space-age coat racks and flat-screen TVs make the Superior apartments truly inviting; Standards have less panache but are just as large. Personal touches, such as fresh flowers in rooms, daily housekeeping and a complimentary self-service continental breakfast, add to an already homely atmosphere. Service is professional, prompt and lacking any pomp.

THEATER-HOTEL Map pp258-9   Hotel €€
☎ 405 36 48; www.theaterhotelwien.at; 08, Josefstädter Strasse 22; s/d €184/196; 🚋 J
For lovers of theatre, this hotel will rank among the best in Vienna. Theatre memorabilia lines the hallways, stairwells and rooms, and Art Nouveau touches hark back to the days when the stage was all the rage. Rooms are filled with dark-wood furniture and Art Nouveau picture panels, both of which are offset by pale-cream shading. Most are on the small side but a handful come with the added bonus of a small kitchen. Theatre-Hotel also has many of the facilities its more modern counterparts offer, such as sauna, solarium, bar and café-restaurant.

HOTEL RATHAUS Map pp258-9   Hotel €€
☎ 400 11 22; www.hotel-rathaus-wien.at; 08, Lange Gasse 13; s/d €138/198; 🚋 46
Rathaus is a shrine to Austrian winemakers. Each of the 33 stylish rooms in this newly

revamped boutique hotel is dedicated to a quality Austrian winemaker and the mini-bar is stocked with premium wines from the growers themselves. The interiors are an elegant mix of dark woods, pale yellows and personal touches (cut flowers, designer vases and the like), creating a functional and appealing setup. The hotel offers wine tastings in its designer bar and excursions to Austria's nearby wine-growing regions.

OUTSIDE THE GÜRTEL

You won't be in the thick of things if you stay in these heavily residential outlying suburbs, but you will be amongst the Viennese, whether it is in the predominantly rich 13th and 19th districts, the working-class neighbourhoods of the 10th to 12th, or the Turkish and Balkan influenced 15th and 16th. You'll also have the advantage of close proximity to some of Vienna's larger natural attractions, the Wienerwald (Vienna Woods) and Lainzer Tiergarten, and easy escape by car to excursion destinations.

HIETZING
PARKHOTEL SCHÖNBRUNN

Map pp260-1   Hotel €€

☎ 878 04-0; www.austria-trend.at/paw; 13, Hietzinger Hauptstrasse 10-20; s/d from €127/172; Ⓤ U4 Hietzing

Franz Josef specifically built the Parkhotel as his guesthouse in 1907 (any self-respecting Emperor needs all 1441 rooms in the palace for himself), which explains the Schönbrunn-yellow façade and ubiquitous portraits of the penultimate emperor throughout the interior. Rooms are fairly standard and reasonably spacious and come with modern furniture, twin beds and plenty natural light; balconies are attached to those facing busy Hietzinger Haupt-strasse. The hotel's four suites, which take pole position on the building's corners, are a far more interesting option.

PENZING
SOPHIENALPE Map pp252-3   Hotel €

☎ 486 24 32; www.sophienalpe.at; 14, Sophien-alpe 13; s/d €41/67; bus 243, 443

This hunting lodge of sorts, with its wood trimmings and cheerful rows of flowering

pot plants, provides a taste of the Austrian countryside without having to wander too far from the capital. Rooms are one step up from basic but are more than adequate, with natural-wood furniture and large twin beds hidden under fluffy duvets and pillows; all are en suite. The restaurant, which alludes to hunting tales (both tall and short), specialises in 'wild' meats, best appreciated in the autumn months. A car is really needed to get around, and it's only open from May to November.

RUDOLFSHEIM-FÜNFHAUS
DO STEP INN Map pp260-1   Hostel €

☎ 982 33 14; www.dostepinn.at in German; 15, Felberstrasse 22/6; hostel s/d €32/39; hotel s/d €39/48; Ⓤ U3, U6 Westbahnhof

Handy to Westbahnhof and offering some of the cheapest rooms in town is Do Step Inn, a small, clean hostel/hotel. Rooms are gener-ally bright, colourful and simple, and the hotel variety come with a private bathroom. Kitchens are available for use, and staff are quite helpful. Ten percent is added to the price if you're only staying one night.

WOMBAT'S Map pp260-1   Hostel €

☎ 897 23 36; www.wombats.at; 15, Grangasse 6; dm €18, r €48; Ⓖ 52, 58, bus 12A; 🖳

Offering up a bit of Australian hostel vibe in the Capital of Culture, Wombat's is the choice for the savvy backpacker. The inte-rior is a rainbow of pastel colours which immediately liven up the reception, bar, corridors and rooms, and whoever the artist was took to cubism like Castro to communism. Rooms are clean, bright and breezy but don't offer much more than a comfy bed and place to stash your gear. The bar is a big bonus, with pool tables, music and chummy pals on bar stools. Bike rental is available and staff are experienced and relaxed.

ALTWIENERHOF Map pp260-1   Hotel €€

☎ 892 60 00; www.altwienerhof.at; 15, Herklotz-gasse 6; s/d €74/119; Ⓤ U6 Gumpendorfer Strasse, Ⓖ 6, 18

Altwienerhof is a pseudo-plush family-run hotel just outside the Gürtel. Room decor harks back to a bygone era when the Orient Express was all the rage; miniature chan-deliers, antique pieces, floral bed covers and couches, and lace tablecloths all do a fine job of adding a touch of old-fashioned romance. Breakfast is taken either in the conservatory or large inner courtyard, depending on the weather.

OTTAKRING
SCHLOSSHERBERGE AM
WILHELMINENBERG Map pp252-3   Hostel €

☎ 485 85 03700; shb@verkehrsbuero.at; 16, Savoyenstrasse 2; dm from €20.50, s/d from €43/62; bus 46B, 146B; 🖳

This HI hostel in the grounds of Schloss Wilhelminenberg may be a long way from the city centre, but the glorious views of the city and easy access to the Wienerwald make up for it. Like most of Vienna's hostels, the rooms are modern with a minimum of extravagance, and include solid wooden bunk beds, attached bathrooms, individual lockers, and enough colour to take away the blandness. It's also a perfect spot for families, with a minigolf course, table tennis, a PlayStation and large meadows.

HOTEL SCHLOSS
WILHELMINENBERG Map pp252-3   Hotel €€

☎ 485 85 03-0; www.austria-trend.at/wiw; 16, Savoyenstrasse 2; r from €120/150; bus 46B, 146B

Schloss Wilhelminenberg is a fully-fledged palace with unbridled views of the entire city and a resortlike ambience. The reception and café are suitably palatial (featuring high ceilings, detailed wall- and ceiling-inlays, chandeliers) and while rooms are in contemporary style they complement rather than detract from the building's neo-imperial architecture. The standard rooms on the top floor are small but have excellent views, and the more expensive maisonette variety are unusually narrow but they do have exceptionally high ceilings and loft beds.

DÖBLING
LANDHAUS "FUHRGASSL-HUBER"
Map pp252-3   Pension €€

☎ 440 30 33; www.fuhrgassl-huber.at; 19, Rathstrasse 24; s/d from €77/115; bus 35A

The thick, whitewashed walls, rows of flowering pot plants and creeping vines of Fuhrgassl-Huber look more suited to the valleys of Tyrol. Inside it's no different; panelled-wood ceilings are ever-present, folk art adorns the walls, ornamental carpets warm tiled floors, and staff don traditional garb. Flowery designs are the norm in the pension's cosy rooms, and the huge buffet breakfast (taken in the pension's secluded garden on warm mornings) will please the most uptight gourmet. At night, a world of *Heurigen* (wine taverns) is only a step away.

Excursions

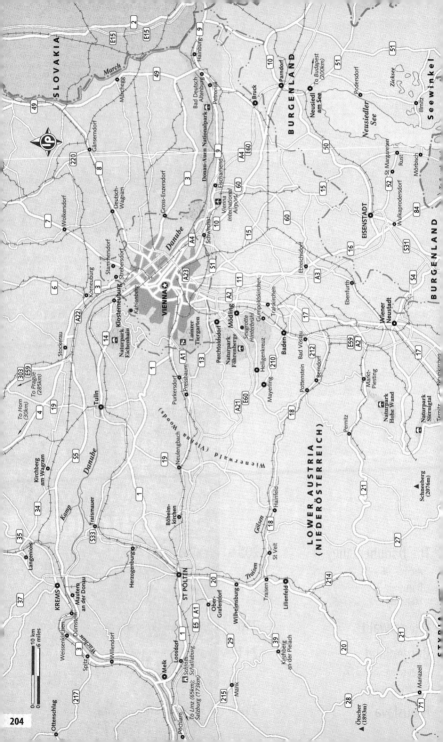

Excursions

Vienna is blessed with a bountiful array of day-trip destinations and activities. Nature lovers will enjoy the Wienerwald (Vienna Woods; p210) to the west of the city, which offers a wealth of hiking and cycling opportunities, and to the east the Neusiedler See (p211), a shallow steppe lake with boating and bird watching.

The Danube Valley, (below), to the northwest of Vienna, is dotted with historical towns, such as Krems, Dürnstein and Melk, and lorded over by crumbling castles; a river cruise down the Danube provides a snapshot of it all. It's also a major centre for wine; its hills are covered in vineyards, from which some of the country's best wines are produced. Wine again features heavily in Burgenland, particularly at the lakeside town of Rust (p211).

The Czech Republic, Slovakia, and Hungary are all within a two-hours' drive from Vienna. Bratislava (p214), Slovakia's capital, is a bustling Eastern European city with a long history, while Sopron (p214), across the border in Hungary, still retains its medieval heart.

THE DANUBE VALLEY

The Danube Valley, or the *Wachau* as its known locally, is arguably the prettiest stretch along the entire course of the Danube and a Unesco World Heritage Site. Here the dustless highway is bent and twisted between high hills whose slopes are layered with vineyards, and whose peaks are topped with castles.

Highlights are numerous, but rivalling the architecture of Krems, Dürnstein and Melk is the region's wining and dining. Some of the country's finest wines originate along the banks of the Danube, and the seasonal fare, using the freshest ingredients from the valley, attracts gourmands from across Austria.

TRANSPORT – THE DANUBE VALLEY

Distance from Vienna to Krems 64km; to Dürnstein 73km; to Melk 83km
Direction West
Bicycle A bicycle path runs along both sides of the Danube from Vienna to Melk, passing through Krems, Dürnstein, Weissenkirchen and Spitz (these are all on the northern bank). Many hotels and *Pensionen* (guesthouses) are geared towards cyclists, and most towns will have at least one bike-rental shop. For more information, pick up a copy of *Donauradweg – Von Passau bis Bratislava*, which provides details of distances, hotels and information offices along the route. Copies are available in tourist offices in the Wachau (and also Tulln); the text is in German only. Bicycles can also be taken on trains to and from Vienna.
Boat From mid-May to mid-September DDSG Blue Danube (p219) runs a Sunday service (8.35am from Vienna, 4.40pm from Dürnstein; one-way/return €19.50/26, 5¾ hours) between Vienna and Dürnstein, stopping at Krems (1.55pm, returning 5pm).

A number of boat companies, including DDSG Blue Danube, operate boats from Krems to Melk, stopping in at Dürnstein and Spitz, from April to October. Boats leave Krems at 10.15am all season, and from late April to September two extra sailings cater to the added demand, departing at 1pm and 3.45pm. Return sailings are at 1.50pm the whole season, and 11am and 4.25pm from late April to September (one-way/return €16.50/22, three hours).

Bikes can be taken on board all sailings free of charge.
Car For Krems and Dürnstein take the A22 north out of Vienna towards Stockerau, then the S5 west to Krems. From Krems, the Bundesbahn 3 continues west and passes through Dürnstein, Weissenkirchen and Spitz. Melk is best reached by the A1 autobahn which connects Vienna with Salzburg; access the A1 from Penzing.
Train Over 20 direct trains every day travel between Franz-Josefs-Bahnhof and Krems (one hour). Only one train daily (7.35am) connects Dürnstein (the station is called Dürnstein-Oberloiben) with Franz-Josefs-Bahnhof; normally a change at Krems is required (13 daily, 1¼ hours).

At least 14 direct trains from Vienna's Westbahnhof (1¼ hours) travel to Melk daily. It's also possible to take a train to St Pölten, and change there.

A leisurely way to see the Danube Valley is by boat (p205). Cruising down the Danube with a glass of Riesling in one hand and a camera in the other can be the highlight of a trip to Vienna. From the capital it is easily organised; DDSG Blue Danube (p219) and the Österreiche Bundesbahn (ÖBB; Austrian Federal Railway; p222) offer a combined train–boat–train ticket (adult/child €39.80/20.70) for one-way train connections to Krems and Melk, and the boat trip in between the two. Tickets can be purchased at any train station or from the DDSG Blue Danube office. Sporty types may opt to tour the valley by bike (see p205).

Tourismusregion Wachau-Nibelungengau (☎ 02713-300 60 60; www.wachau.at; Schlossgasse 3, Spitz an der Donau; ☯ 9am-6pm Mon-Fri, 10am-noon & 1-7pm Sat) is the central tourist office and stocks brochures covering the entire region.

KREMS

Krems is one of the larger towns in the Wachau region and has a historical core dating back over 1000 years. It's on the northern bank of the Danube, surrounded by terraced vineyards, and has been a centre of the wine trade for most of its history.

The town is comprised of three parts: Krems to the east, the smaller settlement of Stein 2km to the west, and the connecting suburb of Und – an unusual name that inspires the joke: 'Krems and (und in German) Stein are three towns'. Together, they create an attractive setting with a peaceful air; add to this a huge selection of wines from the region and the result is a town well worth spending some hours exploring. The **Krems Tourismus** in Kloster Und supplies visitors with a map pinpointing all the architectural and cultural attractions around town, but it's just as rewarding to simply wander the cobbled streets, quiet courtyards and ancient city.

Krems has several churches and museums worth diving into. The **Pfarrkirche St Veit** on the hill at Pfarrplatz is baroque in style, with frescoes by Martin Johann Schmidt, an 18th-century local artist who used the pseudonym Kremser Schmidt. **Piaristenkirche**, up behind St Veit's on Frauenbergplatz, has Gothic vaulting, huge windows and baroque altars. The

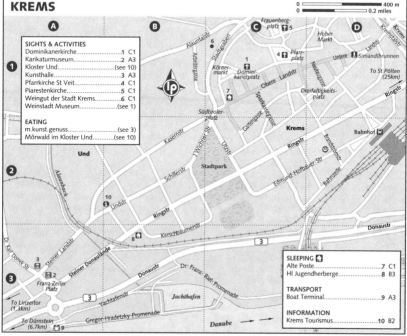

Weinstadt Museum, housed in a former Dominican monastery, contains collections of religious and modern art, (including works by Schmidt) and wine-making artefacts. East of the main centre is the **Karikaturmuseum** (Caricature Museum); it holds the largest collection of cartoons by Manfred Deix, a legendary Austrian cartoonist with an eye for the absurd and a knack for sharp social commentary. The town's arts centre, the **Kunsthalle**, is also located here.

Much of Krems' economic strength comes from its wine culture, and many shops offer wine tastings; both **Kloster Und** and **Weingut der Stadt Krems** have wines to sample and buy.

Sights & Information

Krems Tourismus (☎ 02732-826 76; www.tiscover.com /krems; Undstrasse 6; ☺ 9am-6pm Mon-Fri, 11am-5pm Sat, 11am-4pm Sun May-Oct, 8.30am-5pm Mon-Fri Nov-Apr)

Weinstadt Museum (☎ 02732-801 567; Körnermarkt 14; adult/child €4/3; ☺ 9am-6pm Tue, 1-6pm Wed-Sun Mar-Nov)

Karikaturmuseum (☎ 02732-908 020; www.karikatur museum.at in German; Steiner Landstrasse 3a; adult/concession/child €8/7/3.50; ☺ 10am-6pm)

Kloster Und (☎ 02732-701 90-0; www.klosterund.at; Undstrasse 6; ☺ 1-7pm Wed-Sun)

Kunsthalle (☎ 02732-908 010; www.kunsthalle.at; Steiner Landstrasse 3; adult/concession/child €8/7/3.50; ☺ 10am-6pm)

Weingut der Stadt Krems (☎ 02732-801 441; www.wein gutstadtkrems.at; Stadtgraben 11; ☺ 9am-noon & 1-5pm Mon-Fri, 9am-1pm Sat)

Statue and fresco at Piaristenkirche, Krems (opposite page)

Eating

Mörwald im Kloster Und (see box below)

m.kunst.genuss (☎ 02732-908 010-21; Steiner Landstrasse 3; lunch buffet €7, mains €5-10; ☺ 10am-6pm) Another from the Mörwald family (below), with simple lunch buffet produced with the freshest ingredients and accompanied by selective regional wines. Housed in the Kunsthalle.

Sleeping

HI Jugendherberge (☎ 02732-834 52; oejhv.noe.krems @aon.at; Ringstrasse 77; dm €15; ☺ Apr-Oct) Excellent hostel with facilities for cyclists and clean, basic dorm rooms.

Alte Poste (☎ 02732-822 76; www.altepost-krems.at in German; Obere Landstrasse 32; s/d €42/70) Guesthouse located in a historic 500-year-old house with an enchanting courtyard and cosy rooms.

DETOUR: GOURMET DANUBE

The Danube Valley is well known for its culinary delights and viticulture, both of which heavily follow the seasons. A day spent sampling both can be a very rewarding experience, but for the best quality it pays to be a little picky.

Mörwald im Kloster Und ☎ 02732-704 93; Undstrasse 6; mains €20-30; ☺ noon-2pm, 6-10pm Tue-Sun) in Krems combines a stylish interior with an impressive selection of wine. Its European cuisine is outstanding, and its head chef, Leonard Cernko, was voted 2006 Cook of the Year by Gault Millau. Across the Danube in Mautern, **Landhaus Bacher** (☎ 02732-829 37; Südtiroler Platz 2; mains €20-30; ☺ 11.30am-2pm & 6.30-9.30pm Wed-Sun) has won numerous awards (including two Michelin stars) for its creative take on staple Austrian dishes, and its summer garden, complete with walnut trees, is a joy in summer.

Weissenkirchen features two top eateries. Family-run **Weingut Jamek** (☎ 02715-2235; Joching 45, Weissenkirchen; mains €12-23; ☺ 11.30am-4pm Mon-Thu, 11.30am-11pm Fri) is an old fashioned establishment with a relaxed air, shady garden, and vineyard; its Riesling is one of the more highly rated in the region. Not far from Jamek, **Holzapfels Prandtauerhof** (☎ 02715-2310; Joching 36, Weissenkirchen; mains €15-25; ☺ 11.30am-10.30pm Wed-Sat, 3-10.30pm Sun) occupies a baroque villa and serves classic Austrian food with a modern twist; its sheltered inner courtyard is often full in summer.

East of Dürnstein, **Brustbauer** and **Loibnerhof** (p209) are further examples of quality dining in the Danube Valley.

Excursions

THE DANUBE RIVER

DÜRNSTEIN

Dürnstein achieved 12th-century notoriety for its imprisonment of King Richard the Lionheart of England. Today, this compact, picturesque village is one of the prime destinations in the Wachau region.

High on the hill, commanding a marvellous view of the curve of the Danube, stand the ruins of **Kuenringerburg**, where Richard was incarcerated from 1192 to 1193. His crime was insulting Leopold V; his misfortune was being recognised despite his disguise when journeying through Austria on his way home from the crusades. His liberty was achieved only upon the payment of a huge ransom which funded the building of Wiener Neustadt. The hike up from the village takes 15 to 20 minutes.

In the village, Hauptstrasse is a cobbled street with some picturesque 16th-century houses, wrought-iron signs and floral displays. The dominating feature of Dürnstein however is the blue spire of the **Chorherrenstift** (Abbey church). Inside, its baroque interior effectively combines white stucco and dark wood, and its balcony enjoys a grand view of the Danube.

Travelling west from Dürnstein along the banks of the Danube, the steep hills are densely covered with vineyards. Riesling and Veltliner, two of Austria's top wines, are grown in these parts, and served in traditional *Heurigen* (wine taverns). Six kilometres on from Dürnstein is **Weissenkirchen**, a peaceful town that hasn't changed much in the last 100 years. Its centrepiece is a fortified **parish church** rising from a hill, with a labyrinth of covered pathways leading to its front doors. This Gothic church was built in the 15th century and has an impressive baroque altar. Directly below the church is the tiny **Wachau Museum**, which showcases artists of the Danube School. A further 5km west is **Spitz**, a village surrounded by vineyards and lined with quiet, cobblestoned streets. Its **parish church** is noteworthy for its unusual chancel, which is out of line with the main body of the church. Also note the 15th-century statues of the 12 apostles lining the organ loft. Continuing on another 5km towards Melk and **Willendorf** soon appears, where the 25,000-year-old sandstone statue of Venus was discovered.

Ruins of Kuenringerburg overlooking Dürnstein and the Danube River (this page)

Sights & Information

Chorherrenstift (☎ 02711-375; Stiftshof; adult/child €2.40/1.50; ☻ 9am-6pm Apr-Oct)

Dürnstein Information Office (☎ 02711-200; Dürnstein Bahnhof; ☻ 11am-6pm Mon-Sat mid-May–Sep, 1-6pm Mon-Sat mid-Apr–mid-May & 1st half Oct) Located east of town near the train station.

Wachau Museum (☎ 02715-2268; Weissenkirchen 32; adult/child €4/1.10; ☻ 10am-5pm Tue-Sun Apr-Oct)

Weissenkirchen Parish Church (☎ 02715-2203; Weissenkirchen 3; admission free; ☻ 8am-7pm Easter-Oct, 8am-5pm Sat & Sun Nov-Easter)

Eating

Brustbauer (☎ 02732-873 00; Oberloiben 2; mains €8-15; ☻ 11am-10pm Apr-Oct) Gorgeous garden laden with tables and fruit trees, and with views of the Danube; simple homemade Austrian fare and fine wines.

Loibnerhof (☎ 02732-828 90; Unterloiben 7; mains €11-23; ☻ 11.30am-9pm Wed-Sun) Large restaurant in a 400-year-old house, and an attractive garden, 1km east of Dürnstein in Unterloiben. The *Butterschnitzel* (a schnitzel of veal or pork, lightly buttered and then fried) is a speciality.

Sleeping

Pension Böhmer (☎ 02711-239; pension.boehmer@ onemail.at; Hauptstrasse 22; s/d €30/40) Family-run *Pension* with good rooms and a well-stocked wine shop.

Gasthof Sänger Blondel (☎ 02711-253; www .saengerblondel.at; Klosterplatz; s/d €63/92) Right in the heart of Dürnstein; old fashioned rooms and decent restaurant with garden.

MELK

Lying in the lee of its imposing monastery-fortress, Melk is arguably the most essential excursion destination from Vienna.

The **Stift Melk**, perched on a hill, dominates the town and provides an excellent view of the surrounding area. It was once the residence of the Babenberg family, but the Benedictine monks transformed it into a monastery in 1089 and it has stayed that way ever since. Receiving a major overhaul in the 18th century, it's an example of baroque gone mad, with endless prancing angels and gold twirls, but is very impressive nonetheless. The absolute highlights are the library and the mirror room, both of which have an extra tier painted on the ceiling (by Paul Troger) to give the illusion of greater height. The ceilings are also slightly curved to aid the effect. Imperial rooms, where various dignitaries (including Napoleon) stayed, contain museum exhibits. Guided tours (often in English, but phone ahead to be sure) of this Benedictine abbey explain its historical importance and are well worth the extra money.

The countryside surrounding Melk is home to some fine palaces. **Schloss Schallaburg**, 5km south of Melk, is a 16th-century Renaissance palace with magnificent terracotta arches and prestigious temporary exhibitions. There's also a permanent exhibition of toys through history and a reduced combination ticket with Stift Melk monastery is available. Just under 5km northeast is **Schloss Schönbühel**, on the southern bank of the Danube, along with a 17th-century Servite monastery (the Servites were a mendicant order of friars), and the ruins of the 12th-century **Burg Aggstein**.

Sights & Information

Burg Aggstein (admission €2; ☻ dawn-dusk)

Melk Tourist Office (☎ 02752-523 07-410; www.tiscover .com/melk in German; Babenbergerstrasse 1; ☻ 9am-7pm Mon-Sat, 10am-noon & 5-7pm Sun Jul & Aug, 9am-noon & 2-6pm Mon-Fri, 10am-noon & 4-6pm Sat & Sun May, Jun & Sep, 9am-noon & 2-6pm Mon-Fri, 10am-noon Sat Apr & Oct)

Schloss Schallaburg (☎ 02754-6317; www.schallaburg.at; Anzendorf; adult/concession/child €8/7/3.50, combined ticket with Stift Melk €13.60; ☻ 9am-5pm Mon-Fri, until 6pm Sat)

Schloss Schönbühel (admission free; ☻ dawn-dusk)

Stift Melk (☎ 02752-555 232; www.stiftmelk.at; adult/ child €7/4.10, with guided tour €8.80/5; ☻ 9am-6pm May-Sep, 9am-5pm Apr & Oct, guided tours only Nov-Mar)

Reservations for tours in English are advisable (call ahead). The last admission is one hour before closing.

Eating

Tom's Restaurant (☎ 02752-524 75; Hauptplatz 1; menus from €25; ☻ noon-3pm & 6.30-10pm Thu-Tue) Three- to nine-course set menus showcasing food from the region; overlooks the town's main square.

Sleeping

Stadt Melk (☎ 02752-525 47; www.hotelstadtmelk.com, in German; Hauptplatz 1; s/d from €55/85) Friendly, small and pink *Pension*/hotel above Tom's Restaurant.

Zur Post (☎ 02752-523 45; info@hotelpost-melk.at; Linzer Strasse 1; s/d from €55/88) Family-run four-star hotel with very comfy rooms and bicycles for hire for €10 per day.

DETOUR: WEINVIERTEL & WALDVIERTEL

The Weinviertel (wine quarter), a flat expanse bordering the Czech and Slovak republics to the north and northeast of Vienna, is an agricultural area known for its wines. The Waldviertel (woods quarter), running north from the Danube Valley to the Czech border, is a region of rolling hills and rural villages. Sights are few, but combined they make an excellent escape the madding crowds in Vienna.

Benedictine **Stift Altenburg** (☎ 02982-3451; www.stift-altenburg.at in German; Stift 1; adult/senior/student/family €7/6/3/14, guided tours extra €1.50; ✆ 10am-5pm Apr-Oct, to 6pm mid-June–Aug; tours 11am, 2pm & 3pm Sat & Sun Apr-Oct) was founded in 1144 but much of the extensive baroque architecture seen today dates from 1650. Close to Altenburg, the Renaissance **Schloss Rosenburg** (☎ 02982-2911; www.rosenburg.at, in German; Rosenburg am Kamp; tours adult/senior/child/family €10/8.50/5/24, extra €2 for falconry & pageantry; ✆ 9am-5pm May-Sep (till 6pm weekends), 9.30am-4.30pm Apr & Oct) has splendid falconry shows at 11am and 3pm. About 18km east of Rosenburg, the **Österreiche Motorradmuseum** (Motorbike museum; ☎ 02984-2151; www.motorradmuseum.at in German; Museumgasse 6, Eggenburg; adult/concession/child €5/4/2; ✆ 8am-4pm Mon-Fri, 10am-5pm weekends mid-Jan-mid-Dec) showcases over 300 immaculately restored bikes, including the Böhmerland 600, the longest bike in the world.

Waldviertel Tourismus (☎ 02822-541 09; www.waldviertel.or.at in German; Sparkassenplatz 4), 50km northwest of Krems in the town of Zwettl, has plenty of information on the region, while it's Weinviertel counterpart, **Weinviertel Tourismus** (☎ 02552-3515; www.weinviertel.at in German & Czech; Kolpingstrasse 7), resides in Poysdorf, 60km due north of Vienna. The best way to explore the regions is under your own steam as many places can only be reached by irregular bus services. Towns served by train include Horn (six trains daily; 1¼ hours) and Rosenburg (six trains daily; 1hour) from Krems and Eggenburg (15 daily trains; 1¼ hours) from Vienna. Very irregular buses run to Altenburg (7 minutes) from Horn.

WIENERWALD

The Wienerwald, a 1250 sq km forest to the west and southwest of Vienna, attracts Viennese eager to enjoy its peaceful woodlands. Hiking and biking possibilities abound, and in keeping with the Austrian need for order, paths are well marked and start at the city border. Attractive settlements, such as the wine-growing centres of Perchtoldsdorf, Mödling and Gumpoldskirchen, speckle the area. **Mayerling** would be left off tours to the Wienerwald if it were not for its bloody history. In 1889, Archduke Rudolf, 30-year-old son of Emperor Franz Josef and heir to the throne, died in a mysterious double suicide with his mistress, 17-year-old Baroness Marie Vetsera. The hunting lodge in which the suicide took place was turned into a convent; it still operates today but there's not much to see.

About 6km northeast of Mayerling is **Heiligenkreuz**, the site of a 12th-century **Cistercian Abbey.** The abbey is the final resting place of most of the Babenberg dynasty who ruled Austria until 1246. The church and cloister are a combination of Romanesque and Gothic styles and the abbey museum contains models by Giovanni Giuliani, who also created the trinity column in the courtyard.

Between Mödling and Heiligenkreuz is the **Seegrotte Hinterbrühl**, Europe's largest underground lake. The site was used by the Nazis in WWII to build aircraft.

For more on mountain biking in the Wienerwald, and a suggested walk, see p112.

Sights & Information

Cistercian Abbey (☎ 02258-870 3-0; www.stift-heiligen kreuz.at in German; Heiligenkreuz 1; tours adult/child €6.20/3; tours 10am, 11am, 2pm, 3pm & 4pm Mon-Sat, 11am, 2pm, 3pm & 4pm Sun)

Seegrotte Hinterbrühl (☎ 02236-263 64; www.see grotte.at; Grutschgasse 2; tours adult/child €7/4.50; ✆ 9am-5pm Apr-Oct, 9am-noon & 1-3pm Mon-Fri, 9am-3.30pm Sun Nov-Mar)

Wienerwald Tourismus (☎ 02231-621 76; www.wienerwa ld.info; Hauptplatz 11, Purkersdorf; ✆ 9am-5pm Mon-Fri)

TRANSPORT – WIENERWALD

Distance from Vienna to Heiligenkreuz 27km

Direction Southwest

Bus The Baden-Alland Bundesbus, which runs from Mödling (reached from Südbahnhof) to Alland eight times daily, stops at Heiligenkreuz (27 minutes) and Hinterbrühl (17 minutes).

Car It's best to explore this region by car. Take the A2 south out of Vienna and exit onto the A21 at the Vösendorf junction; the A21 leads directly to Hinterbrühl and Heiligenkreuz (Mayerling is a short drive southwest of Heiligenkreuz).

BURGENLAND

NEUSIEDLER SEE

This, the only steppe lake in Central Europe, is not only a popular summer holiday getaway for many Viennese and a top wine-growing region, but it's also a favourite breeding ground for nearly 300 species of birds.

Neusiedler See is a shallow lake (1.8m at its deepest) that has no natural outlet, giving the water a slightly saline quality. It's ringed by a wetland area of reed beds, particularly thick on the western bank, which provides an ideal breeding ground for birds. Bird-watchers flock to the area to catch a glimpse of the multitude of species; the national park **Seewinkel**, on the east shore, is a grassland interspersed with a myriad of smaller lakes and a popular spot for birds and bird-voyeurs.

Water sports are very popular activities here, with boats and windsurfers for hire at various resorts around the lake. The area's main town is **Neusiedl am See**, at the lake's northern end, but **Podersdorf**, 12km southeast of Neusiedl, is the largest centre for water sports on the lake. Cycling is another popular outdoor activity in these parts; a cycle track winds all the way around the reed beds, making it possible to complete a circuit of the lake, but remember to take your passport as the southern section is in Hungary. Pick up a copy of *Radtouren,* a handy map of the lake with cycle paths and distances marked, from any tourist office on the lake.

Much of the western side of Neusiedler is given over to vineyards. **Rust**, 30km southwest of Neusiedl, has some 60 wine growers nearby. The town's prosperity has been based on wine for centuries; in 1524 the emperor granted local vintners the exclusive right to display the letter 'R' on their wine barrels, and corks today bear the same insignia. From the end of March to late August storks descend on Rust to rear their young. If you stroll around town during this time, you'll see twig-nests perched precariously on chimney tops and, if you're quiet, hear the clicking of expectant beaks. A good vantage point is attained from the tower of the **Katholische Kirche** on Rathausplatz. The **Fischerkirche** at the opposite end of Rathausplatz is the oldest church in Rust (12th to 16th centuries) and contains some faded, yet beautiful, frescoes.

Entrance to a wine tavern in Rust (this page)

Excursions

BURGENLAND

Sights & Information

Fischerkirche (Rathausplatz, Rust; adult/child €1/0.50; ☺ 10am-noon, 2.30-5pm Mon-Sat, 11am-noon, 2-5pm Sun May-Sep, 11am-noon, 2-3pm Mon-Sat, 11am-noon, 2-4pm Sun Apr & Oct)

Katholische Kirche (Haydngasse, Rust; admission €1; ☺ summer only)

Nationalpark Neusiedler See-Seewinkel (☎ 02175-344 20; www.nationalpark-neusiedlersee.org in German; Illmitz; ☺ 8am-5pm Mon-Fri, 10am-5pm Sat & Sun, Apr-Oct, 8am-4pm Mon-Fri Nov-Mar)

Neusiedler See Tourismus (☎ 02167-86 00; www .neusiedlersee.com; Obere Hauptstrasse 24; ☺ 8am-5pm Mon-Fri, 9am-5pm Sat, 9am-noon Sun Jul-Aug, 8am-4pm Mon-Sat, 9am-noon Sun Apr-Jun & Sep-Oct)

Rust Tourismus (☎ 02685-502; www.rust.at in German; Conradplatz 1, Rathaus; ☺ 9am-noon & 1-6pm Mon-Fri, 9am-noon & 1-4pm Sat, 9am-noon Sun Jul & Aug, 9am-noon & 1-5pm Mon-Fri, 9am-noon & 1-4pm Sat May, Jun & Sep, 9am-noon & 1-4pm Mon-Fri Mar, 9am-noon & 1-4pm Mon-Sat Apr & Oct, 9am-noon & 1-4pm Mon-Thu, 9am-noon Fri Nov-Feb)

Eating

Zur Dankbarkeit (☎ 02177-22 23; Hauptstrasse 39, Podersdorf; mains €8-21; ☺ 11.30am-2pm & 5.30-9pm Fri, 11.30am-9pm Sat & Sun) Lovely old guesthouse with regional cooking.

Inamera (☎ 02685-64 73; Oggauer Strasse 29, Rust; mains €12-25; ☺ 6-10pm Wed & Thu, 11.30am-2.30pm & 6-10pm Fri & Sat, 11.30am-10pm Sun) Upmarket restaurant with fantastic tree-shaded garden and contemporary cuisine.

Sleeping

Alexander (☎ 02685-301; www.pension-alex ander.at, in German; Dorfmeistergasse 21; s/d from €41/60; P) Four-star establishment with garden and sauna.

Seewirt (☎ 02177-2415; www.seewirtkarner.at; Strandplatz 1, Podersdorf; s/d from €41/82; P) Luxury establishment for the price; next to the ferry terminal on the lake, with well-appointed rooms.

TRANSPORT – NEUSIEDLER SEE

Distance from Vienna to Neusiedl am See 50km

Direction Southeast

Bus Buses run approximately hourly to and from Eisenstadt (30min) for Rust, and then on to Mörbisch (an extra 10min).

Car For Neusiedl and Podersdorf, take the A4 southeast out of Vienna till the Neusiedl am See exit; signposts direct you from there. For Rust and Mörbisch, head south out of Vienna on the A2 and exit onto the A3 at the Guntramsdorf junction. When the A3 ends, follow the signs to Eisenstadt (east), exit the road at Eisenstadt Süd and continue east, passing through Trausdorf and St Margareten before arriving in Rust.

Ferries During the summer months ferries link Rust with Podersdorf, Podersdorf with Breitenbrunn, and Mörbisch with Illmitz.

Train Neusiedl is the only town on the lake reachable by train. Nine direct trains (40min) leave from Südbahnhof daily.

EISENSTADT

Tourism in Eisenstadt is primarily centred on one factor – the town's association with Josef Haydn.

Haydn revealed that Eisenstadt was 'where I wish to live and to die'. He achieved the former, being a resident for 31 years, but it was in Vienna that he finally tinkled his last tune. He also rather carelessly omitted any directive about his preferred residency after death. His skull was stolen from a temporary grave shortly after he died in 1809, and later became a museum exhibit in Vienna. The headless cadaver was subsequently returned to Eisenstadt (in 1932), but it wasn't until 1954 that the skull joined it.

Haydn's white marble tomb can now be seen in the **Bergkirche**. The church itself is remarkable for the Kalvarienberg, a unique Calvary display; access is via a separate entrance to the rear of the church. Life-sized figures depict the Stations of the Cross in a series of suitably austere, dungeon-like rooms.

You can't miss the baroque, 14th-century **Schloss Esterházy**, which dominates the town. Today, the palace is still owned by the powerful – and rich – Hungarian family Esterházy.

Without a doubt the highlight here is the frescoed **Haydn Hall**, which has the second-best acoustics of any concert hall in Austria (after Vienna's Musikverein). The **International Haydn Festival** (☎ 02682-618 66; www.haydnfestival.at) is an annual event staged here around the middle of September.

Not far from the palace, Haydn's former residence has been turned into a museum, the **Haydn-Haus**. It contains a few of his personal belongings but really only caters to Haydn fans. Behind the palace is a large, relaxing park, the **Schlosspark**, the setting for the **Fest der 1000 Weine** (Festival of 1000 Wines; ☎ 0664-540 40 68; www.burgenlaendische-weinwoche .at in German) in late August.

Sights & Information

Bergkirche (☎ 02682-626 38; www.haydnkirche.at in German; Joseph Haydn Platz 1; adult/child €2.50/2; ⊗ 9am-noon & 1-5pm mid-Apr–Oct)

Burgenland Tourismus (☎ 02682-633 84-29; www.burgen land.info; Schloss Esterházy; ⊗ 9am-5pm Apr-Oct, 9am-2pm Mon-Fri Nov-Feb, 9am-5pm Mon-Fri Mar) Covers the Burgenland province, and has information on the Neusiedler See.

Eisenstadt Tourismus (☎ 02682-673 90; www .eisenstadt-tourism.at; Schloss Esterházy; ⊗ 9am-5pm Apr-Oct, 9am-2pm Mon-Fri Nov-Feb, 9am-5pm Mon-Fri Mar) Offers maps and tours of the town.

Haydn-Haus (☎ 02682-719 3900; www.haydnhaus.at; Joseph Haydn-Gasse 19-21; adult/child €4/3; ⊗ 10am-6pm Apr-Oct, 10am-5pm Mon-Fri Nov-Mar)

Schloss Esterházy (☎ 02682-719 3000; www .schloss-esterhazy.at; Schloss Esterházy; adult/child €7.50/7; tours by appointment) The tour visits 25 rooms, including the Haydn Hall and palace chapel.

Eating

im esterházy (☎ 02682-628 19; Esterházyplatz; mains €7-16; ⊗ 11.30am-11pm) Opposite the Schloss Esterházy; arched ceilings, natural light, fine service and the likes of pasta with *gambas* (shrimps) and organic beef steak with summer vegetables.

Bodega La Ina (☎ 02682-623 05; Hauptstrasse 48; mains €8-20; ⊗ 10am-midnight Tue-Sat) Mediterranean and Austrian cuisine accompanied by Burgenland wines and a courtyard setting.

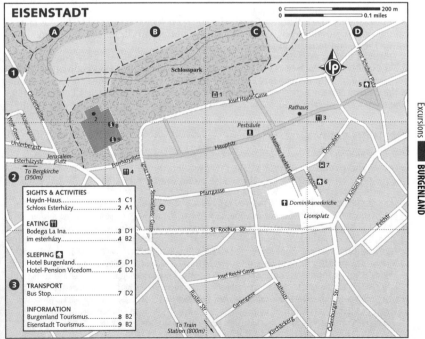

EISENSTADT

0 — 200 m
0 — 0.1 miles

Schlosspark

Josef Haydn-Gasse

Rathaus

Pestsäule

Hauptstr

To Bergkirche (350m)

Pfarrgasse

Dominikanerkriche

Lionsplatz

St-Rochus-Str

Josef Reichl-Gasse

To Train Station (800m)

SIGHTS & ACTIVITIES	
Haydn-Haus	1 C1
Schloss Esterházy	2 A1

EATING 🍴	
Bodega La Ina	3 D1
im esterházy	4 B2

SLEEPING 🛏	
Hotel Burgenland	5 D1
Hotel-Pension Vicedom	6 D2

TRANSPORT	
Bus Stop	7 D2

INFORMATION	
Burgenland Tourismus	8 B2
Eisenstadt Tourismus	9 B2

Sleeping

Hotel-Pension Vicedom (☎ 02682-642 22; www
.vicedom.at; Vicedom 5; s/d from €30/52) Comfortable
Pension/hotel with breakfast buffet and simple, adequate
rooms.

Hotel Burgenland (☎ 02682-696 0; www.hotel
burgenland.at; Franz Schubert-Platz 11; s/d from
€87/97; 🛁 🖳) Modern hotel with a slant towards
business clients in the very centre of town.

TRANSPORT – EISENSTADT

Distance from Vienna to Eisenstadt 60km
Direction Southeast
Bus Frequent direct buses depart from Südtiroler
Platz in Vienna (70min).
Car Head south out of Vienna on the A2 and exit onto
the A3 at the Guntramsdorf junction. When the A3
ends, follow the signs to Eisenstadt (east).
Train There are no direct trains from Vienna to Eisens-
tadt; change at Neusiedl am See (1hr 35min; trains con-
nect with those heading to and from Südbahnhof).

BRATISLAVA

Slovakia's capital is a vibrant, pulsing city
just over an hour from Vienna by train. Its
historical centre is small, easy to explore on foot and crammed with historical buildings, many
of which have received a well-earned makeover in recent years with the help of EU money.

From Hlavná stanica, Bratislava's main train station, it's around a 20-minute walk to
Hurbanovo námestie, the northern edge of the old town. Dominating the city from above
is **Bratislava Castle**, the city's most prominent sight. Its shape, reminiscent of a four-poster bed,
was well established by the 15th century but most of what you see today is a reconstruction
from the 1950s. The castle's best feature is the views from its hefty ramparts; the vastness
of the communist **Petržalka** housing estate lies to the south, while the old town spreads east.
On the ground floor is the **Treasury of Slovakia**, containing a small but important collection of
archaeological finds dating from 5000 BC and earlier – the *Venus of Moravany*, a 25,000-
year-old fertility statue of a naked woman, is a highlight. The top floors are occupied by the
Historical Museum, which covers folk crafts, furniture, modern art and history and also includes
the all-important ice-hockey hall of fame.

Židovská, the most direct path from castle hill to the old town, passes through what
remains of the former Jewish quarter. What is reputedly the skinniest house in Central
Europe contains a little **Museum of Clocks** and nearby, the **Museum of Jewish Culture** houses moving
exhibits about Slovakia's Jewish community lost during WWII, the buildings demolished
in the 1960s, and Judaism in general.

Down in the old town **St Martin Cathedral**, the city's finest Gothic structure, dominates. Of
the museums here, the best is the **Municipal Museum**, located in the 14th-century town hall. It
comes complete with Renaissance courtyard and green-roofed neogothic annexe. Next door
is the **Primatial Palace**, where Napoleon signed a peace treaty with Austria's Franz I in 1805.
The town's only surviving tower gate, **Michael Tower**, has a 14th-century base, a 16th-century

DETOUR: SOPRON

Many Austrians associate Sopron, a town 27km southeast of Eisenstadt in Hungarian territory, with hairdressers and
dentists – both are cheaper, and often better, than their German-speaking counterparts. Unfortunately most Austrian
day-trippers return home without a glance at the city, which has a charming medieval heart.

The best place to begin a tour of Sopron – and get your bearings – is to climb the 200 steps of the narrow circular
staircase to the top of the 60m-high **firewatch tower** (tűztorony; ☎ 0036-99-311 327; Fő tér; adult/senior or student
500/250Ft; ⏰ 10am-8pm Tue-Sun May-Aug, 10am-6pm Tue-Sun Apr, Sep & Oct) at the northern end of Fő tér, the
central square. Back on ground level, an exploration of the inner town's cobblestone streets reveals some inviting
sights. The **Storno Collection** (Storno Gyűjtemény; ☎ 311 327; adult/senior or student 800/400Ft; ⏰ 10am-6pm
Tue-Sun Apr-Sep, 10am-2pm Tue-Sun Oct-Mar), on the second floor of Storno House, contains a Gothic treasure-trove
of religious items, and the **Old Synagogue** (Ó Zsinagóga; ☎ 311 327; Új utca 22; adult/senior or student 400/200Ft;
⏰ 10am-5pm Tue-Sun May-Sep, 10am-2pm Tue-Sun Oct) and **New Synagogue** (Új Zsinagóga; Új utca 11), both built
in the 14th century, are open to the public. A number of smaller museums also habitat the central area.

Information on Sopron is available from **Tourinform** (☎ 0036-99-517 560; sopron@tourinform.hu; Ferenc Liszt
Conference & Cultural Centre, Liszt Ferenc utca 1; ⏰ 9am-5pm Mon-Fri year-round, 9am-3pm Sat & Sun Jun–mid-Sep)
near the centre of town. At least 11 direct trains daily (1½ hours) connect Sopron with Vienna's Südbahnhof.

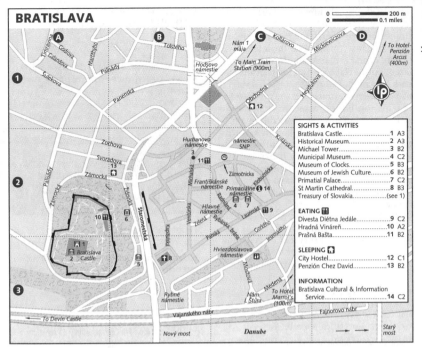

BRATISLAVA

0 — 200 m
0 — 0.1 miles

To Hotel-
Penzión
Arcus
(400m)

To Main Train
Station (900m)

SIGHTS & ACTIVITIES

Bratislava Castle	1 A3
Historical Museum	2 A3
Michael Tower	3 B2
Municipal Museum	4 C2
Museum of Clocks	5 B3
Museum of Jewish Culture	6 B2
Primatial Palace	7 C2
St Martin Cathedral	8 B3
Treasury of Slovakia	(see 1)

EATING

Divesta Diétna Jedále	9 C2
Hradná Vináreň	10 A2
Prašná Bašta	11 B2

SLEEPING

City Hostel	12 C1
Penzión Chez David	13 B2

INFORMATION

Bratislava Cultural & Information Service	14 C2

To Devín Castle

Nový most   Danubio   Starý most

top and an 18th-century steeple. Climb to the top for views across the rooftops and a small display of antique swords, armour and guns.

Dating from Roman times is **Devín Castle**, 9km west of town. Most of the castle you see today dates from the 15th and 16th centuries, although within its grounds is a restored 13th-century citadel. Its cliff-top views back across the Danube towards Vienna are quite enchanting; the best transport to the castle is by **ferry** (adult/student return 150/95Sk; 10am & 2.30pm Tue-Sun May-Aug).

Bratislava also has its quirky side. **Nový most**, (Nový Bridge; 1972), which spans the Danube between the old town and Petržalka, is an unbalanced modernist structure with what looks

View of Michael Tower looking along Michalská, Bratislava (this page)

like a 1970s B-grade-film flying saucer hovering above it. Hard to miss are the old town's strange bronze statues: the **Watcher** peeps out of an imaginary manhole at the intersection of Panská and Sedlárska; the **Frenchman**, a replica of one of Napoleon's soldiers, leans on a park bench; the **Photographer** stalks his subject paparazzi-style around a corner; **Schöner Náci** tips his top hat on a square; and a **soldier** stands guard in front of a water fountain.

The currency is Slovak koruna (crowns; the country is set to adopt the Euro in 2009), which are easily changed at banks and bus, boat and train stations. Nationals of EU countries don't require a visa to enter Slovakia; citizens of Australia, Canada, New Zealand and the US don't need a visa for tourist visits of up to 90 days. South African citizens can stay in the country for up to 30 days without a visa. In theory EU citizens only require an identity card to visit Slovakia, but in practice it's still best to carry a passport.

Sights & Information

Bratislava Castle (Bratislavský hrad; grounds admission free; 9am-8pm Apr-Sep, to 6pm Oct-Mar)

Bratislava Culture & Information Centre (BKIS; 00421-2-5249 5906; www.bkis.sk) Centre (Klobučnícka 2; 8.30am-6pm Mon-Fri, 9am-3pm Sat); Main Train Station (Hlavná stanica; 8am-7.30pm Mon-Fri, 8am-5pm Sat Jun-Sep, 8am-4.30pm Mon-Fri, 9am-2pm Sat Oct-May)

Devín Castle (00421-2-6573 0105; Muranská; adult/student 80/30Sk; 10am-5pm Tue-Fri, until 6pm Sat & Sun mid-Apr-Oct)

Michael Tower (Michalská veža; 00421-2-5443 3044; Michalská 24; adult/student 40/20Sk; 10am-5pm Tue-Fri, 11am-6pm Sat & Sun)

Municipal Museum (00421-2-5920 5130; Hlavné nám; adult/student 50/20Sk; 10am-5pm Tue-Fri, 11am-6pm Sat & Sun)

Museum of Clocks (Múzeum hodín; 00421-2-5441 1940; Židovská 1; adult/student 40/20Sk; 10am-5pm Tue-Sun)

Museum of Jewish Culture (Múzeum Židovskej kultúry; 5441 8507; www.chatamsofer.com; Židovská 17; adult/student 200/20Sk; 11am-5pm Sun-Fri)

Primatial Palace (Primaciálny Palác; Primaciálne námestie 1; adult/student 40Sk/free; 10am-5pm Tue-Sun)

Historical Museum (00421-2-5441 1441; www.snm .sk; adult/student 100/40Sk; 9am-6pm Tue-Sun)

Slowakische Zentrale für Tourismus (0041-1-513 95 69; www.slovakiatourism.sk; 04, Prinz-Eugen-Strasse 70; 9am-1pm & 2-5pm Mon-Fri) Slovak Tourism Board's representative in Vienna.

TRANSPORT – BRATISLAVA

Distance from Vienna 65km
Direction East

Boat For information on boats to Bratislava see p219.
Bus For information of bus connections to Bratislava's airport see p218
Car Head east on the A4 from Vienna until the Fischamend junction, where you continue on Bundesbahn 9, which passes through Petronell and Hainburg and eventually ends at the Slovakia border, just south of Bratislava.
Train From Südbahnhof, over a dozen trains daily (1¼hrs) travel to both Bratislava's main train station, 1km north of the old town, and its Petržalka station, 3km south of the old town.

St Martin Cathedral (Dóm sv Martina; Rudnayovo námestie; admission 60Sk; 9-11am & 1-5pm Mon-Sat, 1-5pm Sun)

Treasury of Slovakia (currently closed for renovation; check with the Information Centre for up-to-date details)

Eating

Divesta diétna jedáleň (Laurinská 8; mains 60-80Sk; 11am-3pm Mon-Fri) Central buffet with constant queues for its healthy vegetarian food.

Prašná Bašta (00421-2-5443 4957; Zámočnicka 11; mains 105-215Sk) Good, reasonable Slovak food, a charming round vaulted interior and one of the most private inner courtyards in the city.

Sleeping

City Hostel (00421-2-5263 6041; www.cityhostel.sk; Obchodná 38; s/d 1000/1690Sk;) Small, modern singles and doubles that are more basic hotel than hostel; each has its own bathroom, but TV costs extra and breakfast isn't available.

Penzión Chez David (00421-2-5441 3824; www.chez david.sk; Zámocká 13; s €64-74, d €78-88) Small but comfortable rooms at this cool blue (and Jewish) pension. Kosher food is available from its attached restaurant.

Hotel-Penzión Arcus (00421-2-5557 2522; www.hotel arcus.sk; Moskovská 5; s 1400-1800Sk, d 2600Sk) Friendly, popular hotel near the bus station and only 15 minutes' walk from the old town. Some of the dated rooms come with balcony.

Hotel Marrol's (00421-2-5778 4600; www.hotelmarrols .sk; Tobrucká 4; s 7000Sk, d 7300-9600Sk;) Retro refinement, black-and-white movie stills, sleek leather chairs, sumptuous fabrics: Hotel Marrol's is straight off the silver screen – circa 1940. The Jasmine spa downstairs is welcome relief after a day of sightseeing.

Directory

Directory

TRANSPORT
AIR

Vienna is well connected to the rest of the world and can be reached by no-frill and full-frill airlines. Bratislava, Slovakia's capital, only 60km east of Vienna, is a highly feasible alternative to flying into Austria. To find a flight online, try the following:

Expedia (www.expedia.com/www.expedia.co.uk) Lists major airline flights from the UK and USA; the earlier you book the better.

Flight Centre (www.flightcentre.com) Respected operator handling direct flights, with sites for Australia, New Zealand, the UK, the USA and Canada.

Last Minute (www.lastminute.com) One of the better sites for last minute deals, including hotels.

Flycheapo (www.flycheapo.com) No-frills website for no-frill airlines.

Opodo (www.opodo.co.uk) UK-based company with excellent deals for European destinations.

BOOKINGS ONLINE

Flights, tours and train tickets can be booked online at www.lonelyplanet.com/travel_services.

Airlines

Air Berlin (☎ 701 26 888; www.airberlin.com)

Air France (Map pp254–5; ☎ 502 22-2400; www.airfrance .com; 01, Kärntner Strasse 49)

Alitalia (Map pp254–5; ☎ 505 17 07; www.alitalia.com; 01, Kärntner Ring 2)

Austrian Airlines (Map pp252–3; ☎ 05 17 89; www.aua .com; 10, Fontanastrasse 1)

British Airways (Map pp254–5; ☎ 7956 7567; www .britishairways.com; 01, Kärntner Ring 10)

German Wings (☎ 820 24-0554; www.germanwings.com)

KLM (☎ 0900-359 556; www.klm.com)

NIKI (☎ 701 26 888; www.flyniki.com)

Sky Europe (☎ 998 555 55; www.skyeurope.com)

Swiss (Map pp254–5; ☎ 0810-810 840; www.swiss.com; 01, Marc-Aurel-Strasse 4)

Airports

20km southwest of the city centre at Schwechat is **Vienna International Airport** (flight inquiries ☎ 7007 22233; www.viennaairport .com). Facilities include a handful of restaurants and bars, banks and ATMs, money-exchange counters, a supermarket, a post office, car rental agencies and a 24-hour left-luggage counter. Getting to or from the airport is possible using the following transport options:

Bus Link (☎ 05 17 17; www.oebb.at; one-way/return €6/11, children under six free, children 6-15 €3/5.50; from Westbahnhof ☉ 5am-11pm, from Südbahnhof ☉ 5.15am-11.15pm, from Schwedenplatz ☉ 5am-11.30pm, from UNO City ☉ 6.35am-6.35pm, every 30 min) The Westbahnhof service calls in at Wien Südbahnhof station.

C&K Airport Service (☎ 444 44; www.ck-airportservice .at; one-way €27, up to four persons) C&K car service is a better, cheaper option than a taxi as its rates are fixed. On arrival at the airport, head to its stand to the left of the exit hall; when leaving Vienna, call ahead to make a reservation.

City Airport Train (CAT; ☎ 252 50; www.cityairporttrain .com; return adult/child €16/9, booked online €15/8; ☉ 5.38am-11.08pm, every 30 min) Departs from Wien-Mitte; luggage check-in facilities and boarding card issuing service.

Schnellbahn 7 (☎ 05 17 17; www.oebb.at; one-way €3, €1.50 with city transport passes; ☉ 4.32am-9.56pm Mon-Sat, every 30 min) Cheapest way to get to the airport; departs from Wien Nord and passes through Wien-Mitte.

Airport Letisko Bratislava (☎ 0421 2 4857 3353; www .airportbratislava.sk), serving Bratislava, is connected to Vienna's International Airport by 11 buses daily (one-way /return €9/16).

THINGS CHANGE...

The information in this chapter is particularly vulnerable to change. Check directly with the airline or a travel agent to make sure you understand how a fare (and ticket you may buy) works and be aware of the security requirements for international travel. Shop carefully. The details given in this chapter should be regarded as pointers and are not a substitute for your own careful, up-to-date research.

CLIMATE CHANGE & TRAVEL

Climate change is a serious threat to the ecosystems that humans rely upon, and air travel is the fastest-growing contributor to the problem. Lonely Planet regards travel, overall, as a global benefit, but believes we all have a responsibility to limit our personal impact on global warming.

Flying and climate change

Pretty much every form of motorized travel generates CO_2 (the main cause of human-induced climate change) but planes are far and away the worst offenders, not just because of the sheer distances they allow us to travel, but because they release greenhouse gases high into the atmosphere. The statistics are frightening: two people taking a return flight between Europe and the US will contribute as much to climate change as an average household's gas and electricity consumption over a whole year.

Carbon offset schemes

Climatecare.org and other websites use 'carbon calculators' that allow travellers to offset the level of greenhouse gases they are responsible for with financial contributions to sustainable travel schemes that reduce global warming – including projects in India, Honduras, Kazakhstan and Uganda.

Lonely Planet, together with Rough Guides and other concerned partners in the travel industry, support the carbon offset scheme run by climatecare.org. Lonely Planet offsets all of its staff and author travel.

For more information check out our website: www.lonelyplanet.com.

BICYCLE

Vienna is easily handled by bicycle – over 700km of cycle tracks crisscross the city, making it a breeze to avoid traffic, but not always pedestrians. Many one-way streets do not apply to cyclists; these are indicated by a bicycle sign with the word *ausgen* alongside it. The Walking & Cycling Tours chapter offers two cycle tour suggestions for the city (p113 and p115), while popular cycling areas include the 7km path around the Ringstrasse, the Donauinsel (Danube Island), the Prater and along the Donaukanal (Danube Canal).

Hire bikes from any of the following:

Copa Cagrana Rad und Skaterverleih (Map pp252–3; ☎ 263 52 42; www.fahrradverleih.at in German; 22, Am Kaisermühlendamm 1; 1hr/½-/full-day rental from €4.80/14.40/24; ◷ 9am-6pm Mar & Oct, 9am-8pm Apr & Sep, 9am-9pm May-Aug) Also has roller blades for hire (from €6 per hour).

Pedal Power (☎ 729 72 34; www.pedalpower.at; 02, Ausstellungsstrasse 3; 1hr/½-/full-day rental €5/17/27; ◷ 8am-7pm Apr-Oct) Also offers tours of the city; see p52 for more information. Child seats and helmets are €4 extra a piece.

Vienna City Bike (☎ 0810-50 05 00; www.citybikewien .at in German; 1st hr free, 2nd hr €1, 3rd hr €2, 4th hr and above €4) Blue and yellow bicycles provided by the City of Vienna to promote cycling in the city; currently 45 bike stands are scattered throughout the city. A credit card or a bank card from an Austrian bank is required to rent bikes; just swipe your card in the machine and follow the instructions (in a number of languages). If neither suits, a Tourist Card, available from **Royal Tours** (Map pp254–5; ☎ 710 46 06; 01, Herrengasse 1-3; ◷ 9-11.30am, 1-6pm) for €2 per day, allows tourists to rent bicycles without using a credit card. A lost bike will set you back €600.

Bicycles can be carried on carriages marked with a bike symbol on the S-Bahn and U-Bahn from 9am to 3pm and after 6.30pm Monday to Friday, after 9am Saturday and all day Sunday for half the adult fare. It's not possible to take bikes on trams and buses.

BOAT

The Danube is a traffic-free access route for arrivals and departures from Vienna. Eastern Europe is the main destination; **Twin City Liner** (Map pp254–5; ☎ 588 80; www.twincityliner .com; 01, Schwedenplatz; one way/return from €15/30; ◷ 8am-4.30pm) connects Vienna with Bratislava in 1¼ hours from June to October while **DDSG Blue Danube** (Map pp254–5; ☎ 588 80; www.ddsg-blue-danube .at; 01, Friedrichstrasse 7; one way/return €79/99; ◷ 9am-6pm Mon-Fri) links Budapest with Vienna April to October.

The Danube is connected to the Rhine by the River Main tributary and the Main-Danube canal in southern Germany; imaginatively named ships like the MS *Sound of Music* and MS *River Empress* cruise along this route, from Amsterdam to Budapest, between May and November. Bookings can be made through **Noble Caledonia** (☎ 020-7752 0000; www.noble-caledonia.co.uk) in Britain and **Uniworld** (☎ 1-800-360 9550; www.uniworld.com) in the USA.

For boat trips through the Wachau region northwest of Vienna see the Excursions chapter (p205).

BUS

Vienna has no central bus station; your arrival destination will depend on which company you're travelling with.

Eurolines (Map pp262–3; www.eurolines.com; ☎ 798 29 00; www.eurolines.at; 03, Erdbergstrasse 202; ☻ 6.30am-8.30pm Mon-Fri, 6.30-11am & 4.30-8.30pm Sat & Sun) has basically tied up the bus routes connecting Austria with the rest of Europe. Its main terminal is at the U3 U-Bahn station Erdberg but some buses stop at Südbahnhof, on Arsenalstrasse (Map pp262–3).

Post buses (☎ 711 01; www.postbus.at in German; information line ☻ 7am-8pm) are Austria's regional buses and basically go everywhere regional trains don't.

CAR & MOTORCYCLE
Driving

A car is the best way to see the many of the sights mentioned in the Excursions chapter but in Vienna itself it's best to stick with the excellent public transport system. The city is riddled with one-way streets (the Innere Stadt is a veritable rabbit-warren of these), the Viennese are aggressive drivers at the best of times, parking is difficult and/or expensive in the centre and speeding trams (which have priority) are never far away. Note that vehicles must wait behind trams when they stop to pick up or set down passengers and Austrians drive on the right.

Always carry proof of ownership of a private vehicle and your driver's licence. EU licences are accepted in Austria while all other nationalities require a German translation or an International Driving Permit (IDP). Third-party insurance is a minimum requirement in Europe: you'll need proof of this in the form of a Green Card.

The blood-alcohol limit in Austria is 0.05%. Speed limits are 50km/h in built-up areas, 100km/h on country roads *(Bundesbahn)* and 130km/h on the autobahn. On some country roads speed is restricted to 70km/h. Crash helmets are compulsory on motorcycles and children under the age of 14 and/or shorter than 1.5m must have a special seat or restraint.

A motorway tax *(Vignette)* is imposed on all autobahn travel; 10 day/two month/year passes cost €7.60/21.80/72.60. They're available from most petrol stations; note that hired cars come with a year *Vignette*.

Hire

For the lowest rates, organise car rental before departure. Holiday Autos (www.holidayautos.com) offers highly competitive rates, as does easyCar (www.easycar.com).

All the big names in car hire are present in Austria (and have desks at the airport) and advanced reservations can be made online:

Avis (Map pp254–5; ☎ 0800 0800 87 57; www.avis.at; 01, Opernring 3-5; ☻ 7am-6pm Mon-Fri, 8am-2pm Sat, 8am-1pm Sun)

Denzeldrive (Map pp262–3; ☎ 050105 4000; www.denzeldrive.at in German; 03, Erdbergstrasse 189-193; ☻ 7am-7pm Mon-Fri, 8am-2pm Sat & Sun)

Europcar (Map pp254–5; ☎ 714 67 17; www.europcar.at in German; 01, Schubertring 9; ☻ 7.30am-6pm Mon-Fri, 8am-1pm Sat, 8am-noon Sun)

Hertz (Map pp254–5; ☎ 512 86 77; www.hertz.at; 01, Kärntner Ring 17; ☻ 7.30am-6pm Mon-Fri, 9am-3pm Sat & Sun)

Rates start at around €60 per day but decrease for longer rentals. Check extra charges before signing an agreement; Collision Damage Waver (CDW) is an additional charge starting at around €22 per day, theft protection another €7 to €8 and drivers under the age of 25 are often required to pay an additional €4 to €5 per day.

The minimum age for renting is 19 for small cars and 25 for prestige models and a valid licence of at least a year is required. If you plan to drive across the border, especially into Eastern Europe, let the rental company know beforehand and double-check any add-on fees.

Directory

TRANSPORT

Parking

Districts 1-9 and 20 are pay-and-display short-stay parking zones (*Kurzparkzone*) where a parking voucher (*Parkschein*) is required; other districts are general parking zones, but also contain some *Kurzparkzone*, mainly on the larger streets (look for blue signs circled in red with a single diagonal line). *Parkscheine* come in 30/60/90 minute lots (€0.40/0.80/1.20) and can be purchased from most *Tabakladen* (tobacconists), banks, train stations and Wiener Linien ticket offices. A free 10-minute voucher is also available. To validate a voucher, just cross out the appropriate time, date and year and leave it on your dashboard. The parking restrictions are in force from 9am to 7pm Monday to Friday (maximum 1½ hours parking) in the Innere Stadt and from 9am to 8pm Monday to Friday (maximum two hours) in other districts. Traffic wardens are quite vigilant and eager to hand out fines (€20 to €170).

The MuseumsQuartier, Südbahnhof and Westbahnhof all sport private parking garages, as does the Ringstrasse; expect to pay anything between €2 and €5 per hour.

Automobile Associations

Two automobile associations serve Austria. Both provide free 24-hour breakdown service to members and have reciprocal agreements with motoring clubs in other countries; check with your local club before leaving. If you're not entitled to free assistance, you'll incur a fee for call outs which varies depending on the time of day. These are the two associations:

ARBÖ (Map pp260–1; 24-hr emergency assistance ☎ 123, office ☎ 891 21-0; www.arboe.at in German; 15, Mariahilfer Strasse 180; ⏰ 8am-6pm Mon-Fri, 9am-noon Sat)

ÖAMTC (Map pp254–5; 24-hour emergency assistance ☎ 120, office ☎ 711 99-0; www.oeamtc.at; 01, Schubertring 1-3; ⏰ 8am-6pm Mon-Fri, 9am-1pm Sat)

PUBLIC TRANSPORT

Vienna has a comprehensive and unified public transport network that is one of the most efficient in Europe. Flat-fare tickets are valid for trains, trams, buses, the underground (U-Bahn) and the S-Bahn regional trains. Services are frequent and you rarely have to wait more than 10 minutes. Public transport starts around 5am or 6am; buses (with the exception of night buses) and trams finish between 11pm and midnight and S-Bahn and U-Bahn services between 12.30am and 1am.

Transport maps are posted in all U-Bahn stations and at many bus and tram stops. Free maps and information pamphlets are available from **Wiener Linien** (☎ 7909-100; www.wienerlinien.at in German; information line ⏰ 6am-10pm Mon-Fri, 8.30am-4.30pm Sat & Sun), located in nine U-Bahn stations. The Karlsplatz, Stephansplatz and Westbahnhof information offices are open 6.30am to 6.30pm Monday to Friday and 8.30am to 4pm Saturday and Sunday. Those at Schottentor, Praterstern, Floridsdorf, Landstrasse, Philadelphiabrücke and Erdberg are closed on weekends.

Tickets & Passes

Tickets and passes can be purchased at U-Bahn stations – from automatic machines (with English instructions and change) and occasionally staffed ticket offices – and in *Tabakladen*. Once bought, tickets need to be validated before starting your journey (except for weekly and monthly tickets); look for small blue boxes at the entrance to U-Bahn stations and on buses and trams. Just pop the end of the ticket in the slot and wait for the 'ding'. It's an honour system and ticket inspection is infrequent, but if you're caught without a ticket you'll be fined €62, no exceptions.

Tickets and passes are as follows:

Single Ticket (*Einzelfahrschein*) – €1.50; good for one journey, with line changes; costs €2 if purchased on trams and buses (correct change required)

Strip Ticket (*Streifenkarte*) – €6; four single tickets on one strip

24-Hour Ticket (*24 Stunden Wien-Karte*) – €5; 24 hours unlimited travel from time of validation

72-Hour Ticket (*72 Stunden Wien-Karte*) – €12; 72 hours unlimited travel from time of validation

Eight-day Ticket (*8-Tage-Karte*) – €24; valid for eight days, but not necessarily eight consecutive days; punch the card as and when you need it

Weekly Ticket (*Wochenkarte*) – €12.50; valid Monday through Sunday only

Monthly Ticket (*Monatskarte*) – €45; valid from the 1st of the month to the last day of the month

Vienna Shopping Card (*Wiener Einkaufskarte*) – €4; for use between 8am and 8pm Monday to Saturday; only good for one day after validation

The Vienna Card *(Die Wien-Karte)* – €16.90; 72 hours of unlimited travel from time of validation plus discounts; see Discount Cards (p225) for more information

Children aged six to 15 travel for half-price, or for free on Sunday, public holidays and during Vienna school holidays (photo ID necessary); younger children always travel free. Senior citizens (women over 60, men over 65) can buy a €2 ticket that is valid for two trips; inquire at transport information offices.

Buses

Buses go everywhere, including inside the Innere Stadt, and either have three digits or a number followed by an 'A' or 'B'. Very logically, buses connecting with a tram service often have the same number, eg bus 38A connects with tram 38, bus 72A with tram 72.

Night Buses

Vienna's comprehensive Nightline service takes over when trams, buses and the U-Bahn stop running. Twenty-three routes cover much of the city and run every half hour from 12.30am to 5am. Schwedenplatz, Schottentor and the Staatsoper are starting points for many services; look for buses and bus stops marked with an 'N'. All transport tickets are valid for Nightline services.

S-Bahn

S-Bahn trains, designated by a number preceded by an 'S', operate from train stations and service to the suburbs or satellite towns. If you're travelling outside of Vienna, and outside of the ticket zone, you'll probably have to purchase an extension; check on maps posted in train stations.

Trams

There's something romantic and just plain good about travelling by tram, even though they're slower than the U-Bahn. Vienna's tram network is extensive and it's the perfect way to view the city on the cheap (see p53 for suggestions for touring the city by tram). Trams are either numbered or lettered (eg 1, 44, J, D) and services cover the city centre and some suburbs.

U-Bahn

The U-Bahn is a quick and efficient way of getting around the city. There are five lines, U1 to U6 (there is no U5); the U2 line is currently being extended and by 2008 will run to the Ernst-Happel-Stadion in the Prater and by 2009 to Aspernstrasse in the eastern reaches of the Donaustadt district. Platforms have timetable information and signs showing the different exits and nearby facilities. The whole U-Bahn system is a nonsmoking zone.

TAXI

Taxis are reliable and relatively cheap by Western European standards. City journeys are metered; flag fall costs €2.50 from 6am to 11pm Monday to Saturday and €2.60 any other time, plus a small per km fee. A small tip is expected; add on about 10% to the fare. Taxis are easily found at train stations and taxi stands all over the city, or just flag them down in the street. To order one call ☎ 31 300, 60 160 or 40 100. Don't count on taxis taking credit cards.

TRAIN

Like much of Europe, Austria's train network is a dense web reaching the country's far-flung corners. The system is fast, efficient, frequent and well used. **Österreiche Bundesbahn** (**ÖBB; Austrian Federal Railway**; 24hr information ☎ 05 17 17; www.oebb .at) is the main operator, and has information offices all of Vienna's main train stations. Tickets can be purchased at ticket offices or on the train, but the latter will normally cost a little extra. Reservations incur a minimum fee of €3.40, and are recommended for travel on weekends.

Vienna's three main train stations are Westbahnhof, Südbahnhof and Franz-Josef-Bahnhof. **Westbahnhof** (Map pp260–1; information office ☉ 5am-midnight) services trains to Western and northern Europe and western Austria and is connected to Vienna's public transport system by U-Bahn and tram. **Südbahnhof** (Map pp262–3; information office ☉ 5am-midnight) services trains to Italy, the Czech Republic, Slovakia, Hungary and Poland and has tram and bus stops. **Franz-Josefs-Bahnhof** (Map pp258–9) handles regional and local trains, including trains to Tulln, Krems and the Wachau region. All three stations have left-luggage lockers (24 hours; €2 to €3.50), ATMs, currency-exchange counters, post offices and plenty of places to grab a snack. They usually close their doors from around 1am to 4am.

Smaller stations include **Wien Mitte** (Map pp254–5), **Wien Nord** (Map pp258–9) and **Meidling** (Map pp260–1). All have U-Bahn stops and the former two have connections to the airport.

TRAVEL AGENTS

Restplatzbörse (Map pp254–5; ☎ 580 850; www .restplatzboerse.at, German only; 01, Opernring 3-5; ☻ 9am-7pm Mon-Fri, 10am-1pm Sat) Specialises in bargain flights and has 10 outlets across Vienna, including one at the airport.

Österreichisches Verkehrsbüro (Map pp254–5; ☎ 588 00-775; www.verkehrsbuero.at in German; 04, Friedrich-strasse 7; ☻ 9am-5pm Mon-Fri) Major national agency organises everything under the sun.

STA Travel (Map pp254–5; ☎ 401 48-6000; www.statravel .at in German; 04, Rilkeplatz 2; ☻ 9am-6pm Mon-Fri) STA has discounted flights for students. The staff is helpful, friendly and speaks English. There are four branches in Vienna.

PRACTICALITIES
ACCOMMODATION

Accommodation alternatives in the Sleeping chapter are separated into district groupings, and ordered by budget (lowest to highest). The average price for a double room in the Innere Stadt is around €150, but there are cheaper rooms in the surrounding districts. Peak season is June to September, Christmas and New Year, and Easter; expect high prices and a lack of availability at popular times. Over winter, rates can drop substantially and many places offer discounts and specials for longer stays. Some, especially the five-star hotels, offer special weekend rates, or 'two nights for the price of one' packages. It's definitely worth inquiring about cheaper rates before signing on the dotted line. Prices quoted in the Sleeping chapter are summer rates.

Note that reservations are binding and compensation may be claimed by the hotel if you do not take a reserved room, or by you if the room is unavailable.

BUSINESS

Vienna is Austria's business hub and a traditional stepping stone between Eastern and Western Europe. It's also a major conference location, something Vienna's promotional machine pushes; the city's conference capabilities are seen as one of its five USPs (Unique Selling Points). For more information on conferences and conventions, contact the Vienna Convention Bureau (☎ 211 14; www.vienna.convention .at), which is part of the Vienna Tourist Board.

The Austrian Business Agency's (Österreichische Wirtschaftswerbungs) website, www.aba.gv.at/en/pages, is a good introductory point for starting a business in the country as it has contact listings and general information. Helpful organisations in Vienna include:

American Reference Center (Map pp258–9; ☎ 405 30 33; www.usembassy.at; 08, Schmidgasse 14; ☻ 8.30am-5pm Mon-Fri) Reference centre linked to the US embassy, with publications in English about or from the USA. It's a resource for people undertaking research and not for the general public; appointments are necessary.

American Chamber of Commerce (Map pp258–9; ☎ 319 57 51; www.amcham.or.at; 09, Porzellangasse 35; ☻ 9am-noon Mon-Fri) Offers a directory of American companies in Austria for a small fee.

British Embassy Commercial Section (Map pp262–3; ☎ 716 13 6161; www.britishembassy.at; 03, Jauresgasse 12; ☻ 9am-1pm, 2-5pm Mon-Fri) Holds a directory of British companies operating in Austria.

Hours

Hours are similar to the rest of Europe:

Banks 8am or 9am to 3pm Monday to Friday, with extended hours until 5.30pm on Thursday. Many smaller branches close from 12.30pm to 1.30pm for lunch.

Cafés 7am to midnight.

Post Offices 8am to noon and 2pm to 6pm Monday to Friday; some also open 8am to noon Saturday. The **main post office** (Map pp254–5; 01, Fleischmarkt 19) is open 24 hours, and branches at Westbahnhof, Südbahnhof and Franz-Josefs-Bahnhof have extended hours.

Pubs and Clubs Opening times vary; close is normally between midnight and 4am throughout the week.

Restaurants Generally 11am to 3pm and 6pm to midnight.

General Office Hours 8am to 3.30pm, 4pm or 5pm Monday to Friday.

Shops Normally open 9am to 6pm Monday to Friday and until 5pm Saturday. Some have extended hours on Thursday or Friday until 9pm.

Supermarkets 7.30am or 8am to 6pm or 7pm Monday to Friday, till 5pm Saturday. Closed Sunday.

Centres

The Vienna International Airport has a number of business centres; the **Airport VIP Business Centre** (☎ 7007 23300/400/406; www.viennaairport.com), the **Danube Aviator Club** (☎ 01 7007 23300; wwwviennaairport.com) and the **Vienna Airport World Trade Center** (☎ 7007 36000; www.world-trade-center.at). The **NH Vienna Airport** (☎ 701 510; www.nh-hotels.com) also has conference facilities. The **Regus Business Centre** (Map pp254–5; ☎ 53 712-0; www.regus.com; 01, Schottenring 16) can provide office rental and business services.

CHILDREN

For more years than anyone would care to remember, the Viennese had the reputation of loving their dogs more than their children. This attitude has thankfully changed in recent times, and now children are given more reign to just be kids. Facilities have also improved, with new trams easily accessible for buggies or prams (the older ones, however, are a nightmare); the U-Bahn and buses are also parent friendly. Children receive discounts on public transport (p221), some restaurants have children's menus and often children under 12 can stay in their parents' hotel room free of charge. Breast-feeding in public is a common sight and nappy changing ruffles few feathers. There's even an information centre, the WienXtra-Kinderinfo (p231), for parents and their offspring. Baby-sitters for visitors are however hard to arrange; the best idea is to check with the hotel you're staying at.

An increasing number of Vienna's museums, attractions and theatres cater to children and feature exhibitions and events specifically aimed at the little 'uns; places such as the Kunsthistorisches Museum (p73) and the Albertina (p63) have children's programs over the summer months. The city boasts three children's museums – Zoom (p77), Schönbrunn Kindermuseum (p102) and Minopolis (p83) – and there is plenty of outdoor space for running off excess energy. The Prater (p79) has wide-open playing fields, playgrounds and a fun-fair, and Lainzer Tiergarten (p99) and the Donauinsel (p82) are popular with families seeking for fresh air. Swimming pools are dotted across the length and breadth of the city and offer free access to children under 15 over the summer school holidays.

The Sights and Entertainment chapters feature more options, and we've included a 'Top Picks for Children' (p82) in the Sights chapter.

For helpful travelling tips, pick up a copy of Lonely Planet's *Travel with Children* by Cathy Lanigan.

CLIMATE

Austria falls within the central European climatic zone, though the eastern part of the country (where Vienna is situated) has a Continental Pannonian climate, characterised by a mean temperature in July that hovers around 20°C and annual rainfall usually under 800mm.

The differences in temperature between day and night and summer and winter are greater here than in the west of the country. July and August can be very hot, and a hotel with air-conditioning would be an asset at this time. Winter is surprisingly

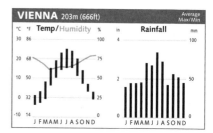

cold, especially in January, and you would need to bring plenty of warm clothing. Damp maritime winds sometimes sweep in from the west, and the *Föhn*, a warm wind from the south, is not an uncommon occurrence throughout the entire year. The average rainfall is 710mm per year, with most falling between May and August, causing the Danube to flood in recent years.

COURSES

Many places offer German courses, and they can usually offer the option of accommodation for the duration of the course. These are two of the better-known course providers:

Berlitz (Map pp254–5; ☎ 0820-820 082; www.berlitz .at; 01, Graben 13; ☉ 8am-8pm Mon-Fri) Offers a range of private, intensive and evening courses and has four offices in Vienna.

Inlingua Sprachschule (Map pp254–5; ☎ 512 22 25; www.inlingua.at; 01, Neuer Markt 1; ☉ 9am-6pm Mon-Fri) Courses run for a minimum of two weeks, and can either be taken during the day or at night. Classes are limited to eight students; individual tuition is also available.

Check the *Gelbe Seiten* (Yellow Pages) under *Sprachschulen* (language schools) for more listings.

See the Eating chapter for cooking courses (p128).

CUSTOMS

Theoretically there is no restriction on how much you can bring into Austria from other EU states. However, to ensure these goods remain for personal use, guideline limits are 800 cigarettes (25 cigarettes if entering by car or ship), 200 cigars, 1kg tobacco, 10L of spirits, 90L of wine, 110L of beer and 20L of other alcoholic beverages. The same quantity can be taken out of Austria, as long as you are travelling to another EU country.

For duty-free purchases made outside the EU, you may bring 200 cigarettes or 50 cigars or 250g tobacco, plus 2L of wine and 1L of spirits into Austria. Items such as weapons, drugs (both legal and illegal), meat, animal products and certain plant material are subject to stricter customs control.

DISCOUNT CARDS

The Vienna Card (*Die Wien-Karte*; €16.90) allows three days unlimited travel on the public transport system (including night buses) and provides discounts at selected museums, cafés, *Heurigen* (wine taverns), restaurants and shops across the city, and on guided tours and the CAT (p218). The discount usually amounts to 5% to 10% off the normal price, or a free gift. It can be purchased at Tourist Info Wien (p231), many hotels, and at Wiener Linien ticket offices (p221).

ELECTRICITY

The voltage used in Vienna and throughout Austria is 220V. Sockets are the round two-pin type, which are standard throughout most of Continental Europe. North American 110V appliances will need a transformer if they don't have built-in voltage adjustment.

EMBASSIES

The Austrian Foreign Ministry website (www.bmaa.gv.at) has a complete list of embassies and consulates.

Australia (Map pp254–5; ☎ 506 740; www .australian-embassy.at; 04, Mattiellistrasse 2)

Canada (Map pp254–5; ☎ 531 38 3000; www.kanada.at; 01, Laurenzerberg 2)

Czech Republic (Map pp260–1; ☎ 899 581 11; www .mzv.cz/vienna; 14, Penzingerstrasse 11-13)

France (Map pp254–5; ☎ 502 75 200; www.consulfrance -vienne.org; 01, Wipplingerstrasse 24-26)

Hungary (Map pp254–5; ☎ 537 80 300; kom@huembvie .at; 01, Bankgasse 4-6)

Italy (Map pp262–3; ☎ 713 56 71; www.ambvienna .esteri.it; 03, Ungargasse 43)

Slovakia (Map pp252–3; ☎ 318 90 55; www.vienna.mfa .sk; 19, Armbrustergasse 24)

Slovenia (Map pp254–5; ☎ 585 22 40; vdu@gov.si; 01, Nibelungengasse 13)

Switzerland (Map pp262–3; ☎ 795 05-0; www.eda .admin.ch/wien; 03, Prinz-Eugen-Strasse 7)

UK (Map pp262–3; ☎ 716 130; www.britishembassy.at; 03, Jauresgasse 12)

USA (Map pp254–5; ☎ 319 39; www.usembassy.at; 4th fl, Hotel Marriott, 01, Gartenbaupromenade 2-4)

EMERGENCY

In case of emergency, dial the following:

Ambulance *(Rettung)* ☎ 144

Doctor *(Ärzte-Notdienst)* ☎ 141

Fire *(Feuerwehr)* ☎ 122

Police *(Polizei)* ☎ 133

Women's Emergency Line *(Frauennotruf)* ☎ 71 719

GAY & LESBIAN TRAVELLERS

Vienna is a city that is reasonably tolerant towards gays and lesbians, more so than the rest of Austria, and gay bashing is virtually unknown here (in contrast to the situation in ostensibly more gay-tolerant cities such as Amsterdam or Berlin). The situation is improving all the time; the restricting federal statute 209, which set the consenting age for sex between men at 18 (it is 14 for heterosexuals) was repealed in 2003. There is no set age of consent for lesbian sex, apparently because the legislators decided there was no discernible difference between mutual washing of bodily parts and intimate sexual contact. While lesbians welcome the lack of legislation, they see this as a typical (male) denial of female sexuality.

Information on the *Schwullesbische Szene* (gay and lesbian scene) is quite comprehensive. The Vienna Tourist Board produces the handy *Queer Guide,* a booklet listing gay bars, restaurants, hotels and festivals, and the *Gay Guide,* a city map with gay locations marked. Both are freely available at the Tourist Info Wien office (p231), from the organisations listed below and at many gay and lesbian *Lokale* (bars). *Xtra* (www.xtra-news.at, in German), a free monthly publication, is an additional supplement packed with news, views and listings. For online resources, try www.gayboy.at, www.rainbow.or.at and www.gaynet.at which can provide further information and up-to-date news on events.

Events to look out for on the gay and lesbian calendar include the Regenbogen Parade (Rainbow Parade), the Life Ball, Wien ist Andersrum and Identities (Vienna's Queer Film Festival); the City Calendar (p9) has more details. Bars, venues and clubs are listed throughout the Entertainment chapter.

Organisations

Homosexuelle Initiative Wien (HOSI; Map pp258–9; ☎ 216 66 04; www.hosiwien.at in German; 02, Novaragasse 40; ☿ from 8pm Tue, from 7pm Wed, from 5.30pm Thu, from 9pm Fri) HOSI is a politically minded gay and lesbian centre with regular events.

Rosa Lila Villa (Map pp260–1; www.villa.at in German; 06, Linke Wienzeile 102) Probably the best organisation in Vienna for information, the Rosa Lila Villa has telephone counselling, a small library with books in English, and advice and information on what's on offer in the city. The **lesbian centre** (☎ 586 81 50; lesbenberatung@villa.at; ☿ 5-8pm Mon, Wed & Fri) is on the ground floor, and the **gay men's centre** (☎ 585 43 43; schwulenberatung@villa.at; ☿ 5-8pm Mon, Wed & Sat) is on the 1st floor.

HOLIDAYS

The Viennese take their holiday time seriously; and the entire city basically shuts down on public holidays. The only establishments remaining open are bars, cafés and restaurants, and even some of these refuse to open their doors. Museums like to confuse things – some stay closed while others are free. The big school break is July and August; most families go away during this time so you'll find the city is a little quieter, but the downside is that a high percentage of restaurants and entertainment venues close. Consult the City Calendar (p9) for details on festivals and events.

Public holidays are:

New Year's Day *(Neujahr)* 1 January

Epiphany *(Heilige Drei Könige)* 6 January

Easter Monday *(Ostermontag)*

Labour Day *(Tag der Arbeit)* 1 May

Ascension Day *(Christi Himmelfahrt)* sixth Thursday after Easter

Whit Monday *(Pfingstmontag)* sixth Monday after Easter

Corpus Christi *(Fronleichnam)* second Thursday after Pentecost

Assumption *(Maria Himmelfahrt)* 15 August

National Day *(Nationalfeiertag)* 26 October

All Saints' Day *(Allerheiligen)* 1 November

Immaculate Conception *(Mariä Empfängnis)* 8 December

Christmas Day *(Christfest)* 25 December

St Stephen's Day *(Stephanitag)* 26 December

INTERNET ACCESS

Vienna is well geared to travellers wishing to stay in touch via email while on holiday. Many of the main streets leading away from the city centre outside the Gürtel are lined with cheap, albeit slightly grungy, call centres doubling as internet cafés. The centre of the city is less stocked, but by no means a desert; **BigNet**, with branches at Hoher Markt (Map pp254–5; ☎ 533 29 39; 01, Hoher Markt 8) and Kärntner Strasse (Map pp254–5; ☎ 503 98 44; 01, Kärntner Strasse 61) has internet access for €5.90 per hour from 9am to 11pm, and **Speednet Café** (www .speednet-café.com) has a branch lurking at the back of Westbahnhof (Map pp260–1; ☎ 892 56 66; 15, Europlatz, Westbahnhof; ☼ 7am-midnight Mon-Sat, from 8am Sun) and also in the Innere Stadt (☎ 532 57 50; 01, Morzinplatz 4; ☼ 8am-midnight Mon-Fri, 10am-midnight Sat & Sun) and in Landstrasse (☎ 218 46 8640; 04, Landstrasse Hauptstrasse 92; ☼ 8am-10pm Mon-Fri, 10am-10pm Sat & Sun). Free access is available at Café Florianihof (p141), Flex (p164) and rhiz (p164; free after 9pm), but there aren't many terminals. Bücherei Wien (p91) also has free internet access; just turn up with your passport and log on.

All top hotels have plugs for connecting your laptop to the Internet, but as yet it's not possible to organise an ISP in Austria for a short period (minimum contracts run for 12 months). AOL's access number in Vienna is ☎ 071-891 50 52, Compuserve's ☎ 071-891 51 61 and EUnet's ☎ 899 330.

There are almost 200 wireless connections – WLAN hotspots – in Vienna; for a complete list search for 'public internet access' on www.wien.gv.at/english.

MAPS

For most purposes, the free *Stadtplan* (city map) provided by the tourist office will be sufficient. It shows bus, tram and U-Bahn routes, has a separate U-Bahn plan and lists major city-wide sights. It also has a blow-up of the Innere Stadt. For a street index, you'll need to buy a map. Freytag & Berndt's 1:25,000 fold-out map, available at most book stores, is very comprehensive, but its *Buchplan Wien* (scale 1:20,000) is the Rolls Royce of city maps and is used by locals.

MEDICAL SERVICES

EU and EEA (European Economic Area) nationals receive free emergency medical treatment, although payment may have to be made for medication, private consultations and nonurgent treatment. To receive treatment, you'll need to present a European Health Insurance Card (called the *e*card in Austria) to take advantage of reciprocal health agreements in Europe; arrange one before leaving home. Nothing, however, beats having full health insurance.

If you're staying a long time in Vienna it would facilitate matters if you get a certificate from the health insurance office, the **Gebietskrankenkasse** (Map pp252–3; ☎ 601 22-0; www.wgkk.at in German; 10, Wienerbergstrasse 15-19; ☼ 7.30am-2pm Mon-Wed & Fri, 7.30am-4pm Thu). This office can also tell you the countries that have reciprocal agreements with Austria (the USA, Canada, Australia and New Zealand don't).

Emergency Rooms

The following hospitals *(Krankenhäuser)* have emergency rooms open 24 hours a day, seven days a week:

Allgemeines Krankenhaus (Map pp258–9; ☎ 404 00; 09, www.akhwien.at; Währinger Gürtel 18-20)

Lorenz Böhler Unfallkrankenhaus (Map pp258–9; ☎ 331 10; www.ukhboehler.at, in German; 20, Donaueschingenstrasse 13)

Unfallkrankenhaus Meidling (Map pp252–3; ☎ 601 50-0; 12, Kundratstrasse 37)

If you require a pharmacy *(Apotheke)* after hours, dial ☎ 1550 (German speaking).

METRIC SYSTEM

The metric system is used. Like other Continental Europeans, Austrians indicate decimals with commas and thousands with points. You will sometimes see meat and cheese priced per *Dag*, which is an abbreviation referring to 10g (to ask for this quantity say '*Deca*').

MONEY

Austria's currency is the euro, which is divided into 100 cents. There are coins for one, two, five, 10, 20 and 50 cents, and €1 and €2. Notes come in denominations of €5, €10, €20, €50, €100, €200 and €500.

See the Quick Reference (inside front cover) for exchange rates at the time of going to press. For the latest rates, check out www.oanda.com.

ATMs

*Bankomat*s (ATMs), which accept credit, debit and Eurocheque cards, are never very far away in Vienna – just look for a neon sign with two green and blue stripes sticking out from a bank facade. *Bankomats* can also be found in the main train stations and at the airport.

Check with your home bank before travelling to see how much the charge is for using a *Bankomat* in Vienna; normally there's no commission to pay at the Austrian end.

Changing Money

Banks are the best places to exchange cash, but it pays to shop around as exchange rates and commission charges can vary a little between them. Normally there is a minimum commission charge of €2 to €3.50 so try to exchange your money in large amounts to save on multiple charges.

There are plenty of exchange offices in the Innere Stadt, particularly around Stephansplatz and on Kärntner Strasse. Westbahnhof also has one (7am-10pm), as does Südbahnhof (6.30am-10pm). Commission charges are around the same as banks, but quite often their exchange rates are uncompetitive.

American Express (Map pp254–5; 515 400-40; vienna@axrep.at; 01, Kärntner Strasse 21-23; 9am-5.30pm Mon-Fri, 10am-3pm Sat) exchanges cash as well as travellers cheques (Amex travellers cheques for free, cheques of other institutions incur a small charge). It also has a travel section and financial services, and will hold mail (not parcels) free of charge for up to one month for customers who have an American Express card.

Credit Cards

Visa, EuroCard and MasterCard are accepted a little more widely than American Express and Diners Club, although a sur-prising number of shops and restaurants refuse to accept any credit cards at all. Plush shops and restaurants will usually accept cards, though, and the same applies for hotels. Train tickets can be bought by credit card in main stations.

To report lost or stolen credit cards, call the following:

American Express 0800 900 940

Diners Club 501 35 14

MasterCard 0800 218 235

Visa 0800 200 288

NEWSPAPERS & MAGAZINES

English-language newspapers are widely available in Vienna, usually late in the afternoon of the day on which they're published. The first to hit the stands are the *Financial Times* and the *International Herald Tribune*. *USA Today*, *Time*, *Newsweek*, the *Economist* and most British newspapers are also easy to find. You'll find most titles sold at newsstands and pavement sellers, particularly around the main train stations and at U-Bahn stations on the Ringstrasse.

Of the several German-language daily newspapers available, the magazine-size *Neue Kronen Zeitung* has the largest circulation by a long shot despite its sensationalist slant and lack of hard news. Serious papers include *Der Standard* and *Die Presse;* the former usually takes a stance on the left-hand side of the fence, the latter on the right. For entertainment listings and on-the-button political and social commentary, the winner hands down is Vienna's own *Der Falter*. This weekly publication comes out on Wednesday and is only in German, but the listings are quite easy to decipher. *City* is a cheaper, slimmed-down *Der Falter,* with none of the politics and less listings coverage. *Augustin,* Vienna's version of the *Big Issue,* is partially produced and sold by the homeless who receive a portion of the sales. Vienna's only home-grown paper in English, *Austria Today* (www.austriatoday.at), is only available online.

Austrian newspapers are dispensed from bags attached to pavement posts on weekends, and rely on the honesty of readers to pay for the copies they take.

POST

Austria's postal service (www.post.at) is reliable and easy to use. Post offices are commonplace, as are bright yellow postboxes. Stamps can also be bought at *Tabakladen*. Sending letters (up to 20g) within Austria or Europe costs €0.55 and worldwide €1.25. The normal weight limit for letter post *(Briefsendung)* is 2kg; anything over this limit will be sent as a package (from €4 within Austria, from €11.80 anywhere else). Up to 20kg can be sent via surface mail *(Erdwegpakete)*.

Poste restante is *Postlagernde Briefe* in German; address letters *Postlagernde Sendungen* rather than post restante. Mail can be sent care of any post office and is held for a month; a passport must be shown on collection.

The following post offices have longer hours:

Franz-Josefs-Bahnhof Post Office (Map pp258–9; 09, Althanstrasse 10; ☽ 7am-8pm Mon-Fri, 9am-2pm Sat & Sun)

Main Post Office (Map pp254–5; ☎ 0577 677 1010; 01, Fleischmarkt 19; ☽ 6am-10pm)

Südbahnhof Post Office (Map pp262–3; 10, Wiedner Gürtel 1b; ☽ 7am-8pm Mon-Fri, 9am-2pm Sat & Sun)

Westbahnhof Post Office (Map pp260–1; 15, Europlatz; ☽ 7am-10pm Mon-Fri, 9am-8pm Sat & Sun)

RADIO

State-run stations include Ö1 (87.8 and 92 FM), which provides a diet of highbrow music, literature and science, and Ö3 (99.9 FM), a commercial outfit with pop music. Radio Wien (89.9 and 95.3 FM) is another state-run station, as is FM4 (103.8 FM). FM4 is the pick of the crop for alternative music and topical current affairs; it broadcasts in English from 1am to 2pm and has news on the hour in English from 6am to 7pm.

SAFETY

You'd be hard pressed to find a safer capital city in Europe than Vienna. At night it's not uncommon to see women walking home alone or elderly people walking dogs or using public transport. Tourists normally only experience petty crime, such as pickpocketing (especially at the

Naschmarkt) or the very rare money scam (which have been reported around Westbahnhof).

There are, however, a few places to avoid, especially at night. Karlsplatz station and U6 Gumpendorfer Strasse are well-known spots for drugs and drug addicts, as is the Prater and Praterstern. Südtirolerplatz and the S-Bahn and tram stations along Margareten and Wieder Gürtel can be quite unnerving after dark.

TELEPHONE

Austria's country code is ☎ 0043, Vienna's is ☎ 01. Free phone numbers start with ☎ 0800 or 0810, while numbers starting with ☎ 0900 are pay-per-minute. When calling from overseas drop the zero in the Vienna code; ie the number for Vienna's main tourist office is ☎ 0043 1 211 14 555. When calling a Vienna number from within Vienna, the Vienna code is not required; however, when calling Vienna from elsewhere in Austria (or from a mobile) the code needs to be used. Directory assistance is available on ☎ 11 88 77 and international assistance on ☎ 0900 11 88 77.

Telekom Austria (☎ 0800-100 100; www.telekom.at in German) is Austria's main telecommunications provider and maintains a variety of public telephones throughout Vienna. These take either coins or phonecards and a minimum of €0.20 is required to make a local call. Many post offices have phone booths where both international and national calls can be made; rates are cheaper from 6pm to 8am Monday to Friday, and on weekends. Another option is call centres; they're generally found in the outlying districts and offer very competitive phone-call rates.

To reverse the charges (ie call collect), you have to call a freephone number to place the call. Some of the numbers are listed below (ask directory assistance for others):

Australia ☎ 0800 200 202

Ireland ☎ 0800 200 213

New Zealand ☎ 0800 200 222

South Africa ☎ 0800 200 230

UK ☎ 0800 200 209

USA (AT&T) ☎ 0800 200 288

USA (Sprint) ☎ 0800 200 236

Mobile Phones

Austria's network works on GSM 1800, and is compatible with GSM 900 phones (*Handy* in German), but generally not with systems from the USA or Japan. *Handy* numbers start with 0699, 0676, 0664, 0660 and 0650. The major *Handy* networks – Drei, One, A-1 and T-Mobile – sell SIM cards with €10 worth of calls for €39. Telering, a smaller operator, has SIM cards for €30 with €30 worth of calls. Refill cards can be purchased from supermarkets and Trafik (a chain of tobacconists) for €20 or €40. Reciprocal agreements with overseas providers do exist, but its best to check with your local network before leaving home. Also, confirm your phone is unlocked before buying an Austrian SIM card; your home network will do this.

Phonecards

There's a wide range of local and international phonecards. You can save money and avoid messing around with change by buying a phonecard *(Telefon-Wertkarte)*; they come in various denominations, some of which give you extra calls for your money.

TELEVISION

Austria's state-run channels, ÖRF1 and ÖRF2, are never going to win any international broadcasting awards. ÖRF1 has sitcoms (both American and European), plenty of sport, dubbed movies (including *Colombo* almost every Sunday night) and a mixture of game, cooking and dating shows. ÖRF2 is more cultured, and regularly features documentaries, black-and-white Austrian movies, talk shows, operas, and unwatchable Alpine folk-music shows.

Many homes (and hotels) have satellite or cable and can pick up a whole host of TV channels from Germany and elsewhere, plus MTV, Eurosport, CNN, NBC and ATV, Austria's first domestic cable/satellite station.

TIME

Austrian time is on Central European time, one hour ahead of GMT/UTC. If it's noon in Vienna it is 6am in New York and Toronto, 3am in San Francisco, 9pm in Sydney and 11pm in Auckland. Clocks go forward one hour on the last Saturday night in March and back again on the last Saturday night in October.

Note that in German *halb* is used to indicate the half-hour before the hour, hence *halb acht* (half eight) means 7.30, not 8.30.

TIPPING

Tipping is part of everyday life in Vienna; tips are generally expected at restaurants, bars (even ordering a beer at the bar normally incurs a tip), cafés and in taxis. In service establishments, it's customary to round up smaller bills (to the nearest 50 cents or euro) when buying coffee or beer, and to add 10% to the bill for full meals; taxi drivers will expect around 10% extra. Tips are handed over at the time of payment: add the bill and tip together and pass it over in one lump sum. It doesn't hurt to tip workers, hairdressers, hotel porters, cloakroom attendants, cleaning staff and tour guides a euro or two.

If you think the service stinks, voice your disapproval by not tipping.

TOILETS

Around 330 public toilets are scattered throughout Vienna, of which over 90 are wheelchair accessible. If they're attended, a small fee is required to use them, normally around €0.50. The toilet block on Graben (p58), designed by Adolf Loos, is an *Jugendstil* (Art Nouveau) masterpiece and worth visiting even if you don't have to go. The Rathaus Information Office (opposite) produces a handy *Toiletten-Stadtführer* city map with toilets marked on it. Remember, *Damen* is for women and *Herren* is for men, although sometimes it's hard to tell which is which; some bars and cafés either hide the markings behind posters and graffiti, or don't even bother to give an indication.

TOURIST INFORMATION

Airport Information Office (⏰ 8.30am-9pm) Located in the arrivals hall.

Jugendinfo (Map pp254–5; ☎ 1799; www.jugendinfo wien.at in German; 01, Babenbergerstrasse 1; ⏰ noon-7pm Mon-Sat) Jugendinfo is tailored to those aged between 14 and 26, and has tickets for a variety of events at reduced rates for this age group. Staff can tell you about events around town, and places to log onto the internet.

Niederösterreich Werbung (Map pp254–5; ☎ 536 100; www.niederoesterreich.at; 01, Fischhof 3/3; 🕙 8.30am-5pm Mon-Thu, until 4pm Fri) Provides information on Niederösterreich (Lower Austria), the province surrounding Vienna.

Rathaus Information Office (Map pp254–5; ☎ 525 50; www.wien.gv.at; 01, Rathaus; 🕙 8am-6pm Mon-Fri) The City Hall provides information on social, cultural and practical matters, and is geared as much to residents as to tourists. There's an info-screen with useful information.

Tourist Info Wien (Map pp254–5; ☎ 211 14; www.wien .info; 01, Albertinaplatz; 🕙 9am-7pm) Vienna's main tourist office, with a ticket agency, hotel booking service, free maps, and every brochure under the sun.

WienXtra-Kinderinfo (Map pp254–5; ☎ 4000 84 400; www.kinderinfowien.at; 07, Museumsplatz 1; 🕙 2-7pm Tue-Thu, 10am-5pm Fri & Sat) Marketed firstly at children (check out the knee-high display cases), *then* their parents, this child-friendly tourist office has loads of information on kids activities and a small indoor playground.

TRAVELLERS WITH DISABILITIES

Vienna is fairly well geared for people with disabilities *(Behinderte)*, but not exceptionally so. Ramps are common but by no means ubiquitous; most U-Bahn stations have wheelchair lifts but trams and buses don't (though buses can lower themselves for easier access and the newer trams have doors at ground level); many, but once again not all, traffic lights 'bleep' to indicate when pedestrians can safely cross the road.

The tourist office can give advice and information. Its detailed booklet *Vienna for Visitors with Disabilities*, in German or English, provides information on hotels and restaurants with disabled access, plus addresses of hospitals, medical equipment shops, parking places, toilets and much more. Send an email (info@wien.info) for more details.

Organisations

Bizeps (Map pp260–1; ☎ 523 89 21; www.bizeps.at, in German only; 07, Kaiserstrasse 55/3/4a; 🕙 appointments only 10am-4pm Mon-Thu, 10am-1pm Fri) A centre providing support and self-help for people with disabilities.

Faktor i (Map pp260–1; ☎ 274 92 74; www.faktori.wuk .at, in German only; 05, Rechte Wienzeile 81; 🕙 1-5pm Mon & Tue, 9am-7pm Thu, information line 🕙 9am-5pm Mon & Tue, 9am-1pm Wed, 9am-7pm Thu) Faktor i is aimed at offering information to young people with disabilities.

VISAS

Visas for stays of up to three months are not required for citizens of the EU, the EEA (European Economic Area), much of Eastern Europe, Israel, USA, Canada, the majority of Central and South American nations, Japan, Korea, Malaysia, Singapore, Australia or New Zealand. All other nationalities require a visa. The Ministry of Foreign Affairs website, www.bmaa.gv.at, has a list of Austrian embassies where you can apply.

If you wish to stay longer you should simply leave the country and re-enter. EU nationals can stay indefinitely, but are required by law to register with the local magistrate's office *(Magistratisches Bezirksamt)* if the stay exceeds 60 days.

Austria is part of the Schengen Agreement which includes all EU states (minus Britain and Ireland) and Switzerland. In practical terms this means a visa issued by one Schengen country is good for all the other member countries and a passport is not required to move from one to the other. Things are a little different for the 10 EU member states which joined in 2004; a passport is still required to move in and out of these countries, but check with your local embassy for more up-to-date information.

WOMEN TRAVELLERS

Overall, Vienna is a very safe city and women travellers should experience no special problems. Attacks and verbal harassment are less common than in many countries. However, normal caution should be exercised in unfamiliar situations.

The **Frauen Büro** (Map pp254–5; ☎ 4000 83 515; 08, Friedrich-Schmidt-Platz 3; 🕙 8am-4pm Mon-Fri) has loads of pamphlets and brochures (mostly in German) on women's issues and can help with many problems you may have. A 24-hour hotline for women is the *Frauennotruf* (Women's Emergency Line; ☎ 71 719).

WORK

EU nationals can work in Austria without a work permit or residency permit, though as intending residents they need to register with the police.

Non-EU nationals need both a work permit and a residency permit, and will find it pretty hard to get either. Inquire (in German) about job possibilities via local Labour Offices; look under 'Arbeitsmarkt-service' in the White Pages for the closest office. The work permit needs to be applied for by your employer in Austria. Applications for residency permits must be applied for via the Austrian embassy in your home country.

Teaching is a favourite of expats; look under 'Sprachschulen' in the *Gelbe Seiten* for a list of schools. Outside that profession (and barkeeping), you'll struggle to find employment if you don't speak German. There are some useful job websites:

www.ams.or.at (in German) Austria's Labour Office

www.jobfinder.at (in German) Directed towards professionals

www.jobpilot.at (in German) Another for professionals

www.virtualvienna.net Aimed at expats, with a variety of jobs, including UN listings

Language

Language

It's true – anyone can speak another language. Don't worry if you haven't studied languages before or that you studied a language at school for years and can't remember any of it. It doesn't even matter if you failed English grammar. After all, that's never affected your ability to speak English! And this is the key to picking up a language in another country. You just need to start speaking.

Learn a few key phrases before you go. Write them on pieces of paper and stick them on the fridge, by the bed or even on the computer – anywhere that you'll see them often.

You'll find that locals appreciate travellers trying their language, no matter how muddled you may think you sound. So don't just stand there, say something! If you want to learn more German than we've included here, pick up a copy of Lonely Planet's user-friendly *German Phrasebook*.

SOCIAL
Meeting People
Hello.
Guten Tag.
Goodbye.
Auf Wiedersehen.
Please.
Bitte.
Thank you (very much).
Danke (schön).
Yes/No.
Ja/Nein.
Do you speak English?
Sprechen Sie Englisch?
Do you understand (me)?
Verstehen Sie (mich)?
Yes, I understand (you).
Ja, ich verstehe (Sie).
No, I don't understand (you).
Nein, ich verstehe (Sie) nicht.

Could you please ...?
Könnten Sie ...?
  repeat that
  das bitte wiederholen
  speak more slowly
  bitte langsamer sprechen
  write it down
  das bitte aufschreiben

Going Out
What's on ...?
Was ist ... los?
  locally
  hier

this weekend
dieses Wochenende
today
heute
tonight
heute Abend

Where are the ...?
Wo sind die ...?
  clubs
  Klubs
  gay venues
  Schwulen- und Lesbenkneipen
  restaurants
  Restaurants
  pubs
  Kneipen

Is there a local entertainment guide?
Gibt es einen Veranstaltungskalender?

PRACTICAL
Numbers & Amounts
1	eins
2	zwei
3	drei
4	vier
5	fünf
6	sechs
7	sieben
8	acht
9	neun
10	zehn
11	elf
12	zwölf
13	dreizehn

14	vierzehn
15	fünfzehn
16	sechzehn
17	siebzehn
18	achtzehn
19	neunzehn
20	zwanzig
21	einundzwanzig
22	zweiundzwanzig
30	dreizig
40	vierzig
50	fünfzig
60	sechzig
70	siebzig
80	achtzig
90	neunzig
100	hundert
1000	tausend

Days

Monday	Montag
Tuesday	Dienstag
Wednesday	Mittwoch
Thursday	Donnerstag
Friday	Freitag
Saturday	Samstag
Sunday	Sonntag

Banking

I'd like to ...
Ich möchte ...
  cash a cheque
  einen Scheck einlösen
  change money
  Geld umtauschen
  change some travellers cheques
  Reiseschecks einlösen

Where's the nearest ...?
Wo ist der/die nächste ...? m/f
  automatic teller machine
  Geldautomat
  foreign exchange office
  Geldwechselstube

Post

I want to send a ...
Ich möchte ... senden.
| parcel | ein Paket |
| postcard | eine Postkarte |

I want to buy a/an...
Ich möchte ... kaufen.
aerogram	ein Aerogramm
envelope	einen Umschlag
stamp	eine Briefmarke

Phones & Mobiles

I want to make a ...
Ich möchte ...
  call (to Singapore)
  (nach Singapur) telefonieren
  reverse-charge/collect call (to Singapore)
  ein R-Gespräch (nach Singapur) führen

I want to buy a phonecard.
Ich möchte eine Telefonkarte kaufen.

Where can I find a/an ...?
Wo kann ich ... kaufen?
I'd like a/an ...
Ich hätte gern ...
  adaptor plug
  einen Adapter für die steckdose
  charger for my phone
  ein Ladegerät für mein Handy
  mobile/cell phone for hire
  ein Miethandy
  prepaid mobile/cell phone
  ein Handy mit Prepaidkarte
  SIM card for your network
  eine SIM-Karte für Ihr Netz

Internet

Where's the local Internet café?
Wo ist hier ein Internet-Café?

I'd like to ...
Ich möchte ...
  check my email
  meine E-Mails checken
  get Internet access
  Internetzugang haben

Transport

What time does the ... leave?
Wann fährt ... ab?
boat	das Boot
bus	der Bus
train	der Zug

What time does the plane leave?
Wann fliegt das Flugzeug ab?

What time's the ... bus?
Wann fährt der ... Bus?
first	erste
last	letzte
next	nächste

Where's the nearest metro station?
Wo ist der nächste U-Bahnhof?

Are you free? (taxi)
Sind Sie frei?
Please put the meter on.
Schalten Sie bitte den Taxameter ein.
How much is it to ...?
Was kostet es bis ...?
Please take me to (this address).
Bitte bringen Sie mich zu (dieser Adresse).

FOOD

breakfast	Frühstück
lunch	Mittagessen
dinner	Abendessen
eat	essen
drink	trinken

Can you recommend a ...?
Können Sie ... empfehlen?

bar/pub	eine Kneipe
café	ein Café
coffee bar	eine Espressobar
restaurant	ein Restaurant
local speciality	eine örtliche Spezialität

What's that called?
Wie heisst das?
Is service included in the bill?
Ist die Bedienung inbegriffen?

For more detailed information on food and dining out, see the Eating chapter, p117.

EMERGENCIES

It's an emergency!
Es ist ein Notfall!
Call the police!
Rufen Sie die Polizei!
Call a doctor/an ambulance!
Rufen Sie einen Artzt/Krankenwagen!
Could you please help me/us?
Könnten Sie mir/uns bitte helfen?
Where's the police station?
Wo ist das Polizeirevier?

HEALTH

Where's the nearest ...?
Wo ist der/die/das nächste ...?

(night) chemist	(Nacht) Apotheke
dentist	Zahnarzt
doctor	Arzt
hospital	Krankenhaus

I need a doctor.
Ich brauche einen Arzt.

Symptoms

I have (a) ...
Ich habe ...

diarrhoea	Durchfall
fever	Fieber
headache	Kopfschmerzen
pain	Schmerzen

GLOSSARY

Abfahrt – departure (trains)
Achterl – 125mL glass of wine
Ankunft – arrival (trains)
Altwaren – second-hand goods
Apotheke, Apotheken (pl) – pharmacy
Ausgang – exit
Autobahn – motorway

Bahnhof – train station
Bankomat – ATM
Bauernmarkt, Bauernmärkte (pl) – farmers market
Besetzt – occupied, full (ie no vacancy)
Bezirk, Bezirke (pl) – (town or city) district
Beisl, Beisln (pl) – Viennese term for beer house
Biedermeier – 19th-century art movement in Germany and Austria; decorative style of furniture from this period
Briefsendung – letter; item sent by letter post
Briefmarken – stamps
Bundesbahn – country roads
Buschenshank – family-run wine taverns located in semi-rural areas on the city outskirts

Busch'n – green wreath or branch, hung over the door of wine taverns
BZÖ – Alliance for the Future of Austria (political party)
Christkindlmarkt – Christmas market
Dag – abbreviation for 10g
Damen – women
Denkmal – memorial
Einbahnstrasse – one-way street
Eingang, Eintritt – entry
Fahrplan – timetable
Fahrrad – bicycle
Feiertag – public holiday
Fiaker – horse and carriage
Flakturm, Flaktürme (pl) – flak tower
Flohmarkt – flea market
Flugpost – air mail
Föhn – hot, dry wind that sweeps down from the mountains, mainly in early spring and autumn
FPÖ – Freedom Party (political party)
FKK (Freikörperkultur) – free body culture

Gästehaus – guesthouse, perhaps with a restaurant
Gasthaus, Gasthäuser (pl) – inn or restaurant, without accommodation
Gasthof – inn or restaurant, usually with accommodation
Gelbe Seiten – Yellow Pages
Glühwein – mulled wine

Haltestelle – bus or tram stop
Hauptbahnhof – main train station
Hauptpost – main post office
Herren – men
Heuriger, Heurigen (pl) – wine tavern

Jugendherberge – youth hostel
Jugendstil – Art Nouveau

Kellner/Kellnerin – waiter/waitress
Konsulat – consulate
Krankenhaus, Krankenhäuser (pl) – hospital
Krügerl – 500mL glass of beer
Kurzparkzone – short-term parking zone

Lokal, Lokale (pl) – bar or pub
Luxuszimmer – luxury rooms

Maut – toll (or indicating a toll booth); also Viennese dialect for a tip (gratuity)
Melange – Viennese version of cappuccino
Mensa, Mensen (pl) – university caféteria
Menü – meal of the day; the menu (ie food list) is called the *Speisekarte*
Mehrwertsteuer – MWST, value-added tax
Münze – coins

ÖAMTC – national motoring organisation
ÖAV – Austrian Alpine Club
ÖBB – Austrian federal railway
ÖVP – Austrian People's Party (political party)

Parkschein – parking voucher
Pension, Pensionen (pl) – B&B guesthouse
Pfarrkirche – parish church
Polizei – police
Postamt – post office
Prolos – Viennese word for working class

Radverleih – bicycle rental
Rathaus – town hall
Ruhetag – 'rest day', on which a restaurant is closed

Saal, Säle (pl) – hall or large room
Sacher Torte – rich chocolate cake with layers of apricot jam
Sammlung – collection
Säule – column, pillar
Schiff – ship
Schloss – palace or stately home
Schrammelmusik – popular Viennese music for violins, guitar and accordion
Schwullesbische Szene – gay and lesbian scene
Selbstbedienung (SB) – self-service (restaurants, laundries etc)
SPÖ – Social Democrats (political party)
Sprachschulen – language schools
Stadtheurigen – basic wine taverns or multilevel cellars
Stammlocal – regular watering hole
Studentenheime – student residences
Szene – scene (ie where the action is)

Tabak/Tabakladen – tobacconist(s)
Tagesteller/Tagesmenü – the set meal or menu of the day in a restaurant
Telefon-Wertkarte – phonecard
Tierpark/Tiergarten – animal park/zoo
Tor – gate

Urlaub – holiday
U-Bahn – underground rail network

Viertel – 250mL glass (drinks); also a geographical district (quarter)
Vignitte – motorway tax

Wanderung – hiking
Wien – Vienna
Wiener Schmäh – the dark, self-deprecating Viennese sense of humour
Wiener Werkstätte – workshop established in 1903 by Secession artists
Wäscherei – laundry
Würstelstand – sausage stand

Zahnarzt, Zahnärte (pl) – dentist
Zimmer frei/Privat Zimmer – private rooms (accommodation)
Zeitung – newspaper

Behind the Scenes

THE LONELY PLANET STORY

The story begins with a classic travel adventure: Tony and Maureen Wheeler's 1972 journey across Europe and Asia to Australia. There was no useful information about the overland trail then, so Tony and Maureen published the first Lonely Planet guidebook to meet a growing need.

From a kitchen table, Lonely Planet has grown to become the largest independent travel publisher in the world, with offices in Melbourne (Australia), Oakland (USA) and London (UK). Today Lonely Planet guidebooks cover the globe. There is an ever-growing list of books and information in a variety of media. Some things haven't changed. The main aim is still to make it possible for adventurous travellers to get out there — to explore and better understand the world.

At Lonely Planet we believe travellers can make a positive contribution to the countries they visit — if they respect their host communities and spend their money wisely. Every year 5% of company profit is donated to charities around the world.

THIS BOOK

This fifth edition of *Vienna* was researched and written by Neal Bedford – a resident of Vienna – with assistance from Janine Eberle, who wrote the Shopping chapter. Neal also wrote the previous edition, and co-authored *Vienna 3* with Mark Honan, the author of the first two editions. This guidebook was commissioned in Lonely Planet's London office, and produced by the following:

Commissioning Editor Janine Eberle

Coordinating Editor David Carroll

Coordinating Cartographer Julie Dodkins

Coordinating Layout Designer Yvonne Bischofberger

Managing Editors Barbara Delisson, Geoff Howard

Managing Cartographers Mark Griffiths, Adrian Persoglia

Assisting Editor Kate Cody

Assisting Layout Designers Wibowo Rusli, Cara Smith

Cover Designer Mary Nelson-Parker

Project Manager Fabrice Rocher

Language Content Coordinator Quentin Frayne

Thanks to Glenn Beanland, Daniel Fennessy, Wayne Murphy, Trent Paton, Lyahna Spencer, Celia Wood

Cover photographs DJ and bartender at Artclub Future-garden in Mariahilf, Greg Elms/Lonely Planet Images (top); Roman-inspired sculptures from Greek mythology, Schloss Schönbrunn, Jon Davison/Lonely Planet Images (bottom); Red Vienna tram in front of Burgtheater, Martin Brent/Getty Images (back)

Internal photographs by Greg Elms/Lonely Planet Images, except for the following:
p215 Glenn Beanland/Lonely Planet Images; p18, p22, p26, p138, p154 (#2) Martin Brent/Getty; p2 (#1, 3), p35,
p52, p67, p95, p147, p148 (#1, 2, 3), p149 (#2), p150 (#1, 4), p151 (#2), p152 (#1, 2), p153 (#2, 3, 4), p154 (#3), p180 Greg Elms/Lonely Planet Images; p2 (#4) Hemis/Alamy; p31, p211 Mark Honan/Lonely Planet Images; p2 (#5) Hannah Levy/Lonely Planet Images; p10, p44, p207, p208 Diana Mayfield/Lonely Planet Images; p151 (#3) Wiesenhofer/ANTO.

All images are copyright of the photographer unless otherwise indicated. Many of the images in this guide are available for licensing from Lonely Planet Images: www.lonelyplanetimages.com.

THANKS
NEAL BEDFORD

Thanks Mum & Dad, Tina, Zsuzsa, Tom P, Peter, Sladjan, Marty, Anne, Dan, Matt, Rose, Marek, Tom, Astrid, Clara, Winston/Beany-Boy, Flo, Vivi, Bruno, Marion, the Eisvogel crew, Alexa, Axel, Barbara, Colin, Mark, Hannes, Myrta, and the Kuzaras.

Special thanks to Sebastian Schlachter-Delgado, Peter Göbel, Helmut Österreicher, Babara Pruchner, Christian Cummins, Sabina Egger, Brigitte Schreger, Harald Hütterer, Renate Hofbauer, and the excellent in-house team of David Carroll and Julie Dodkins.

A big round of applause to my wonderful CE and co-author Janine Eberle for all her help, advice, and energy she brought to this project.

I dedicate this book to Tiffany.

JANINE EBERLE

Thanks to Imogen Hall and Fiona Buchan, whose fabulous idea it was that I take a dedicated shopping visit to Vienna, and also to Neal Bedford who gave me some great tips, was a pleasure to work with, and who introduced me to the delights of the *Heuriger*.

OUR READERS

Many thanks to the travellers who used the last edition and wrote to us with helpful hints, useful advice and interesting anecdotes:

Dominik Anker, Manfred Bosch, John Chiu, J Diggle, Rebecca Dinar, Donald Fisher, Mike Fitzgerald, Grahame Foster, Jose Garrido, Jay Gatz, Malcolm Gesthuysen, George Hart, Jarrod Hepburn, Peter Keenan, Lorenzo Lelli, Paul Levatino, Lee Maher, Wilfried Mayr, Tom Mcdonnell, Bob Morris, Berit Nielsen, Louise Potterton, Merron Selenitsch, April Semanision, Michael Sherman, Luisa Sprugasci, Peter Taylor, John Venham, Paul Wells, Sofia Windstam, Andrew Young

ACKNOWLEDGMENTS

Many thanks to the following for the use of their content:

Vienna U & S Bahn map © Wiener Linien

SEND US YOUR FEEDBACK

We love to hear from travellers — your comments keep us on our toes and help make our books better. Our well-travelled team reads every word on what you loved or loathed about this book. Although we cannot reply individually to postal submissions, we always guarantee that your feedback goes straight to the appropriate authors, in time for the next edition. Each person who sends us information is thanked in the next edition — and the most useful submissions are rewarded with a free book.

To send us your updates — and find out about Lonely Planet events, newsletters and travel news — visit our award-winning website: www.lonelyplanet.com /contact.

Note: We may edit, reproduce and incorporate your comments in Lonely Planet products such as guidebooks, websites and digital products, so let us know if you don't want your comments reproduced or your name acknowledged. For a copy of our privacy policy visit www.lonely planet.com/privacy.

Notes

Notes

Index

See also separate indexes for Eating (p248), Drinking (p249), Entertainment (p249), Shopping (p250) and Sleeping (p250).

Index

Index

000 map pages
000 photographs

250

MAP LEGEND

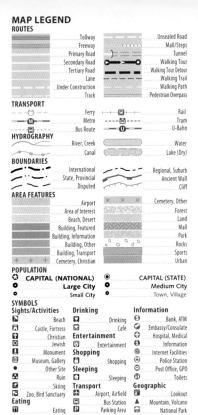

ROUTES

Tollway	Unsealed Road
Freeway	Mall/Steps
Primary Road	Tunnel
Secondary Road	Walking Tour
Tertiary Road	Walking Tour Detour
Lane	Walking Trail
Under Construction	Walking Path
Track	Pedestrian Overpass

TRANSPORT

Ferry	Rail
Metro	Tram
Bus Route	U-Bahn

HYDROGRAPHY

River, Creek	Water
Canal	Lake (Dry)

BOUNDARIES

International	Regional, Suburb
State, Provincial	Ancient Wall
Disputed	Cliff

AREA FEATURES

Airport	Cemetery, Other
Area of Interest	Forest
Beach, Desert	Land
Building, Featured	Mall
Building, Information	Park
Building, Other	Rocks
Building, Transport	Sports
Cemetery, Christian	Urban

POPULATION

○ **CAPITAL (NATIONAL)**	◉ **CAPITAL (STATE)**
● **Large City**	● **Medium City**
○ Small City	○ Town, Village

SYMBOLS

Sights/Activities
- Beach
- Castle, Fortress
- Christian
- Jewish
- Monument
- Museum, Gallery
- Other Site
- Ruin
- Skiing
- Zoo, Bird Sanctuary

Eating
- Eating

Drinking
- Drinking
- Café

Entertainment
- Entertainment

Shopping
- Shopping

Sleeping
- Sleeping

Transport
- Airport, Airfield
- Bus Station
- Parking Area

Information
- Bank, ATM
- Embassy/Consulate
- Hospital, Medical
- Information
- Internet Facilities
- Police Station
- Post Office, GPO
- Toilets

Geographic
- Lookout
- Mountain, Volcano
- National Park

Maps

GREATER VIENNA

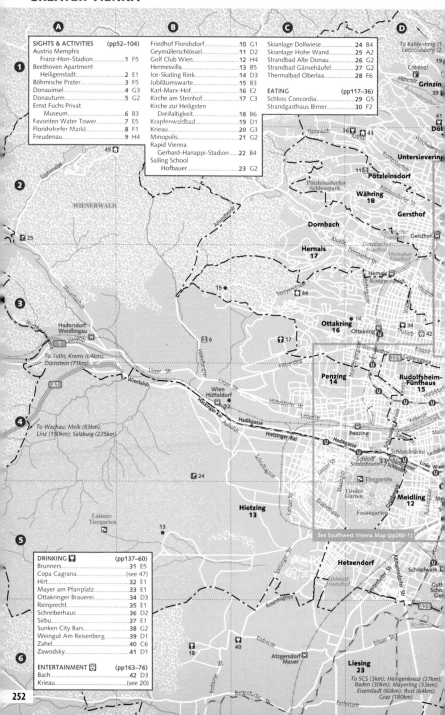

To Kahlenberg (1.
Leopoldsberg (2.

Cobenzl
Höhenstr
Grinzin

To Tulln; Krems (64km);
Dürnstein (73km);

To Wachau; Melk (83km);
Linz (150km); Salzburg (275km);

WIENERWALD

Hadersdorf
Weidlingau

Wien
Hütteldorf

Lainzer
Tiergarten

See Southwest Vienna Map (pp260-1)

Untersievering

Pötzleinsdorf

Währing
18

Gersthof

Dornbach

Hernals
17

Ottakring
16

Penzing
14

Rudolfsheim-
Fünfhaus
15

Meidling
12

Hietzing
13

Hetzendorf

Schöpfwerk

Liesing
23

To SCS (3km); Heiligenkreuz (27km);
Baden (30km); Mayerling (33km);
Eisenstadt (60km); Rust (64km);
Graz (180km);

Atzgersdorf
Mauer

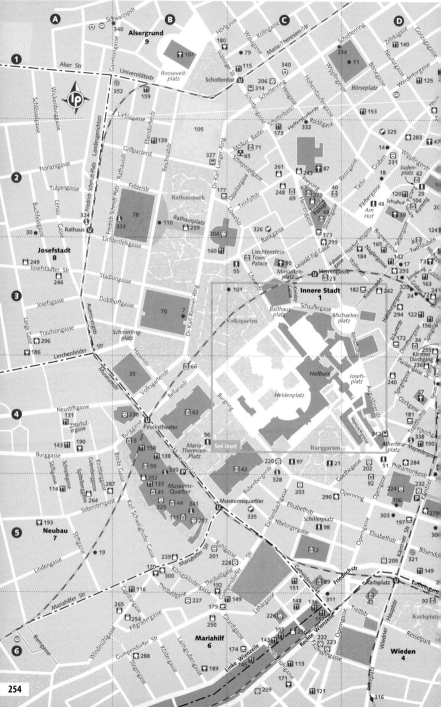

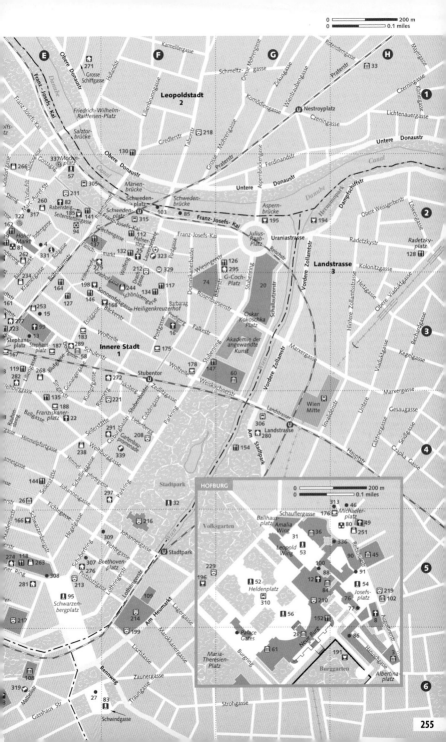

CENTRAL VIENNA

CENTRAL VIENNA

NORTHEAST VIENNA

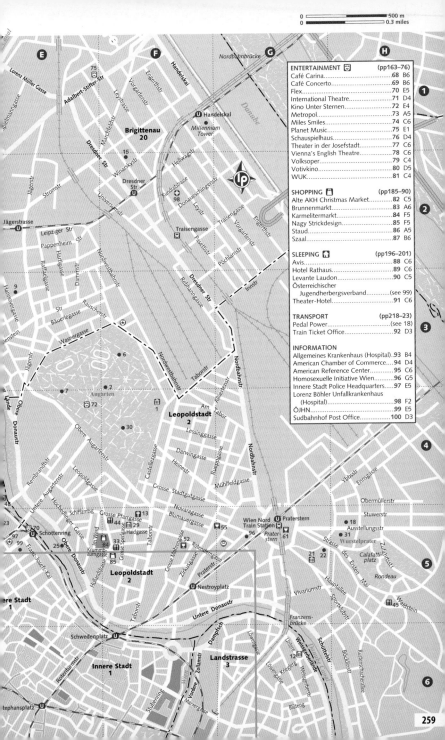

ENTERTAINMENT	(pp163–76)
Café Carina	68 B6
Café Concerto	69 B6
Flex	70 E5
International Theatre	71 D4
Kino Unter Sternen	72 E4
Metropol	73 A5
Miles Smiles	74 C6
Planet Music	75 E1
Schauspielhaus	76 D4
Theater in der Josefstadt	77 C6
Vienna's English Theatre	78 C6
Volksoper	79 C4
Votivkino	80 D5
WUK	81 C4

SHOPPING	(pp185–90)
Alte AKH Christmas Market	82 C5
Brunnenmarkt	83 A6
Karmelitermarkt	84 F5
Nagy Strickdesign	85 F5
Staud	86 A5
Szaal	87 B6

SLEEPING	(pp196–201)
Avis	88 C6
Hotel Rathaus	89 C6
Levante Laudon	90 C5
Österreichischer Jugendherbergsverband	(see 99)
Theater-Hotel	91 C6

TRANSPORT	(pp218–23)
Pedal Power	(see 18)
Train Ticket Office	92 D3

INFORMATION	
Allgemeines Krankenhaus (Hospital)	93 B4
American Chamber of Commerce	94 D4
American Reference Center	95 C6
Homosexuelle Initiative Wien	96 G5
Innere Stadt Police Headquarters	97 E5
Lorenz Böhler Unfallkrankenhaus (Hospital)	98 F2
ÖJHN	99 E5
Sudbahnhof Post Office	100 D3

259

SOUTHWEST VIENNA

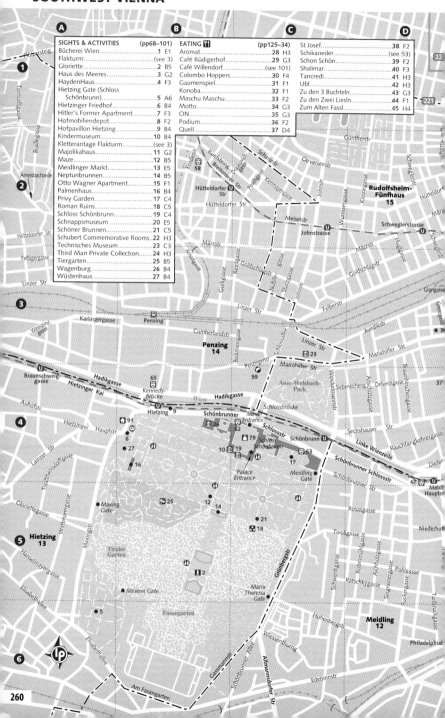

SOUTHEAST VIENNA

Hofburg

A

Stephansplatz

Innere Stadt
1

Burggarten

Stubentor

Stubenring

Vordere Zollamtstr

Wien
Mitte

Landstrasse

See pp2

Hetzgasse

Blütengasse 15
Löwengasse 14

Marxergasse

Unter Weissgerber

Weissgerberlände

Schüttelstr

Böcklinstr

Rudolfinkschaftsalle

Rotunden-
brücke

Rotunden-
brücke

Opernring

Kärntner Ring

Schubertring

Lothringerstr

Stadtpark

Landstrasse
3

Rasumofskygasse

Kundmanngasse

Rochusgasse

20

Hörnesgasse

Erdbergstr

Geusaugasse

Erdberger
Lände

Friedrichstr

Karlsplatz

Karlsplatz

Lothringerstr

Am Heumarkt

Reche Bahngasse

Linke Bahngasse

Reisnerstr

Salesianergasse

Neulinggasse

Neulinggasse

Hainburger Weg

Wisser

Erdbergstr

gasse

Haidingergasse

Margaretenstr

Wiedner Hauptstr

Panigl-
gasse

Karlsgasse

Gusshausstr

Schwindg

Wohlleben

Prinz-Eugen-Str

18

Agentinierstr

39

17

23

Rennweg

29

Jauresgasse

10

40

19

8 9

Arenbergpark

37

Landstrasser

Barmherzigengasse

Apostelgasse

Kardinal-
Nagl-Platz

Baumgasse

Petrusgasse

Schleifmühlg

Paulanergasse

Frankenberggasse

Taubstummeng

Taubstummengasse

Barichgasse

Juchgasse

Schützen-
gasse

Boerhaavegasse

Eslarngasse

Steingasse

Obere Bahngasse

Oberzellergasse

Waag-
gasse

Floragasse

30 26

Wieden

Mayerhofgasse

Wieden
4

Theresianumgasse

Belvederegasse

Graf-Starhemberg-Gasse

Mommsengasse

Prinz-Eugen-Str

Goldeggasse

4

Weyringergasse

Schloss
Belvedere

Botanic
Gardens

5

16

2

Alpine
Garden

Obere Bahngasse

Rennweg

Gerlgasse

Jacquingasse

Fasangasse

Keilg

Hegergasse

Kölblgasse

Mohsgasse

Hohlweggasse

Kircherngasse

A. Blamur-Gasse

Rennweg

Hauptstr

Schimmel

Aspangstr

Hauptstr

Landstrasse
3

Schönburgstr

Johann-Strauss-Gasse

Rainergasse

Blechturmgasse

Kolschitzkygasse

Schellinggasse

Wiedner Gürtel

Südtiroler
Platz

Südtiroler
Platz

Laxenburger Str

Sonnwendgasse

Wiedner Gürtel

Landstrasser Gürtel

38

34

Südbahnhof

Arsenalstr

1

Schweitzer
Garten

Kelsenstr

Cherggasse

Landstrasser

Lebensstr

Faradaygasse

Gänsbachergasse

Geiseistr

Br

13

Arsenal

Lilienthalgasse

Franz-Grill-Str

Landgutgasse

Scardsburggasse

Dampfgasse

Hasengasse

Jagelgasse

Götzgasse

Kepler-
gasse

Keplerplatz

Favoriten
10

Columbusgasse

Favoritenstr

Favoritenstr

Humboldtgasse

Gudrunstr

Erlachgasse

Pernerstorfergasse

Quellenstrasse

Buchengasse

24

Wielandgasse

Herndlgasse

Erlachgasse

Gellertgasse

Gudrunstr

Neilreichgasse

Hetzgasse

Rotenhofgasse

Davidhofgasse

Leebgasse

Reumannplatz

28

3

Reumann-
platz

Buchengasse

Steudelgasse

Absberggasse

Quellenstr

Schrötterstr

Inzersdorfer Str

Angeligasse

Laxenburger Str

Ettenreichgasse

Rotenhofgasse

Davidhofgasse

Favoritenstr

Antons-
platz

Laaer-Berg-Str

Kudlichgasse

Puchsbaumgasse

See Central Vienna Map (pp252-3)

1

2

3

4

5

6

A

B

C

D

262

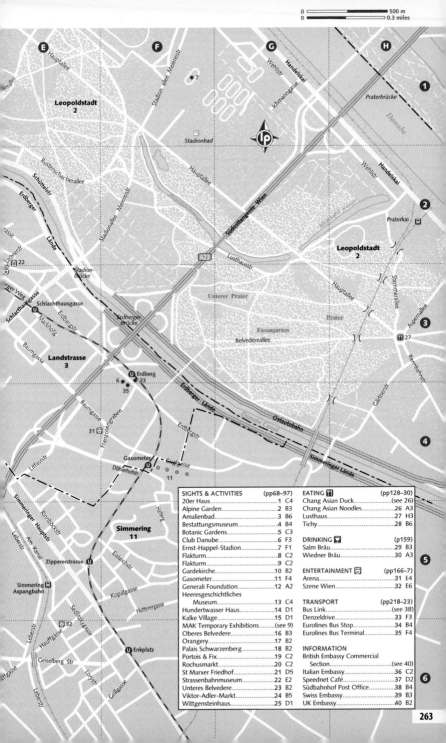

SIGHTS & ACTIVITIES	(pp68–97)
20er Haus	1 C4
Alpine Garden	2 B3
Amalienbad	3 B6
Bestattungsmuseum	4 B4
Botanic Gardens	5 C3
Club Danube	6 F3
Ernst-Happel-Stadion	7 F1
Flakturm	8 C2
Flakturm	9 C2
Gardekirche	10 B2
Gasometer	11 F4
Generali Foundation	12 A2
Heeresgeschichtliches Museum	13 C4
Hundertwasser Haus	14 D1
Kalke Village	15 D1
MAK Temporary Exhibitions	(see 9)
Oberes Belvedere	16 B3
Orangery	17 B2
Palais Schwarzenberg	18 B2
Portois & Fix	19 C2
Rochusmarkt	20 C2
St Marxer Friedhof	21 D5
Strassenbahnmuseum	22 E2
Unteres Belvedere	23 B2
Viktor-Adler-Markt	24 B5
Wittgensteinhaus	25 D1

EATING	(pp128–30)
Chang Asian Duck	(see 26)
Chang Asian Noodles	26 A3
Lusthaus	27 H3
Tichy	28 B6

DRINKING	(p159)
Salm Bräu	29 B3
Wiedner Bräu	30 A3

ENTERTAINMENT	(pp166–7)
Arena	31 E4
Szene Wien	32 E6

TRANSPORT	(pp218–23)
Bus Link	(see 38)
Denzeldrive	33 F3
Eurolines Bus Stop	34 B4
Eurolines Bus Terminal	35 F4

INFORMATION	
British Embassy Commercial Section	(see 40)
Italian Embassy	36 C2
Speednet Café	37 D2
Südbahnhof Post Office	38 B4
Swiss Embassy	39 B3
UK Embassy	40 B2

263

VIENNA METRO MAP

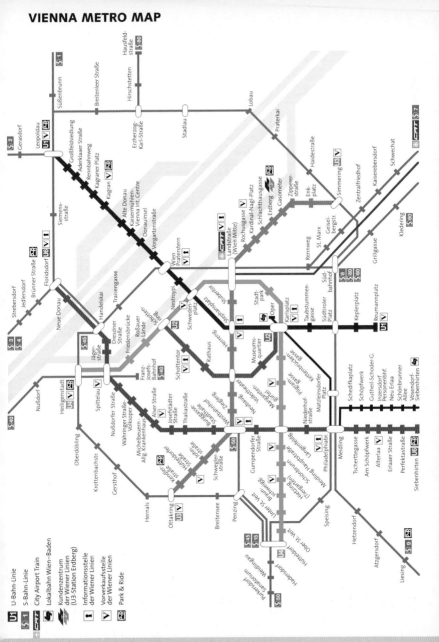

SCHNELLVERBINDUNGEN IN WIEN

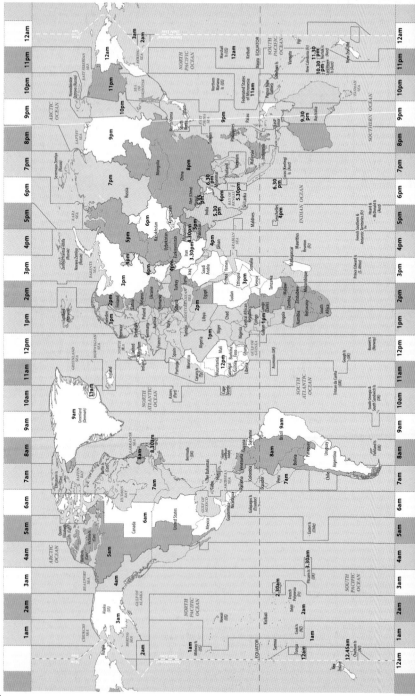